THE HARLEM RENAISSANCE
IN THE AMERICAN WEST

The Harlem Renaissance, an exciting period in the social and cultural history of the U.S., has re-established itself over the past few decades as a watershed moment in African American history. However, many of the African American communities outside the urban center of Harlem that participated in the Harlem Renaissance between 1914 and 1940 have been overlooked and neglected as locations of scholarship and research.

The Harlem Renaissance in the American West: The New Negro's Western Experience will change the way students and scholars of the Harlem Renaissance view the efforts of artists, musicians, playwrights, club owners, and various other players in African American communities all over the American West to participate fully in the cultural renaissance that took hold during that time.

Bruce A. Glasrud is Professor Emeritus of History at California State University, East Bay, and retired Dean of the School of Arts and Sciences at Sul Ross State University.

Cary D. Wintz is Distinguished Professor of History at Texas Southern University. Together Cary Wintz and Bruce Glasrud are the editors of *African Americans and the Presidency* (Routledge).

NEW DIRECTIONS IN AMERICAN HISTORY

THE HARLEM RENAISSANCE IN THE AMERICAN WEST

The New Negro's Western Experience

Edited by
Bruce A. Glasrud and
Cary D. Wintz

Routledge
Taylor & Francis Group

NEW YORK AND LONDON

First published 2012
by Routledge
711 Third Avenue, New York, NY 10017

Simultaneously published in the UK
by Routledge
2 Park Square, Milton Park, Abingdon, Oxon OX14 4RN

Routledge is an imprint of the Taylor & Francis Group, an informa business

© 2012 Taylor & Francis

The right of the editors to be identified as the authors of the editorial material, and of the authors for their individual chapters, has been asserted in accordance with sections 77 and 78 of the Copyright, Designs and Patents Act 1988.

Library of Congress Cataloging in Publication Data
The Harlem Renaissance in the American West: the new Negro's western experience/edited by Bruce A. Glasrud and Cary D. Wintz.
    p. cm.—(New directions in American history)
    Includes bibliographical references and index.
    1. African Americans—West (U.S.)—Social life and customs—20th century.   2. African Americans—West (U.S.)—Intellectual life—20th century.   3. Harlem Renaissance.   4. African Americans—West (U.S.).   5. African American arts—West (U.S.).   6. African American authors—West (U.S.).   7. African Americans—Music.   8. West (U.S.)—Race relations.
    I. Glasrud, Bruce A.   II. Wintz, Cary D., 1943–.
    E185.86.H325 2011
    305.896′073078—dc23   2011027822

ISBN: 978–0–415–88687–1 (hbk)
ISBN: 978–0–415–88688–8 (pbk)
ISBN: 978–0–203–80558–9 (ebk)

Typeset in Bembo and Stone Sans
by Florence Production Ltd, Stoodleigh, Devon, UK

Printed and bound in the United States of America on acid-free paper
by Walsworth Publishing Company, Marceline, MO

CONTENTS

ACKNOWLEDGMENTS

As always, we received considerable help in preparing and publishing this book. For that assistance we wish to thank a number of people. Without the scholarship and ability of the authors, of course, the book would not have been feasible. We are grateful for the cooperation of the thirteen authors whose studies are featured in our book. University of Washington history professor, BlackPast.org creator, and friend and colleague Quintard Taylor encouraged, made suggestions, and supported our effort. Three readers asked pertinent questions, made a few suggestions, and recommended publication. They helped us determine and identify our approach. Carol Roark, Manager of the Texas/Dallas History and Archives Division of the Dallas Public Library, and Dan Morgenstern, Director of the Institute of Jazz Studies at Rutgers University, provided valuable assistance in the selection of photographs for this project. Once more, Kimberly Guinta, editor-in-chief at Routledge, listened, asked questions, and supported our idea and then manuscript. Thanks, Kimberly, and thanks also to the staff at Routledge who took our manuscript and produced an exciting book. For any errors or omissions we remain responsible.

Bruce A. Glasrud, Seguin, Texas
Cary D. Wintz, Houston, Texas

INTRODUCTION

The Harlem Renaissance in the West

Cary D. Wintz and Bruce A. Glasrud

The Harlem Renaissance was the most important period in twentieth-century African American intellectual and cultural history. Initially scholars perceived it as a Harlem-centered literary movement with strong racial and political under-tones that began following the end of World War I and persisted into the late 1930s. The emergence of Harlem as the preeminent African American urban center concurrently with the rise of New York City as the literary and cultural center of the country focused attention on Harlem and its community of black writers and poets. The concurrent emergence of a revitalized and more militant African American struggle for equality, also largely headquartered in New York, provided the political environment for the movement. The Great Migration that fueled the rapid growth of the African American population in northern cities and transformed Harlem into the "Black Metropolis" contributed to both the literary activity and the political organizations. The Harlem Renaissance, or, as some preferred, the "New Negro" movement, appeared at the nexus of these political, social/demographic, and artistic trends.

Recent scholarship has modified this traditional view of the Harlem Renaissance in two significant ways. First, literature, while still an important part of the Renaissance, was only one of a number of outlets for black creativity. Music (especially blues and jazz) and musical theater were also central to the movement, while other art forms such as painting, sculpture, theater, dance, and film all contributed to African American artistic expression in the interwar years. Second, while Harlem and New York were certainly a center for black intellectual and artistic activity, the Harlem Renaissance was truly a national phenomenon. Recent books have discussed the New Negro movement in Washington and Chicago, and attention has been focused on Philadelphia and other northern centers of African American population. As more has been written about music during the Harlem Renaissance era, it has become clear that New York was more of a destination than an incubator for black musicians and black music. Likewise, black film and filmmakers had little connection with Harlem. Both the blues and jazz had their origins in the rural areas and the cities of the South. New Orleans, Memphis, St. Louis, the Mississippi Delta and East Texas were the incubators of much of the distinctive trends in black music. Finally, very few of the creative artists of the Harlem Renaissance were from Harlem. Instead, like most of Harlem's population in the 1920s and 1930s, they migrated there from other parts of the country, and from outside the United States. And equally important, not all of these creative African Americans remained in Harlem; in fact, some never went there.

The purpose of this volume is to expand the study of the Harlem Renaissance —beyond other northern cities, and beyond the American South—to the American West. We argue that the Harlem Renaissance, or the New Negro literary and artistic movement, was a truly national phenomenon and must be understood as such. Much as scholars have long since ceased to perceive the African American experience or the issue of racial injustice merely as a southern phenomenon, African American literary and artistic creativity too must be examined on a national level. This volume represents another step in that direction by focusing its attention on the Harlem Renaissance in the West.

The Harlem Renaissance

The Harlem Renaissance has no clearly defined beginning or end. Instead, a number of events signaled the beginning of the movement. The first took place in music, as the blues and jazz made their way from cities such as New Orleans, Memphis, St. Louis, and Chicago to New York City—particularly Harlem. Pioneered by W. C. Handy and other musicians, the blues emerged at the end of the nineteenth century and became popular during the second decade of the new century in Harlem clubs and a few years later through the sales of phonograph records by blues singers Mamie Smith and Bessie Smith. Jazz moved north from New Orleans to Harlem, with James Reese Europe in 1905 one of the first to play jazz in the city. In 1921 Eubie Blake and Noble Sissle carried the soul of this new music to standing-room-only audiences on Broadway in an all-black musical revue, *Shuffle Along*. Both the poet Langston Hughes and the influential poet and diplomat James Weldon Johnson saw the incredibly popular *Shuffle Along* as a sign of the emerging Harlem Renaissance.

The second event that marked the beginnings of the Renaissance was the 1924 Civic Club dinner held to acknowledge the upsurge in black literary activities. In the early 1920s a series of unconnected literary events—the publication of Claude McKay's volume of poetry, *Harlem Shadows* (1922) and Jean Toomer's novel *Cane* (1923), and the initial published works of other young black writers— signaled an unusual level of black literary activity. The Civic Club dinner, in addition to formally acknowledging the literary activity that was already underway, furthered the movement by bringing together the three major players in the literary renaissance: the black literary-political intelligentsia; white publishers and critics; and young black writers. Originally conceived by Charles S. Johnson of the Urban League to recognize Jessie Fauset on the occasion of the publication of her first novel, *There Is Confusion*, the event expanded to include recognition of the broad array of new literary talent in the black community and to present this talent to New York's white literary establishment. The impact was significant. At this dinner Alain Locke was offered the opportunity to guest-edit an issue of the *Survey Graphic*, a liberal journal of social issues. Locke devoted the resulting "Harlem issue," published in March 1925, to defining the aesthetic of black literature and art. Other black writers made contacts at the dinner that resulted in published books in the coming months.

The third and most important sign of the Harlem Renaissance was the increase in the artistic accomplishments of the talented African Americans in all fields of the arts, and the popularity that these works generated. One success led to another. *Shuffle Along*, for example, led to nine more Broadway musicals written by blacks and featuring black performers during the following three years. In addition, in an effort to capitalize on the success of *Shuffle Along*, white writers and producers turned to black themes and black performers for several significant productions. Jerome Kern and Oscar Hammerstein did so in 1927 for their hit *Showboat*; Irving Berlin cast blues singer Ethel Waters in *As Thousands Cheer* (1933); and George and Ira Gershwin brought their great opera *Porgy and Bess* to Broadway in 1935. Black writers achieved similar success in literature. Although no single work had the impact on literature that *Shuffle Along* had on musical theater, during the fifteen years beginning in 1922 the sixteen best-known black authors of the Harlem Renaissance published more than fifty books with mainstream commercial publishers. As with musical theater, their work stimulated white authors to produce works focusing on the African American experience. DuBose Heyward's best-selling 1925 novel *Porgy*, Carl Van Vechten's controversial *Nigger Heaven* (1926); Julia Peterkin's Pulitzer Prize–winning 1928 novel *Scarlet Sister Mary*, and Fannie Hurst's very successful *Imitation of Life* (1933) represent the most significant examples of this development.

By the mid-1920s the Harlem Renaissance was in full swing. Music and musical theater paved the way, followed by literature, and then by the visual arts, drama, and film. Fundamental to this artistic surge was the migration of African American people to New York and other northern cities, as well as to cities in the south and west. This great migration has been well studied at least in terms of its demographic impact on the north and its role in creating Harlem as *the* "Negro Metropolis" and the focal point of the Harlem Renaissance. It is also important to recognize the migration of African Americans of talent who fueled the Harlem Renaissance, and made it a national rather than a regional movement. In its simplest form this was a migration from the provinces to the metropolis, bringing, for example, Langston Hughes from Kansas to Harlem, James Weldon Johnson from Jacksonville, Florida to New York, and Louis Armstrong from New Orleans to New York. The reality was far more complicated. Few of the artists who created the Harlem Renaissance were born or raised there. Almost all migrated there from somewhere else. Furthermore, while some of these migrants permanently settled in New York, many passed through the city, or moved in and out. And, even those who made New York or Harlem their home spent considerable time on the road away from the city. Not only was the Harlem Renaissance a national movement but it and its participants were extremely mobile.

There are several figures who exemplify this mobility. Langston Hughes spent most of his youth in Kansas before attending high school in Cleveland. He relocated to Harlem, but then traveled to Europe and also lived for a time in Washington, DC. In the mid-1920s he returned to Harlem, but then spent considerable time as a student at Lincoln University outside Philadelphia. In the early 1930s Hughes left New York and, except for brief trips back, remained away for ten years. He traveled across the world, and spent some time in the Caribbean and in California. In the early 1940s he returned to Harlem. Claude McKay was born in Jamaica. He was already a published poet when he came to the United States in 1912 to attend college, first in Alabama, then in Kansas. In 1914 he moved to Harlem, but his literary contacts were mostly among the Greenwich Village leftists. In 1922 he left for the Soviet Union and spent the rest of the decade in Europe and North Africa. While abroad he published his best-known works including his novel *Home to Harlem*. He returned to New York in 1934. Neither Hughes nor McKay is that unusual. Their publishers were in New York, but they did not consistently live there. Two others, singer and actor Paul Robeson and dancer and performer Josephine Baker, migrated to New York and began their careers there, then chose to become ex-patriots. Robeson had established himself as a singer and actor when he moved to England in 1928 because of his dissatisfaction with racism and segregation in the United States. He returned during World War II. Josephine Baker relocated to Paris from Harlem in 1925 at the age of nineteen as a career move. There she became a phenomenal international star. She became a French citizen and remained in France during the war and for the rest of her life.

If the Harlem Renaissance had no clearly defined beginning, it also lacked a uniform philosophy or artistic signature that set it apart from other literary and cultural movements. While many tried, efforts to define precisely the nature of the literary and artistic creativity of the Harlem Renaissance met with frustration. There was no common literary style or political ideology associated with the movement; it was a reflection of identity far more than an ideology or a literary or artistic school. What united participants was their sense of taking part in a common endeavor and their commitment to giving artistic expression to the African American experience. This identity is much stronger among writers and poets than among musicians and performers. Perhaps the best statement defining the perception of the movement among its practitioners was Hughes's essay "The Negro Artist and the Racial Mountain," published in *The Nation*, June 23, 1926. This essay was an artistic declaration of independence—from the stereotypes that whites held of African Americans and the expectations they had for their creative works, as well as independence from the expectations that black leaders and black critics had of black writers and the expectations black writers had for their own work. As Hughes concluded:

> We younger Negro artists who create now intend to express our individual dark-skinned selves without fear or shame. If white people are pleased we are glad. If they are not, it doesn't matter. We know we are beautiful. And ugly too. The tom-tom cries and the tom-tom laughs. If colored people are pleased we are glad. If they are not, their displeasure doesn't matter either. We build our temples for tomorrow, strong as we know how, and we stand on top of the mountain, free within ourselves.

The determination of black writers to follow their own artistic vision, and the diversity that this created, was a principal characteristic of the Harlem Renaissance. It was also reflected in the great range of artistic forms associated with the movement—literature, theater, musical theater, art, sculpture, photography, film, and music—as well as the variety within each of these fields. If there was a unifying feature it was to express that African American experience in all of its variety through the creative arts. While there was no single political ideology or social issue associated with the movement, in one form or another sometimes explicitly and sometimes with great subtlety, race and its implications to the African American experience always were present. And while there was not always a direct relationship, the Harlem Renaissance was impacted by the struggle for racial equality in the early twentieth century.

The ill-defined beginning of the Harlem Renaissance is reflected in its equally imprecise ending. Some historians attempted to define the end as the onset of the great depression or the Harlem Race Riot of 1935, but the reality is far more complicated. Others link it to the death or departure from Harlem of major Renaissance figures in the late 1920s or 1930s. In spite of all these problems, creative production did not cease overnight. Almost one-third of the major works published during the Renaissance appeared after 1929, and Hurston's *Their Eyes Were Watching God*, arguably the best novel of the period, came out in 1937. Black music continued in popularity through the 1930s and beyond, especially the increasingly sophisticated sounds of Armstrong and Ellington, and Jacob Lawrence produced his best paintings in the 1930s and early 1940s. Some see the Harlem Renaissance moving west to Chicago in the 1930s and early 1940s. In the final analysis the Harlem Renaissance ended when most of those associated with it left Harlem or stopped writing and the new young artists who emerged in the 1930s and 1940s did not connect with the movement.

African Americans in the American West

For the purposes of this study we have defined the West essentially as the line of states extending north from Texas and the states west of this tier. We added Minnesota, especially the urban area of Minneapolis-St. Paul, to this group since it defines the eastern edge of the northern Great Plains, much as Texas defines the eastern extent of the historically Hispanic Southwest. In all, eighteen states are examined: Texas, New Mexico, Arizona, California, Nevada, Utah, Colorado, Oklahoma, Kansas, Nebraska, South Dakota, North Dakota, Minnesota, Montana, Wyoming, Idaho, Washington, and Oregon. In many ways these states are a varied lot. However, there are unifying elements. Except for Texas, and to a much lesser degree Oklahoma and Kansas, none of these states experienced the plantation slavery associated with the antebellum South. Another characteristic of this region is that black residents made up a very small portion of the overall population. In 1930, Texas had the largest black population, yet blacks made up less than 15 percent of the state's population; in Oklahoma blacks comprised slightly more than 7 percent. In eleven of the remaining states blacks made up less than 1 percent of the population. However, as small as this population was, it was highly urbanized (excluding Texas and Oklahoma, which still had large rural black populations); in 1930 almost 90 percent of western blacks resided in urban areas. Western states also participated in the black migration that characterized the early twentieth century. Although far more blacks migrated to the North and Great Lakes regions during this period, the black population of the West increased over 60 percent between 1900 and 1930.

The distribution of the African American population in the West is important for understanding the region's role in the Harlem Renaissance. The Harlem Renaissance was an urban phenomenon. While a large metropolis was not essential for a region to be impacted by the movement, there needed to be a large enough concentration of African Americans for a sense of community to develop and for organizations and institutions to form that could sustain black culture and ferment political or civil rights activity. Individual artists can exist and thrive in non-urban areas. Anita Scott Coleman enjoyed success as a short story writer and poet in New Mexico prior to relocating to Los Angeles in 1926. In New Mexico she grew up on a ranch and attended college in Silver City, which with a population of forty-six blacks in 1920 was not large enough to support a black newspaper or many social or political institutions. Coleman was able to connect with the black literary world through newspapers and national black magazines such as *The Crisis*, *The Messenger*, and *Opportunity* and achieved much of her literary success while in New Mexico. Novelist Wallace Thurman spent most of his childhood in Salt Lake City (718 blacks in 1920) before moving to Los Angeles and then to Harlem, while Langston Hughes spent much of his childhood in Lawrence, Kansas (1,466 blacks in 1920).

TABLE 0.1 African American Population of Western States, 1900–1940

	1940		1930		1920		1900	
	Black Population	% Black	Black Population	% Black	Black Population	% Black	Black Population	% Black
Texas	924,391	14.4	854,964	14.7	741,694	15.9	620,722	20.4
Oklahoma	168,849	7.2	172,198	7.2	149,408	7.4	55,684	7.0
California	124,306	1.8	81,048	1.4	38,763	1.1	11,045	0.7
Kansas	65,188	3.6	66,344	3.5	57,925	3.3	52,003	3.5
Arizona	14,993	3.0	10,749	2.5	8,005	2.4	1,848	1.5
Nebraska	14,171	1.1	13,752	1.0	13,242	1.0	6,259	0.6
Colorado	12,167	1.1	11,828	1.1	11,318	1.2	8,570	1.6
Minnesota	9,928	0.4	9,445	0.4	8,809	0.4	4,959	0.3
Washington	7,424	0.4	6,840	0.4	6,883	0.5	2,514	0.5
N. Mexico	4,672	0.9	2,850	0.7	5,733	1.6	1,610	0.8
Oregon	2,565	0.2	2,234	0.2	2,144	0.3	1,105	0.3
Utah	1,235	0.2	1,108	0.2	1,466	0.3	672	0.2
Montana	1,120	0.2	1,256	0.2	1,658	0.3	1,523	0.4
Wyoming	986	0.4	1,250	0.6	1,375	0.7	940	1.0
Nevada	664	0.6	516	0.6	346	0.4	134	0.3
Idaho	595	0.1	668	0.2	920	0.2	292	0.2
S. Dakota	474	0.1	645	0.1	832	0.1	465	0.
N. Dakota	201	0.0	377	0.1	377	0.1	286	0.1

Source: U.S. Census Bureau, Sixteenth Census of the United States—1940—Population, Volume II: Characteristics of the Population. Available at www.census.gov/prod/www/abs/decennial/1940.html.

TABLE 0.2 African American Population of Western Cities, 1930–1940

	1940		1930	
	Black Population	% Black	Black Population	% Black
Houston	86,302	21.9	63,337	21.7
Los Angeles	63,774	4.2	38,894	3.1
Kansas City★	62,659	12.0	58,446	11.2
Dallas	50,407	14.9	38,742	14.9
Oklahoma City	19,344	7.9	14,662	7.9
San Antonio	16,235	7.8	17,978	7.8

Notes: ★Includes Kansas City, Kansas and Kansas City Missouri

Source: *Sixteenth Census of the U.S.*

While individual writers, musicians, and artists came from small black communities across the West, larger urban areas supported more active literary and artistic communities. The four largest black urban areas in the West in the 1920s and 1930s (Houston, Los Angeles, Kansas City, and Dallas) had vibrant and varied artistic scenes that mixed local talent with touring artists, musicians and writers. They had their own infrastructure of clubs and performance venues, black newspapers, and branches of black organization such as the National Association for the Advancement of Colored People (NAACP), the Urban League, and Garvey's Universal Negro Improvement Association (UNIA). They provided local blacks (and often whites) with a taste of Harlem night life. Other concentrations of urban black western communities and their residents met with similar experiences, but usually on a smaller scale.

The African American population was not distributed evenly through the western states; Texas had the largest black population by far. In 1940 it accounted for almost 70 percent of the West's black population. The states north of Texas also had substantial black populations, especially Oklahoma, followed by Kansas. Nebraska and Minnesota had much smaller black populations than their neighbors to the south, but more than the states to their west. By 1940 California trailed only Texas and Oklahoma in black population; of the rest only Arizona and Colorado had more than 10,000 blacks. The seven northern plains and mountain states (the Dakotas, Idaho, Nevada, Wyoming, Montana, and Utah) had a total black population of 5,275 in 1940, and consequently had far less well organized black communities. However, by 1941 Las Vegas, with less than 200 blacks, had a "Cotton Club" and hosted a concert by Pearl Bailey. On the west coast most blacks were concentrated in Los Angeles, which had over 60,000 black residents in 1940 and a very active artistic and cultural community in the South Central area of the city. The San Francisco Bay area, San Diego, Portland, and Seattle had smaller but also active black communities.

The Harlem Renaissance in the West

The goal of this study is to shift the focus of the Harlem Renaissance away from Harlem to the cities and states of the American West. It is inspired by the broadened view of the early twentieth century African American literary and artistic movement that has established that while the Renaissance was centered in New York it was a national phenomenon. As noted above, while all of the writers and artists associated with the movement spent significant time in Harlem, and most considered themselves part of the Renaissance, many also spent significant parts of their career away from Harlem. As we look at the black experience in the West it becomes clear that not only did many participants in the Harlem Renaissance have western roots or western connections but in communities across the West African Americans were involved in black art, literature, and music both as consumers and as artists themselves. In her book, *From Greenwich Village to Taos: Primitivism and Place at Mabel Dodge Luhan's*, Flannery Burke observed that the term Harlem Renaissance "is a misnomer that fails to acknowledge the cultural activities of African Americans prior to the 1920s and in areas outside New York City." This volume is concerned with the latter facet of Burke's comment, that "areas outside New York City" have not been investigated as well as they might.

Given the relatively small African American population in the West, a disproportionate number of black writers and artists had roots in the West before they came to Harlem. The best known of these is Langston Hughes. Not only did Hughes spend most of his childhood in Lawrence, Kansas, but he celebrated his western roots in his writing. The title poem of his first book of poetry, "The Weary Blues," was inspired in large part by a street-corner musician he encountered during a childhood visit to Kansas City. His first and most important novel, *Not Without Laughter*, was set in a fictionalized Lawrence, Kansas, and addressed the issue of migration to the urban north, and the way that the arts provide an escape from poverty for talented African Americans. Aaron Douglas, who became a friend of Hughes in Harlem, grew up a few miles west of Hughes in Topeka, Kansas. Douglas studied art at the University of Nebraska and then taught art in Kansas City before moving to Harlem in 1924. Two other close friends of Hughes met in Los Angeles before they moved to Harlem. Arna Bontemps was born in Louisiana, but spent his childhood and early adult years in Los Angeles; Wallace Thurman grew up in Salt Lake City, but moved to Los Angeles to attend college. Both moved to Harlem in 1924, and both set at least parts of their novels in the West.

In addition to African Americans who were born or raised in the West, there are others who spent a significant portion of their careers there. Many black musicians performed in western cities, but at least three had deeper ties there. Jelly Roll Morton, one of the founding fathers of American jazz, spent the six years from 1917 to 1923 based in Los Angeles. Louis Armstrong left Harlem and the famed Connie's Inn to become the orchestra leader at the version of the Cotton

Club in Los Angeles. Armstrong returned to Hollywood frequently during his career to appear in films. Between 1932 when he made his film debut through 1945 he participated as actor or musician in sixteen Hollywood films. Black filmmaker Oscar Micheaux left his native Illinois to become a homesteader in South Dakota in 1905. Micheaux's career as a sodbuster lasted only about five years, but it gave him material for two novels and one motion picture.

The experiences of individual writers and artists indicate clearly that the Harlem Renaissance extended into the West. This study, however, focuses on the western cities and states, not individual artists, and its purpose is to capture the African American cultural and artistic creativity in black communities in this region of the country. In Texas, for example, the urban centers of Dallas, Fort Worth, Houston and San Antonio vibrated with cultural energy. They were not alone: El Paso poet Bernice Love Wiggins published a volume of poetry in 1925. The Alain Locke of Texas, famed folklorist J. Mason Brewer, published a volume of black Texas poetry, *Heralding Dawn*, while teaching at an Austin college. From his base in Marshall, Texas, the home of two African American universities, Harlem Renaissance poet Melvin Tolson invited lecturers such as Langston Hughes to campus.

Going north from Texas, in other Great Plains states, Oklahoma's black communities in Oklahoma City and Tulsa heralded this new period of artistic energy. Author Ralph Ellison grew up playing in a jazz band there. As we noted, Kansas produced writers and artists who ultimately left the state to become key persons in the Harlem Renaissance. Wichita, Lawrence, Topeka, and especially Kansas City fostered their own black renaissance. Omaha, with a large, vibrant black population, and Lincoln became centers of the artistic, musical, and literary contributions. Black students at the University of Nebraska, as well as those at Kansas, Iowa, and Minnesota, made their own special contributions. In Minnesota, Minneapolis developed its own musical sound.

The movement stretched farther west. Denver, Helena, and Laramie featured black bands and other artistic developments. In the southwest, Jean Toomer spent considerable time in Taos; short story writer and poet Anita Scott Coleman, from Silver City, New Mexico, eventually published over thirty short stories in leading periodicals of the day. Black Albuquerque published a newspaper. Tucson and Phoenix became renaissance hubs in Arizona. As in Texas, three California cities became prominent parts of the "New Negro" movement of the 1920s and 1930s— San Diego, Los Angeles, and San Francisco/Oakland. Los Angeles, as Quintard Taylor reminded us, became home to "a fledgling Harlem Renaissance." It was more than fledgling; black authors and entertainers frequently arrived in the west coast city. Short-lived magazines such as *Ink Slinger* and *Flash* tried to establish a place for artistic endeavors. San Diego, a vital center for the emergence of California Soul, attracted prominent musicians. San Francisco and Oakland also witnessed and participated in renaissance activities. Up the coast, in Portland and in Seattle, famed writers and participants such as Horace Cayton and his family brought the renaissance to the Pacific Northwest.

The fourteen essays of *The Harlem Renaissance in the West* are organized to reflect the scope and the diversity of the African American cultural experience in the western half of the United States. The first five essays explore the Harlem Renaissance in five major western cities: Houston, Dallas, Kansas City, Los Angeles, and the San Francisco Bay area. The first four had the largest urban African American populations during the period of the Harlem Renaissance in the West, while the Bay Area, with a smaller black population, had a particularly vibrant artistic community. The next nine chapters move geographically across the region as they explore black culture in the west. Beginning in Oklahoma with its large African American population, we continue north, first to Nebraska and then to the Twin Cities. The four chapters that follow begin in the southwest, first with the San Antonio/Austin area, which had a smaller African American population and demographics more akin to Albuquerque than to the other Texas cities, then west to New Mexico and Arizona, then north to the Denver area, and further north to Montana and Wyoming. The final two chapters move down the Pacific Coast, from Seattle and Portland in the Pacific Northwest to San Diego at the Mexican border.

Each essay is unique, but each explores the Harlem Renaissance in the West from one or more of the following perspectives. First and most important is the African American creative arts within the community and its surrounding area, including those developments and artists that remained in the community as well as those that came out of the community and moved on to Harlem, Chicago, or other centers of African American literary and artistic creativity. Second is the question of how the larger Harlem Renaissance impacted local African American communities. This can include visits, performances, or exhibits by Harlem Renaissance figures as well as book clubs, reviews, news reporting, media events, educational activities, the impact of black cultural magazines such as *The Crisis* and *Opportunity*, and other ways that the community interrelated with the Harlem Renaissance. Third is the process through which blacks in western urban centers reflected or absorbed the themes and ideas associated with the Harlem Renaissance/New Negro movement in terms of culture and the creative arts among African Americans, the impact of the black artists and/or performers who visited those cities, and the broader political and racial developments that were a part of that time period. The final perspective is the degree to which the larger white community responded to or interacted with the developments of African American literature, visual arts, theater, and especially music. Overall one notices that the western renaissance spirit, though connected to the national rebirth and to Harlem, was also important and significant in its own way.

1

HARLEM IN HOUSTON

Charles Orson Cook

The decade and a half following the outbreak of World War I witnessed the most dynamic growth rate in Houston's history. The city's total population in 1915 was barely 100,000, but by the early 1930s it had increased more than three-fold, making it the largest city in Texas, second largest in the South, and among the twenty largest in the nation. African Americans had traditionally been an important component of Houston's population. In 1870, for instance, census records indicate that almost 40 per cent of the Bayou City's residents were black, a proportion that declined over the next half-century, but in total numbers the Afro-Houstonian community grew exponentially. In 1930, there were over 60,000 blacks living in Houston, mostly in the city's Third, Fourth, and Fifth Wards near downtown. The clear bulk of this population increase was the product of a significant demographic shift among southern African Americans in the first few decades of the twentieth century that brought tens of thousands of black people into the nation's cities. The best-known example of that shift occurred when blacks, mostly from the southern Atlantic states, began an important migration to the Harlem district of New York City, which made it what James Weldon Johnson called "Black Manhattan," and "The Culture Capital" of Negro culture. This so-called Harlem Renaissance and the accompanying New Negro Movement of the interwar era was the most vivid representation of the kind of cultural explosion that came with the transition to an urban milieu that changed much of black life in early twentieth-century America. Almost as significant were similar demographic patterns that brought impressive numbers of southern Negroes, mostly from the mid-South, to other northern cities such as Chicago, Cleveland, and Detroit, all of which had smaller, though no less vibrant, versions of Harlem. Less well known, however, were the growing black populations of places such as Houston in the trans-Mississippi South and West. One study of Afro-Houstonians for the period 1914–1941, for example, has concluded that probably as many as 25,000 blacks moved to Houston, primarily from rural East Texas and neighboring Louisiana.

Like most of her sister cities in the North and East, Houston's main attraction for black migrants was economic. The hope of employment in the Southern Pacific rail yards in the Fifth Ward, and the burgeoning petroleum and shipping industries along Houston's new ship channel, were among the largest potential employers in Texas, particularly in the aftermath of World War I. By the late 1920s, Houston was the home of one professional black baseball team (and several amateur and semi-professional clubs), one African American owned insurance company, three black high schools (one in each of the Third, Fourth, and Fifth Wards), one junior college, three newspapers (one of which, the *Informer*, was the oldest in the trans-Mississippi West), an active chapter of the NAACP, a Colored Branch of the Houston Public Library, black chapters of the YMCA and YWCA, a black hospital, and countless restaurants, bars and speakeasies, grocery stores, churches, and funeral parlors. African American fraternal, civic, and professional clubs and organizations abounded. Superior Productions Company, which produced Texas's first African American film in 1921, was also based in the Bayou City. In short, there was an active, even flourishing black community in Houston, and there was clearly an emerging black middle class composed of lawyers, physicians, clergymen, and teachers. One local black booster bragged in 1928 that Houston was the home to twenty-two African American physicians, fourteen dentists, seven pharmacists, and four lawyers. Moreover, he boasted, Houston had more black teachers with degrees than any city in the South and more 1928 high school graduates than any metropolitan area in the country. Moreover, he pointed to many black designed and owned commercial buildings as tangible proof that Afro-Houstonians were sharing in the city's growing prosperity. Another insightful black observer in 1931 described Houston in remarkably modern terms when he characterized it as "a big sprawling city" that had many of the characteristics of a boomtown: ramshackle housing and inadequate municipal services but an exciting, go-for-the-main-chance atmosphere. Despite the fact that the Great Depression had made work much harder to find and that job competition among immigrant and native-born workers was keen, our observer concluded that race relations were comparatively good and that Negroes had more opportunities in Houston than most other cities.

It is, of course, unclear just how realistic such optimistic economic assessments of Houston's growing black community actually were. Like many cities, Houston had its share of blatant racism, both officially in the form of rigid segregation laws and informally in a thousand ways, some of them dangerously violent. The specter of the 1917 Camp Logan race riot, which left nineteen dead and many more wounded, hung over the city for years as a reminder of the dreaded potential of racial violence. Moreover, the brutal and blatant nature of the 1928 lynching of Robert Powell on the eve of the Democratic National Convention was another grim reminder of the darker side of Houston's racial climate. The power and influence of the renewed Ku Klux Klan in the Bayou city, particularly in the early 1920s was undeniable, too. But it is obvious, and to some degree remarkable, that in spite of such an oppressive atmosphere, Houston did offer a rich and complex cultural life for both established African American elites and newcomers on the make.

For most of the early twentieth century, the Fourth Ward, located just southwest of downtown, was the undisputed center of Houston's black commercial and cultural life. It incorporated much of the post Civil War "Freedmen's Town," which in the aftermath of the Civil War was home to many emancipated slaves. In the first decade of the twentieth century, Houston's first black high school was located there and so was the original Colored Branch of the public library. The largest and most influential black churches were in the Fourth Ward, and there too were most of the important black businesses, including the Pilgrim Life Insurance Company whose Houston headquarters were located in an imposing four-story structure that included an auditorium for public speakers and entertainers. By the late 1920s there were also six black movie theaters in the district, and several nearby white venues offered late night segregated shows for black audiences. Fourth Ward movie houses were so popular with blacks that in 1921 the Houston Censor Board was moved to ban any films starring the former boxer turned actor Jack Johnson for fear they might generate racial unrest. There was the Lincoln Theatre, too, owned and operated by blacks and widely regarded as the most modern and best equipped of all the black theaters in the city. The Lincoln, the site of many of the most ambitious theatrical and film events of the time, was for more than a decade a Fourth Ward cultural landmark. To be sure, by the late 1920s, the Third Ward had surpassed the Fourth in population and was beginning to attract a growing number of middle class blacks. Symbolized by the opening of the new Jack Yates High School, the dedication of the Houston Negro Hospital, and the creation of the Houston Junior College for Negroes, the Third Ward in the 1920s was increasingly attractive to Afro-Houstonians. As early as 1920, in fact, the Third Ward was showing clear signs of cultural life when an advertisement appeared in the city's foremost black newspaper, the *Houston Informer*, for a "Grand Moonlight Picnic" at Emancipation Park with a dancing contest to music supplied by Calvin's Lucky Five, "Those Jazzing Boys from Dixie." The Fifth Ward, located to the immediate north of downtown Houston, continued to be the home of many working class African Americans and would eventually become the residence to more blacks than any other neighborhood. But until the Great Depression at least, the Fourth Ward retained its status as the symbolic heart of Houston's black community.

A clear personification of Houston's black renaissance was the life and career of Milton Larkin. At age four, in 1914, young Milton and his three siblings moved with their widowed mother from Navasota, Texas to Houston's Fifth Ward to

FIGURE 1.1 The King and Carter Jazz Orchestra was one of the musical groups that emerged in Houston in the early 1920s. The Robert Runyon Photograph Collection [RUN05020], courtesy of The Briscoe Center for American History, The University of Texas at Austin

join family members in search of economic security. Mother Larkin worked for a time as a domestic, but died prematurely in 1921, leaving her children, including Milton, in the care of her sister. Milton eventually graduated from Houston's newest black high school, Phillis Wheatley High, in 1927. He was largely a self-taught musician who was inspired to play the jazz trumpet after hearing the legendary New Orleans trumpeter Bunk Johnson play a Houston gig. Even before high school graduation, Larkin had become part of Houston's black cultural community as a versatile and talented member of several local bands. By the mid-1930s he was best known locally as the leader of his own jazz ensemble, which played in several Houston nightspots, including the popular Harlem Grill and the Ethiopian Cafe in the Fourth Ward. In these early years, Larkin was joined in his band by two other musicians, Arnett Cobb on tenor saxophone, an alumnus of Wheatley High School, and the guitarist "Sonny Boy" Franklin, a Yates High School product. The saxophonist Illinois Jacquet, who also grew up in Houston, was another standout in Larkin's ensemble who later established a national reputation. One indication of Larkin's growing popularity was the fact that he and his band were chosen by the local NAACP chapter to provide the entertainment for its 1937 fundraiser. But by decade's end, Larkin had migrated north to Chicago's South Side where he launched a successful career as a nationally recognized band leader whose reputation for blues and big-band swing music extended over several decades.

Victoria Spivey was another accomplished musician who emerged from Houston's black working class. Victoria's parents, Grant and Adie Spivey, were former slaves who had acquired land in both Louisiana and Texas before hard times in the 1890s stripped them of most of their assets. In 1896, the Spiveys migrated to Houston in search of work, which Grant found as a part-time railroad flagman. Father Spivey presided over a family of musicians who performed frequently in local churches and community picnics. Victoria was born in Houston in 1906 and joined the family band as a pianist and organist at a very young age. Grant died suddenly in a work-related accident, leaving his family in desperate financial straits. At twelve, Victoria sought and found work as a pianist at Houston's Lincoln Theatre, but she was soon appearing in speakeasies, bordellos, and clubs in Houston and nearby Galveston. She quickly developed a reputation as a blues vocalist who was inspired by the earthy recordings of Ida Cox and the live performances in Houston of Texas guitarist "Blind Lemon" Jefferson and the New Orleans jazz trumpeter Louis Armstrong, with whom she had performed onstage. Before she was twenty, "Vickie" Spivey had developed a "road blues" style all her own, which often included allusions to the migratory nature of the black experience and featured controversial lyrics that were often blatantly sexual. In 1926 Spivey left Houston for St. Louis where she recorded several of her own songs for Okeh records, including her classic "Black Snake Blues" and the one surviving nod to her Houston origins, "Big Houston Blues." By World War II, she had graduated to more mainstream record companies such as RCA Victor and Decca. In 1930, she had a cameo role in the first Hollywood film with an all-black cast, *Hallelujah*, produced by the white director King Vidor, and shortly thereafter she was in the live jazz revue *Hellzapoppin*. During the blues revival of the 1960s, Spivey launched her own recording label, Spivey Records, and reprised many of her own songs, sometimes in collaboration with such white celebrities as Bob Dylan.

In many ways, the career of Beulah "Sippie" Wallace was remarkably similar. Born Beulah Thomas in 1898 in Houston, Sippie was part of a large, musically talented family, which included her brothers George and Hersal, both of whom were pianists/composers. Wallace got her professional start playing the piano for the Shiloh Baptist Church in the Fifth Ward. In her early teens she was already a follower of musical tent shows and soon was building a reputation as a blues singer in many of those same itinerant productions. At age fifteen, she moved to New Orleans with her brothers, and two years later married Matt Wallace, her second husband, who became her manager and who successfully guided her into blues stardom. Shortly thereafter, Sippie was in Chicago's bustling jazz scene and in 1923 made her first recording for Okeh records. Her early career included recordings and live appearances with such jazz legends as Louis Armstrong and

Clarence Williams. After a twenty-year retirement in Detroit, she was coaxed back into music in the 1960s by Victoria Spivey on whose record label the ageing Wallace made a comeback in this country and abroad. She died suddenly on tour in Germany in 1986.

Not surprisingly, among the most celebrated cultural expressions of Houston's renaissance were those of visiting celebrity artists who added a sense of legitimacy and sophistication to the black community. To cite one example, the arrival in the spring of 1932 of Langston Hughes, the poet laureate of the Harlem Renaissance, was greeted with much fanfare in the Houston area. Hughes's visit was actually just one stop on a speaking tour of the South that he made in late 1931 and early 1932, in part to acquaint himself with southern black culture but also to sell his own books to admiring audiences. Hughes stopped at Prairie View State College near Houston at the invitation of the Gilpin Dramatic Club, where he gave a poetry reading that was followed by a social mixer with faculty and students. Hughes's program at Prairie View—which he repeated in many of his other stops—came in essentially two parts. The first was the author's reminiscences about his own journey of discovery as a writer, and the highlight of the second part of his presentation was the reading of some of his best-known protest verse, including "Elevator Boy," and "Suicide." The college newspaper described the event as the best of the year and was effusive in its praise for the poet and his work. Several days later he was in Houston itself where he gave a similar program and sold several volumes of his work at the Pilgrim Auditorium in the Fourth Ward. The *Houston Informer* noted that the young poet attracted an enthusiastic crowd and demonstrated his brilliant ability to manipulate language. The *Informer*'s reporter observed that "perhaps Langston Hughes cannot be called great now," but he was certainly destined for a brilliant future. She also observed that among the most interesting parts of the poet's presentation was a collection of African and Caribbean artifacts, which caught the audience's attention and which had helped inspire some of Hughes's race poetry. Hughes made other stops ninety miles away in Beaumont and in the East Texas town of Tyler before continuing his journey to its ultimate termination in California. In 1938, the multi-talented James Weldon Johnson was in Prairie View to dedicate a new building and to speak on "The Negro: The Test of Democracy in America." Marian Anderson, the much acclaimed black contralto, made five appearances in Houston in the decade before the outbreak of World War II, some to integrated audiences. She was in Houston first in 1929, but she returned in 1931 to help raise money for the Bethlehem Settlement House for black children with a program that was mostly classical but did include popular love ballads and Negro spirituals. For one performance scheduled in 1937 at the City Auditorium, *The Pittsburgh Courier* predicted, "she will receive all the homage due a renowned singer . . .; the Philadelphia singer will receive such a welcome [in Houston] that has seldom been accorded a celebrity." Each of three black Houston high schools formed Marian Anderson Clubs in honor of her concerts in the Bayou City. The Georgia born tenor Roland Hayes, perhaps the first black classical singer to achieve an international reputation, also performed several times in Houston. His first appearance in the Bayou City was a concert in 1931 to a racially integrated audience in excess of 5,000. A second Houston performance four years later, however, attracted less than half that number. Black Houstonians were especially enthusiastic about a 1930 classical performance by Florence Cole-Talbert, whom the *Informer* called "the greatest operatic soprano the race has ever produced" and "among the greatest singers the world has ever known." Perhaps the *Informer*'s enthusiasm for Madam Talbert was in part traceable to the fact that her piano accompanist was Miss Ernestine Covington, "celebrated local pianist and music instructor at Bishop College in Marshall, Texas." The *Informer* apparently did not have to mention that Miss Covington was also the daughter of one of Houston's most prestigious black families.

The famous Smart Set Company of Whitney and Tutt (actually an African American production company owned by half-brothers Salem Tutt Whitney and J. Homer Tutt) was in Houston on February 24, 1926 to put on its hit black song and dance review, "Bamboula," in the City Auditorium. The composer J. Berni Barbour was in Houston in April of that same year promoting his operettas, and, according to *The Pittsburgh Courier*, "creating quite a stir with one of his new songs, 'Heavenly Houston.'" Cab Calloway and his swing orchestra from Harlem's famed Cotton Club made a triumphant tour of Texas in the spring of 1933, which included a full week of performances in the white Metropolitan Theater in Houston, but which also included a separate two-night dance engagement at the black Pilgrim Auditorium in the Fourth Ward. Calloway's show, in fact, was so popular that it forced the Metropolitan to moderate its policy of strictly segregated audiences. Calloway himself cynically noted that the almighty dollar was more important to many Houston whites than racial purity. Noble Sissle, the famous co-author with Eubie Blake of the smash 1922 Harlem musical hit *Shuffle Along*, brought his orchestra to Houston in February, 1937 and played to enthusiastic crowds at the same venue. Popular vocalists Billy Banks and Lena Horne shared top billing and helped pack the house for a Friday night performance. Lesser companies such as Irving Miller's *Broadway Rastus* revue and the Texas-based "Harlem Playgirls," an all-female swing band, made single one-night stands in Houston in the 1930s as well.

Although it was quite rare for Texas black painters to leave their mark on regional culture, there is some evidence that black art had a following in Houston in the era between the wars. In September, 1930, the Houston Museum of Fine Arts sponsored a two-day exhibit of seventy-three submissions from black artists and sculptors from all areas of the country who were finalists for the prestigious Harmon Award. Given by the William E. Harmon Foundation for excellence in several areas, the Harmon Award is widely credited with encouraging excellence in the arts during the period of the Harlem Renaissance. The Houston show was one of the first major traveling exhibitions of black art in the nation, and it attracted rapt attention throughout the black cultural community. No doubt much of the local enthusiasm for the exhibit was tempered by the reality of the Houston Museum's strict racial admissions policy, which allowed "colored patrons" unfettered access on only a single day each month; admission to the museum on other days required a formal application. Such a policy meant that few of Houston's black schoolchildren or adults, for that matter, had an opportunity to see the exhibit. In 1933, however, the Colored Branch of the Houston Public Library hosted a show of eight artists, and among them were examples of the painting of Samuel Countee, who had several works in the Harmon competition as well. Countee was born in Marshall, Texas in 1909 but moved to Houston's Fourth Ward in his childhood. He was a graduate of Booker T. Washington High School and had studied painting at the Houston Museum of Fine Arts. Eventually, Countee graduated from Bishop College and continued his art studies at several prestigious institutions, including the Boston Museum and Harvard University. This exhibit became an annual affair at the Colored Branch Library for several years thereafter, and in 1937 the event featured the work of a Galveston elevator operator and self-taught artist Frank Sheinall. In that year too, the library's exhibit had expanded to include a music program and three guest speakers. Both Countee and Sheinall were also featured in the 1936 Texas Centennial Exposition in Dallas. Their paintings at the Exposition were on display in the Negro Hall of Life alongside such Harlem Renaissance luminaries as the muralist Aaron Douglas and sculptor Henry O. Tanner. The Renaissance Society of the University of Chicago also included Countee paintings in an exhibition of African American art in early December, 1936. Other exhibitions of his work were at Smith College, Howard University, and Atlanta University. Countee served in World War II, and one of his murals still hangs in the restored officers club at Fort Leonard Wood in Missouri. One account of his life also suggests that at one point in his military career, probably in 1943 or 1944, he was assigned to produce several murals for the palace of the Shah of Iran. He ultimately settled in New York City where he became an art teacher and popular portraitist. One of his works, a portrait of Louis Armstrong's fourth (and last) wife Lucille, hangs today in the Louis Armstrong House Museum in Queens, New York. Countee died of cancer in New York in 1959.

Live theater emerged in the 1930s as another significant component of Houston's cultural renaissance. The *Pittsburgh Courier* noted in 1930 that the Houston Negro Little Theatre Movement had its first planning meeting at the Blue Triangle YWCA. The next year the same group sponsored a drama workshop at Booker T. Washington High School in the Fourth Ward and launched its first season in the Pilgrim Auditorium with a series of one-act plays, including *No Count Boy* and *White Dresses* by Paul Green and *The Slave* by Elizabeth Yates. Later in the same year the Houston theatrical company hosted a similar troupe from San Antonio that performed Green's Pulitzer Prize winning drama *In Abraham's Bosom*. Declining attendance forced a total reorganization of the Houston theater in 1934, but the company emerged from that process determined to keep black drama alive in the Bayou City. An important organizer in the theater's revival was James Hulbert, the librarian at the Carnegie Colored Library, who offered space for the development of dramatic productions. The inaugural season of the revived company began with an attempt to generate interest in its activities by offering free admission to the one act melodrama *No Sabe*. The fact that it attracted an audience of 250 suggests that interest in live black theater was still very much in evidence in Houston. The revived company's next production was Oscar Wilde's *Lady Windermere's Fan*, which played before near capacity audiences in the Pilgrim Auditorium. More importantly, a group of affluent black Houstonians agreed to underwrite the Negro Theatre's activities, thus assuring the survival of black drama in Houston for the immediate future. When the city's Recreation Department attempted to stimulate interest in acting in 1940 by sponsoring a drama tournament for young black Houstonians, members of the Little Negro Theatre acted as judges of the amateur one-act productions in the Emancipation Park clubhouse. Clearly, despite several daunting obstacles, live theater was in Houston's black community to stay.

Regrettably, there were few published black writers of note in Houston or in Texas generally during the period between World Wars I and II. But there was clearly an interest among Afro-Houstonians in the written word as an expression of their unique cultural consciousness. Already cited above is the popular fascination with Langston Hughes's triumphant 1932 tour and the interest in James Weldon Johnson's dedicatory speech at Prairie View State College. But Afro-Houstonians demonstrated their interest in literature in other ways as well. In Houston schools Paul Dunbar Clubs and Phillis Wheatley Clubs honored famous black writers and also attempted to stimulate interest in writing generally. Perhaps the most visible initiative to attract attention to the importance of writing in the black experience was the policy of the *Houston Informer* to encourage literary submissions from its readers and its occasional practice of publishing the works of more established writers. On March 6, 1920, for instance, the *Informer* published a poem by the well-known El Paso poet Bernice Love Wiggins whose "Ethiopia Speaks" made a bold race-conscious statement with these opening stanzas about lynching:

> Lynched!
>   Somewhere in the South the "Land of the Free,"
>   To a very strong branch of a dogwood tree
> Lynched! One of my sons—
>   When the flag was in danger they answered the call
>   I gave them my black sons, ah, yes, I gave them all
>   When you came to me.
>
>   You called them the sons of a downtrodden race,
>   The Negro you said, in his place must stay.

> To be seen in your midst is deemed a disgrace,
> I remembered, O yes, still I gave them that day
>> Your flag to defend.

In 1931, the *Informer* published several installments of a serial melodramatic mystery story "Satan's Henchman" by Art Naylor, whose plot revolved around romance and crime in the fictional Negrolian Life Insurance Company. The story's hero was James Oliver, "the idol of his widowed mother," who "by hard work holds the responsible position of cashier" and who was engaged to be married to the daughter of the company's president. When 10,000 dollars of the firm's money turned up missing, the stage was set for young James to save the day by identifying the embezzler and exposing his crime to the authorities. "Satan's Henchman" was far from highbrow literature, but it was apparently popular with many of the newspaper's readers. In 1932 the *Informer* ran several poems by J. Walter Fridia, a Waco physician, and eventually Dr. Fridia had his own column called "Weekly Rhymes." Among the most racially inspired of his verses was his "Much in a Name," which included the following lines:

> Ambition it will always check,
> It's like a millstone around your neck,
> You cannot rise, you cannot go,
> As long as you are called, "Negro."

Beginning in 1935 and continuing for several years, the *Informer* included a weekly column called "Dreamship," which sought poetic contributions from readers. Among those was Walter Waring's poem "Query," which boldly addressed black frustrations over lynching:

> Downtown white people
> All stared at my dark skin,
> Women, men, all stared
> Because I was a Negro, too,
> And one had been lynched
> That day somewhere.

Despite its popularity, "Dreamship" was suspended during World War II, a casualty of wartime paper rationing, but the column's popularity clearly demonstrated that black Houstonians had an abiding interest in the written word, especially when it addressed their aspirations and frustrations. When the *Informer* returned to the promotion of black writing in the postwar years, its readership responded with renewed fascination.

Part of the success of the black renaissance in Houston is clearly attributable to a handful of individuals who acted, sometimes behind the scenes and often indirectly, to facilitate the expansion of African American cultural life. Some of them, such as C. F. Richardson, the editor and publisher of the *Houston Informer* (and later the *Defender*), are well known by historians. Richardson's fiery editorials about racial solidarity and his willingness to supply supportive and sympathetic publicity during the 1920s for many Houston black artists are virtually a matter of public record. Only slightly less obvious was the support and encouragement of Jennie Belle Covington and her husband Dr. Benjamin Covington whose efforts seldom caught the headlines but were quietly significant. The Covingtons moved to Houston in 1903, and Dr. Covington's medical practice quickly catapulted them into the city's African American elite. The popular couple were among the first of their class to move to the Third Ward where they built an imposing home on Dowling Street and promptly bought the first automobile owned by blacks in Houston (it was a 1908 Maxwell). Moreover, Dr. Covington was one of the founders of a black Third Ward landmark, the Houston Negro Hospital. The Covington home became the unofficial hotel for many visiting artists and celebrities, including Booker T. Washington, Marian Anderson, Paul Robeson, Roland Hays, and Joe Louis. Mrs. Covington and her husband were self-taught musicians who loved all kinds of music, but were exceedingly fond of the classics. Mrs. Covington, in fact, helped form the all-black Ladies Symphony Orchestra, which included both her and her daughter among the principals. She was also one of the founders of the Blue Triangle Young Women's Christian Association, which hosted several artistic events and supported many others in a variety of ways. Jennie Belle Covington was an early member of the Houston Committee on Interracial Cooperation, and for a time served as its chairperson. Her daughter, Ernestine, was an accomplished classical pianist who taught music at Wiley College in Marshall, Texas and often performed in Houston before she married the President of Dillard University in New Orleans.

But almost lost in the story of the New Negro movement in Houston is Olen Pullum DeWalt (O. P. to his friends), successful businessman, cultural entrepreneur, and race activist. DeWalt was born in Livingston, Texas, the youngest son of John and Caroline DeWalt. O. P.'s father died shortly thereafter, forcing the surviving family to relocate several times to various places in East Texas in search of financial security. It was not until O. P. was fourteen or fifteen that he received a systematic education. Through diligence and hard work he managed to finish his secondary school through a series of rapid promotions. After a brief stint as a teacher himself, O. P. was admitted to the state-supported Prairie View State Normal and Industrial College. He graduated in 1910 and headed immediately for Houston with two dollars in his pocket and a determination, as the *Houston Informer* would later put it, "to set himself toward the task of meeting the problems of life in an independent way." After several jobs in retail sales, he settled on a career in real estate and opened offices in the old Olympia Opera House building (it had also been a brewery and warehouse) at 917 Prairie in the

Fourth Ward. In 1916, a group of investors bought the property and began extensive renovations that would eventually add two floors and a theater. Somehow, DeWalt convinced his landlords to make him building manager, and by the early 1920s he became the property's sole owner. By that time DeWalt was an active member of Houston's branch of the NAACP and a resident of the all-black suburb of Independent Heights. Less than a decade later, the *Informer* estimated his net worth at over $200,000. As an index to his community status, Prairie View State College counted him among its most successful alumni; he was head of the college's ex-student association for many years. He was also president of the local NAACP for most of the 1920s and is credited with helping to revive the Houston chapter, which had gone into serious decline early in the decade. Under his direction the Houston chapter took the lead in the defense of several high-profile criminal cases involving black defendants and helped keep community interest high in the unsuccessful attempt to prosecute the perpetrators of the Robert Powell lynching in 1928. He was also in the early vanguard of those seeking to overturn the white primary. As president, he also took the lead in recruiting young people for the NAACP and sponsored several social events to pad the membership rolls. His racial activism aroused the ire of some in the white community, and he received several death threats for his public involvement in civil rights causes. In fact, at one point he was given to carrying a pistol for self-protection, a weapon he never had an occasion to use against whites. By 1930, O. P. was much admired in the black community. Hazel Young, a younger contemporary, remembered him reverently:

> And everybody admired Mr. DeWalt because he had a theater that was nice, you could go in and sometimes after hours, you could have a party, invite your friends and everybody would come to see that person with you. And you would be dressed all up in your evening clothes and go in and see a picture that only your guests would be invited to. That was supposed to be a socialite affair. Mr. DeWalt was a nice person. I can remember him and his wife, and their home was such a nice home. We had our own social life as black people . . .

Lorenzo Greene, who was in Houston in the spring of 1930 to promote the Association of Negro Life and History, met DeWalt for the first time there and was impressed with the Houstonian's dedication to the teaching of black history and culture and with his business sense. According to Greene, "He claims to have the best Negro-owned theater in the South. It is large and well decorated, and contains the latest in sound-recording equipment. [DeWalt] is a fine man, with good business acumen, yet he has never attended a business college." In some ways, the Lincoln Theatre offered conventional entertainment to its patrons, including popular white western films and an occasional blockbuster such as

Les Misérables. DeWalt, however, was also eager to show black films whenever possible. He was especially proud to screen the work of the pioneering filmmaker Oscar Micheaux whose photoplays frequently rested on racial themes and were often controversial, especially among whites. In 1920, for example, the Lincoln was the only venue in Houston to offer Micheaux's first full-length film *Within Our Gates*, which was assumed by many to be the black response to the white D. W. Griffith's 1915 racist smash hit *The Birth of a Nation*. The Lincoln's newspaper advertisement for *Within Our Gates* on March 20, 1920 described the film as "A story of the Negro, written by a Negro, Played by Negroes. This is the most spectacular screen version of the most sensational story on the race question since 'Uncle Tom's Cabin.'" DeWalt's June 9, 1923 *Informer* promotion for Micheaux's *The Virgin of the Seminole* was clearly appealing to racial consciousness by announcing the film as "one of the biggest colored pictures we have ever shown. You'll be surprised at the great progress our race in making in the motion picture world." DeWalt gave similar billing to Micheaux's *30 Years Later* in 1929. The Lincoln was also host to *Hallelujah*, the first Hollywood production to feature an all-black cast. So prominent was the Lincoln Theatre in Houston that the *Informer* editorialized "that there is nothing else like it in Houston, or in Texas for that matter, owned and operated by a Negro, for Negroes." By the late 1920s DeWalt had begun to publish his own weekly newspaper, *The Lincoln Theatre Weekly News*, in which he announced forthcoming movies and other entertainment at his theater. But he also used his paper and his theater to promote political and social issues in which he had an abiding interest. In one issue, for instance, he reminded patrons that they could pay their poll tax at the Lincoln, and frequently he used advertisement space to encourage his readers to join the NAACP. In short, O. P. DeWalt was both a race activist and cultural entrepreneur, and often those two roles were impossible to separate. He was a businessman, and a good one at that, but his quest for turning a profit was always tempered by his commitment to the advancement of his race.

Notoriety, however, could easily breed controversy, jealousy, and sometimes even hatred. On April 23, 1931 DeWalt was shot by one of his long-time employees, Julius Frazier, in the projection room of the Lincoln Theatre. He died the next day in a local black hospital despite multiple blood transfusions. Although the Houston's white newspapers ignored the crime and his subsequent death, the *Houston Informer* and even the *Chicago Defender* gave the story generous coverage. DeWalt's funeral came as close as one could to having a state funeral in black Houston. There were thousands of mourners at the memorial service, and eulogies were as numerous as they were effusive. The NAACP raised money to help finance the prosecution of his murderer, and the community was rife with rumors that DeWalt had been the victim of a white supremacist conspiracy. One version of that rumor had it that DeWalt's attempt to upstage white theaters by booking *Hallelujah* before anyone else may have led directly to his slaying. In a controversial trial verdict a few weeks later his assailant was given a two-year prison sentence, much to the dismay of his friends and admirers who hoped for a more severe punishment. DeWalt, who was buried in Livingston, Texas, was survived by his widow, Maude, and two sons.

Thus, in the two decades before World War II Houston's black community grew in size and in social and cultural complexity. Heretofore, its history in this period has existed in only bits and pieces and its importance has often gone unnoticed. But the example of Houston and its sister cities of the Trans-Mississippi South and West have the potential of expanding and, at the same time, complexifying an important chapter in African American history in the early twentieth century. For years historians and others have focused their attention on this important development from the perspective mostly of the brilliant example of Harlem and a few other places in the North and East. But the history of Houston suggests that the New Negro movement, even the Harlem Renaissance, was not just a regional phenomenon; it was a national one. To be sure, Houston was no Harlem. It did not enjoy the size or the diversity of the black population in Upper Manhattan, and so viewed from a distance it may appear provincial at times, but it is no less useful in understanding the profound effects of urbanization on the black experience.

Further Reading

"A Feeling for Jazz: An Interview with Arnett Cobb." *Houston Review*. Volume XII, Number 3, 1990, pp. 123–143.

Chicago Defender, 1920–1940.

Christian, Garna. " Texas Beginnings: Houston in the World of Jazz." *Houston Review*. Volume XII, Number 3, 1990, pp. 144–166.

Fauser, Erica. "The Man Behind the Curtain: O. P. DeWalt and the Houston Renaissance." Provost Undergraduate Research Project University of Houston, 2009. Copy in possession of author.

Glasrud, Bruce A. "Harlem Renaissance in the United Sates: 8—Texas and the Southwest." In Cary D. Wintz and Paul Finkelman eds. *Encyclopedia of the Harlem Renaissance*, pp. 521–524. Routledge: New York, 2004.

Govenar, Alan. "Blues." *Handbook of Texas Online*. www.tshaonline.org/handbook/online/articles/FF/hpfl.html. Accessed August 24, 2010.

Greene, Lorenzo. "Sidelights on Houston Negroes as Seen by an Associate of Carter G. Woodson in 1930." In *Black Dixie: Afro-Texas History and Culture in Houston*. Texas A&M University Press: College Station, TX, 1992.

Houston Informer, 1920–1940.

McComb, David G. *Houston: A History*. University of Texas Press: Austin, 1980.

The Pittsburg Courier, 1915–1940.

Pruitt, Bernadette. "For the Advancement of the Race: The Great Migrations to Houston, Texas, 1914–1941. *Journal of Urban History*. Volume 31, Number 4, May, 2005, pp. 435–447.

Richardson, Clifton R. "Houston's Colored Citizens: Activities and Conditions among the Negro Population in the 1920s." In Beeth, Howard, and Cary D. Wintz. *Black Dixie: Afro-Texas History and Culture in Houston*. Texas A&M University Press: College Station, TX, 1992.

Saffer, Neil. "Texas Black Culture in Texas: A Lone Star Renaissance." In Glasrud, Bruce A. and James M. Smallwood. *The African American Experience in Texas: An Anthology.* Texas Tech University Press: Lubbock, TX, 2007.

SoRelle, James M. "Race Relations in Heavenly Houston, 1919–1945." In Beeth, Howard, and Cary D. Wintz. *Black Dixie: Afro-Texas History and Culture in Houston.* Texas A&M University Press: College Station, TX, 1992.

Strom, Steven. *Houston Lost and Unbuilt.* University of Texas Press: Austin, 2010.

Welling, David. *Cinema Houston: From Nickelodeon to Megaplex.* University of Texas Press: Austin, TX, 2007.

Wintz, Cary D. "Fourth Ward Houston." *Handbook of Texas Online.* www.tshaonline.org/handbook/online/articles/FF/hpfl.html. Accessed August 24, 2010.

Young, Hazel. Oral History interview. October 5, 2007. Houston Public Library Oral History Project. http://digital.houstonlibrary.org/cdm4/item_viewer.php?CISOROOT=/oralhistory&CISOPTR=22&CISOBOX=1&REC=13. Accessed August 5, 2010.

2

NORTH TEXAS'S BLACK ART AND LITERATURE DURING THE 1920S AND 1930S

"The Current Is Much Stronger"

Michael Phillips

Dominated by bankers and realtors with limited exposure to the urban culture of metropolises such as New York and Paris, for much of the twentieth century white Dallas held a philistine reputation regarding art. "I'll support the damned opera if I don't have to listen to it," Dallas Mayor R. L. Thornton once famously said in the 1950s. The ruling business clique saw paintings and sculptures as mere adornments to the city, like costume jewelry, not enterprises worthy in and of themselves. Dallas's white artists fled the city to find appreciation and an audience. Meanwhile, white art patrons in Dallas expected the music and paintings they subsidized to be non-controversial and apolitical. In 1955, right-wing pressure from groups such as the Public Affairs Luncheon Club forced The Dallas Museum of Fine Arts to remove works by supposedly leftist painters such as Diego Rivera and Pablo Picasso.

In contrast, especially in the 1920s and 1930s, African American art in Dallas became a passionate cause and was, by design, political and provocative. Unlike New York's Harlem neighborhood, Dallas served as a transit point for black authors, sculptors and kindred spirits. The important figures of Dallas's black art scene passed through the city but generally put down roots elsewhere. Many, particularly blues performers, lived perpetually on the road. This gave many of the big players in Dallas's artistic community a working-class lifestyle, bringing them closer to the down-and-out drifters, fighters and rebels they wrote and sang about. Dallas—and more broadly North Texas—is important to this time period: because of its status as a destination for rural African Americans seeking higher-paying city jobs in the 1920s and 1930s; for the blues music created there in this time period; and for the impact on American literature of writers such as John Mason Brewer and Melvin Tolson after their sojourns in the region.

During the Harlem Renaissance period, African Americans in Dallas and across North and Central Texas searched for their cultural roots in Africa and celebrated what they considered authentic black culture among field hands, the urban poor, janitors, maids, and petty criminals seeking a niche in which they could survive. African American women's clubs such as the Phillis Wheatley Art Club, Royal Arts Club, the Cecelian Choral Club and the Eady Mary Art and Culture Club proliferated in the 1920s and 1930s and stimulated discussion of poetry, novels and paintings. The community heatedly debated issues in art, with an African American weekly newspaper, the *Dallas Express*, serving as the forum for these passionate exchanges.

On March 15, 1919 the *Express* ran a column "Devoted To Colored Race Literature And Dedicated To Those Who Are Providing It," by Philadelphia writer M. G. Duggars. The column reveals the range of issues the black arts community engaged in during this period. In rapid fashion, Duggars praises black newspapers such as *The Philadelphia Tribune* that used "great discretion" in accepting advertisements from companies selling hair straighteners and skin-bleaching treatments aimed at giving African Americans a "whiter" appearance. (Ironically, the *Dallas Express* would be filled with such ads for decades.) Insisting that whites show African Americans respect, Duggars advised his readers to avoid any newspaper that "prints 'Negro' without using a capital 'N.' Why not take a race paper and escape the indignity[?]" Through columns such as Duggars's, the *Dallas Express* not only made its audience aware of Harlem Renaissance writers such as Langston Hughes but also raised the readership's awareness of the political implications for their works and the responsibility all prominent African Americans and black institutions had towards "racial uplift."

The *Express* gave news space to generally unpublished poets, some of whom urged readers to preserve a respect for the black cultural past. An intense exchange in North and Central Texas developed between traditionalists and modernizers. One contributor to the *Express*, Sarah Collin Fernadis, attacked attempts to fuse black gospel songs from the slave era with modern jazz rhythms. The gospel "freedom songs" mixed faith in God's justice with demands for political freedom in the here-and-now, but in a poem published by the *Express* on January 20, 1923, Fernadis feared that reframing such powerful lyrics in a jazz setting would compromise the dignity of the older material:

> So, they've sought a new sensation
> [in] this modern jazz craze
> In the ruthless syncopation of
> Those sweet old plaintive lays
> That the souls of their forefathers
> 'neath affliction's heavy rod
> coined from bitterness of sorrow
> as they reach for touch with God . . .

Referencing gospel classics such as "Swing Low, Sweet Chariot," and "Steal Away to Jesus," Fernadis ends her plea on a plaintive note: "O ye unthinking inheritors of this rare and sacred tract—/Of a race's soul's outpouring—/jazz in pleasure if you must/But . . . leave, O leave untouched, unsullied, those dear songs your fathers gave."

Amateurs such as Fernadis were not alone in looking towards the past to find cultural authenticity. Prolific author, folklorist, historian and poet John Mason Brewer did not care for his contemporaries in the Harlem Renaissance, complaining in 1932 to his mentor J. Frank Dobie about "how unrepresentative the loudly-heralded literature out of Harlem" was and "how false both in psychology and language." Brewer perhaps misjudged his New York contemporaries as elitists. Brewer himself embraced the dialect of the downcast in a series of books, journals and privately published works produced from the 1930s until the 1960s. He never openly discussed the political implications of his tales, but his effort to get the intonation just right in his stories reveals a defiant attitude toward white America. He believed that the stories told by black slaves and their sharecropper descendants could stand any comparison to the supposedly more sophisticated art of white museums and symphony halls.

Brewer served as the Dallas Renaissance artist *par excellence*. Brewer's mother Minnie taught school for fifty years. She viewed her son—born March 24, 1896, in the Central Texas town of Goliad—as one of her most important pupils. She guided John to "Negro history books and the poems and stories of Paul Laurence Dunbar as soon as he could read," according to Brewer biographer James Byrd. Brewer's father took on a legion of humble jobs, including mail carrier, grocer, wagoner, and barber, as he struggled to support six children. The elder Brewer stoked young John's imagination with tales of his career driving cattle to Kansas at the height of the cowboy era. After graduating from Wiley College in Marshall, Texas, Brewer won appointment as professor at Samuel Huston (now Huston-Tillotson) College in Austin after World War I. In perhaps the most critical moment of his life, in 1931 he formed a friendship with Dobie, Texas's chief folklore collector and interpreter, and one of the state's most widely regarded authors. Dobie liked his young colleague personally and admired his scholarship. As a white man with extensive connections in the academic and publishing worlds, Dobie played a key role in getting Brewer's future books published.

Brewer spent much of the 1930s in the Dallas-Fort Worth area, and taught Spanish at the segregated Booker T. Washington High School in Big D even as his first books were being published. During this time and throughout his career, he did field work across Texas, collecting stories dating back to slavery times. Brewer's advanced education and his success as a writer never altered his working-class identity. Throughout his subsequent works, he portrayed the powerful as ruthless con artists. In one of his earliest works, *Negrito: Negro Dialect Poems of the Southwest* (published in 1933), the rich lose their souls as they grasp for power. In a series of quatrains, Brewer rebuked a series of archetypes, taking one swipe at African American politicians who appealed to black pride while catering to the demands of the white power structure. In "Politician" he points out the politician who plays the role of the race man in front of his black constituents: "Den sells 'em for uh drink."

When circulating in the white world, Brewer warned his readers, black people needed to put the larger black community ahead of even their own career ambitions and to remember that intelligence, talent, humor, and hard work would more than likely be met with indifference, fear, or disrespect by the city's ruling class. With material benefits small or non-existent, achievement had to be its own reward, Brewer argued, through his tale, "The Hays County Courthouse Janitor." In this story, "Unkah Sug Miller," a janitor at the Hays County Courthouse in the Central Texas town of San Marcos, is confronted by a county judge who hates him. The judge warns the janitor that even though he has never missed a day of work in twenty-five years, he will be fired unless he learns to read and write. The judge sees to it that Sug gets sacked, and four years elapse before the two confront each other on a San Marcos street.

The judge, to his great surprise, learns that Miller has become a wealthy farmer. He praises Sug who has "come up in de worl' fas'—'taint no tellin' what you'd of been sho 'nuff, if'n you'd of knowed how to read an' write." Sug is unimpressed with the judge's reaction. "Ah knows zackly what Ah'd of been," Sug says. "Ah'd of still been de janitor at the Hays County Coa'thouse."

The tale reminds one of Malcolm X's bitter joke: "What would you call an educated Negro with a B.A., an M.A., a B.S. or a Ph.D.? You call him a nigger." Sug knew that white society set a low upper limit on black prestige. The mythic American land of opportunity had no place for African Americans. A literate janitor would still be nothing more than a floor sweeper to the white world.

Brewer sought to empower his black readers, even if he tempered his encouragement with heavy doses of realism. Some readers might interpret the conclusion of the "Janitor" story as surrender to fatalism. Such an interpretation would ignore the fact that once Miller exits the white world, his genius realizes its potential and he becomes a prosperous farmer. Brewer walked a tightrope. He did not defend segregation but he informed his black audience that African American poverty directly resulted from white oppression.

Brewer's works reflect an incipient black nationalism. The title of his poetry collection "Negrito" referred to the Negritude movement, a black-affirming approach to art, inspiring African-descended intellectuals on both sides of the Atlantic. Like other Negritude writers, Brewer sought to blow away white racism and discrimination not by imitating Anglo society but by establishing a new blackness. With an unblinking lack of sentimentality, he sought cultural and political equality on black terms.

The complex meaning of black identity remained central to Brewer's art. If Jim Crow laws implied that the "white" and "black" races were clearly separate and easily defined, centuries of white sexual assault committed against black women during and after slavery created a more complex, multi-racial world. A universe of color existed within Texas's African American community. In North Central Texas, ethnic tension sometimes existed between darker-skinned individuals and those with lighter, so-called "high yeller" complexion, and the skin bleach ads in the *Dallas Express* suggested higher esteem for "whiter" skin. In the eyes of artists such as Brewer, however, this spectrum of pigment instead stood as mute testament to white oppression and a shared alienation from mainstream culture. Brewer expressed this unity in "Apostolic," a 1936 poem in which he describes an African American church congregation displaying all the hues produced by white sexual subordination:

> [A] seething mass of black, brown and yellow beings
> Shouting tunes, mysterious mixtures of Jazz, Religious and Jungle
>   melodies

Ironically, Brewer shares this concern with one of the other great writers from North Texas during the Harlem Renaissance period, poet and Wiley College professor Melvin Beaunorus Tolson. In many ways, Tolson—who filled his verse with erudite references to ancient classics and displayed a deep knowledge of world literature—represented the "unrepresentative" elite black artist Brewer so disliked. However, Brewer and Tolson, whose championship debate teams at Wiley in Marshall, Texas, were depicted in the 2007 film *The Great Debaters* starring Denzel Washington, shared much in common. The meaning of black identity also concerned Tolson, whose epic poem "Harlem Gallery" explored themes similar to those in Brewer's "Apostolic." Unlike Brewer, however, Tolson explicitly rejected race as a meaningful biological concept. A Marxist for much of his adult life, Tolson saw race as a social construction, a fabricated identity used to internally divide the working class along color lines. If Brewer never seriously questioned what made an individual "black," that issue serves as a central concern in the "Psi" section of "Harlem Gallery." Here he addresses the ambiguity of racial identity, which shifts depending on situation and perspective. In this poem, Tolson suggests that both "whiteness" and "blackness" lack validity as categories. The white voice uses stereotypical black dialect ("in deah ole Norfolk") while the black voice uses elite grammar. The narrator describes himself as a chameleon, able to assume any identity, which Tolson suggests is a mindset the opposite of that of the white South, which seeks to chain individuals to racial categories for the purpose of dividing and conquering the working masses.

Born in Missouri, Tolson graduated from Lincoln University in Pennsylvania in 1924, winning an appointment to teach English and speech at Wiley College, 152 miles east of Dallas. He stayed there until 1947. Tolson became one of the most acclaimed Texas authors of his age, black or white. "Tolson's poetic lines and images sing, affirm, reject, predict, and judge experience in America, and his poetry is direct and humanistic," proclaimed esteemed Harlem Renaissance novelist Richard Wright. "All history, from Genesis to Munich, is his domain. The strong men keep coming and Tolson is one of them."

Although able to defuse conflicts with his charm, Tolson did not shy from bluntly confronting what he saw as evil. At one point, Tolson organized a boycott of Marshall merchants to force them to provide better and more courteous treatment of black customers, a movement that inspired talk of lynching. He ran the risk of lynching again in 1938 when, as an invited speaker at a high-school commencement in Rustin, Louisiana, he strongly condemned a lynching that had taken place near the small town the day before. "Where were you good folks when these men were lynched?" he asked the audience, which included the white sheriff, police chief and president of the school board. Warned by locals that they faced violent reprisals, Tolson and an armed Wiley student who escorted him to the event made a quick exit, driving along back roads in the dead of night back to Texas.

While Brewer only implied rape as the cause of black color diversity, Tolson is bolder and more explicit. Referring to the naked women who stood before white bidders during slave sales across antebellum America as "The dark hymens on the auction block," Tolson mournfully asked in the same poem:

> [W]hat midnight-to-dawn lecheries,
>   in cabin and big house,
> produced these brown hybrids and yellow motleys
>   White Boy,
> *Buchenwald* is a melismatic song . . .

Tolson's concerns are more universal than Brewer's. Brewer grounds much of his writing firmly in the Texas setting, and even if he complicates black identity, the white world appears relatively homogenous in his poems and folktales. Tolson, however, sees poor African Americans as part of a globally oppressed working class, divided from their white and brown brethren only through the conscious manipulations of elites. In the above passage's reference to the Buchenwald concentration camp, Tolson links Southern racism to eliminationist Nazism. In a melismatic song, one sings a single syllable of lyrics to a series of notes. Tolson suggests that Louisiana lynchers are simply another face of the same fascist monstrosity stalking Europe in the early and mid-1940s.

Racism, Tolson argued in his poetry and his newspaper columns, was the common enemy of all underpaid and overworked humanity. As he observes in "The Underdogs," the poem that closes "Harlem Gallery," Jews, Slavs, Italians and even "poor white trash" in America have been deceived by plutocrats who play these marginalized groups against each other in order to disenfranchise and keep wages low.

Brewer was implicitly political, and Tolson was explicitly so. Brewer dealt with the hardships and tragedies of black life in America with humor, while Tolson responded with blunt rage and calls for revolution. Lillian B. Jones Horace, an African American novelist in Fort Worth active in that city's black theater circle, fantasized about a more just and fair life for African Americans "returning" to Africa. A teacher born in Jefferson, Texas, about 168 miles northeast of Dallas near the Louisiana border, Horace moved with her family to Fort Worth early in her childhood. She attended Prairie View Normal School near Houston and Bishop College in Marshall before beginning her teaching career in Tarrant County in 1905. An English teacher and dean of girls at I. M. Terrell High School in Fort Worth, she established the campus's drama department and the school's first drama club. Horace, then twenty years old, starred as the Old Testament title character in an African American production of the musical *Queen Esther* produced by the namesake of the Terrell School at Fort Worth City Hall, Professor Terrell. The local African American press praised the production, describing it as an "excellent entertainment" that "would have done credit to amateur singers anywhere." Horace also guided the I. M. Terrell Dramatic Club's original operetta *The Stolen Princess*, staged during the troupe's inaugural season in 1922. Horace's ideas seem to have been deeply influenced by Marcus Garvey, the Jamaica-born founder of the United Negro Improvement Association, which claimed thirty branches across the country by 1919. Garvey, who heavily influenced the Nation of Islam sect, taught that "black is beautiful." Opposing the Euro–American view that Africa represented a civilization wasteland where inhabitants lived in the Stone Age until the arrival of Europeans, Garvey told his followers that Africans had built a noble civilization and that white culture was diseased. Racism was so deeply entrenched in white society, he preached, that it was useless to appeal to their sense of justice.

Garvey felt that blacks would be free only if segregated from whites while in the United States, and once even met with Klan leaders to discuss common strategy to achieve racial separation. Ultimately, the only hope for African Americans, he said, was for blacks in the United States to return to Africa and build a new nation of their own, a program he called "Negro Zionism." Garvey called this theoretical nation the "Empire of Africa" and crowned himself provisional president of that state in 1921.

Garveyites were active in Dallas, and the thoughts and deeds of Garvey received heavy coverage in the *Dallas Express*. In this atmosphere, a time when Texas ranked third among the states in the nation in numbers of lynchings per year, Horace wrote the utopian novel *Five Generations Hence*. The title reflects Horace's hope that African Americans would be resettled in the home continent in five generations. In the novel, the heroine, Miss Noble, shared a recent vision with a friend:

> It seemed a week of horrors to our people throughout the land, of which I read in the daily papers: there had been a lynching not far away and it seemed that the end of my endurance was reached when members of my

race, men and women and even children, were attacked upon the streets of one of our leading cities, brutally assaulted, and forced to flee like hunted beasts . . . I saw the Negro for more than fourteen generations of oppression attended by theft from their native shores and crack of the whip about their heads.

[Then] I saw a people, a black people, tilling the soil with a song of real joy upon their lips. I saw a civilization like to the white man's about us today, but in his place stood another of a different hue. I beheld beautifully paved streets, handsome homes beautified and adorned, and before the doors sported dusky boys and girls . . . I was as if thunder struck when a still small voice, yet seeming to penetrate my inmost soul, cried in thunderous accents, "Five Generations Hence." I was stunned as the truth began to dawn: the land was Africa, the people were my own returned to possess the heritage of their ancestors.

Marxists such as Tolson ridiculed such Garveyism. Unlike Horace, Tolson and Brewer saw America as a land that belonged as much to blacks as to whites. Furthermore, like W. E. B. Du Bois, Tolson would argue that hoping for a mass migration of African Americans across the Atlantic was a futile pipedream. White supremacy threatened people of color globally. Even as Horace wrote her novel, brutal British, French and Belgian colonial regimes had raped Africa, stolen its resources, and exploited its people.

If white Texas lacked a vibrant artistic tradition in the early twentieth century, Afro-Texans in the 1920s and 1930s spawned a vital creative outpouring that encompassed not just novels, folktale collections and poetry but also nurtured one of the most important blues and jazz music scenes in the United States. Deep Ellum, a collection of pawnshops, liquor joints, nightclubs and gambling dens east of downtown Dallas at the time of the Harlem Renaissance, became a well-known (to African Americans) performance venue for such musical heavyweights as Bessie Smith, Leadbelly, Blind Lemon Jefferson, Aaron "T-Bone" Walker and the legendary songwriter and composer Robert Johnson. Johnson recorded thirteen of his best-known songs, such as "Love in Vain" and "Me and the Devil Blues" over a two-day period at the Warner Brothers Film Exchange building at 508 Park in Dallas in June, 1937, the year before his death at the age of twenty-seven. Because of new technology, blues and jazz artists from around the country could be heard in Dallas on 78 rpm records. One of the earliest producers of so-called "race records," the Okeh label, advertised heavily in the *Dallas Express*. But even without a gramophone, black and white residents and visitors to Dallas could enjoy the same artists live at a number of music clubs lining the Deep Ellum district.

If authors such as Brewer and Tolson depicted a world in which racial antagonism created unbridgeable distance between the black and white worlds, Deep Ellum became one of the few places where white and black cultures openly

FIGURE 2.1 The Harlem Theater in the Deep Ellum district of Dallas in the 1930s. The Harlem Theater was one of the venues for the rich African American cultural scene in Dallas during the Harlem Renaissance. From the collections of the Texas/Dallas History and Archives Division, Dallas Public Library

nourished each other and even blended. Deep Ellum became "the gathering place of blacks from all over the country, for Mexicans fleeing oppression in Mexico, for Jews who established businesses and poor whites looking for 'action,'" wrote Robert Prince, a local historian from the nearby State-Thomas district. "The white-owned stores on Elm served both black and white patrons," Dallas music historians Alen B Govenar and Jay F. Brakesfield wrote in their monograph *Deep Ellum and Central Track: Where the Black and White Worlds of Dallas Converged.* ". . . The black music played in Deep Ellum was also a force in the development of Western swing . . . Deep Ellum, then, was a crossroads, a nexus, where peoples and cultures could interact and influence each other in relative freedom."

Performers in Deep Ellum sang of an irredeemably corrupt world. "If you go down on Deep Ellum/To have a little fun/Have your fifteen dollars ready/when that policeman comes," warned the ballad "Deep Ellum Blues." The police, according to the song, were not there to protect black men and women but to engage in corrupt shakedowns. For blacks in Dallas, the presumption of innocence represented a pleasant fantasy; racial biases haunted any African American caught in the Kafkaesque Texas justice system.

"I wonder why they electrocute a man at the one o'clock hour of night?" asked Blind Lemon Jefferson, a frequent performer in Deep Ellum. A native Texan, Jefferson then answers the question posed in "'Lectric Chair Blues" with a cold bluntness:

> Because the current is much stronger,
> when the folks has turned out all the lights

By the 1930s, many black homes in Texas still lacked electricity, but the white man made sure the juice would be there when it came time to kill black convicts. Another blues legend regularly played in the hot Deep Ellum music scene, Huddie Ledbetter (better known as Leadbelly). Leadbelly first encountered a jazz band in Dallas in 1910, and he became a regular performer at speakeasies, nightclubs and other music venues there, beginning in 1920. Sent to prison three times during his adult life, he gained more experience than he wanted with the separate and unequal systems of justice offered blacks and whites in America. In an old European folk song recast within the black lyrical tradition by Leadbelly, "Gallis [Gallows] Pole," a condemned black man is saved from hanging only through bribery. The narrator pleads with members of his family for money:

> Mother did you bring me silver?
> Mother did you bring me gold?
> What did you bring me mother,
> [To] keep me from the gallis pole?

In his notes for the song, Leadbelly wrote, "In the olden days when you put a man in prison behind the bars in a jailhouse if he had 15 or 25 or 30 dollars you could save him from the gallows pole because they were gonna hang him if he don't bring up a little money." Lynchings, the "sudden" death of blacks in police custody or while being pursued or arrested, and white juries' greater readiness to send black defendants (as opposed to white defendants) to Death Row, represent only the top of a lengthy menu of ways white Dallasites murdered black residents.

According to a 1927 report by the Civic Federation of Dallas's Interracial Committee, 66 percent of Dallas's black residents lived in buildings lacking bathtubs, water, and toilets. With most neighborhoods closed to blacks due to segregation laws, just under 30,000 African Americans crammed into the 3.5 square miles set aside for them, families doubling and tripling up in rental units that became flashpoints for tuberculosis, diphtheria, scarlet fever, and other contagious diseases. Such suffering provided deep source material for Dallas's blues performers. Even when blacks fell ill in Dallas, they could not be assured that they would receive life-saving medical care. In her autobiography *Lady Sings the Blues*, the great jazz vocalist Billie Holiday tells the story of her father's illness.

Himself an accomplished musician, Clarence Holiday came down with pneumonia during a tour of club dates in North Texas in 1937 and died as he traveled
from hospital to hospital looking for one that would admit black patients.
"And it wasn't the pneumonia that killed him, it was Dallas, Texas," Billie Holiday
said. Holiday later said that she decided to record her famous, mournful jeremiad
against lynching, "Strange Fruit," because of the institutional murder of her father
in Dallas.

Few singers in his era were as outspoken or direct politically as Leadbelly.
This real-life singer-songwriter built such a reputation for toughness that he became
the central character in tall tales Brewer included in *American Negro Folklore*. His
songs often took the form of musical journalism, peppered with pungent social
commentary, as in his classic commentary on segregated Washington, DC,
"Bourgeois Blues":

> Well, me and my wife we were standing upstairs
> We heard the white man say'n I don't want no niggers up there
>   Lord, in a bourgeois town
>   . . . .
>   I got the bourgeois blues

Songs such as "Bourgeois Blues" constituted a call to action, made by a hard-as-
nails ex-convict who survived several near-death experiences fighting and clawing
his way through poverty shacks and the racist Texas prison system. Leadbelly's
work is available to audiences today largely because of the recordings made by
white folklorists and musicologists John and Alan Lomax. Meanwhile, the Dallas
theater scene of the mid- and late 1920s came the closest to producing the
collaboration of white and black artists that Harlem Renaissance writers such as
Alain Locke hoped for as a means of creating a movement for social justice.

In Dallas, the white arts community had moved well past the population as a
whole in its receptivity to African American art and awareness of the hardships
facing blacks. In its debut 1923–1924 season, the Little Theatre staged *Judge Lynch*,
a one-act play written by *Dallas Times Herald* entertainment editor John William
Rogers, Jr., concerning an innocent black man unjustly hanged by a mob after
being accused of committing murder during the theft of a watch. In 1929 and
1930, a white high school English teacher in Dallas, Kathleen Witherspoon,
authored a play about racial injustice called *Jute*. The script concerned the title
character, a mixed-race young woman, secretly the offspring of one of the most
powerful white people in a small Georgia town, Judge Richardson. Jute's sexually
promiscuous behavior with the white men in town leads to her expulsion. Written
in dialect, the play lapsed into condescension and stereotype at times, but
remained a searing critique of sexual double standards and the hypocrisy regarding
interracial sex in the Jim Crow era, a time when white men assumed a right to
erotically exploit black women while black men risked their lives if they looked

in the direction of a white woman. In April 1930 the Oak Cliff Little Theatre put on a production of *Jute* with an all-white cast that included Witherspoon playing the lead role in blackface. In the first months of 1931, the Dallas Negro Players staged the same play with an all-black cast. Black theatrical groups struggled for financial survival in the 1920s and, like white production companies in the city, folded during the Great Depression. But groups such as the Negro Players represented the increased interest in art and literature inspired by the Harlem Renaissance. *Jute* remained a popular choice for local audiences. However, as *Dallas Morning News* theater critic John Rosenfield noted, when the Oak Cliff Little Theatre tried to stage this play about racial intolerance again four years later, this time with an interracial cast, producers "ran into a stupid but stubborn invocation of the Jim Crow law" and the revival had to be cancelled.

Black art in Dallas during the pre-World War II era reached an apotheosis with the 1936 Texas Centennial Exposition and the construction of the "Hall of Negro Life" at the city's Fair Park. Businessman and Dallas civil rights leader A. Maceo Smith won a $100,000 appropriation from the state legislature to build an exhibit hall celebrating black history. The state withdrew its financial support, however, when Smith refused to back down after endorsing a black candidate, Ammon S. Wells, running in a special election for the Texas House.

The state legislature passed a $3 million appropriation for the Centennial in April 1935, with not a penny reserved for the Hall of Negro Life. However, with the Centennial taking place during the Depression, many local businessmen worried the event would be a financial flop and that the fair would need the support of local blacks. A white oilman, Walter D. Cline of Wichita Falls, agreed to win federal support for the Negro Hall if African Americans successfully sold $50,000 worth of bonds backing fairground construction. The bonds sold, and the United States Congress passed a $3 million package for the fair, including $100,000 for the Hall of Negro Life.

Given only 90 days before the start of the centennial celebration, work crews constructed a 10,000-square-foot exhibition hall. Exhibit organizers had to accept white contractors to build the hall, including a painter who splashed the interiors with bright red and green because, he said, black people liked loud colors and would need "something pretty to look at." (Ironically, those colors would be associated with the African independence movement two decades later.) The original interior was redecorated with more subdued hues when the exhibit officially opened on "Juneteenth" (the anniversary of the date when the Union Army first implemented the Emancipation Proclamation in Texas, on June 19, 1865).

Disdained by some black intellectuals in Texas who wanted to distance their community from slavery, Juneteenth had long served as a black working-class celebration of freedom. The confluence of Juneteenth (a day that resembles July 4th parties with its family-oriented feasts and church services) and the intelligentsia-crafted exhibit, which depicted blacks since slavery as acquiring civilization rather than descending from noble cultural traditions, captured the class tensions intrinsic in the Harlem Renaissance. Opening day featured track and boxing events. A troupe of black actors established supposed "high art" credentials with a production of *Macbeth*, and judges crowned a bathing beauty queen the "Cleopatra of the Centennial"—perhaps a subtle way to inform audiences that black Africans formed part of the Egyptian royal family. Jazz great Cab Calloway performed his masterpieces while the Jubilaires choral group celebrated traditional black music such as spirituals drawn from the days of slavery. Event organizers did not segregate the celebration into mutually exclusive categories of highbrow and lowbrow art.

The hall's organizers hoped to fill black patrons with pride and to educate white visitors. They knew they had to contend with a white-concocted master narrative that depicted Africans as living in the Stone Age until the arrival of the European slave ships in the 1400s and as having acquired the veneer of civilization due to the patient tutelage of their white masters in America. The emphasis on cultural progress since 1865 perhaps unintentionally demeaned African culture and the society that had been created by the slaves. Based on white reactions to the hall, however, it appears that the African American organizers of the exhibit knew their majority audience well.

Immediately at the front door, visitors encountered a sculpted plaster model of a black man "with broken chains from slavery, ignorance, and superstitions falling from his wrists." This sculpture depicted the folklore John Mason Brewer saw as essential to the black soul as cultural baggage that should be thrown off as soon as possible. Pamphlets touted rising African American literacy rates while other exhibits displayed black inventions and bragged of the achievements of black leaders.

A series of murals along the walls of the lobby by New York artist Aaron Douglas, a major figure of the Harlem Renaissance, became the one point in the Hall where the black hope for the future did not at least partly imply a denigration of the past. Douglas's work, inspired to a large degree by West African art, proved both eye-catching and subversive. His mural "Negro's Gift to America" portrayed African Americans as contributors to the nation's music, art and religion. His previous paintings displayed a deep appreciation of the spiritual continuity of African religious ceremonies and the rhythms of African American spirituals, and the painter celebrated black popular culture. In the Hall's murals, Douglas made the African and slave ancestors of 1930s Afro-Texans a felt presence, the protective guardians of an unbent black soul.

The painter used the slave past to advocate for black freedom in early twentieth-century America. Alonzo J. Aden, a curator at the Hall of Negro Life, noted in a published description of the work that Douglas placed a woman in the center of one mural. Previously, Aden said, "the Negro woman has occupied the lowest position. Here she is given a place of honor." The woman holds a baby in her outstretched arms in "a plea for equal recognition . . . The child is a sort of banner, a pledge of Negro determination to carry on . . . in [a] struggle toward truth and light." Below the painting Douglas placed a banner with a roll call of great black artists, inventors and thinkers such as poet Paul Laurence Dunbar, abolitionist leaders Sojourner Truth, Harriet Tubman and Frederick Douglass and Dr. Daniel H. Williams, an acclaimed African American surgeon from Chicago. "Into Bondage" depicted Africans facing the shore as a slave ship approached, while "Aspiration" featured silhouettes gazing upward at a futuristic castle on a mountain summit, while below chained hands reach toward the sky.

William A. Webb, who took over as Centennial director from Walter Cline, did everything he could to obscure the exhibition hall. A man described as still fighting the Civil War, Webb demanded the planting of a cluster of cedar trees directly in front of the exhibit. Nevertheless, the hall drew more than 400,000 people during the course of the exposition, about 60 percent of them white. Whites often found the experience disturbing. Earline Carson, a librarian who staffed the information desk at the Hall, remembered an angry fit thrown by one white woman from nearby Corsicana, Texas. "She advanced a few feet into the hall and was standing as one transfixed, looking all about her," Carson said. "All of a sudden she exclaimed . . . 'No! No! Niggers did not do this.'" Some visitors expressed even a new doubt about white supremacy. "Why if you were to give Negroes an equal chance, they would surpass white people," one woman declared.

The Hall of Negro Life stood as an island of integration, the one place where whites and blacks peacefully mingled. Otherwise, African Americans faced the usual humiliating hassle of finding restrooms and concessions open to them. Black critics, who saw the exhibit as collaboration with Jim Crow, also attacked the hall. In a letter to the *Dallas Express*, Charles H. Bynum, a teacher at Booker T. Washington High, dismissed officials associated with the hall as "Uncle Toms" who rationalized the "gross injustices" suffered by black visitors to the fair. Bynum argued that no exhibit should have been opened if it took place in a larger context of segregation. Ghettoizing tributes to black achievement in one building while African American visitors were reminded of their social inferiority by segregated restrooms, water fountains and ice cream stands represented a Pyrrhic victory at best, Bynum suggested.

The Bynum view of men like A. Maceo Smith unfortunately, proved surprisingly durable. African American civil rights leaders in Dallas would languish in obscurity compared to their peers in other southern cities, or would be accused of collaborating with their oppressors. Until the mid-1990s, Dallas's African American community attracted little interest from historians. Neither black nor white art produced in Dallas drew much attention from national critics. The city's black political leadership drew little comment, and what attention it received proved negative. Longtime Dallas journalist Jim Schutze's 1986 book *The Accommodation: The Politics of Race in an American City* did not label men such as Maceo Smith "Toms," but it did accuse that generation of black leaders of exchanging the fight for social justice for a promise of relative physical safety.

White Dallas in the 1930s had a less sanguine view of the black generation that fueled the city's cultural flowering in the 1920s and 1930s. The Hall of Negro Life may have embraced the condescending white narrative of "Negro Progress" but it also became a venue where whites and blacks could find tributes to—and the words of—black radicals such as W. E. B. Du Bois and singer Paul Robeson. Apparently the exhibit frightened not only the stray visitor from Corsicana. The Hall of Negro Life proved too dangerous to survive. What could not be hidden by cedar trees had to be demolished. When officials announced that the Centennial Exposition would continue in 1937 as the Greater Texas and Pan American Exposition, a wrecking crew tore the Hall down, the only original permanent structure that was immediately destroyed.

Deep Ellum, where in the early twentieth century the most influential blues, swing and jazz musicians of the Southwest first found voice and an audience, fell victim to a combination of macroeconomics and urban planning that focused on the needs of affluent whites at the expense of the black and white urban working class. In 2010, the Warner Brothers Film Exchange, where Robert Johnson and Charlie Parker recorded, was across from The Stewpot, a resource center for the homeless. The Exchange was boarded up and facing possible demolition. (By late 2010, First Presbyterian Church of Dallas was attempting to buy the structure and said it would restore the old studio.) The Deep Ellum of the 1920s and 1930s was eroded piece by piece until it became another urban ghost like the Hall of Negro Life.

The Great Depression drove the district's big theaters out of business even as doctors' and lawyers' offices in the neighborhood shut down and relocated near the black middle-class Mecca of State-Thomas. Unoccupied buildings lent a seedy character to the businesses that remained, while the advent of television in the 1950s changed entertainment habits for blacks and whites. The newly constructed Central Expressway, the first sections of which were operational by 1950, also sealed off the Deep Ellum district from the rest of downtown Dallas. By the 1970s, the district featured vacant lots and empty warehouses, only to be gentrified first into a collection of music clubs and then a chic cluster of lofts, cafes and avant-garde art galleries. Developers in the 1980s even toyed with erasing the Deep Ellum name, which originated from local black and/or Jewish pronunciations of "Elm Street," hoping to coin a whiter, more upscale moniker.

John Mason Brewer's works remain, but they now reside primarily in seldom-inspected special-collections sections of libraries. Contemporary readers, black and white, have largely forgotten Brewer. The home where he grew up and where he spent much of his adult life, the John Henry Brewer and Minnie Tate House at 1108 Chicon St. in Austin, made the National Register of Historical Places in 1995, but remains vacant and has been sadly neglected, the remains decaying and splattered with graffiti.

In a city with as thin an artistic tradition as Dallas, one that seeks cultural prestige and lacks the aesthetic confidence even of its western neighbor Fort Worth, it would seem that civic leaders might memorialize the black creative output of the early twentieth century. Instead, like much of the Dallas past, this period has been tossed in an Orwellian Memory Hole. Perhaps there is a reason deeper than boredom with history. The physical erasure of all but the most wispy traces of Dallas's artistic flowering in the 1920s and 1930s suggests that the movement was not the accommodating work of Uncle Toms but the blossoming of Texas black insurgency, an adamant revolt against the city's crassly mercantilist values. Historian Harvey Graff recently suggested that Dallas is a city at war with its past. That war has left the city's black artistic heritage literally buried under rubble.

Further Reading

Acheson, Sam, *et al.* with an introduction by John Rosenfield. *Three Southwest Plays.* Dallas, TX: Southwest Review, 1942.

Asch, Moses and Alan Lomax. *The Leadbelly Songbook: The Ballads, Blues and Folksongs of Huddie Ledbetter.* New York: Oak Publications, 1962.

Boswell, James David. "Negro Participation in the 1936 Texas Centennial Exposition." Master's report, University of Texas at Austin, 1969.

Brewer, J. Mason. *Negrito: Negro Dialect Poems of the Southwest.* San Antonio, TX: Naylor Printing Company, 1933.

———. *Heralding Dawn: An Anthology of Verse.* Dallas, TX: June Thomason Printing, 1936.

———. "John Tales," in Mody C. Boatright, ed., *Mexican Border Ballads and Other Lore,* Publications of the Texas Folklore Society, Vol. XXI. Austin, TX: Texas Folklore Society, 1946.

———. *The Word on the Brazos: Negro Preacher Tales from the Brazos Bottoms of Texas.* Austin, TX: The University of Texas Press, 1953.

Byrd, James. *J. Mason Brewer: Negro Folklorist.* Austin, TX: Steck-Vaughn Company, 1967.

Dallas Express, issues from 1919 to 1925.

Farnsworth, Robert M. *Melvin B. Tolson, 1898–1966: Plain Talk and Poetic Prophecy.* Columbia, MO: University of Missouri Press, 1984.

Govenar, Alan B. and Jay F. Brakesfield. *Deep Ellum and Central Track: Where the Black and White Worlds of Dallas Converged.* Denton, TX: University of North Texas Press, 1998.

Graff, Harvey J. *The Dallas Myth: The Making and Unmaking of an American City.* Minneapolis, MI: University of Minnesota Press, 2008.

Jones, Jan. *Renegades, Showmen and Angels: A Theatrical History of Fort Worth from 1873–2001.* Fort Worth, TX: Texas Christian University Press, 2006.

Kessler, Carol Farley. *Daring to Dream: Utopian Fiction by United States Women Before 1950.* Syracuse, NY: Syracuse University Press, 1995.

Phillips, Michael. *White Metropolis: Race, Ethnicity and Religion in Dallas, 1841–2001.* Austin, TX: The University of Texas Press, 2006.

"Power Still Growing, The Excitement Unabated: Texas," *Life Magazine,* July 1, 1966, 59.

Schutze, Jim. *The Accommodation: The Politics of Race in An American City.* Secaucus, NJ: Citadel Press, 1986.

Thomas, Jesse O. *Negro Participation in the Texas Centennial Exposition.* Boston, MA: The Christopher Publishing House, 1938.

Tolson, Melvin B. *"Harlem Gallery" and Other Poems of Melvin B. Tolson* (Raymond Nelson, ed.) Charlottesville, VA: University Press of Virginia, 1999.

3

THE WESTERN BLACK RENAISSANCE IN THE KANSAS CITY REGION

Marc Rice

When Kansas City bandleader Bennie Moten died suddenly on April 1, 1935, thousands of African Americans turned out for one of the most extravagant funerals that the city's black community had ever witnessed. As the African American newspaper the *Kansas City Call* reported, the loss of one of the region's most famous musicians was deeply felt: "Many who were unable to gain entrance into the church formed a line on both sides of the street for blocks to view the procession as it passed. Many who stood on the sidewalks as the funeral cortege crawled by wept openly." The procession traveled through the 18th and Vine neighborhood, the black commercial and cultural center of western Missouri and eastern Kansas. It passed churches, businesses, restaurants, dance clubs, theaters, and social institutions that had supported Moten during his entire career. And as the cortege traveled slowly through the streets of Kansas City, it was honored by one of the largest and most vibrant black communities west of the Mississippi River.

By the 1930s, the African American population in the region of western Missouri and eastern Kansas had been expanding for decades. Like black communities all across the country, those in large urban centers such as Kansas City, medium-sized cities such as Topeka, and smaller towns such as Lawrence faced the travesties of segregation and discrimination. And like others, they created their own social, economic, and civic systems to thrive in the face of segregation. And like others, they strived for social uplift, envisioning a better life someday for themselves, and their children. And as in other places, the arts were here an important means of exerting views, expressing culture, and defining community. But unique to this region was the focus on music, particularly jazz, as a cultural and civic expression. Although there were many types of artistic outlets for blacks in the Kansas City region, it was music that seemed to be everywhere, played, sung, or danced by everyone.

Thus the account of Bennie Moten's funeral in the *Call* illustrates for us his role as a musician and respected community leader among African Americans in the Kansas City area. The episode reveals the decades of economic growth, organizational development, and focus on social uplift that had led to this moment, in which a strong and vibrant community paid respect to one of its key members. And, indeed, Moten and jazz were a vital part of the region's black cultural expression. Their music, and the music made by countless others in the region, served to entertain, to educate, and to inspire pride among African Americans, as they sought to achieve a better life for themselves and their children, in the midst of fierce discrimination from all sides.

By the early 1920s, the beginnings of Moten's career, and jazz in the Kansas City area, African Americans had established churches, schools, businesses, and social institutions, all of which interacted with music in some way. The black population of the region had grown considerably since the mid-nineteenth century, led first by the Exoduster migration movement to Kansas, and then by the Great Migration during and after World War I. Concerts of spirituals and sacred classical music were essential components of church life. Musical education from grade school to college was highly valued, and the region's schools produced many professional singers and musicians. African American businesses were expanding, and business leaders, held in high esteem by the community, were important patrons of all types of music. The local chapters of the NAACP, the Urban League, the Garveyites, and other organizations that focused on social uplift were highly active, and used music to connect with their community, and especially for fundraising events. And dozens of men's lodges and ladies' auxiliaries were a key part of the region's social fabric, working towards the empowerment of the community through charity and activism. They too used music to communicate and to motivate their members.

There are many reasons why the Kansas City area and the surrounding region had such a strong relationship with music in the context of social uplift. First, the area had been a goal of African American migration since the 1870s. Kansas was the destination of the Exoduster movement, to which thousands of blacks who saw the formerly free state as a place of opportunity migrated from 1879 to 1880. Many Exodusters settled in eastern Kansas, especially in Topeka and other towns just west of Kansas City. And as an urban center with a large meat-packing industry, Kansas City itself received thousands of migrants during the 1920s. In fact, from 1910 to 1930 the city's black population grew from 23,556 to 38,574, according to the U.S. Census.

Kansas City was also a central stop on the vaudeville circuit, which served the mid- and southwest regions of the country in the early twentieth century. The Theater Owner's Booking Association, or TOBA, the black-owned vaudeville company, used the city as a hub of a traveling circuit that went from Texas to Minnesota. In Kansas City they performed for black-only audiences at the Lincoln Theatre, in the city's African American business district. These events not only brought musicians and other entertainers to town, they served as a source of pride for the community. As a 1929 review in the *Call* of a show featuring the team Butterbeans and Susie demonstrates, musical theater could and did communicate the principles of social uplift to its audience:

> The audience was in rare good humor and was applauding generously each "wise crack." Then came a remark about what rights were due the Negro, the injustice he is suffering, and the relief he ought to have. It was worded cleverly as Butter Beans and Susie would do, and the house literally "went wild . . ."

By the early 1920s the Lincoln Theatre was just one of hundreds of black-owned businesses that defied the city's strict segregation policies. A person walking down 18th street through the heart of the city's African American business district would see clothing stores, shoe shops, restaurants, physicians, dentists, grocers, laundries, the Winston Holmes music store, the Hotel Street, the Gem Theater, the offices of the Urban League, the American Legion, and the Masonic Temple. Nearby would be the Paseo Dance Hall, Homer Roberts's car dealership, the T. B. Watkins funeral home, and the Musician's Protective Union building. As described by Roy Wilkins, the future head of the NAACP who began his career as a writer for the *Call*, a large segment of the black community were "well educated, intelligent, hardworking, successful people whose standard of living matched anything in the surrounding white community—and whose ethics were higher than those of the local white community."

The church played a vital role in both the spiritual and the cultural life of the community. By the late 1920s there were about forty black churches in Kansas City, the most prominent of which were the Second Baptist and the Allen Chapel. Musical and theatrical productions were an important artistic contribution that the churches provided. For example, in 1927, a production entitled *St. Paul's Appeal Before King Agrippa*, written by Kansas City native Ona B. Wilson, utilized a cast of forty actors and the Ebenezer Sunday School Orchestra. The production was sponsored by several churches, and the African American chapter of the Knights of Pythias. Another example is the 1934 production of the renowned music teacher N. Clark Smith's *Negro Choral Symphony*, held at the Bethel A.M.E. church. Witnessed by over 700 people, according to the *Call*, the production applied Smith's music to a dramatic presentation in five scenes, representing the experiences of African American people. The scenes were set in an African jungle, at an auction block, in a cotton field, and at a levee, portraying the black experience in a context of racial pride. It combined the choirs of the

Bethel A.M.E. church with an orchestra of local musicians. As the *Call* later pointed out, such productions represented:

> a step forward for the community to provide its own cultural events. Segregation keeps us out of most entertainment, and then chides us because we do not know how to act when we are welcome. This lack we can ourselves supply . . .

In early October, 1928, the Moten Orchestra played a "Monster Benefit" for the Brotherhood of Sleeping Car Porters Union. As the advertisement for the event in the *Call* makes clear, the Union was seen as a contributor to social uplift, and a source of pride for the community:

> You are urged to buy tickets, whether you attend or not:
>
> **Because** You will be fighting against the oppression of ALL laboring Negroes
> **Because** You will be helping directly the upkeep of churches, fraternal and social organizations
> **Because** You will be aiding in the general education of our children the country over
> **Because** Only organized Negro resistance will successfully overcome organized white unfairness
>
> (capitals and bold type in original)

The music program at the city's designated black Lincoln High School was one of the strongest in the country, responsible for educating dozens of future musicians, including members of the Moten and Basie bands. Led by innovative band director and composer N. Clark Smith until 1922, and then William L. Dawson, whose *Negro Folk Symphony* received its premier in 1934 under Leopold Stokowski with the Philadelphia Orchestra, the program provided students with formal music training and ensemble experience. The program featured a symphony orchestra, a marching band, and a chorus, and the teachers held private lessons and classes in music theory. The ensembles frequently performed in the community; for example, in 1925 the orchestra furnished the music for *Milestones*, which the *Call* reported as "a pageant of Negro progress" that was staged in Kansas City, Missouri, Kansas City, Kansas, and Wichita.

The Urban League of Kansas City was a prominent coalition of whites and African Americans that maintained an agenda of aiding the poorer blacks, particularly those who had recently migrated from the South. The League's Community Center on 18th Street sponsored day nurseries and clubs for boys, girls, and mothers, and training schools for janitors, domestics, and other types of trades available to blacks. The League frequently held fundraising events that featured music. For example, in December, 1934, a "Program of Negro Dance and Drama" was presented, with a church choir singing choral arrangements of spirituals, a piano suite by local choral director Eric Franklin, two plays about black family life, a reading of poetry by Langston Hughes, and pieces by black composers Samuel Coleridge-Taylor and William Marion Cook. Presiding over the program was H. O. Cook, the principal of Lincoln High School, who stated: "the realms of the spiritual and cultural as avenues of expression . . . are likewise opportunities for race distinction."

The Kansas City chapter of the NAACP formed in the early 1920s. The chapter concerned itself with fundraising drives for local projects, and also to support the national organization. Throughout the 1920s and 1930s there were many membership drives, during which the *Call* strongly urged its readers to join. There were also fundraising events that featured music, dancing and other forms of entertainment.

With the rise of the local chapter, the national meeting of the NAACP was held in Kansas City in 1923. It included as guest speakers James Weldon Johnson, W. E. B. Du Bois, and George Washington Carver. Over 10,000 people attended, including *Call* reporter Roy Wilkins, who must have seen the event as a life-changing experience:

> I had never seen anything like it. A haunting chorus of 200 Negroes in white robes sang [African American choral composer Robert] Dett's "Listen to the Lambs . . ." the old accommodating ways of Booker T. Washington were swept aside by the fighting doctrine of Du Bois . . . ten thousand Black people rose to their feet. They cheered and clapped until their voices were hoarse and their hands stinging with pain.

By 1925 the NAACP had become an important part of the political expression in the community. An editorial in the *Call* (perhaps written by Wilkins) exhorted its readers to become involved:

> Except one hold himself cheaply, he will join the NAACP. It is less for the dollar membership fee, than for the force that each person gives the cause, that all should join in the coming membership drive . . . it is because the NAACP has the desire to better the condition of the Negro in America, and because it has won some considerable successes, that the membership of us all in it is vital.

In addition to the political meetings, the city's NAACP also sponsored musical events that raised money for the organization's national fund. One such affair, in 1931, was a "Cabaret Minstrel," a kind of variety show in which "one hundred or more people . . . entertained with pop songs and light classics." And as jazz and dancing became more popular, benefit dances were held. For example, in 1927 there was a costumed dance, dubbed a "Greenwich Village Dance" featuring the Bennie Moten Orchestra. As the advertisement read:

> Fifty cents only, a reasonable fee,
> Good 'cause you will be helping the NAACP.
> Everybody come, whate'er your size,
> The best costume there brings a grand prize.

Men's and women's benevolent organizations were vitally important supporters of jazz and dancing in the region. Their contribution has been overlooked, in favor of a narrative that sees the rise of Kansas City as a jazz center as a result of vice and political corruption. It is true that with the onset of the Great Depression, and the strengthening of the Pendergast government, which controlled the city's vice establishments, jazz performance in the region became increasingly affiliated with criminal activity. But during the 1920s, African American social organizations developed and supported elaborate dance halls, and hired musicians to perform for the community, frequently for the purpose of charitable causes.

In Kansas City, the Knights of Pythias, the Elks Lodge, Masonic Lodge, and Beau Brummels club were the men's organizations most active in the sponsoring of charitable dances. They focused much of their efforts on the betterment of the community's schools, hospitals, and other institutions. As William M. Brooks, the head of the Kansas City Elks in the late 1920s, stated:

> the Elks believe in education of the youth and charity for the needy. At the present time our order is maintaining 39 young Negro boys and girls in colleges and universities . . . We need the whole hearted support of Greater Kansas City.

The men's organizations had been sponsoring dances since the early 1920s, and they played an important role in the evolution of the Bennie Moten Orchestra, the city's most successful band of the decade. The group began in 1918 as a trio performing ragtime music, but soon switched to a style that accommodated the dances popular among the black upper classes at that time, schottisches and waltzes. There was a formality to these dances, as according to the *Call*, the patrons were led by "Profs. Buckner and Beach," who introduced "all the latest dances," and in fact taught the dancers and controlled the activity on the floor. Soon the "New Way Dancing Club" was formed, which advertised in the *Call*, "Plenty of Soda Pop and good old punch. Note: We wish the patronage of respectable people only." Held at the Labor Temple, a building that served as a meeting place for the city's unions, the group was an immediate hit with the community, and social dancing became an essential part of African American social life.

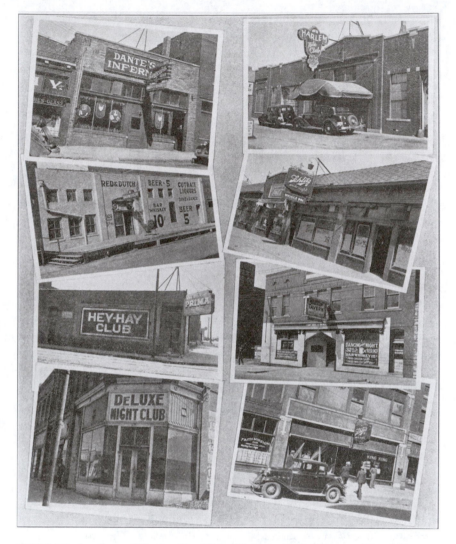

FIGURE 3.1 A collage of Kansas City Night Clubs in 1935. The top right photo depicts the Harlem Club on 12th Street. This club and the others were typical of the nightlife during Kansas City's Jazz Age in the late 1920s and early 1930s. Photograph was made from image as published in the "Future" newsweekly, Vol. 1, No. 12, March 29, 1935, p. 1, MVSC F051 F996. Kansas City Public Library, General Collection (P1), Taverns—Harlem Nite Club, #1

Although the Moten trio also performed the blues in more illicit establishments, the steady employment offered by the organized dances allowed the group to become financially stable. The popularity of the group and the dances soon caught the eye of the benevolent societies. In February 1922, the Knights of Pythias gave a "Grand Ball" at the Temple, and in April several groups worked together to stage a fashion show for the benefit of the Wheatley Provident Hospital, an important institution in the community. Also in 1922 the Moten band, now having expanded to five pieces, performed for the Elks "Priest of Pallas Charity Ball" and had received the title of the "Elks Official Orchestra." There was also the first of many Halloween Dances, a benefit for the Niles Orphan Home, held at the Shriner's Hall in Kansas City, Kansas.

In 1923 African American record store owner Winston Holmes had taken the band under his wing. He had his own studio, the Merritt Recording Company, which specialized in recording local blues singers and sermons of local preachers. He trained the band, perfecting their sound for the studio, and then introduced them to field agents for Okeh Records, the first company to bring the blues to a national audience. The Orchestra was hired to make several recordings, and their success became a source of pride for their community. As the *Call* reported:

> [Holmes] has pioneered in making a place for Kansas City talent in the recording laboratories of the large record companies. His efforts deserve the commendation of the business people of the city, as he is interested only in putting forward the best talent of the race.

In March 1924 a new dance hall, the Paseo Dancing Academy, was purchased and opened up for the exclusive patronage of the black community. It quickly replaced the Labor Temple as the place where middle and upper class African Americans danced schottisches, foxtrots, and eventually the Charleston. For the Moten Orchestra, the hall became a kind of "home field," offering steady employment, and the opportunity to establish its reputation. And many of their dances would be sponsored by the community's benevolent organizations.

As the *Call*'s announcement makes clear, the Paseo Dance Hall would be a source of pride and community expression:

> Society is demanding higher standards in all of its social phases. BENNIE MOTEN and his MUSICAL COHORTS, have raised the standard of Dance Please and announced the lease of the BIG HALL . . . for the indulgence of COLORED DEVOTEES OF TERPSICHOREAN DELIGHT. This is indeed the Hall of Halls—with every up-to-the-moment CONVENIENCE for PATRONS . . . With the best possible dance floor, the best installed acoustics for carrying the best Music—a good time is assured at all times.
>
> (capitals in original)

By January 1925 the Moten Orchestra was performing at the Paseo Hall every Sunday and Thursday. In March the band played a "Spring Fashion Show" for the Parliamentary and Culture Clubs, a benefit for the Douglass Hospital and Orphan Home of Kansas City, Kansas. They played a "Barn Dance" sponsored by the Harmony Literary Art Club, one of many dances that had themes, in which patrons and band members dressed accordingly, in this case in overalls and straw hats. The also played a "Charleston Wedding" sponsored by the Twelve Charity Girls. The Charleston dance, first featured in the African American Broadway hit *Shuffle Along*, had thus come to the Midwest. The advertisement for the dance reports that it was "The sensational amusement event everybody is talking about . . . Nothing like it [has] ever before [been] seen west of New York."

In 1926 the Moten Orchestra signed a contract with Victor Records, a much larger and more prominent company than Okeh. They recorded with Victor until 1932, thus becoming the only band from the Midwest to produce more than a few sides during their career. In fact, they ultimately made 106 recordings, and through them gained national recognition that rivaled many of the East Coast bands such as Fletcher Henderson. Naturally there was a dance to celebrate the new contract, for as the *Call* stated, "Bennie has reached the position in the musical world desired by every orchestra director—that of being recognized by the big record companies." For the dance the *Call* requested that "all turn out and give Bennie and his orchestra a rousing welcome. The first colored orchestra outside of New York to record for Victor. It has taken Bennie years of effort to reach his goal. Let's go!"

During 1927 the band played on Tuesdays and Thursdays at the Del Ray Gardens in Kansas City, Kansas, and performed at the Paseo Hall for dances sponsored by the Phalanx Club, the Varsity Club, and the Elks Charity Ball. Their summer job was at Liberty Park, the only public park in Kansas City to accept African Americans. But the signing of the new contract meant more touring for the Orchestra. In 1928 the band took a nine-month tour of the East Coast, playing in Pennsylvania and New York, returning in the fall to play the "Monster Benefit" for the Brotherhood of Sleeping Car Porters Union, and a rally for the Democrat party sponsored by the Elks.

In addition to these engagements, in the autumn of 1928 the Orchestra became the first African American ensemble to play in one of the city's white-only establishments, the El Torreon Ballroom. The band worked consistently at the El Torreon through 1929, and their dances were broadcast over radio station KMBC. This information was taken from the white *Kansas City Star*, which only wrote about the city's blacks when they either committed crimes or entertained the white community.

While the Moten Orchestra was otherwise engaged, several other bands rose to take its place at the Paseo. Most notable was the George E. Lee Orchestra, Moten's chief rival, featuring George's sister Julia as a vocalist, Bill Little and His Little Bills, and Chauncey Downs and His Rinky Dinks. Indeed, Kansas City's

African American musicians' union Local 627 saw a dramatic rise in membership during the late 1920s, ultimately reaching over 300 members.

By 1928 Local 627 was sponsoring an annual "Musician's Ball." These affairs were important in establishing reputations among dancers and booking agents. At its peak the Ball featured six bands, playing alternately in musical "battles" for the approval of several thousand dancers. As the *Call* reported about the 1929 dance:

> The crowd did everything but hang on the ceiling. The lobby was jammed; the dance floor was jammed; the seats along the wall were jammed; and the balcony was groaning from too much population. And maybe you think those six orchestras didn't play with that sort of crowd for inspiration! There were more varieties of melody, rhythm, blues, and stomp music than the old dance palace had heard in a long time.

Concepts of social uplift were found not just in Kansas City but also throughout the region. Small towns such as Lawrence, Leavenworth, and Olathe were farming communities, but they did have active social organizations and free schools. There was communication throughout the region via the black newspapers, and frequent travel to attend major events in the cities.

The area's second-largest African American population was in Topeka, Kansas, which was a focal point of black culture in eastern Kansas. The town was a main stopping point for the Exodusters in the 1860s, and would be the setting for *Brown vs. the Board of Education* in the 1950s. In the 1920s and 1930s, although jazz and dancing did not play as prominent a role in the city's cultural life as in Kansas City, there was a very active Knights of Pythias group, several women's clubs, and schools and churches that sponsored a wide variety of musical and theatrical events.

In August, 1921 the Knights of Pythias and Court of Calanthe held their national meeting in Topeka. The African American newspaper the *Topeka Plain Dealer* announced, "it is an honor to welcome . . . one of the greatest Colored organizations in the United States, which is doing so much for the uplift of humanity and for the betterment of both races," and described the condition of blacks in the state for the visitors:

> A history of Kansas, beginning with John Brown, driving rebels and slaveholders out, noted for its freedom and liberty, stands high in the ranks of education, all children of school age shall have an education . . . so Kansas is classed as an intelligent and progressive state, both from an education and financial point. All of her colleges and public institutions are free to everybody, especially where the public pays the taxes . . . There is no segregation after grade school in many communities.

A notice in the African American newspaper the *Topeka Plain Dealer* from 1922 demonstrates an awareness of the artistic movements occurring in Harlem. Although a bit mysterious (What was the music? What was the "line of blues"?) and not exactly accurate (Hughes was born in Joplin, Missouri, and raised in Lawrence), the notice does reveal the importance placed on education, and the progress of black artistic culture:

> We are running a cut of Langston Hughes, a young man that was born in Lawrence, Kansas twenty-one years past. He is now a composer and is writing some classy music as well as a line of Blues which is being sung all over the country. We would like for our music lovers of Kansas and the West to use his music.
>
> His mother, Mrs. Carry Langston Hughes, was born and reared in Lawrence, Kansas. She was one of the first colored lady graduates of Kansas University. Her son is a prominent young man and has built up a wonderful reputation which will put him in a class of the famous men of the race in years to come if he continues to build up as he is now doing.

The *Plain Dealer* often ran poetry from local authors, frequently unattributed. This particular piece from 1923, with its themes of music and race, seems clearly influenced by the Harlem Renaissance:

The Black Voice

It was a far off voice.
And it cried.
　　Give me black soul music,
　　The melody of the guitar.
It was a soft sweet voice,
And it crooned,
　　Give my black soul understanding
　　Of a creed that says it is the color,
　　and not the man.
It was a mellow, heart-rung voice,
And if pleaded,
　　Oh God! Give me love and forgiveness
For a race that tramples upon nature's mystery of black.

Also coming to the region was the Broadway show *Shuffle Along*, which played both Kansas City and Topeka in the spring of 1923, helping to spread the new Charleston dance. As the *Plain Dealer* advertised, "Positively never before in the history of the stage has there been produced anything so artistically amazing. Gorgeous and Entertaining as the brilliant and magnificent music comedy which took New Year by storm at the Grand theater . . ."

The men's and women's clubs were the center of Topeka's black cultural life. Their meetings were opportunities for people from around the region to gather and be entertained, often for the sake of charity. For example, The Elks, the American Legion, and the women's club gathered in December, 1923 for a Carnival to benefit the Topeka Nursery and Crittenton Home. This event featured local marching bands and "singers from Wichita and Kansas City." A Knights of Pythias meeting in 1926 featured the Principal of the Atchison High School making "a wonderful address on the Life and Character of Frederick Douglass," followed by judge T. W. Beel of Leavenworth who "paid a glowing tribute to the Life and Character of John Brown at Harper's Ferry." According to the *Plain Dealer* there were visitors from all over the state, and "quite a crowd" from Kansas City and Lawrence, who also heard music furnished by local church choirs.

Marching bands played a prominent role in Topeka's musical culture. Parades featuring bands from Topeka, Kansas City, Kansas, and the smaller towns in the region were a staple of any holiday or important event. The Knights of Pythias, the Elks, and several of Topeka's other men's groups had their own marching bands, which often paraded during charity events. As the *Plain Dealer* describes, bands such as the Kansas Army Band, which could play Mendelssohn, Tchaikovsky, and Negro Spirituals, were a great source of pride for the region:

> Kansas never heard such fine and harmonious music played before by any band. "Home Sweet Home," as played by the bands of all foreign countries, was something that bewildered the audience . . . Prof. G. W. Jackson, of the famous 23rd Kansas Band [was] present and said to the audience "This band is the cream of the U.S. Army." . . . The colored race is proud of this band along with the fair-minded whites.

Eastern Kansas was also home to Western University, perhaps the earliest black school west of the Mississippi river. The activities of its students were frequently covered in the *Plain Dealer*, and the school cultivated the concepts of racial uplift through its strict curriculum, academic standards, and superior music department. Developed by Robert G. Jackson, who was well known as an educator throughout the region, the music department offered studies in piano, organ, composition, harmony, and music history. There was a marching band initiated in 1914 by the future illustrious teacher and composer N. Clark Smith. And its most famous group was the Jackson Jubilee singers, who toured throughout the country, in the fashion of their predecessors from Fisk University. Quite often the Jackson singers performed in Kansas and Missouri, always drawing large crowds.

Topeka had an active theatrical scene. There was the Apex Theater, black owned and operated, which featured live acts on Sundays, and movies throughout the week. In addition to the live performers, simply the act of patronizing the theater, as opposed to the white owned theaters, was seen as a point of civic duty, as the *Plain Dealer* makes clear:

> We are proud that our Theater is now in the same class with all other theaters in Topeka and we can see just as good shows there as at any other theater. Now we do not have to be stuck of in one corner of the house, or wait until a certain time to go to the show. We are at liberty to go any time the doors are open and sit just wherever we please . . . Recently, the Apex permitted a Fashion Show given by Mrs. Cleo Todd which was an overwhelming success, the house being crowded to the extent that many were unable to gain admittance . . . We highly commend Mr. and Mrs. B. F. Payne for the success they are making of the Apex Theater. Let's push them up still farther. What do you say?

As in Kansas City, the theater could entertain, educate, and uplift the Topeka community, especially when written and performed by local people. Unlike the more segregated Kansas City, open-minded whites sometimes also attended these shows. In the spring of 1926, a "historical pageant" titled *Out of the Past*, written by Topeka native Lillian J. Craw, debuted to fine reviews in the *Plain Dealer*.

> [The drama] was indeed complimentary to the intelligence and dignity of the colored people of Topeka. . . . There was a crowd something like over two thousand paid admissions. Everyone played their part well. There were three or four hundred white people present and all stayed until the last and enjoyed the play from start to finish. This play had effect upon the younger generation from the fact that they never knew the hardships and struggles their fore-parents went through to educate them to earn a livelihood. In this play they discovered that their former parents had no opportunity and education or business of any kind but now to witness a reproduction of what happened a few years ago or as little as sixty five years ago and see the improvement is certainly wonderful when put on by the descendents of former slaves.

With the onset of the Great Depression, many of the institutions that had supported the black artistic movement in the Kansas City area were hit hard. White Kansas City was temporarily spared the most devastating effects of the Depression by a corrupt city government that issued municipal bonds for new construction, keeping whites employed. During this time whites had money, and many spent it at the city's afterhours drinking and vice establishments, which also employed jazz musicians. Blacks, however, were "last to be hired and first to be fired," as the *Call* put it. The Paseo Hall, the Musician's Balls, and the charity events that so characterized black life in the 1920s were casualties of the rising unemployment. The Moten Orchestra disbanded in 1931, briefly reforming to play at the city's new "black and tan" clubs, segregated dinner theaters that imitated the Cotton Club in New York City.

Although Pendergast's vice establishments were located in the black neighborhoods, many who lived there resented the rising crime and violence that they brought. And of course only the musicians saw any financial benefit. An editorial in the *Call* from 1930 summarizes the devastating impact of political corruption in the neighborhood:

> Because Negroes have the least financial and political weight, ties between the police and the racketeers endanger us most of all . . . Our residence district . . . suffers the contamination of white vice resorts. In addition, our own racketeers very naturally bid for protection, and the double burden is too much if the police are more interested in getting money than in safeguarding the public. The good citizen who has only his vote with which to win the attention of public officials . . . has been hopelessly displaced by the racketeer with his campaign gifts and herd of followers.

The discovery in 1936 that the municipal bonds issued earlier in the decade were worthless led to the downfall of the Pendergast regime, and the beginning of severe economic depression in Kansas City. By the 1940s, even most of the vice establishments were gone. However, in the 1990s the 18th and Vine neighborhood was revitalized, with the restoration of the Gem Theater, the Blue Room jazz club, and museums dedicated to jazz and the Negro baseball league. Today Kansas City is recognized as a major contributor to the history of jazz. Although its most famous musicians, Count Basie, Lester Young, and Charlie Parker, gained their reputations in the 1930s and 1940s, after having left Kansas City, it is a certainty that their art owed a great debt to a community that made jazz, and music, an essential part of its cultural expression.

Further Reading

Brady, Marilyn Dell. "Organizing Afro-American Girls' Clubs in Kansas in the 1920s." *Frontiers: A Journal of Women Studies* 9 (1987, 69–73).

Coulter, Charles E. *Take Up the Black Man's Burden: Kansas City's African American Communities 1865–1939*. (Columbia and London) University of Mississippi Press, 2006.

Driggs, Frank, and Chuck Haddix. *Kansas City Jazz: From Ragtime to Bebop*. (Oxford and New York) Oxford University Press, 2005.

Painter, Nell Irvin. *Exodusters: Black Migration to Kansas After Reconstruction*. (New York) Alfred A. Knopf, 1977.

Pearson, Jr. Nathan. *Goin' to Kansas City*. (Champagne/Urbana) University of Illinois Press, 1994.

Walker-Hill, Helen. "Western University at Quindaro, Kansas (1865–1943) and Its Legacy of Pioneering Musical Women." *Black Music Research Journal* 26 (Spring, 2006, 7–37).

4

THE NEW NEGRO RENAISSANCE
IN LOS ANGELES, 1920–1940

Douglas Flamming

In the 1920s, the black community in Los Angeles was well positioned to absorb the cultural currents flowing out of Harlem, and it was also able to send its own artistic talent to Manhattan. These two trends—black L.A.'s increasingly close relationship with New York and the migration of L.A.'s black literati to Harlem —both proved significant. The first trend contributed to a growing nationalization of African American politics and culture, a nationalization that held important ramifications for long-term twentieth-century race relations. The second trend was of more immediate importance, for the work of black westerners in Harlem in the mid-to-late 1920s would reorient the trajectory of the Renaissance itself.

In the 1930s, as the Renaissance faltered in Harlem, Los Angeles became a refuge for black westerners who had ventured to New York; they hoped to keep the spirit of Harlem alive on the West Coast. Some tried to break into screenplay writing in Hollywood; others, embracing the promise of the Left, took an ocean liner to the Soviet Union to write and produce a film about racism in the American South; still others hunkered down and tried to write their way through the economic and racial crises of the era. Central Avenue's jazz clubs kept hopping, but for the writers who had experienced Harlem in the 1920s, L.A. in the 1930s proved unable to uphold the Renaissance spirit.

This essay will cover the L.A. Renaissance in three broad strokes. First, it will demonstrate the influence of Harlem on black Los Angeles in the 1920s, highlighting the development of a close—though sometimes contentious— relationship between the African American leadership in the two cities. Second, it will discuss the exodus of black artistic talent from L.A. to Harlem and suggest how black westerners ignited a new and daring phase of Renaissance literature— the birth of the "New Negro" phase of the Renaissance. Finally, it will show

how these maverick westerners returned to L.A. during the Great Depression, believing that Hollywood and the West Coast was the last best chance to keep the Renaissance spirit alive.

The Origins of L.A.'s Black Community

Modern Los Angeles was born in the 1880s, when railroads connected the sleepy town to the rest of the nation. Frenzied real-estate speculation followed, and the rush was on for cheap land and Southern California's magnificent climate. A man-made harbor gave the city global trade positioning, and a massively engineered aqueduct brought a steady gush of water (courtesy of Northern California) for the region's citrus industry and for its rapidly growing population. Trainloads of easterners arrived daily—northerners fleeing cold winters, southerners fleeing a depressed economy or an oppressive racial regime or both. Refugees and dreamers from all over the globe found their way to Los Angeles, especially from Mexico, Europe, and Japan. The open spaces and the churning economy absorbed them all. As the journalist Carey McWilliams would later observe, the history of modern Los Angeles was essentially one big boom interrupted only by the occasional, short-lived bust.

Between 1880 and 1920, Los Angeles' black community outgrew all others in the Far West—both in terms of population and organizational development. From one hundred black residents in 1880, black Los Angeles grew to nearly 7,600 in 1910 and to almost 16,000 in 1920. This population growth was accompanied by the creation of community-building organizations: The rise of impressive Negro churches and black-owned newspapers, known as Race papers, were especially important; a vibrant and long-standing branch of the Afro-American Council stamped the early activism of the community, as did the rise of activist Colored Women's Clubs.

There was a middle class character to the black community of Los Angeles. It took some money and gumption to travel from Dixie to the West Coast, and the migrants in the late nineteenth and early twentieth century saw themselves as part of the Talented Tenth—the Race leaders whose education, entrepreneurship, and vision would lead American blacks toward fuller civil rights and a higher social status in the nation, or, in the case of Los Angeles, in the West. Few black leaders in early L.A. were actually middle-class by economic standards; they were middle-class in terms of values and outlook. They were church-building, church-going strivers; they emphasized education as the means to both group progress and individual success; they were joiners, with faith in progress; they were speculators, with a sharp eye toward real estate investment. They were, especially, home owners. The Los Angeles community had one of the highest percentages of home ownership in the nation, even though most blacks could only find work in low-level occupations. At the turn of the century, black Los Angeles was led by a blue-collar bourgeoisie; gradually, a small group of rising professionals and successful entrepreneurs took the lead, but the outlook of the community did not really change.

The relationship between Harlem and Central Avenue began in earnest with the creation of the local NAACP chapter in 1913. Organized in 1910 and headquartered in New York City, the NAACP quickly became known to blacks throughout the nation by virtue of its monthly publication, *The Crisis*, edited by W. E. B. Du Bois, the nation's foremost black intellectual and civil rights activist. In 1913, Du Bois took a West Coast tour and received something like a hero's welcome in black Los Angeles. While in L.A., Du Bois also became enamored with Central Avenue itself, and he struck up a warm and lasting friendship with community leaders John and Vada Somerville. Shortly thereafter, the community organized a local branch of the NAACP. With the Somervilles among the active leaders of the organization, the L.A. Branch of the NAACP soon emerged as the strongest in the Far West and captured the attention of black leaders in New York.

By the mid-1910s, black America stood on the verge of an historic demographic movement: The Great Migration. With the outbreak of World War I in Europe in 1914, American industry boomed to meet Europe's war needs. At the same time, the industrialists' supply of cheap European labor was cut off, requiring that corporations looked to southern blacks for the grunt work. The result was that roughly a half a million black southerners moved to northern industrial cities during the war, and the flow continued after the war ended in 1918. Whites in northern cities quickly adopted restrictive real estate covenants to keep the black newcomers hemmed in, giving rise to the northern black ghettos.

The West, by contrast, did not receive many newcomers because of this Great Migration. Steady migration from south to west continued, especially to Los Angeles, and blacks who already lived in the West were able to get jobs in western factories during the war, but the surge of southerners toward northern industrial work was not replicated in the West, where black communities remained small, stable, and mostly middle class. The demographic transformation that gave rise to Chicago's Southside, and to Harlem itself, bypassed western cities. The black West and the black North thus took divergent paths, and those differences persisted through the interwar decades.

Shared by all black Americans, however, was the pain of postwar racism. African Americans believed that their sacrifices for this war to make the world "safe for democracy" would help them attain democracy within the United States itself. To the contrary, violent white racism ran rampant during and after the war. White mobs accosted black soldiers and black communities across the nation: Houston and East St. Louis in 1917; then a burst of bloody riots in 1919—Chicago, Omaha, and rural Arkansas, to name a few. Blacks in L.A. paid close attention to these tragedies and felt a deep disillusionment shared by African Americans throughout the nation. Then came the devastating Tulsa riot of 1921, in which most of that city's black homes and business district were burned to the ground when black men tried to stop the lynching of one of their own. The carnage in Tulsa, which had a prosperous community with parallels to L.A. black middle class development, jolted L.A.'s black community to the core. That violence, in conjunction with the simultaneous rise of the Ku Klux Klan (KKK) in L.A., showed in no uncertain terms that the 1920s were to be a difficult era for African Americans, even those living in the more open society of the Far West. The vibrancy of the New Negro Renaissance that followed might therefore be seen, in part, as a defiant counterattack on the racism sparked by World War I.

The Roaring Twenties in L.A.

The lifeline of black Los Angeles in the 1920s was Central Avenue. A broad, western-sized street, Central ran southward from downtown; it was the high-energy artery of what was then known as the city's "Eastside" (not to be confused with today's "East L.A."). Central was abuzz with street cars, automobiles, horse-drawn wagons, and bicycles, and its wide sidewalks carried a seemingly endless stream of foot traffic. "The Avenue," as people in the community called it, was lined with boarding houses and red-brick business blocks that offered a full accompaniment of mom-and-pop shops, cafes, and clubs. From about 5th Street, where the southern edge of downtown petered out, to about 25th Street, African Americans lived on both sides of The Avenue. Some black Angelenos rented rooms on Central, but most occupied single-family bungalows that fanned out across the district. Within these residential streets stood the Negro churches, many of them impressive sanctuaries, the pride and joy of black Los Angeles. Even in the 1910s, black leaders were referring to Central Avenue as the "Black Belt" of the city.

It would be misleading, however, to think of the Central Avenue community as an all-black section of the city. On the contrary, the racial and ethnic diversity of the district was striking—and certainly set it apart from the racial homogeneity of Harlem. The bungalows stemming off of Central housed one of the most diverse residential areas of any city in the nation. By 1920, virtually all African Americans in L.A. lived along The Avenue, but, taken altogether, they comprised only about 15 to 20 percent of the district's population. Living among them were an eclectic array of white folks: Jews from Russia and the Middle East, Canadians, a wide range of immigrants from Europe, and a host of migrants from the eastern half of the United States—mostly Midwesterners but also whites from the Northeast and the South. The neighborhoods were majority white, but the whites did not form any kind of identifiable cultural or political groups. Spicing up the mix were people of Mexican descent—native born and immigrant—as well as the Japanese. There were also a small number of Chinese, and, during the 1920s and 1930s, a growing number of Filipinos.

For all its demographic diversity, the Central Avenue district was effectively claimed by its African American residents. The majority white population was too diverse and ethnically divided to coalesce into any cohesive cultural or political force, and the ethnic-Mexican and Japanese populations were not citizens or were too far outside of mainstream culture to challenge the blacks as a dominant presence in the district. African Americans in L.A. were overwhelmingly migrants from the South—mostly the urban South—who shared similar pasts, similar political ambitions, and similar hopes for their future in the West. They built impressive churches, established key institutions—such as the Colored YMCA, the Sunday Forum (a weekly public meeting to discuss local and national issues pertaining to the Race)—a community band, a variety of men's fraternities, and an impressively organized network of Colored Women's Clubs. The Race papers of L.A.—especially the *California Eagle*, owned and edited by Charlotta and Joe Bass, and the *New Age*, owned and edited by Frederick Roberts, who, in 1918, became the first African American elected to the California state legislature. There was a black-owned theater at 12th and Central, the unofficial heart of Central Avenue.

The 1920s saw a veritable "Who's Who" of East Coast leadership come to L.A. for a look at this distant place in the sun. Early in the decade, Marcus Garvey, leader of the Universal Negro Improvement Association, arrived to a grand parade down the Avenue. W. E. B. Du Bois visited twice: to stage his pageant, *The Star of Ethiopia* in 1925, and again as a leader of the NAACP for the Association's national convention in 1928—the first time the NAACP had held its annual conclave in the West. Chandler Owen, editor of the black national magazine *The Messenger*, came to L.A. in part to scope out real-estate investment opportunities. Upon seeing the sights along Central, he told his readers that he had "found a veritable little Harlem, here in Los Angeles."

"A Veritable Little Harlem"

The Renaissance in L.A. had a soundtrack and a certain look to it. The soundtrack was jazz—with interludes of high-level gospel. Because jazz grew out of New Orleans, and because so many blacks in L.A. hailed from New Orleans, it was no surprise that the new sounds were heard early on in Southern California. Black Los Angeles had always been a musically inclined community, with well-known music teachers and a deep talent pool. Skilled vocalists, composers, and musicians produced high-level ragtime, gospel, and classical music. Jazz therefore found a welcome home in L.A. Jelly Roll Morton and Kid Orey were early arrivals. The city of Los Angeles would impose a club curfew during the 1920s, but there was easy access to jazz clubs south of the city limits, including the black-owned Leak's Lake Pavilion, where the best musicians gathered to jam for appreciative audiences long after the L.A. clubs had closed for the night.

The "look" of the L.A. Renaissance was the architecture of Paul Williams, whose buildings in the Central Avenue district marked his rise to prominence. Williams was a native son, born in Los Angeles in 1894. His childhood reflected the classic diversity that was L.A.'s Eastside: his schools were mostly white but ethnically and racially mixed; he picked up a little Chinese and German from his neighbors. As a child, before he even knew what architecture was, he sketched every building between his home and grade school. By the time he entered high school, he knew he wanted to become an architect. When his high school guidance counselor asked him what he wanted to be, and he said an architect, the astonished counselor blurted out, "Whoever heard of a Negro architect?" Williams replied that *he* had heard of *one* other Negro architect in America, and that he was sure this country could use at least one more.

Williams persevered and succeeded. Architecture was both a business and an art, and Williams excelled at both. When it became clear in the early 1920s that he had exceptional talent, he got some good breaks and established his own successful practice. By the middle of the decade, there was enough prosperity in the black community for organizations and businesses to commission Williams to design buildings for them. By the end of the decade, he had designed three of the major buildings in black Los Angeles—Second Baptist Church (1924), the 28th Street YMCA (1925), and the Golden State Life Insurance building (1928). For the YMCA, Williams highlighted the race-specific purpose of the building with sculpted representations of African American heroes, including Frederick Douglass and Booker T. Washington.

Although it is getting ahead of our story here, it is worth pointing out that in the 1930s, Williams would become the architect for many white Westside elites, especially those in Hollywood. It became a status symbol to have a "PRW home," especially in the rarified confines of Bel Air and Beverley Hills. That Williams was building mansions where he could not live was a thought that seldom left his mind. As he wrote in 1937:

> I am an architect . . . Today I sketched the preliminary plans for a large country house which will be erected in one of the most beautiful residential districts in the world, a district of roomy estates, entrancing vistas, and stately mansions. Sometimes I have dreamed of living there. I could afford such a home. But this evening, leaving my office, I returned to my own small, inexpensive home in an unrestricted, comparatively undesirable section of Los Angeles [because] I am a Negro.

Three major events of the 1920s illuminated the complicated relationship that developed between Harlem and L.A. The first—not so much an event as a development—was the rapid rise and fall of L.A.'s Garvey movement in the early 1920s. The second was the staging of a theatrical pageant, *The Star of Ethiopia*, which played at the Hollywood Bowl in 1925. The third was the holding of the NAACP's national convention in L.A. in 1928—the first time that influential organization had held its annual meeting in the West. All three events highlighted the growing importance of the West in the black national network, but they also demonstrated specific tensions between the black East and black West during the Renaissance era.

Marcus Garvey's UNIA took black L.A. by storm in the early 1920s. There were good reasons: The general disillusionment from the racial violence of 1919 and the Tulsa riot of 1921, and the appearance of the KKK in L.A., accompanied as it was with the re-release of the racist film *Birth of a Nation*, all stirred black nationalist fervor. In black L.A., the message of black self-sufficiency merged easily with the community's ongoing commitment to Race enterprises (that is, black-owned businesses). A restive black pride was in the wind. Coupled with the prospect of profits on Garvey's proposed Black Star Line, which would create commercial links between African Americans and Africa itself, the black nationalist currents of the day swept the black middle class of L.A. into a warm embrace with the decidedly working-class UNIA, which was headquartered, of course, in Harlem. One of L.A.'s leading ministers even left for Harlem to became one of Garvey's lieutenants in the UNIA.

But the warm embrace quickly chilled. L.A.'s UNIA representative to the national convention of 1923, held in Harlem, was Noah Thompson. Thompson corresponded almost daily with L.A.'s Race papers, and his reports became increasingly critical of the UNIA as the convention wore on. Fully part of Southern California's black middle-class leadership, Thompson was a part-time journalist and a full-time real estate man. As such, he had a keen eye for business and a no-nonsense approach to the UNIA's Black Star Line. Appalled that large amounts of convention time were used for debating UNIA uniforms—how many buttons on an officer's coat, for example—and other trivial matters, Thompson pressed for information on the Black Star Line. He wanted to see the three ships that had been bought with the membership dues; he wanted an official accounting of the business. In the end, the truth hurt: The ships were wrecks, the treasury was all but empty, the Black Star Line was dead in the water.

Outraged, L.A.'s UNIA leaders met in protest and created their own, West Coast version of the organization—the Pacific Coast UNIA, leading thousands of members out of Garvey's organization. Headquarters in Harlem then decertified L.A.'s initial UNIA, and created a new local division, which could boast only about 150 members. The grand parade Garvey was given on Central Avenue, and the packed crowds he attracted when he spoke afterward, was really his attempt to bring L.A. back into the fold. Only in minor matters did this attempt succeed. Some black leaders, including the *Eagle* editor Joe Bass, continued to hound Garvey and celebrated his deportation several years later. It was a lesson New York's black organizations would learn for decades to come: Black L.A. had its own mind about how to do things. W. E. B. Du Bois was next in line to learn the lesson.

In 1925, the Junior Branch of the L.A. NAACP announced that it would stage Du Bois's theatrical pageant, *The Star of Ethiopia*. Initially written in the early 1910s, *Ethiopia* was a sweeping lesson in Negro history, from antiquity in

Egypt to the present-day United States. The pageant required a full orchestra and literally hundreds of cast members; part of the novelty of the program was that the local communities who staged the pageant provided the musicians and actors, who were directed by Du Bois and his theatrical right-hand, Henry Burroughs. Du Bois's larger goal was to educate whites about black history and to inspire blacks themselves. The pageant had played to singular success in New York, Washington, DC, and Philadelphia.

Normally, a "junior branch" was made up of adolescents who conducted membership drives and community-service projects. In L.A., however, the Junior Branch of the early 1920s came to be comprised of local college students who fully embraced the New Negro ideal. In what amounted to a generational dispute, they characterized the adult leaders of the branch as do-nothings, and they resolved, in effect, to take charge of the L.A. Branch and bring it to life. To show how things were done, they set about presenting Du Bois's pageant at the Hollywood Bowl. The *Eagle* reported that the announcement "swept intelligent Los Angeles like wild fire." Two Junior Branch members had already been to New York, where both met with Du Bois and received his permission to stage the program. In the beginning, the branch leaders in L.A. were mostly proud of their assertive New Negroes, but soon a feud broke out between the Juniors and Du Bois over who would really be in charge of the pageant.

The Juniors were well along the way to producing the pageant when Du Bois sent Burroughs to L.A. to take charge of the production. The Juniors, who believed Du Bois had given them permission to stage the production themselves, expressed outrage. Du Bois, being Du Bois, held firm. L.A.'s Junior Branch, however, would not kowtow to Dr. Du Bois's power and prestige. When Du Bois and the Juniors reached an impasse, the Junior Branch boycotted the pageant altogether, taking most of the young people in L.A. out with them—including most of the orchestra. Du Bois and Burroughs persisted with a skeletal cast and orchestra.

At least Du Bois got a good newspaper spread about the pageant in the *Los Angeles Times*, penning a Sunday edition article that explained the meaning of what he called—apparently for the first time in print—"A Negro Art Renaissance." He began by debunking the commonly held idea that the rise of African American art and literature dated from Emancipation in 1865. It began, rather, in ancient Africa. American slavery had caused "a vast hiatus in Negro development," he argued, but African artistry was never completely destroyed or forgotten. Now African artistry was reasserting itself with unprecedented "a renaissance of Negro genius, linking the past and the present." The surge in Negro arts, therefore, was not a matter of blacks trying to imitate white arts; it was a blossoming of deeply held black traditions and skills. The result, Du Bois insisted, was that whites must view blacks as their artistic equals—and thus their equals more broadly.

That was the larger civil-rights ideal that Du Bois envisioned for the Renaissance, but in L.A. in 1925, *The Star of Ethiopia* was a bust. Du Bois and

Burroughs staged two shows at the Hollywood bowl, and the attendance at both ran under 2,000. The Junior Branch boycott won the day against Harlem's general. Du Bois was miffed, the Senior Branch officially disbanded the Junior Branch, and the L.A. Branch was disgraced. Du Bois soon tired of this "Renaissance" (the L.A. production of *Star of Ethiopia* probably played a role in that respect) and lost faith that art—rather than civil rights activism—could actually change racial conditions.

But if Du Bois was losing faith in the transformative power of art, most blacks were not. In the summer of 1926, for example, the *Pacific Defender*, a local Race paper, waxed ecstatic over the black Choir Contest held at the Hollywood Bowl. It was not simply that First AME's famous Eighth and Towne Choir had won the competition with a stunning performance. Nor was it simply that a mixed-race crowd of 10,000 had witnessed "this great musical treat." It was rather that the contest, "contributed by the Black citizens of this city" stood "as evidence of the race's advancement in the world of art." This was not a trivial triumph, for "the beautiful voices blended together in harmonious expression, rolling up and out of the throats of bright-eyed, smiling artists, answering to the baton of their leaders, was an evidence of the Race's right to demand its place in the American citizenship."

In the *Defender*'s view, exemplary music—high-church expertise and tightly orchestrated Negro spirituals—could be a force for black civil rights. Any race of people capable of such artistry, the *Defender* insisted, had every right "to demand its place" in society. White people exposed to black cultural virtuosity would abandon their assumptions of Negro inferiority; they would begin to see blacks as fully human, as a people entitled to first-class citizenship. If political activism could not win African Americans their civil rights, if economic progress could not persuade whites that blacks deserved a place at the American table, then maybe black culture could. This was a powerful idea. It was also, by the mid-1920s, a common idea among the city's middle-class blacks. Here was another battle line on which they could fight the good fight.

The NAACP continued to fight the fight, both nationally and in L.A. The L.A. Branch, under the leadership of a new and aggressive branch president, H. Claude Hudson, became more active and aggressive than ever. The local branch raised large amounts of money for the national office, attacked beach segregation with an act of civil disobedience (an act for which Hudson was arrested), and even took on the L.A. Police Department on the issue of police brutality. NAACP membership in L.A. soared. Du Bois got over the *Star of Ethiopia* debacle and remained friends with John and Vada Somerville, who remained leaders in the local branch. The upshot was that the L.A. Branch was redeemed, and it began to angle to get a chance to host the annual national NAACP convention.

John Somerville promised to build a brand new hotel in Los Angeles to house the delegates if the NAACP would hold its convention in L.A. in 1928. The deal was done, and a whirlwind of construction began on what would soon be the Hotel Somerville, located at 41st and Central Avenue. The location was significantly south of the existing black business district, but the area was still largely undeveloped, land was cheap, and, in any case, the hotel was so nice compared to any other black-owned business in the city (or anywhere else in America, for that matter) that the location soon became a magnet for other black-owned businesses (including, across the street, the new dental office of NAACP president H. Claude Hudson) and black homes. The Hotel Somerville became the new center for black Los Angeles, including the local jazz scene. It became, in the late 1920s, the most visible sign of the L.A. Renaissance.

The NAACP convention of 1928 was a huge success on every count. Somerville's hotel, opened scarcely a week before the convention, was brand new and, especially on the inside, beautiful—an open-air alcove with palms and a fountain; Spanish style interior for the downstairs dining area and ballroom and for the mezzanine that overlooked it; one-hundred rooms on three upper floors; a roof-top garden. Du Bois gushed over it, calling it a "jewel." The turnout for the convention was higher than expected, given the distance to L.A. from the East, and the program was chock full of popular and influential speakers. The entertainment included jazz and dance. Delegates from back East were enthralled, and, for the moment, but only a moment, it seemed the distance between East and West—between Harlem and L.A.—had all but vanished.

From L.A. to Harlem

Even as the Harlem Renaissance was reshaping black Los Angeles, black writers from L.A. and other western cities were reshaping the Harlem Renaissance. The two most influential writers who left L.A. for Harlem were Arna Bontemps and Wallace Thurman. Both left in the mid-1920s, and in Harlem they joined a Renaissance in full swing—but a Renaissance led by middle-age leaders, such as Du Bois, who believed black art should reflect high aspirations of the Talented Tenth, in order to break down white stereotypes about black inferiority. Bontemps and Wallace, both in their early twenties, viewed their art differently. They joined a group of other young writers and artists—several of them also from the West—who shared their impatience with Talented Tenth respectability and who, quite purposefully, inaugurated a new phase of the Renaissance, which the historian David Levering Lewis has called the "New Negro Renaissance."

For Bontemps and Thurman—like their western-born Renaissance counterparts, Langston Hughes and Aaron Douglass—the goal was not civil rights; it was instead a desire to discover, and connect with, what they considered to be authentic Negro culture. The roots of this desire could be found in their western upbringing.

Arna Bontemps was born in Alexandria, Louisiana, in 1902, but at the age of four, he moved with his parents to Los Angeles. There, in Southern California, Arna was raised on the fringe of the black community. Neither his parents nor grandparents associated much with the African Americans who were building the Central Avenue community. Paul Bontemps, Arna's father, became a pioneering black minister in the Seventh Day Adventist church—a man who sought to make a clean break with the South and his past. Arna lived in majority white areas, with few black companions, and he attended schools that were mostly white. When Arna reached high school, his father sent him to an Adventist boarding school north of Los Angeles, where he acquired an excellent education but also where he began to feel robbed of his birthright, his Negro heritage. He had spend his years around his Uncle Buddy Ward, also from Louisiana, who shared nothing of his father's respectability and was given to fast living, gambling, swearing, and the telling of lively tales about voodoo and ghosts. For Arna, Uncle Buddy came to represent authentic Negro culture—southern style—whereas his father came to represent a repudiation of black southern culture. His college years, spend at an otherwise all-white Adventist school in the far reaches of northern California, only reinforced Arna Bontemps's longing for all that was black.

"Before I finished college," he later wrote, "I had begun to feel that in some large and important areas I was being miseducated, and that perhaps I should have rebelled." His Western education had given him permission to dream of being a writer. But at the same time he felt, and would always feel, that the West had somehow robbed him of his birthright—a personal connection to Negro life. His father's coldness for things "colored" clashed with his love for Buddy and his curiosity about black history.

The result was Arna's sharply bifurcated view of heritage, region, and identity. "In their opposing attitudes toward roots my father and my great uncle made me aware of a conflict in which every educated American Negro, and some who are not educated, must somehow take sides," Arna wrote in the last decade of his life. "By implication at least, one group advocates embracing the riches of the folk heritage; their opposites demand a clean break with the past and all it represents." By the time he graduated from Pacific Union, there was no possibility that he would choose the latter. "So," Bontemps remembered later in life, "what did one do after concluding that for him a break with the past and the shedding of his Negro-ness were not only impossible but unthinkable?" His own answer came in 1924, when he left a post-office job in Los Angeles to become a writer in the Harlem Renaissance.

As Bontemps later described it, Harlem in 1924:

> was like a foretaste of paradise. A blue haze descended at night and with it strings of fairy lights on the broad avenues. From the window of a small room in an apartment on Fifth and 129th Street I looked over the rooftops of Negrodom and tried to believe my eyes. What a city! What a world!

He went to the Harlem public library and found young black women employed at the front desk, a sight unknown back home. Better yet, the young woman who accepted his application for a library card recognized his name from his recently published poem in *Crisis*. It was a sweet beginning, and things only got better as he quickly became an accepted figure in Renaissance circles. By day, he taught at Harlem Academy, an Adventist school. By night, he roamed with the poets. Before long he got married and roamed less, but he continued to love Harlem and to write about the heritage of race.

Wallace Thurman grew up in Salt Lake City and moved to L.A. after graduating from high school. Salt Lake must have felt much like a prison to him. Thurman was an irreverent literary genius surrounded by fervent Mormons; he had a very dark complexion but was surrounded by family members who prized their light complexions. He came to L.A. to take classes at the University of Southern California (USC) and to find a more open, intellectual climate for his prodigious, politically charged talents. But he found L.A. disappointing. By his reckoning, the black college students at USC were merely social climbers and the city's black middle class residents were "fuddlers"—the term he used to condemn what he considered to be their shallow intellectual life and their bungled attempts at bourgeois culture. He worked for a time in the same post office in which Bontemps worked, and, like Bontemps, he longed for Harlem and arrived there shortly after Bontemps.

Bontemps and Thurman were different in almost every way. Bontemps was a disciplined Adventist and a married man with a day job. Thurman imbibed all the booze and sex Manhattan had to offer—male and female, black and white—and lived on a sarcastic prayer. Bontemps was healthy and happy and well settled; Thurman had tuberculosis, laughed too loudly to keep from crying, and lived with an aggressive impermanence. Bontemps carried the weight of his mulatto heritage; Thurman carried the weight of his very dark skin. But the two shared a bookish intelligence and undeniable literary talent. In addition, they shared western upbringings in which their families kept them at the margins of the black mainstream. Both sought to remedy that in Harlem—by simply being in the Black Capital of the World and also by writing their way into Negro-ness.

For Bontemps in particular, this meant embracing the racial implications of Modernism—the desire for what was primitive, the search for basic human truths that had been hidden behind the façade of industrial civilization. The basic goal was to restore "primitivism" to a soulless world. Broadly put, the new ethic ran as follows: the modern world was on the verge of disaster because the European pursuit of civilization had crushed the primitive and natural aspects of life that were critical to humanity's well being; Negroes—African and American alike— had preserved at least some of their primitivism; by presenting that primitivism in their art and letters, New Negroes might save modern civilization from its drought of soul. A resurgence of primitivism (and a romanticization of it) was not Du Bois's idea of Renaissance, but it *was* what Bontemps had in mind—in a literary sense—in the late 1920s. In giving voice to primitivism—to what they considered the authentic and almost-extinct voice of African Americans—the black

Westerners sought at last to find their own true selves, to save Negro Americans from their ongoing loss of Negro-ness, and perhaps to save the soul of the nation. "The idea," Bontemps later recalled, "intoxicated us."

Du Bois's view had been that black art should serve political purposes. It could be an effective way to undermine white racist stereotypes. This dominant assumption among leading black intellectuals rendered some subjects taboo, including black promiscuity, drunkenness, and southern-style primitivism in general. But the young (mainly western) blacks who dominated the post-1925 Renaissance had no desire to distance their art from the earthier aspects of African American culture. Indeed, they had moved to Harlem to close the gap between themselves and Afro-southern folk culture. Artistically, they loved jungle scenes, jazz rhythms, blues sensibilities, sensuality, thick dialect.

Following Thurman's lead, the young leaders of New Negro Renaissance launched in 1926 their own literary journal, *FIRE!!* It lasted only one issue (with most issues going up, literally, in flames) and won them the ire of the Talented Tenth generation. That same year, Bontemps's friend Langston Hughes published his first book of poems, *The Weary Blues* (1926), which plunged readers into the world of the black masses, linking African jungle moons and tribal dances with Harlem cabarets and jazz-filled nights. The debate over "racial" art boiled up in New York's intellectual circles, but Arna Bontemps never wavered in his belief that "colored" representations (as he and his friends defined them) were much needed in literature.

Thurman's failure with *FIRE!!* was not the end of him. In 1929 he scored two major successes: a Broadway play, *Harlem*, and his first novel, *The Blacker the Berry . . .: A Novel of Negro Life*. Still his most famous work, *Blacker* took dead aim at the taboo subject of skin color within the black community. The protagonist, a female based loosely upon Thurman himself, arrives in L.A. to attend USC but, due to her dark complexion, is ostracized by the light-skinned, socially adept crowd of black college students. Eventually, she moves to Harlem, thinking it will offer a more open-minded culture. But she does not fit in Harlem, either, and her life veers toward self destruction. Near the end of the novel, in a moment of despair, she sees a flashing neon sign: "Western Union." And she wonders, should she return to the West? Can she start over and find a home there? No, she decides, no. The West had failed her. She is in permanent exile within black America.

Bontemps's first novel *God Sends Sunday* (1931) underscored his commitment to racial art by presenting as its main theme the southern misadventures of his Uncle Buddy. Bontemps did not care to write about a westerner who moved to Harlem, as did Thurman. Nor did he use the black West as his setting, as Langston Hughes did in his first and only novel, *Not Without Laughter* (1930). Bontemps wanted to write about the South, the region he once called "that vast everglade of black life." *God Sends Sunday* is about Afro-southern folk culture. The protagonist is his Uncle Buddy, thinly veiled as a jockey named

Little Augie. Virtually all of the characters are sporting men and painted women, whose earthy dialect and violent behavior flow like the Mississippi as they wander up and down the Delta between New Orleans and St. Louis. Little Augie races horses, chases women, gambles, and fights—his luck with horses and women running hot and cold until he finally hits rock bottom. Then he goes west to find his sister.

At last Augie arrives in Los Angeles, or rather in Mudtown, "the Negro neighborhood" outside of Watts. Mudtown, he discovers, "was like a tiny section of the deep south literally transplanted." With his sister, Leah, and her grandson Terry (close representations of Arna's grandmother and Arna himself), Augie plans to settle down at last—but he cannot. His restless, volatile personality leads him once again into drunkenness and trouble. In a fight over a young woman, he cuts up a neighbor—perhaps mortally—with a beet knife. Facing nothing but trouble in Mudtown, Augie flees to Mexico, hitching a ride to the border with his only possession—the freedom of movement.

The curious thing about *God Sends Sunday* is that it is not about the black West, which Bontemps knew best, or about the northern ghetto, which surrounded him as he wrote, but about the black South, which he had never seen. Even the part of the novel situated in Southern California is really about the South, not the West. The novel's "Mudtown" is obviously based on the Furlough Track where Arna had lived for a time with his grandmother and Buddy; but the real Furlough Track, as later described by Arna himself, was nothing like a transplanted section of the Deep South.

The novel received mixed, sometimes heated, reviews. Du Bois hated it. Having bestowed prizes on Bontemps's early poetry, he now fumed that *God Sends Sunday*—and by implication its author—was "a profound disappointment." He admitted that Little Augie's character had "a certain pathetic touch," but emphasized that "nearly all else is sordid crime, drinking, gambling, whore-mongering, and murder." He was shocked that Bontemps had included:

> not a decent intelligent woman; not a single man with the slightest ambition or real education . . . In the "Blues" alone Bontemps sees beauty. But in brown skins, frizzled hair and full contoured faces, they are to him nothing but ugly, tawdry, hateful things, which he describes with evident caricature.

Du Bois called Bontemps a race hater, but nothing could be further from the truth. Du Bois mistook Bontemps's joyful representation for hateful misrepresentation. Bontemps later sighed: "Du Bois did not fail to express pained displeasure—in much the same terms as my own upright father used when he read it—and I, in my exhilaration, was convinced that neither quite understood." In fact they did not understand. Bontemps wrote what he did in *God Sends Sunday* not because he despised poor southern blacks but because he loved them, even envied them. He felt they still possessed what he had lost growing up out West—a culture linked to primitivism, an enduring tie to an African past, an undeniable sense of self.

By the time Bontemps was defending his novel, the Great Depression was shutting down the Harlem Renaissance. Bontemps's Adventist school closed, and he accepted a teaching position at an Adventist college in Huntsville, Alabama. There, in the Deep South, he gained a very different perspective on the region. Langston Hughes left Harlem as well, and when Wallace Thurman's tuberculosis caught up with him, he returned to Utah to recuperate with family—not a particularly edifying experience for him. Once he was well enough, he moved back to L.A. to try to break into the screenwriting business in Hollywood. That did not pan out, so he returned to Harlem to write a final novel—which lambasted the Renaissance itself—and to die, which he did in 1934, largely unnoticed, in a public hospital. If that were not enough to signal the end of the Renaissance, the Harlem ghetto riot of 1935 surely did.

A New Renaissance in L.A.?

In the 1930s, Los Angeles became a productive center for the black arts. Wallace Thurman remained in town and worked in Hollywood until 1934. Arna Bontemps returned the following year, fleeing the South to write his masterwork, *Black Thunder*. Langston Hughes spent much of the 1930s in California, mostly Los Angeles. William Grant Still of New York, the most talented black composer of the twentieth century, moved permanently to Los Angeles in the mid-1930s. In addition, largely unknown local writers, such as Bruce Forsythe and Elizabeth Adams, struggled to be heard. *New Age* editor and retired politician Frederick Roberts sponsored a popular radio show that featured black musical talent. Simply put, the New Negro Renaissance that swept Harlem in the 1920s did not really die out in the 1930s; it just moved to Los Angeles.

But there was more involved here than a mere shift from East Coast to West Coast. The Harlem experience could not be duplicated in Los Angeles because Southern California was not Manhattan. New York had all the natural ingredients for making a visible and influential artistic movement: It was home to every major publishing house in America, as well as the three national black monthlies—*Crisis*, *Opportunity*, and *Messenger*; it had the black Talented Tenth, with W. E. B. Du Bois at the helm, who were eager to promote young African American talent; it had Broadway, which was an obvious, if reluctant, employer of black writers and performers; it had Greenwich Village, whose leftist and bohemian culture offered some support to aspiring African Americans. Harlem in the mid-1920s also had a group of young and talented black artists who banded together in a conscious effort to turn the art world on its head. Taken together, these factors created a gravitational pull that gave the Harlem Renaissance a sense of centrality and community.

FIGURE 4.1 Between July 1930 and March 1931, Louis Armstrong shifted his base
of operations from Connie's Inn in Harlem to Sebastian New Cotton
Club in Los Angeles. Armstrong directed the orchestra there as he had
at Connie's Inn. Los Angeles' Cotton Club was located on Washington
Blvd. in Culver City. Courtesy of Louis Armstrong House Museum

Los Angeles lacked Manhattan's support system for artists, which meant that
its Renaissance lacked the sense of cohesion and purpose that the Harlem
experience had. In Los Angeles, there were no major publishing houses or patrons,
black or white. Hollywood was more hostile to blacks than Broadway. Los Angeles
had no Greenwich Village. Indeed, it had no Harlem. Central Avenue, for all its
jazz clubs and black businesses, was far more diverse than black Manhattan, and
its black community was far more decentralized. Harlem pulled artists together
and won them notice, while also placing certain restrictions on their creative
directions. Los Angeles absorbed black artists into anonymity and set them adrift
in the weightless sunlight. It gave them more freedom to work as they pleased,
but it offered fewer opportunities to make a name and no chance at all to feel
the energizing force of coordinated effort. It was not simply that the Renaissance
continued in Los Angeles but also that Los Angeles gave rise to a very different
sort of Renaissance: a more individualistic, decentralized effort, an outpouring
of literature and music so defuse and unconnected that it defied even the notion

of a cultural "movement." Even so, there was plenty of artistic action in black L.A. during the Depression decade, and it bears examination.

As a young man, Arna Bontemps had chafed at his parents' decision to leave the South, and he had longed for a connection to the southern culture his parents had left behind. That yearning manifested itself in *God Sends Sunday*, with its unsophisticated, nostalgic representation of Little Augie and the black South. Then Bontemps moved his family to Huntsville, Alabama, to take a teaching position at Oakwood College, an Adventist school. Suddenly, Bontemps found himself with a wife and family to support and protect in the racist cauldron of the Deep South. In Alabama, he loved black southerners and the southern landscape, just as he always imagined he would, but he found the extreme prejudice and racial subjugation suffocating. Suddenly, his parents' decision to move west did not seem so strange.

Living in the South had changed Arna Bontemps's outlook on life, and it would change his literature as well. Almost instinctively, he had begun to explore the history of slave rebellions, especially the campaign of Gabriel Prosser, the Virginia slave who sought freedom through an armed uprising in 1800. Sensing his changed mood, and unnerved by his continued associations with Harlem Renaissance writers, the Oakwood administration gave him an ultimatum: he could publicly renounce and burn his books written by Renaissance authors, or he could lose his job. Bontemps bought a Ford, loaded up his family, and headed for Los Angeles. Feeling himself a failure, he moved the family into his father's home, sold the Ford and went to work on a novel about Gabriel's revolt. In six months, it was done.

Black Thunder reads as if it were written by a different person than the author who wrote *God Sends Sunday*. In his second novel, Bontemps was no longer interested in preserving quaint features of Afro-southern folk life. *Black Thunder* is about getting free, about harnessing the revolutionary potential of Afro-southern culture. Before 1931, living in the urban West and North, he had longed for a South that might connect him to his cherished African heritage. And while he cherished "primitive" Afro-southerners and would continue writing about them throughout his life, he now understood the flip side of southern primitivism, namely, the terrorism of "primitive" *Anglo*-southerners. That experience prompted a dramatic change of perspective and literary style.

Whereas *God Sends Sunday* presents black speech in a molasses–thick dialect that, were it not of loving intent, might be construed as a mocking caricature, the African Americans in *Black Thunder* speak a carefully crafted and dignified dialect that, like the character of Gabriel himself, maintains a powerful edge from beginning to end. Gone too is the simplistic narrative and one-dimensional characterization of his first novel. In *Black Thunder* Bontemps drew upon all his skill and literary knowledge to create an utterly compelling drama about one man's fateful attempt to set the race free.

In the end, nature itself, like a curse from God, thwarts Gabriel's plan. On the night of his carefully planned attack on Richmond, a thunderstorm of unprecedented severity literally floods out the assault. The major-domo of a neighboring plantation, always an uncertain member of the conspiracy, then reveals the plan to his master. Ultimately, Gabriel dies on the scaffold, but his is a death filled with power, indeed glory. He stands there, a strong man baffled by the turn of events, but unflinching and unafraid. In *God Sends Sunday*, Little Augie's flippant escape to Mexico brings the story to a pathetic close. In *Black Thunder*, Gabriel stands on the gallows as a martyr, "the first for freedom."

Bontemps, however, did not remain in L.A. Once he had received a small advance for the manuscript, he moved the family to Chicago, where he found work as a writer for the Works Progress Administration. He and Langston Hughes had once speculated that they would both find their way to L.A. and collaborate on various projects. But times and circumstances had changed. Arna had no prospects in Southern California; he had a teaching job waiting at an Adventist academy in Chicago. For his part, Hughes was in and out of L.A. He spent a good amount of time overseas, especially when he and his L.A. friend and fellow traveler Loren Miller sailed to the Soviet Union with a crew of other Harlem Renaissance figures, with the intention of making a film (at the invitation of the Soviet state) about southern racism. The film was never made, but Hughes kept moving, on through China, before returning stateside. Loren Miller settled into a dual career as a journalist and a lawyer, succeeding in both. But he and Hughes, like Hughes and Bontemps, were not able to collaborate in literary or journalistic endeavors or provide a creative space around which a new Renaissance movement could gain momentum.

Hughes kept a low profile when he was in L.A., but he got one shot to score big with a Hollywood screenplay. The film was supposed to be about the Old South, and Hughes wanted to make sure it was not of the demeaning happy-slave variety. In this project he worked with the actor and NAACP activist Clarence Muse. Hollywood treated Hughes like dirt; at one lunch, the director of the film chose a restaurant that would not admit Hughes—and the director, caring not at all, simply left Hughes to wait outside. The final product slipped out of Hughes's control, and the film *Way Down South* appeared as the happy-slave film that Hughes sought to avoid, with his name in the screenwriting credits. Fed up with L.A., he fled to the tender mercies of Carmel, up the California coast, and went to work on his memoirs, which would be published as *The Big Sea* and would end with Hughes leaving Harlem, offering no mention at all of his time in L.A. For him, L.A. would never quite be home.

For Elizabeth Laura Adams, whose work was largely unknown and who always operated at the far edge of the Renaissance, Southern California was the only home she knew. A frail loner with high-art tastes who converted to Catholicism and wrote about spiritual matters, Adams had her first success (and crushing defeat) as a poet in 1930. Thereafter, she struggled but kept at it, leaving, in the end, some published poetry and a gentle but revealing autobiography, *Dark Symphony*. A native of Southern California, Adams was born in 1909 in Santa Barbara, spent her childhood years in Los Angeles, returned to Santa Barbara during adolescence, then moved Santa Monica, where she graduated from high school. She spent a few more years in Santa Monica before returning to Los Angeles to find work during the Great Depression. Adams had varied artistic interests. She had to give up her first dream—that of becoming a concert violinist—because of a weak heart condition, the lifelong result of having contracted influenza during the Los Angeles epidemic of 1918. Thereafter, she set her sights on what she called "a literary and dramatic career," although, after a conversion to Catholicism, her deepest (and unfulfilled) desire was to become a nun.

Adams's views on life were shaped by three dominant factors: the loss of numerous family members when she was young; her ongoing search for religious faith; and her youthful optimism that racism could be overcome through pluck and talent. She lost both her father and her infant brother, along with a series of relatives. She disliked her mother's Colored Methodist Episcopal Church, where, in her view, there were too many emotional outbursts for God to get a word in. She gravitated to liturgical services, first of the Episcopalians and ultimately (after being kicked out the Episcopalian congregation because of her race) to the Catholic Church. Upon graduation from high school, where she had excelled in journalism and writing, she was shocked to find that white editors were shocked that a black woman would even ask for a job. She remained optimistic.

Her confidence crashed when Adams witnessed her first success as a poet in 1930. Her poem was titled "Consecrated . . . A Prose Dream of Memories sacred to the Mother of a Priest." The subtitle accurately relates the theme. Race enters into the prose not at all. Its evocation of a holy and spiritual connection to God within the Catholic Church placed it decidedly out of step with the standard Renaissance fare. It was also a longer piece (140 lines) than most New Negro Renaissance poems, which, following the path of Langston Hughes's irresistible style, were usually brief. The poem traces the course of a priest's life through four reveries of his mother—regarding her pregnancy, her son's birth, his emergent manhood, and his symbolic death, due to his decision to become a priest and, in service to God, be dead to the world. In section I, for example, the woman remembers praying to "The Virgin Mother" for "the dream child of my womb" and receiving an answer (a "Mandate Omnipotent") in "the candle's dying breath" that the child would be "Consecrated." Throughout, the language is formal, laced with mysticism and loss. It ends with a "memory of a prayer once prayed." The mother cries out "*Jesu! Maria!*" and hears an answer in the winds—"scurrying from the depths of caverns— / Re-echoing weird cries from spacious valleys— / . . . resound in plaintive murmuring: / *Consecrated! Consecrated!*"

At the most obvious level, Adams's verse reflects her own longing for consecration through a spiritual connection to God through the Church. Perhaps, too, it was a way of working through the loss of so many loved ones at such an early age. The poem seems to carry the memory of her own mother's pain at losing an infant son, for in "Consecrated" the mother loses her son twice—first to the priesthood and then to Death (a word Adams capitalizes in this poem and throughout her 1942 autobiography, *Dark Symphony*). Elizabeth's own sorrow is tangible as well. It is not difficult to hear in these lines the loss of a father she idolized and obeyed, much as a parishioner does a priest. And here, too, is Adams's clear recognition that her search for God, if it be her salvation, will come at a cost, for in the poem the mother's supplication for her unborn son—a prayer that God answers with severe precision—is the source of her joy but also the source of her loneliness.

Adams sent the piece "to a literary club" which solicited work for a contest, and the results were sweet and bitter. The only information she was required to submit was her name and age. First came the sweet. As Adams later recalled:

> one of the judges telephoned the good news that my poem had been accepted and the committee marveled at one so young writing with such "mystical depth"—and wished me to meet them personally, which I did upon a given date.

But then the judges laid eyes on Adams, and everything changed. "On finding out that the writer was not fair of skin," she wrote, "the judges were all shocked into a state of regret." The all-white committee was openly skeptical that a black person could write such poetry, and also doubtful that an African American *should* write such poetry. One told her: "You should use Negro themes . . . [and] confine your writing to sentiments expressing the simplicity and humility characteristic of your people." Another added: "'Write so that readers know you're Colored." A tearful Adams left the committee, and her association with the contest was dropped altogether.

It was the old Renaissance dilemma revisited. If the doors of the art world were open to African Americans, what sort of art should they do? If blacks produced literature of high quality based on the normal European standards, what was "black" about it? If distinguished art grew out of and revealed the innermost struggles of the artist's soul, would not black art have to reflect the daily impact of racism on the black American soul? But if African Americans produced only "black" art, was not that just another kind of segregation, a kind of artistic entrapment imposed by white assumptions about what black artists could and should do? At the height of the Harlem Renaissance, Countee Cullen had said he wanted to be known as a great poet, not a great black poet; Langston Hughes countered that if Cullen did not want to be known for his blackness, then he must want to be white. So the argument continued, among blacks themselves and between blacks and whites.

And always the fundamental question remained: What was black? The panel of judges who faced Elizabeth Adams determined at a glance that she was "black," and they proceeded to treat her with that peculiar blend of paternal disrespect that whites often reserved for blacks, but they had sensed nothing "black" in her poetry. Adams was not the poet they thought she was, and her poem, so effusively praised when they did not know her race, was now not praiseworthy at all. Indeed, they now considered it a rather inappropriate hoax: What was this black person doing submitting a poem that they could not recognize as a black poem?

Six years later, the poetry journal *Westward* published "Consecrated." *Westward* was a solidly established poetry magazine with offices in northern California that published all manner of verse on all manner of topics. It was not a vehicle for the New Negro Renaissance; poetry about race themes was mostly absent from the journal, but the subject matter and points of view expressed in the magazine were eclectic, and the editor cared not at all when Adams confessed in a letter that she was black. If publication in *Westward* was not exactly a breakthrough for Adams, it boosted her confidence and marked the beginning of a more productive literary career.

In *Westward*, Adams also published a triad of poems under the heading, "Yes, I'm Colored," which cleverly answered the poetry jury that had snubbed her in 1930. The first two poems—"Space" and "His Faith"—have nothing racial in them. They briefly explore the questions of spirituality, death, and heaven that so encompassed Adams's life. The third, "Death of a Colored Dancer," then serves as a satirical set piece, playing off the "Yes, I'm Colored" title. The poem describes a black Protestant funeral, at which the "dancer" is carried up to heaven. With references to "The church Brothers and Sisters" and Adam's use of dialect speech and formulaic Negro church scenes ("But while / They moaned an' began to shout / A hollerin' / Aloud to keep Satan out), Adams puts one over on white readers who did not get the joke and who took seriously her sympathetic rendering of the church scenes that she herself found appalling.

Elizabeth Adams was isolated from Renaissance circles, and between her religious quest and her work to support her ailing mother she had little time to associate with other artists even if she wanted to. That said, Adams was a voracious reader who was thoroughly versed in Renaissance works; in her autobiography, she makes liberal use of recent black literature, including pieces that emerged out of the Harlem scene of the 1920s. In a cruel, sad, racist world, black literature became her lifeline. In her autobiography, she recalls that in her most desperate hours, looking for any job she could get in the maw of the Depression (she once mowed a lawn for fifteen cents), she walked the streets of Los Angeles clinging to memorized lines of black poetry, including verses from

Bontemps and Hughes. She herself maintained, "I was misunderstood because I represented the New Negro—the thinking Negro." And she wondered, indeed she had to wonder: "Was life . . . a procession in which ambitious young people of my race had no place?"

That was indeed the question, but blacks in Los Angeles never quit trying to break out of their circumscribed place. One senior leader in black L.A. took an innovative approach. Frederick Madison Roberts was a long-time politician, mortician, and publisher of the Race paper, the *New Age*. He was best known for becoming the first African American elected to the California state legislature (the 74th District, essentially the Central Avenue area) in 1918; he held the post until 1934. In 1937, he began a radio show: "The idea of putting on a radio program that belongs exclusively to our group has long been considered by the publisher of this newspaper," he added. There was such a show in New York, but that was of no use to local talent or local listeners. Roberts wanted a Los Angeles entertainment program that would promote artists from his community. The show would feature "all colored talent," and Roberts promised that important Hollywood, radio, and nightclub talent scouts would be in attendance.

Thus was born *The Radio Amateur Show* (later renamed the *Talent Hour*), which was broadcast over Los Angeles radio station KFVD. Beginning in late April, the show aired Sunday afternoons. Performances were live, with a studio audience in attendance, at the fifth-floor studio of the Auburn–Cord Building at Wilshire and Mariposa. Getting on the inaugural show was simple. One needed only to get two people to buy year-long subscriptions to the *New Age* (at $2 each) and to bring their subscription forms (and the $4) to the studio on the morning of the program. On the eve of the first broadcast, Roberts boasted that the upcoming show was "the talk of the town."

The *Talent Hour* was an immediate hit, exceeding even Roberts's expectations. By the second broadcast, KFVD knew it was on to something, and Roberts vowed to make the show a permanent addition to the airways. Acts ranged from the jazz piano of Lady Will Carr (who said her goal was to be "a female Fats Waller") to the spirituals of the Junior Jubilee Singers. There were tap dancers and church choirs and family singers and all manner of instrumentalists—harpists, organists, violinists, pianists. All told, the Talent Hour offered a feast of local African American musical talent. And Angelenos—black and white and otherwise—tuned their radio dials to KFVD. By mid-May, KFVD claimed 35,000 listeners; one month later it claimed 500,000.

Roberts had an expansive vision of what the show could achieve, not just for black Los Angeles but for the city as a whole. It would bridge the divide between blacks and whites; it would demonstrate the purchasing power and voting power of local African Americans. Through dignified entertainment, whites would change their outlook about blacks. Whites would then hire blacks for decent jobs. Moreover, if whites and blacks could get together in the economic arena "without regard to color lines," then Los Angeles would take new strides toward progress. "If the whole is to be great," Roberts wrote, "then all of the parts must be tied for the common good."

Roberts forthrightly stated that the *Talent Hour* was an assault on the Uncle Tom stereotype. It was proving to whites that their mental image of dim-witted, underachieving Negroes was all wrong. "The *Talent Hour* has become a means of propaganda of a decent sort," Roberts wrote, "that is bringing to Greater Los Angeles the respectable and modern art of the younger generation." Thus, the artists were nothing less than "ambassadors of good will, [who] have demonstrated to a critical world that colored artists have the ability and dignity to compete anywhere on merit."

One gets from Roberts's words a strong dose of *déjà vu*. For here is a clear echo of what W. E. B. Du Bois had claimed for the Harlem Renaissance more than a decade earlier. Roberts made no reference to Du Bois, and he did not seek the roots of black artistry in the ancient civilizations of Africa, as Du Bois had; but he clearly shared Du Bois's old faith that black artistry would break down the walls of white bigotry. That was a heavy burden for black art to bear—in the 1930s or any other decade, in Los Angeles or Harlem. Roberts conceded that the *Talent Hour* could not change the world, or even Los Angeles, overnight. But "as the program appeals to wider and wider audiences, more and more people come to a realization of the inherent integrity" of the African American community.

For our purposes, it is useful to acknowledge the disconnect between Roberts's *Talent Hour* and the larger streams of Renaissance creativity that had swirled through Los Angeles in the 1930s. Hughes was in town through much of 1937 and would have happily read some poetry—perhaps bringing Bontemps back to his home town to add some verse of his own. William Grant Still was now a permanent resident of the city and probably would have orchestrated some music for the show. Roberts seems never to have contemplated such connections. He was bringing local Race talent together in a way no one ever had, but somehow he seemed unaware that many Renaissance leaders had come west to Los Angeles during the 1930s.

Perhaps the *Talent Hour* might be credited with some new trends in the local cultural scene. The rise of Roberts's radio program corresponded with city's first major gallery showing of black art. Working with the prestigious, white-owned Stendahl Gallery, the black YMCA held a contest soliciting paintings and sculptures, which were judged by representatives of the Gallery and then shown (and sold on consignment). The *Talent Hour* also featured many church groups at a time when modern gospel music was becoming a new and important form of music in the city's black churches, a trend that would lay the foundations for Los Angeles' Gospel ascendancy in subsequent decades. Roberts's radio hour was therefore entwined with other black arts initiatives in 1930s L.A., but the striking thing, in the end, was the sudden and unexplained demise of his show.

The *Talent Hour* program gained further momentum through late summer. According to one estimate, it was the number four radio show in all of Los Angeles by early August. The studio could no longer hold the standing-room only crowds that came to see the show in action. A cash-prize contest fueled interest in the show. The Sunday programs throughout July and August served as competitive preliminary rounds, with the top three winners each week continuing to the next round. Winners were chosen by the radio audience, who called in their votes to KFVD. The high interest in the event belied the limited amount of cash to be given away—$50 total prize money, to be divided among the finalists. By the end of August the contest ended, with a church choir taking first prize.

Then the *Talent Hour* vanished. As quickly as it had appeared in April, the radio show disappeared that September. With no word of explanation or apology from Roberts, the *Talent Hour* vanished from the pages of the *New Age*, and from the airwaves as well. It serves as a metaphor for the L.A. Renaissance of the 1930s. Innovative things were happening in the black arts scene throughout the decade, but as a collective movement it never gained traction. Because it was a fragmented Renaissance, it has been forgotten that throughout the 1930s, a loosely tied collection of black musicians, composers, writers, and artists lived in L.A. Mostly these artists lived and worked in separate spheres. They came and went, meeting and collaborating only at fleeting moments. The Harlem Renaissance of the 1920s had a center of gravity. Central Avenue's Renaissance of the 1930s sprawled like Southern California itself.

Whether or not Renaissance art in Los Angeles imitated life, the ways in which black art was produced in Los Angeles did reflect the city itself. What occurred was not simply a Renaissance in Los Angeles, but a *Los Angeles* Renaissance.

The Renaissance in Los Angeles thus revealed both the peaks and valleys of this artistic movement in American culture. It revealed the power, excitement, and reach of all things Harlem, even unto the furthest reaches of the American West. It further demonstrated that the Harlem Renaissance itself was shaped by black westerners who traveled east to find themselves. And in the end, it revealed that New York maintained its dominance as a center of American cultural production. L.A. could not yet fill Manhattan's shoes.

Further Reading

Bogle, Donald. *Bright Boulevards, Bold Dreams: The Story of Black Hollywood*. New York: Ballantine Books, 2006.

Bontemps, Arna. *Black Thunder*. New York, 1936; reprint edition with an introduction by the author, Boston, MA: Beacon Press, 1968.

Bryant, Clora, Buddy Collette, William Green, and Steve Isoardi. *Central Avenue Sounds: Jazz in Los Angeles*. Berkeley: University of California Press, 1998.

De Graaf, Lawrence B., Kevin Mulroy, and Quintard Taylor. *Seeking El Dorado: African Americans in California*. Seattle, WA: University of Washington Press, 2001.

Flamming, Douglas. *Bound for Freedom: Black Los Angeles in Jim Crow America*. Berkeley, CA: University of California Press, 2005.

Garceau-Hagen, Dee, ed. *Portraits of Women in the American West*. New York: Routledge, 2005.

George, Lynell. *No Crystal Stair: African Americans in the City of Angels*. New York: Verso, 1992.

Gregory, James N. *The Southern Diaspora: How the Great Migration of Black and White Southerners Transformed America*. Chapel Hill, NC: University of North Carolina Press, 2005.

Hughes, Langston. *Not Without Laughter*. New York: Alfred A. Knopf, 1969.

Jones, Kirkland C. *Renaissance Man from Louisiana: A Biography of Arna Wendell Bontemps*. Westport, CT: Greenwood Press, 1992.

Lapp, Rudolph M. *Afro-Americans in California*, 2nd ed. San Francisco, CA: Boyd and Fraser Publishing Company, 1987.

Lewis, David Levering, ed. *The Portable Harlem Renaissance Reader*. New York: Viking, 1994.

Nugent, Walter. *Into the West: The Story of Its People*. New York: Alfred A. Knopf, 1999.

Rampersad, Arnold. *The Life of Langston Hughes. Volume I: 1902–1941, "I, Too, Sing America."* New York: Oxford University Press, 1986.

Sides, Josh. *L.A. City Limits: African American Los Angeles from the Great Depression to the Present*. Berkeley, CA: University of California Press, 2003.

Smith, R.J. *The Great Black Way: L.A. in the 1940s and the Lost African-American Renaissance*. New York: Public Affairs, 2006.

Taylor, Quintard. *In Search of the Racial Frontier: African Americans in the American West, 1528–1990*. New York: W. W. Norton, 1998.

Taylor, Quintard and Shirley Ann Wilson Moore. *African American Women Confront the West, 1600–2000*. Norman, OK: University of Oklahoma Press, 2003.

Thurman, Wallace. *The Blacker the Berry . . . : A Novel of Negro Life*. New York, 1929; reprint edition, New York: Macmillan, 1970.

Wheeler, B. Gordon. *Black California: The History of African-Americans in the Golden State*. New York: Hippocrene Books, 1993.

Wild, Mark. *Street Meeting: Multiethnic Neighborhoods in Early Twentieth-Century Los Angeles*. Berkeley, CA: University of California Press, 2005.

5

"ALL GOD'S CHILDREN GOT SWING"

The Black Renaissance in the San Francisco Bay Area, 1906–1941

Douglas Henry Daniels

Some 3,000 miles from the Harlem Renaissance, the black residents of the San Francisco Bay Area are not usually depicted as active participants in this literary and cultural movement. However, research on the subject requires that we reconsider the sole focus on Harlem and New York City, as the Bay Area possessed a dynamic and fertile black cultural milieu despite its small African American population. In fact, these cultural activities began before the 1920s, the period usually considered for the Renaissance, and continued for at least a decade afterwards.

The best-known harbingers of the Renaissance from the West Coast were Bert Williams and George Walker, who met in the Bay Area and got their start in San Francisco. Coming from the Bahamas and raised in Riverside, Williams and his Kansas-born companion, Walker, became famous in New York City and abroad in the first decade of the twentieth century. On the other hand, Arna Bontemps, from Louisiana and Los Angeles, who attended college in nearby Stockton, achieved considerable fame as a writer, and Louise Patterson, a University of California graduate, went to Moscow with Langston Hughes and Bay Area resident Matt Crawford in 1932.

The Bay Area abounded with writers and artists and, equally impressive, with musicians who played ragtime and jazz early in the twentieth century and in the New Orleans style. Poet and short-story writer Richard Nauns Ricks published poems as early as 1902 and continued to write over 400 poems and hundreds of short stories over five decades. Playwright Garland Anderson, an elevator operator in San Francisco, achieved considerable success as a newcomer with his Broadway play, *Appearances*, in 1924—the first African American to present a play in this milieu. In 1928, a portion of his play was actually broadcast in Oakland, marking "a new departure in radio play technique."[1]

In another remarkable achievement, Delilah Beasley, a journalist for the *Oakland Tribune*, researched the history of California's Afro-Americans from the Gold Rush era, collecting newspapers and interviewing old-timers, and publishing a classic, *The Negro Trail Blazers of California*, in 1919. This was the first published work on blacks in the Far West, and one of the few state studies of blacks at the time. Besides establishing that their history dated from the mid-nineteenth century, she chronicled the pioneers' anti-slavery and civil rights activities and the founding of black newspapers, churches, benevolent societies, and women's clubs and covered the achievements of literary and musical personalities as well as the lawyers, politicians, and ministers.

Nor was the Bay Area distant from Harlem's Black nationalist influences, as the Oakland chapter of the UNIA held its Garvey Day meeting in late winter 1932. Radicals such as Revels Cayton became involved in union movements in the 1930s. Also, a number of road shows came to California. *Shuffle Along* was one of them, and there were several that originated on the West Coast.

One of the main writers in the Harlem Renaissance, Langston Hughes, enjoyed lecturing and spending time in the region, speaking throughout the Bay before sojourning at his retreat in Carmel down the coast. These engagements included Berkeley High School, the YWCA in San Francisco, and the University of California, Berkeley. As the *Spokesman* pointed out, "The poems and speeches of Hughes are directed usually to a mixed audience."[2]

Tap dancer extraordinaire Bill "Bojangles" Robinson was one of the Harlem personalities who, while performing at the Orpheum in Oakland, found time to dash (with a police escort) to San Pablo Park in Berkeley, change into his sweat suit, and outrace some local track champions—while running backwards. Of course, he was given a twenty-five-yard handicap, but he still beat them handily, changed clothes, and rushed back to his downtown performance—all in an hour's time. The park was right across the street from the home of the award-winning sculptor Sargent Johnson, who made Berkeley his home in the 1920s.

In 1915, one of the first orchestras of its kind, the So Different Jazz Band, was launched in San Francisco in a club by that name. They performed in Honolulu, taking the new music into the Pacific realm as early as 1917. Several other bands were formed in the Bay Area, some of them composed of New Orleans musicians, and by 1921 Joe "King" Oliver and his Creole band performed in the Bay Area and toured California.

At the same time, while the Renaissance is often viewed as having ended with the Depression, a similar Bay Area movement was quite vibrant during the Depression years, and it was to be found throughout the arts—particularly in music, but also in dance, theatrical productions, poetry, and sculpture and other visual arts. Ricks continued reading and publishing his poems through the 1930s and the war. Bands of Curtis Mosby, Ethel Terrell (also Francisco), and others flourished during the swing era.

Singer Ivie Anderson, known as the "California songbird," came from Gilroy, a farming community south of San Jose; in 1920 she was a resident of Vallejo, a naval ship building site on the Bay, and then a few years later lived in Berkeley and Oakland, California. She started her singing-dancing career in the early 1920s and joined the Ellington Orchestra in 1931, where she remained for eleven years, attaining a status with the band reached by none of the singers who followed her.

Dancer and singer Virginia "Midge" Williams was another Bay Area artist who made the big time—also in New York City, to be exact. First she achieved considerable fame in Oakland and on San Francisco radio in the early 1930s and then in Shanghai and Yokohama in 1933 and 1934. Besides recording with various bands, in 1939 Williams sang with the Louis Armstrong show at the Cotton Club and on tour and then with the Ellington Orchestra—achievements matched by only one other west coast singer, Ivie Anderson.

Then too, in the arts, sculptor Sargent Johnson won a number of awards, beginning with the Harmon Foundation in the 1920s, and he worked on several WPA and public arts projects, having his bas-relief placed on the entrance walls at the Maritime Museum, for example.

There were several distinguishing characteristics of these movers and shakers. For one thing, they pioneered in the new media of radio, singing in the case of Williams, and playing, as well, in the case of Henry Starr, from the late 1920s or early 1930s. Also, they typically left the Bay Area for the more lucrative show business milieu in Los Angeles. Ivie Anderson and Henry Starr both sojourned in Los Angeles, and others, such as Curtis Mosby, ranged up and down the coast as well, sometimes heading for Oregon and Washington state.

Even more significant, if Harlem artists were bound for Europe, as was the case with James Reese Europe's band, Langston Hughes, Claude McKay, and many others, the Bay Area artists and entertainers often toured the Pacific Islands, Asia, or Australia before heading east. For example, Ricks served in the Philippines during the Spanish American War, Anderson went to Australia in 1927, and Midge Williams and her brother danced and sang in Shanghai in 1933. Earl Whaley and Bill Power's jazz bands were among the many that went to Asia. This travel experience expanded the horizons of African Americans to the point they realized they were not the only colored people in the world and that the white-black racial dyad was not the entire story.

This rich and dynamic African American cultural milieu was depicted in the local press in 1935. In late winter in the university town of Berkeley, the Alameda County branch of the National Association for the Advancement of Colored People honored Johnson, and a number of luminaries attended the event. He had just won a medal in a competition of the San Francisco Art Association. He shared first honors with his teacher, the renowned sculptor Benjamin Bufano. Johnson's work, "Forever Free," consisted of "an impressive piece of wood sculpture of a Negro woman, with her children, worked out as a relief around her skirt." William Nauns Ricks read a poem and also in attendance were Otis Oldfield and Rinaldo Cuneo, of the San Francisco School of Fine Arts, baritone Marcus Hall, and Bufano. Johnson, it was said, developed his technique "entirely during evenings and other hours before or after work." His head of "Sammy" was a Harmon Foundation winner in 1928.[3]

Later in the summer that year, *San Francisco Spokesman* columnist Byron "Speed" Reilly described a night on the town after attending a July Fourth prize-fight. First he went to Sutter Street and dined on "a fine chicken dinner" that would have appealed to Harlemites with its "dumplings, 'tators and all the trimmings" at Jack's Tavern. Afterwards, he "dropped down to see [movie star] Stepin Fetchit do his act for the second time." He went backstage and obtained the film star's autographed portrait. Then he went to the Trianon Ballroom, where the West Indian Cricket Club staged a successful dance. "A huge crowd glided over the floor to the tune of Duke Turner's Cavaliers."[4]

After "a dance with a vivacious Peninsula widow who well anyhow, we melted out with the crowd and went over to the Club Alabam." Here West Indian nightclub man Lester Mapp and Louie Verrett greeted them with smiles. The club was packed, and "red hot tunes and that hotcha gel [sic] Billye" sang. After this they went to the Creole, formerly the Plantation, to see Fetchit, and "Step is there all right, dark glasses, chauffeur and all." His pal, Wilbert Baranco, from Oakland ("pick of the piano players in this neck of the woods"), reigned, while Dee Dee Earle sang. Fetchit entertained them a while with his miniature phonograph, and then at 2 am the club closed down.[5]

This dynamic music scene existed in San Francisco from the late nineteenth century. The Barbary Coast was infamous the world over for its varied nightlife, its notorious waterfront dives and saloons, and its colorful denizens. The black clubs of Sam King and Lou Purcell, former Pullman men, throve in this setting, as did Lester Mapp's, which were all on Pacific Street. The Dixie Hotel, known as a black establishment, was at 400 Pacific lower down and on the corner.

There were similar black clubs in Oakland, where the transcontinental railroad ended and many black residents settled. Seventh Street was the heart of the African American district, its Lenox Avenue. The Creole Café, at 1740 7th Street, hosted jazz loving night clubbers shortly after the war. The Blue Bird Café on Seventh Street was "the only place on the coast where you will find an atmosphere of sunny Spain with Spanish maids to serve you." The black-owned dance Mecca, the Dreamland, was also on Oakland's Lenox Avenue. Nearby were the Cozy Hotel and Hotel Harbor, "the spot where the boys gather and besides being taken care of in the rooming line, they spin yarns and talk sports in general, and get information about the many eastern boxing stars."[6] In the 1930s Slim Jenkins opened his club and showcased good food and the best in blues and jazz for three decades.

The San Francisco Bay Area's early twentieth century sojourners and residents included New Orleans composer Jelly Roll Morton, Clem Raymond, and others, and West Indians immigrants played in early jazz bands during the World War era. Of course, Los Angeles was another dynamic black music scene, and it shared its musicians and entertainers with Bay Area nightspots. The reverse was also true, as band leader/drummer Curtis Mosby shuttled back and forth between the two metropolitan areas where he maintained two nightclubs. Mosby also had two bands and co-owned the Melody Music Shop with T. C. Carey in Oakland.

One of the "big three" of the pioneer jazz orchestras, the Original Creole Jazz Band, formed by New Orleans musicians, was first influential on the West Coast, insofar as it was launched in Los Angeles before the war, and it performed in the Bay Area before touring the nation. As noted, none other than Joe "King" Oliver and his band introduced New Orleans music—ragtime, blues, and jazz—to Oakland and San Francisco in 1921 before playing in Los Angeles. This was before Louis Armstrong joined and prior to the band becoming a sensation in Chicago.

In 1915, Oakland resident and pianist Sid LeProtti led the So Different Jazz Band, one of the first to use this new term "jazz," at the Portola L'Ouvre in downtown San Francisco. Jazz historian Tom Stoddard wrote about LeProtti and the members of this band and chronicled the history of other early outfits in his classic, *Jazz on the Barbary Coast*.[7]

LeProtti was born in Oakland in 1886, and his grandmother "was a famous contralto in San Francisco in 1860 . . . the first Negro woman to sing on stage in the state of California." This was testimony to the West Coast musical tradition on his mother's side—the African American. Even his father, a white businessman, played the harp. The grandmother made sure he studied and practiced piano under a German instructor who insisted he learned every song by memory, which served him well later in life. Then he encountered two others that were instrumental in his career—one pianist instructed him on how to improve and another taught him some trick fingering.

At the age of about eight years old (in 1894), little Sid (Louis was actually his first name) heard ragtime for the first time when a visiting youngster played on the family's old Stedman piano. Naturally LeProtti enjoyed performances by visiting celebrities, such as Blind Tom, the piano genius, who held forth at the Presbyterian Church on Clay Street in Oakland. He learned to play ragtime from compositions and, in particular, "Ambolena Snow," which was published in the daily newspaper. His grandmother disapproved of ragtime until she consulted with "old man Lorenzo," who "was a German and a great dancer," and then she changed her mind. She died when LeProtti was sixteen, and from then he was on his own.

He worked for a while in the Judson Iron Works, where he toiled "on the rollin' mill on the hot bed," with sparks flying everywhere. A friend told him of a job playing piano at a place on Fortieth and San Pablo in Oakland, and LeProtti went down and was hired. He played "Maple Leaf Rag," "Ambolena Snow," then waltzes and classics from seven until ten o'clock at night.

One day an old singer with a minstrel show, Henry Stewart, heard him play and told him:

> You know kid, you can play all the notes in the world they put up there in front of you, but you ain't playin' nothin'. That music is just mechanical; the only thing that keeps all the mechanicalism [sic] out of it is you play from memory. . . . If you really want'a play somethin'. . . . You want'a get around some of them ear piano players; you want'a learn to listen and pick up some of their stuff. What you got to do is learn to fake and fill in.[8]

He also told him that he should pick up new songs from others: "It's just a matter of ear trainin'."

He started in Barbary Coast dives around 1906, after the earthquake and fire, until the district was closed down in 1921, and he described in colorful detail the music scene and the goings-on at Sam King and Lew Purcell's, at 520 Pacific, at Lester Mapp's, and Louie Gomez's, on the same street—Pacific. The Oakland pianist explained, "The music readin' era was comin' in about that time, which before that was mostly all fakers or improvisers." He took the place of a non-reading pianist who went to Chicago, and who when he came back, found he had been replaced. "He couldn't make it afterwards. By then, all the band was playin' from [written] music."

In the evening the band played marches, two-steps, mazurkas and waltzes, and occasionally someone would request a "slow drag, or the blues as they called them." The bandleader, who "was very stubborn and hard-headed about playin' tunes," would refuse, but when he took a break, "the gang would say to [LeProtti], 'Play the blues!' or 'Slow drag!'" and when LeProtti complied, the dancers filled the floor. The owner, King, noticed this, told the leader he would have to play more blues, and then gave him his two weeks' notice when he refused. As King died in 1910, this allows us to date how early this change occurred in the music's local history.[9]

Shortly after the earthquake and fire, LeProtti first encountered boogie-woogie when a visitor, Willard Jones, "a mighty fine piano player," came to town. About the same time the Oakland pianist heard a new composition, "Basin Street Blues," in the music store, and he learned it, started playing it at Purcell's, and found it was quite popular. Then it died out, but New Orleans bassist Will Johnson came to town and brought it back to life. "They were the first New Orleans jazz band I ever heard of." Johnson picked at the bass instead of bowing it, and this was new for LeProtti. "To see him in a jazz band pick it like that was somethin'. That's where I got the idea of the four beats." He also introduced a bass to his band "because that was the Louisiana-type."[10]

He claimed, "I can hear the difference in that rhythm was changin' in them days" as bands went from two beats to playing four. When his drummer claimed it was too much work to play four beats, he replaced "Old Pete" with George Huddleston. Then he named his band The So Different Orchestra, and boasted "Them fellas could play everything." He dated this change: "It was along about 1912 when we switched to the New Orleans type of instrumentation." This was five years before the famous recordings of the Original Dixieland Jazz Band, who made the new music a household item from coast to coast.

He observed, "That's [also] the bunch that played the overtures. We had a little six-piece band with piano, drums, string bass, clarinet, a fella who played flute and piccolo, and baritone euphonium." The latter won the Louisiana lottery and had to be replaced by Reb Spikes, originally from Texas, on baritone saxophone.[11]

Band members included Clarence Williams, string bass, Adam "Slocum" Mitchell, the clarinetist from Martinique, and Gerald D. Wells, another West Indian who migrated to the U.S. from Grenada in 1910.

Of Slocum Mitchell, LeProtti recalled that he was "the first man I ever heard slur on a clarinet like you do on a trombone." Whether he learned this in Martinique, New Orleans, or the Bay Area is unclear. Clem Raymond, yet another West Indian, resided at 826 Cypress Street and was listed as a musician in the 1930 census. He was born around 1895 in Saint Pierre, Martinique, came to the U.S. in 1903, and enlisted in the 25th Infantry during the war; he distinguished himself as a saxophonist and clarinetist in the army band.[12] Then there was Huddleston, Spikes, and LeProtti. So by the time Morton and King Oliver came to the Bay Area, local musicians were quite familiar with the New Orleans style.

LeProtti also played at Lew Purcell's, where quadrilles were mixed with slow drags. "One of the famous dances which practically originated out of Purcell's was the Texas Tommy dance," which eventually swept the nation. The mayor of San Francisco sent his guests to the resort to learn the dance, and even Al Jolson and Anna Pavlova endorsed it and incorporated it into their respective performances.[13]

In fact, the evidence suggested local residents not only were familiar with this music before New Yorkers but were quite creative within the new idiom. As early as 1919, two years after the historic Original Jazz Band records were made by white performers, Bay Area bands also claimed to present jazz, such as the Country Club Jazzeurs, who promised dance music and numbered from two to six pieces (presumably instrumentalists). The members were H. F. Pierson, drums, C. O. Long, piano, Norris Hester, violin, and E. S. Whaley, saxophone. Hester was the only one listed as a musician in the *Oakland City Directory, 1921*. Both Pierson and Hester were members of LeProtti's larger orchestra of ten musicians by 1923.

Henry Starr

Unlike LeProtti, singer/pianist Henry Starr became internationally famous. Born in Washington, DC in 1899 to a Mexican father and a Kentuckian, Henry Wilson Starr moved to the Bay Area with his family by 1910. Mr. Starr worked as a government watchman and Mrs. Starr was janitress in an apartment building. The couple raised a family of five sons and purchased their own home on Oakland's Grace Street. Henry signed up for the military in 1918, but it is not clear if he was actually inducted. By 1920, he listed his occupation as musician.

He was pianist and leader of Curtis Mosby's Blue Blowers by 1925 and recorded in 1927—four years after the earliest African American jazz recordings—with this combo. When Louis Armstrong performed at Sebastian's Cotton Club in Culver City in 1931, the band, conducted by Lionel Hampton and George Orendoff, used four pianists—Starr was one of them.

On New Year's Eve, he performed with other entertainers for the inmates at San Quentin Prison, suggesting some concern on his part for the less fortunate members of society. When interviewed in 1932, he reported that his first radio appearance took place in Los Angeles, though he did not give a year. Soon afterwards he signed a radio contract, the first Black entertainer on the Pacific Coast to do so. On the program he advertised special piecrust flour, so he was known as the Pie-man. For eighteen months he was "Boy and Director of Publicity over stations KPO and KYA." He anticipated studying music in Europe to enhance his musical training as well as his radio work.[14]

Starr performed opposite Duke Ellington at a farewell party for the bandleader in San Francisco in 1932. The Oakland pianist was honored indeed when the event was "billed as Duke Ellington–Henry Starr night."[15]

Evidently his influence was not limited to the Bay Area in California. In 1934, he was described as pianist at the "famous and exclusive Club Sevelle," and most remarkably, he was one of the guest artists when Ellington performed at the Motion Picture Arts and Sciences Ball at the Ambassador Hotel in Los Angeles. Touted as "the former 'Hot Spot of Radioland,'" Starr sat at a table with Guy and Carmen Lombardo and Herbert Victor, Mr. and Mrs. Clark Gable, Cary Grant, and others from filmdom.[16]

Eventually he went out on his own, traveling to Chicago "to accept several offers tendered him for appearances in the East."[17] He was said to be considering whether to accept the offers of the Regal Theatre, on the one hand, or the Grand Terrace, on the other. Starr was feted at a number of social affairs in the Windy City in late summer 1934. Then he went to Europe, where he teamed up with singer Ivan Browning, also known in the East Bay.

At a time when nearly one-fourth of the U.S. working population was unemployed, the *Defender* praised him as "the Race's first and highest priced radio singer." His style was compared to Rudy Vallee's in that it was "unique and original," making him a "sensation" in California. "Certain big shots of Hollywood have induced Balaban and Katz to attempt to change Starr's mind about vacationing" in the Windy City, which he claimed was his goal.

This was not his first trip to Chicago. He had come there for a princely salary at a moment's notice once before. Constance Townsend, who was engaged to a wealthy businessman, requested a special favor: that he fly to Chicago in time to sing at the big party honoring her. Starr "received $150 a day for two weeks . . ., even though he only worked a single engagement."[18]

On the West Coast, the *Defender* continued, "He is unquestionably the most popular singer out there and for proof we suggest a few of the engagements he has held." These included the Roosevelt Hotel, the Fifty Fifty Club, and two years at Sebastian's Cotton Club in Culver City. In the course of the interview, Starr avoided talking about himself, choosing rather to praise California's beautiful landscape and fine weather, but he did admit that he had "received as high as $750 weekly for his work over quite a stretch." He was also in the movies with Will Rogers, and he contracted to earn $250 a week for this work. The journalist concluded, "Yes, Henry Starr is the gent who received big money for radio work before the Mills boys and other acts were heard of."

He teamed up with singer Ivan Browning and they toured Europe. Shortly after President Roosevelt announced his plans for the WPA, they dressed in top hat and tails for a command performance before English royalty and at the Palladium in London, at Bal Tabarin in Paris, and in Stockholm and Copenhagen. Browning and Starr sang, and Starr performed on piano, bantering with Browning and talking above the music in the manner of Jelly Roll Morton, Fats Waller and other vaudevillians.

The singing duo went to Denmark in the spring of 1936 before returning to Paris about a month later. In the winter of 1938, heralded as "Songs and Rhythm Kings," they ended a successful engagement at the exclusive Alhambra theatre in Brussels. They were also said to have spent some "happy moments" with Josephine Baker and Caterina Jarboro.

In London they started a four months' stint for English society. Apparently, they sojourned with their families, as "The performers and their families send greetings to friends in America. . . ."[19] They were also featured at the Cotton Club Revue in New York city. For records, Starr played solo, but sometimes the duo teamed with other musicians and sang popular songs, an occasional blues, comedy songs, swing and scat songs, spirituals, semi-songs; semi-classics, and popular ballads.

Recently, his recordings with Curtis Mosby's band have been discovered— probably made in Los Angeles in 1924 or 1925. "Riverboat Shuffle" and "All Night Blues" evidenced how much these Californian musicians had adopted the New Orleans sound shortly after Morton and King Oliver made their first recordings in 1923. In 1927 they recorded "Weary Stomp,' and "Weary Blues," a second version of this composition, and "In My Dreams," by California songwriters Otis and Leon Rene, and "Tiger Stomp," which was, of course, "Tiger Rag."

In 1928 Starr recorded "Blues Eyes," on which he sang and played piano, and two instrumentals, "Mr. Froggie" (Morton's "Frog-i-more Rag") and "Willow Tree," and the next year "When I'm Walking with My Sweetness." Along with Browning, a Wiley College graduate from Texas who made his home in Europe, a guitarist, bassist, and drummer joined him in 1935 on "Let's Go Ballyhoo" and "All Because of You," which the singers co-composed with others; "What Harlem Is to Me," "Truckin'," named after a recent Harlem dance, and "Jungle Nights in Harlem" were recorded in 1939. With their European successes, including BBC appearances and recordings by Regal-Zonophone, they returned to the states in 1939 as Europe edged towards war. Starr continued to play in San Francisco and Bay Area clubs until his death in 1962.

Curtis Mosby

Mosby was a leading bandleader and nightclub man in Oakland, San Francisco, and Los Angeles during the "roaring twenties" and the swing era. Originally from Kansas City, he managed several bands as a drummer in the postwar era and recorded in the mid-1920s with his Blue Blowers. He also managed two nightclubs, both called the Apex, in San Francisco and Los Angeles. He was born in 1892 and worked in Chicago as a musician around the time of the war.

Mosby was not the only bandleader. For example, Ethel Terrell—born in New Jersey, and married to a bassist—was one of the few women in this profession, leading a show band on the eve of the swing era. She came to the Bay Area in the 1920s, and in 1933, the local press reported that Ethel Terrell's Mission Theatre and Wade Whaley's Capitol theater bands were "still going strong." Charley "Duke" Turner and His Musical Cavaliers were also popular among whites.

In 1935, Mosby and his Dixie Land Blue Blowers were at their heights at San Francisco's Capitol Theatre performing along with "The Harlem Rhapsody," a review. They were also scheduled to play at Sweets Ballroom in Oakland. At the Capitol, he put "his boys thru their paces with impunity," and "Like the ole king of hi-de-ho, Callaway, gets his patrons to hi-de-hoing, so Curt had the thousand dancers swaying and carioco-ing to red hot tunes."[20] A line of chorines, Jazzlips Richardson, and the show's glee club, "five clever lads in flashy red coats," made for a "great night."

Ivie Anderson

The women singers who came out of the Bay Area included none other than Ellington's favorite, Ivie Anderson. She was born in Gilroy, just south of San Jose, and attended St. Mary's, where she sang in a glee club. Her talents were recognized, and she received a scholarship to attend Nannie Burroughs Girl Training School in Washington, DC for two years. She also studied voice under

Sara Ritt. As noted, in 1920 she resided with her aunt and uncle in Vallejo, Ca.—just north of Berkeley.[21]

In an interview during the Depression she recalled that "Narrow-minded natives of Oakland" did not permit her to swim in the city's YWCA pool when she was a teenager. A "chorus girl" like her might pollute the water. She may have been one of the dancers in the dress rehearsal of Plantation Frolics, a "creole revue," from Los Angeles, appearing at the "Top of Tait's" in San Francisco. It was staged by Fanchon and Marco, a brother and sister dance team that started producing shows in San Francisco around 1920.

In the early 1920s Fanchon and Marco saw her and signed her up for a road show starring Mamie Smith. When a lead actress became ill, Anderson "stepped in to fill the spot on an hour's notice." She also performed at the Club Alabam and the Cotton Club in Los Angeles.

In mid- or late 1924 she left California with the famous musical, *Shuffle Along*, and, when that show closed, quickly obtained a role in *Struttin' Time*. She also worked with other acts and toured the Keith-Albee circuit. For seven months she "set New York on fire at the Cotton club," and then returned to California in the spring of 1925, claiming that she was "home for keeps." She found work immediately at the Plantation café. As the journalist explained, "Ivie is needed in this part of the country and we are going to try and keep her here from now on and henceforth."[22] She also bought a new Hudson, tangible evidence of her success and sudden affluence during the heyday of the jazz age.

Despite their earlier misgivings, a decade later black residents of the Bay Area greeted her with "with fanfare of drum and trumpet." Dan Burley interviewed her at a prizefight in 1934, which was attended by bandleader Ellington as well. She recalled how she went to audition against her family's wishes and went out with the show *Plantation Revue*, starring legendary blues queen Mamie Smith, for ten weeks.

Mention of her in the Bay Area has not been discovered for the 1920s; she moved to Los Angeles and was featured at the re-opening of Los Angeles' Jazzland, "the most beautiful nite club in the west," with room for a thousand guests, in 1927. The LaFayette Players, from Harlem, were featured as "special guests;" Alton Red's 8 Pods of Pepper provided the music.

That autumn she headed for Australia with the Four Covans, Sonny Clay's band, and the Four Emperors of Music Quartet, steaming from San Francisco for Melbourne in October 1927. The next year she was featured along with Carolynne Snowden at the Apex Night Club on Central Avenue shortly before Christmas. Mosby's Dixieland Blue Blowers performed for several artists, including Anderson, who was described as "in a class by herself . . . that singing dancing bundle of pep."[23]

In 1930 she headed the Los Angeles household at 756 East 52nd Street, living with her young cousin and her grandmother, both of whom were Oklahomans.

She gave her occupation as nightclub singer and dancer. Early in 1931 she was "doing a Florence Mills 'blackbird' skit" with Earl Hines's band, which performed at the Regal and broadcast from the Grand Terrace in Chicago.

She sang with Duke Ellington's band at the downtown Oriental, where "a mob of music-hungry Chicagoans pushed, shoved and thronged the entrance to B. and K.'s Loop theater to get a peek at Harlem's king of jazz." Anderson sang the late Florence Mills's "I'm A Little Blackbird." "And how she sells that number. Forced to take four bows and a speech to get off the stage when spotted on the first show."[24] Late in the summer the *Defender* reported she was "scoring a big hit whenever the Duke appears with her rendition of 'Minnie the Moocher,' and 'I'm A Little Blackbird.'"

That fall, in a separate opinion on her joining the famous orchestra leader, the *California Eagle* claimed Ellington heard Anderson singing at the Apex in Los Angeles and signed her immediately. "She seldom fails to stop the show when she appears in theatres these days, and you only have to hear her sing 'Give Me A Man Like That,' to realize her splendid potentiality as a star."

She was often featured in advertisements for the band (see ad in *Los Angeles Times* March 9, 1932, p. 6 and ad in *California Eagle* April 30, 1934, p. 11) and was without a doubt one of the stars in the Ellington band for nearly ten years. Another high point in her career occurred in 1937 when she was featured in the Marx brothers "A Day at the Races" in a rousing scene with the stable hands singing, dancing, and playing, first with Harpo leading the group with his pennywhistle, then Anderson belting out the song, "All God's Children," followed by a jitterbug sequence. In keeping with the stereotypes of the era, she wears a simple frock instead of the stylishly svelte gowns she wore with the Ellington orchestra. When the sheriff enters the scene, the Marx brothers don axle grease as blackface in an attempt to escape him.

Despite this shameful turnabout, the brothers played an important role in getting Anderson and several Black entertainers in the movie. They "backed our own Ivie Anderson to the extent of $100,000 cold cash and were greatly influential in the hiring of several hundred other Race actors, hands, etc."[25]

Ellington convinced her to wear white gowns, and he insisted that she was a contralto. She wore white ever after with him, and "It turned a skinny little black girl into a queen." And when she sang "Rocks in My Bed," he "would show his teeth, smile in restrained pride." He also began to write for her, and among the results were compositions that became Ellington standards: "In My Solitude," "I Got It Bad and That Ain't Good," and "Rocks in My Bed."[26]

She acquired international fame and, indeed, singular acclaim when she toured abroad for the second time in her career. In 1933 she was the only female soloist to accompany Ellington's band to England. She went again to Europe in 1939 with the Ellington orchestra and returned on the *SS Isle de France* in spring that year.

Actually, the Ellington orchestra was unique, insofar as it included six small combos led by different sidemen, including instrumentalists Johnny Hodges and Barney Bigard, and Anderson. This was quite an achievement for a singer in a band of virtuosos. Her combo was named Ivie Anderson and Her Boys from Dixie.

Her recordings with Ellington began in 1932 with "It Don't Mean A Thing If It Ain't Got That Swing," the hit "Truckin'," as well as "Shoe Shine Boy" in 1936, Ethel Water's "Stormy Weather" (later associated with Lena Horne), and the band leader's popular "Mood Indigo" and "I Got It Bad and That Ain't Good" in 1940 and 1941, respectively. After leaving Ellington in 1942, she recorded with Los Angeles musicians, including Wilbert Baranco and Ceele Burke's orchestras, Phil Moore, Irving Ashby, Lee Young (brother of Lester), Buddy Collette, Charles Mingus, and Lucky Thompson.

In an interview she mentioned the sense of ethnic pride that was at the heart of the Renaissance. Considering hers was one of the few, perhaps the only, black family in Gilroy, and she attended a Catholic school in that agricultural town, this was quite remarkable:

> I'd rather sing to my own people than anyone else. Of course, white audiences pay heavy to hear me, but I get the biggest thrill out of making my own happy and pleasing them. I think my biggest thrill came when I introduced "Stormy Weather" in London, England [1933]. I had never sung it before.[27]

Unfortunately, the singer suffered from chronic asthma, causing her to leave Ellington from time to time, and for the last time in 1942, but not before she was featured in his first lengthy spectacular, *Jump for Joy*, a musical presented in Los Angeles. It was advanced for its time because it was a critique of Jim Crow and deferential politics. She died following an asthmatic attack late in 1949.

Virginia "Midge" Williams

Virginia "Midge" Williams was born in Oregon in 1915 and achieved considerable fame as a singer, starting out with her three brothers as the dancing Williams Quartette and Williams Four in the 1920s. Western migration and settlement in new communities was part of her family's heritage. She was the great grandchild of Benjamin "Pap" Singleton, who founded African American towns in Kansas, and his grandchild, her mother, Virginia, married John Williams and lived in Allensworth, California, the all-black community near Fresno. In fact, they ran a store that included a post office and that actually remains as part of the current tourist display. They moved to Berkeley in the 1920s.

Her mother taught music and dance to East Bay children, including her own four—her daughter, the oldest, and three younger brothers. Mrs. Williams (later Mrs. Thurman) was also active in the Women's Clubs, as was her daughter, best known as Midge. In late November 1932, the first quarterly meeting of the California Northern District National Association of Colored Girls met in Berkeley at San Pablo Club House. Midge was state secretary and recorded the minutes, her mother gave a report, and "Miss Virginia Thurman" also soloed on guitar.

When Irene Bell Ruggles hosted a meeting at her San Francisco home, twenty-five members of the girls' dramatic and art club gathered to hear Midge's mother's report. She spoke "very encouragingly to the girls on club work, relating some of the very constructive things being done by the Oakland-Berkeley groups."[28]

In 1933 Byron O'Reilly of the *Spokesman* praised Williams's mother's abilities as "vaudeville director" and the bandleader Ben Watkins for the music at an Oakland affair. Also, "What the Benefit Mid-Night show last Saturday lacked in attendance, the clever young performers more than made up." When the Rhythm Ramblers cut loose with "Tiger Rag," "the youngsters really put it over. The Williams Four . . . [with] Robert and Charles, featured as usual."

Late the next spring "Robert and Charles of the popular Williams Four" were described as among those amateurs "with high class talent" at the midnight benefit held by the Friendly Committee of St. Augustine's church. Charles also played the groom in a staged presentation of the popular *Minnie the Moocher's Wedding Day*.[29]

Midge Williams received the most praise in the local press. In spring 1933 O'Reilly wrote, "Little Midge Williams received another big hand when she sang 'Going, Gone' over KFRC on the Blue Monday Jamboree last week."[30] The Williams Four became international stars as teenagers two generations before the Jackson Five. A mere few weeks after Langston Hughes's return from Asia in July 1933, the Williamses steamed with their mother and their Oakland pianist Roger Segure to Shanghai. They stopped at Honolulu first, after performing on board their ship, the *SS Taiyo*, to considerable acclaim. In Shanghai "they were at the famous Canidrome and should return home with a neat little nest egg."[31] However, in November their mother became sick and had to depart for Oakland, where she died shortly thereafter. She was buried in Allensworth.

The Williams siblings stayed in Asia because of their four months' contract. The boys came home that winter to attend school, while their sister stayed and recorded, singing in Japanese and English, as well as scatting, in February 1934, on the recordings "St. Louis Blues," "Lazy Bones," "Bye Bye Blues," "Stormy Weather," and "Paradise."

Wearing slacks from the U.S., the singer came to the cosmopolitan city of Shanghai at a time when it was experiencing considerable change—including women's fashions. Trousers for women, the symbol of modernity, became the fashion for upper class urban dwellers in Asia in the 1920s, partly because of their convenience for social dancing, and Williams contributed to the fashion.

Her slacks were so popular that "a big company requested that they be allowed to use the pattern, naming the trousers 'Midge Slacks.'"[32]

In spring 1934 she returned from her successful stint in China and Japan, where she made the Columbia recordings. She was described on her return as "Perhaps a trifle more womanly, but still charming as ever and improved in her profession, Midge is being sought by KFRC."[33] The next month, the *Oakland Tribune* reported, "Midge Williams, miniature Ethel Waters, will make a belated return to the Jamboree, singing the rhythmic 'Mood Indigo.'" This was part of KFRC Blue Monday's Jamboree. No one would have guessed that in less than five years she would be singing with the composer of this composition, Duke Ellington himself.

The Williams Four subsequently went to the Orpheum, appearing on the "Happy Go Lucky" review. San Francisco theater-goers greeted the quartet with enthusiasm, especially Midge, "who has been signed to make a month of personal appearances at the famous Club Trouville on Sutter Streets." Her studio work also increased:

> Beside being on the weekly Hodge Podge, Happy Go Lucky, and Blue Monday Jamboree programs, she is appearing with Frank Castle's show on KYA from 11:30 to 12:00 on Tuesday, Thursday, and Saturday and 10:00 to 10:30 on Sundays all night . . . [illegible] . . . programs. Another new program sends Little Midgey as well as her brothers, Charles and Louis to the popular Edgewater Beach Café next month.[34]

Then tragedy struck the family once again. Charles died in a gun accident at their apartment in San Francisco in late August 1934 while his brothers were looking on. This was the end of the Williamses in show business, but Midge Williams continued on her own. She spent a "successful week" at Sacramento's State Fair with Ben Brower's "Happy-Go-Lucky" troupe in early September. Then she returned to San Francisco to appear on the Brower program in the afternoon and the *Blue Monday Jamboree* the very same evening. Her special arrangement of "Moon Glow [sic] just about stopped the Jamboree program."[35]

The singer was described as "a winsome little brownskin girl of a quiet, ladylike demeanor." Until you're told "'That's the famous Midge Williams,' you would judge her to be a high school girl looking out at the world through wondering questioning eyes, rather than one of the western radio world's best loved artists." She was described as having a "thrilling sweet voice."[36]

Williams went to Los Angeles from Berkeley in fall 1934 "and was the center of attraction at every cabaret or breakfast club she happened to attend." She hurried back to San Francisco to prepare for her Monday broadcast. Everyone who met her became a member of her "army of radio fans." While she lived in Berkeley, it was reported that she received her mail at the KFRC station in Francisco in case any one wanted to write her.[37]

She was one of many hopefuls interviewed by William A. McGuire of Universal Studios for the flicker he was to produce, *The Great Ziegfeld*. The prospects hoped to be called soon. Some were, in fact, called to do a screen test with expenses paid. Williams expected to be contacted, and the *Spokesman* reported that other studio heads also interested in her, and that she might appear in a musical film with Rudy Vallee.

They also indicated that she would make several records for Brunswick. "Midgey answers every ring of the phone and opens every letter with rapid beating heart as she expects the record call at any moment and also one from Hollywood where she recently made a screen test."

Harlem finally took notice of this "petite song stylist from Sunny California" who had recently headed east for her "New York debut" early in spring 1936. Williams was said to be "an outstanding radio artist, having won for herself a great deal of recognition out on the Coast" for her work with "one of the major chains." Unfortunately, she made her debut at the Apollo, "which at its best is not a good place for one to make an impression upon the critics or public on account of the lack of care in the presentation of their weekly shows." Her presentation "suffer[ed] from, bad ... amateurish productions and a very unsatisfactory spot in the show." The *Defender* journalist Allan McMillan maintained "She should have by all means been placed near a closing position," allowing New Yorkers to see "just what she really could do."

Poet Langston Hughes was in Harlem that spring and reported that he:

> also saw quite a little bit of Midge Williams, who is singing twice a week over NBC after making a big hit twice with Rudy Vallee's hour. I wrote the words to her theme song, NIGHT-TIME [sic IN CAPS], and will send your sister a copy as soon as it comes out. (I know you can't play it!)[38]

Around this time, winter 1935–36, she also sang with Noble Sissle's band in New York City. By 1937, she had reached the status where she was mentioned in Archie Seale's "Around Harlem" column as among those whose names were so important that they should appear regularly in the news. Among the others were Charles Buchanan, manager of the Savoy, Fred R. Moore, publisher of the *New York Age?*, Ethel Waters, and Ella Fitzgerald.

The year 1937 was good for her, as she recorded with her Jazz Jesters sidemen on "I'm Getting Sentimental Over You" in the winter, and four other selections, including "That Old Feeling" and "I was Born to Swing" in the summer. That fall when she recorded eight songs, her Jesters included Frankie Newton, trumpet, Buster Bailey on clarinet, Billy Kyle on piano, and John Kirby on string bass, all of whom had made names for themselves. "The Lady Is A Tramp," "An Old Flame Never Dies," "Singin' the Blues," and "The Greatest Mistake of My Life"— all popular songs—were among her repertoire. She recorded "Love Is Like Whiskey," with lyrics by Langston Hughes, early the next year and four more compositions the following spring. In 1940, she recorded with Lil Armstrong, former wife of Louis, and Her Dixielanders, which included Wellman Braud, a bassist formerly with Duke Ellington, and trumpet player Jonah Jones.

Like her mother, she was quite active in the community. In Harlem in winter 1937 she was one of numerous entertainers who donated their time for a Christmas benefit for the poor. Bill "Bojangles" Robinson, Cab Calloway, the Nicholas Brothers, Lionel Hampton, Teddy Wilson, Ella Fitzgerald, Benny Goodman, Noble Sissle and Chick Webb and their bands, and others helped make the occasion a success.

In 1938 she reached the summit in the jazz world as singer with Louis Armstrong and his band. *Down Beat* reported that the trumpet player and his band "sent 'em on down" at the city auditorium in Galveston, Texas, rivaling the impact of Basie's band the previous year. Armstrong's band, "sparked by Pop[s] Foster and his golden doghouse and Midge ('That Old Feelin'') Williams, isn't a half bad aggregation." When she appeared with Armstrong in spring 1939 at the Apollo, the *Defender* described her as a "specialty artist, who is sensational."

Armstrong's review was booked at the Cotton Club. The run was very successful and had to be extended three times. The Cotton Club Parade, as it was known, was "a classic in song dance and Harlemania swing and jitterbugging." Maxine Sullivan received the most attention because she was "sensational." Indeed, "what with Bobby Evans and Midge Williams going places vocally and the one and only Sonny Woods comparison must become dangerous." When Armstrong left the Cotton Club to go to Chicago in 1940, Williams was to stay in New York City at the famous café. Later that spring, however, she was with Armstrong's band again in Chicago and was described as simply "terrific."[39]

In late winter, however, she left the Cotton Club for another top-notch band that was also at the pinnacle of the jazz world, Duke Ellington's. She was a temporary replacement for Ivie Anderson, who was recuperating from an illness. "Ivy [sic] made the tour with the Duke but was barely able to keep her place at the mike because of her illness and once the band started one-nighters she left for New York to undergo treatment." Searching for a replacement, Ellington "scanned a list of likely prospects and decided that Miss Midge Williams was the person." She joined the band on tour.[40]

Williams appeared at the Apollo in summer billed as the "sensational stage and radio vocalist" when Armstrong's band came in for one week. When "King Louis Armstrong" took his entourage to the Paramount later that summer, Williams was described by *Billboard* as "an attractive singer with a winning voice and personality. She does Madame La Zonga . . . and has to beg off."

Late in 1940 they went to the Bay Area and "scored an impressive triumph" during the week's stay at Sweet's Ballroom in Oakland. Williams received recognition comparable to that accorded the famous trumpet player: "Features at the program at Sweet's ballroom were Louis and his horn, Miss Midge Williams, and the sweet crooning Sonny Woods. And boy, they were all well received by the patrons."[41] A few weeks later she was back in New York City with a new hit, "Why Is A Good Man So Hard to Find."

Late that year or early in 1941 she became ill in Detroit and dropped out of sight for a time. Rumor was that she could no longer sing. The *Amsterdam News* claimed that reliable reports placed her at Detroit "hot spots" that spring. "She may return to Harlem soon."

This was one of a number of instances where illnesses plagued her as they did Ivie Anderson, who suffered from asthmatic attacks. In spring 1941 she was said to have "improved after a long siege of illness that had her floored."[42] By December she was at Chicago's Regal Theatre with the Nicholas Brothers, Red Saunders and his band, and several white entertainers.

The next year she married and appears to have retired from show business, but the details are sketchy. Dan Burley, the *Amsterdam News* columnist, wrote "the former singing sensation," now retired, "plays and sings by the open window in her apartment in West 126th Street of mornings and the neighbors turn off their radios to get a freebie listen."[43]

But the retirement did not last long, because in December of 1942 she was said to be "one of the few singers of recognized ability developed in the last ten years," and it was reported that she had "just signed a contract to sing on the Crawford 63 Club Hour heard every Sunday evening, 6 to 6:30 o'clock on WMCA." The contract was for four months with an option. The host "usually has a colored guest star every week." However, "his audiences liked Miss Williams so well that he decided she was the person for the spot."[44]

After this she dropped out of sight, perhaps because of family responsibilities or illness or both, and resided in San Francisco for the remainder of her short life. She taught music in San Francisco and came out of obscurity to sing on the local radio in 1946. She died of tuberculosis in 1952.

William N. Ricks

William N. Ricks was one of the earliest, most active and prolific participants in this renaissance. Little has been written about him, though Beasley included some of his poems in *The Negro Trail Blazers*. He was born in Wytheville, VA in the Blue Ridge Mountains in 1876. Nothing is known about his father, and very little is known of his mother or his siblings. They are not discussed in the few accounts of his life. He mentioned attending school in this post-Reconstruction era, and taking over for a time at the age of fourteen when the teacher was sick. Curiously, this town was also the home of Edith Wilson, wife of President Wilson, and her father, who was a judge. Ricks knew him when he was a small boy, writing Mrs. Wilson that Judge Bolling, her father, was quite kind to him, showing him his collection of swords and guns from Asian nations. "I have since seen many of these countries and have always remembered the information and instruction given me by your father."[45]

His adult social life dated from when he helped the black voters by ensuring they had the Republican ticket for voting; he was also a member of KIBAR Lodge No. 3935 (Grand United Order of Odd Fellows) in Roanoke in 1896. When the Spanish–American War broke out, he wrote years later:

> I enlisted in the U.S. Army on Sept 10, 1898 at Wytheville, Va. and was discharged at Ft. Douglas, Utah on Gen. Order 40 Feb. 1899. Re-enlisted at Roanoke Va. March 1899 and rejoined my company at Fort Douglas some time in April, to July 1, 1899. Sailed for the Philippines July 13, 1899. Served two years and two months in the islands invalided back to the U.S. and discharged from convalescent camp at Angel Island, Calif. In March 1902.[46]

It is not clear whether he saw combat, but clearly this travel from the Blue Ridge Mountains to the American West and out into the Pacific, where he stayed in the Philippines, stopping off in Japan on the way home, was as transformative for the twenty-two year old as it was for other West Coast residents who traveled across the Pacific.

Significantly, only one month after his discharge in San Francisco in 1899, he re-enlisted, rejoining his outfit. This was an index of his patriotism and willingness to serve U.S. military interests, even when they were thousands of miles across the Pacific. His intense patriotism was manifest throughout his life. Despite his age he registered for Selective Service during World War I and met regularly with his fellow veterans at yearly reunions. His poems on the flag and patriotic holidays throughout his career drew upon his patriotism and military service.

His Philippine experience no doubt resulted in his membership in the Oakland Lair of the Military Order of Serpents in the Grand Order of the Serpents, described by the *Tribune* as the "playground" of Spanish American war veterans. Significantly, its rituals were based upon those "of the great Philippine secret society, Khatee Puna." Members included cabinet officers, U.S. senators, a number of state governors, and "army officers from generals down." Even more interesting, "Much of the ritual is carried on in the Philippino [sic] language." Oakland's branch was known as Sabay Sabay Labir No. 2 and won distinction by taking the prizes that the Dons of Peralta offered "for the best organization in the Mummer's parade for two consecutive years." Ricks won election as a member of the new head's staff.[47]

It is evident, also, that the young veteran attended numerous operas and musicals while in San Francisco at the turn of the century. His programs and ticket stubs suggest quite an interest in European classical music: the Grand Opera House presented selections from Mozart, Chopin, Schumann, and Liszt that spring; *Il Trovatore* was presented in June, as was *Rigoletto*. Then in 1905 after his Pacific experience, he appears to have attended the Tivoli Opera House for its first season of grand opera, presenting *Lucia*. He also had brochures for *Aida* and *Carmen L'Africaine*.

He settled in Southern California for a time, assisting in the formation of such organizations as the Forum and the NAACP before he moved to the Bay Area around 1904. In 1905 he was an elevator operator in San Francisco. Then he held a clerical position as head of the junior clerks division in the California Packing Co. in downtown San Francisco until retirement in 1946. He was an activist, not only in the NAACP in California but in his church and several literary societies as well as in veterans associations. He and his wife Elizabeth, who was quite active in literary, club, and church circles in Berkeley from their marriage in 1922, lived in the East Bay, tending the garden and writing. He published hundreds of poems, mostly in local newspapers and also took courses in philosophy and literature at the University of California.

He was a musician, as the frequent musical references in his poetry suggest. He also played cello, performing "Easter Morn" by Samuel Coleridge Taylor at the First AME Church in Oakland on the eve of World War I. Significantly Ricks chose the work of the Afro-English composer, while other performers for the most part selected Europeans such as Wagner, Bach, and Mendelssohn.

A few weeks later, his poem "Memorial Day," coming a few weeks before the beginning of the deadliest war known up to that time, is an eerie foreshadowing of what was to follow for the next four years. The dead who came to visit, he claimed:

> . . . are not dead, tho' fields ran red,
> And their clay soon turned to dust,
> Their spirit lives, and their courage gives,
> New strength to our hope and trust.

He pays homage to the Blue and Gray veterans of the Civil War, but concludes in a fashion fitting for the victims of all wars:

> [We] pray to our God, that war's wreck and rod,
> No more shall break hearts so true.[48]

His poem "Armistice" probably appeared after the war, but it was republished on Armistice Day in 1927 in the *Oakland Tribune*.

In 1910, Ricks lived in an Oakland boarding house with a Swedish woman and her sons, both of whom were tailors, on Chestnut Street. Ricks was classified by the census taker as white. He was also listed as a widower, though we know little of his wife or this first marriage.

His second wife was a captain of the Linden Branch's YWCA membership drive in the autumn of 1927, as well as head of the social committee. She was also responsible for the presentation of the students who met at a conference the year before at Asilomar south of San Francisco.

According to the 1930 MC, the couple resided in their own California bungalow, worth $4,000.00, at 3006 Stanton in South Berkeley in a block that was mainly African American. He worked as a department manager in the Delmonte Packing Co. in downtown San Francisco. He was also a veteran of the Spanish American War, having served in the Far West and in the Philippines.

His talents as a poet were widely recognized at the time. Ricks was one of the winners in a poetry contest announced at a dinner for poets from throughout California. As early as the war years, Eloise Bibb Thompson, of The Lincoln Motion Picture Co., Inc., an African American company, wrote him praising his literary abilities and inviting him to write screen plays: "Let me prevail upon you to use such brilliant talents as yours in the moving picture field, where you will be appreciated and your work amply remunerated." She also offered him a chance to buy stock in the company, because "a stockholder has a better chance of having his plays accepted at some future time than an outsider." She invited their white friends to purchase stock as well and, furthermore, started a service bureau to teach scene writing by correspondence.[49]

Ricks responded that he had, in fact, "thought of attempting a scenario and have made some note involving musical ideas." He lacked the training and the time to do this, however, but he was working on finding the time. He does not seem to have written anything for film in a long writing career, however.

Some of his poems were what would later be termed protest literature. One of his them, "Lynched," was written after a mob murdered a black man in Waco, Texas. It was published in the *California Eagle*, where he compared this atrocity to the crucifixion on Calvary:

> In anger I read of Waco's crime
>   Burning in head and heart;
> And I prayed, O, Lord, O; Lord what time
>   Shall end this devil art.

His poem "The Golden Pool," of which there are two versions, revealed an interest in Africa ("beyond the walls of Tunis") like some of the other Renaissance poets. He also displays a bit of erudition when he refers to the Sahara's golden pool by name, "al-din-orr," and to "the curse of Ram-al-Ra, A prophet in the days of old." The short poem, "Petrified Forest at Bu Salaam" was another example of exotica.

Musical instruments and song abound in his poetry. "A Poem to You" refers to violins; a magic flute, silver bells ring, maidens sing; flutes and harps; a trumpet; songs and chimes; and "The Drummer's Serenade," with a chorus that includes the rhythm of this instrument—"Boom te ta ra boom ta roll" repeatedly as warriors marched and children danced.

Ricks published hundreds of poems, particularly in Bay Area newspapers, but also in *Del Monte Activities*, the publication of the company where he worked, and African American newspapers. His busy schedule was indicated in his handwritten report, "Accomplishments of 1938. Literary only." Dr. Gail Cleland read his poem, "Now That Men Have Wings," to two hundred fliers and their families at the first memorial service at Congregational Church service, Alameda for a captain and his crew who were tragically lost. The mayor of San Francisco released this same poem to the Associated Press after it was published in the *Oakland Tribune*. "The Water Lily" was published in *California Out of Doors*, by the Tamalpais Conservation Club, to which he belonged from 1913. *Important American Poets*, an anthology came out that year with two of his poems, "Spring Be Gentle" and "The Bell."

His poems dealt with a variety of different subjects, some patriotic, such as "Our Country's Flag," some dealing with local scenes, "Market Street on A Rainy Day," others with different topics, such as "To Robbie Burns," "The Cycle of Life," "Machine Guns." "A Valentine for Elizabeth" was one of many poems dedicated to his wife. As he concluded about his love for his spouse, comparing it to a song, he also generalized:

> This I have learned as the years roll along,
> Love grows, but it never grows old,
> The longer the road, the sweeter the song,
> The end of the story is ever told.

His short stories sometimes contained classical references and often were ironic, as in "Hunchback of Leidesdorff Street," and "A Modern Charon," and philosophic as in "The Debutante Fly," but he usually did not deal with racial themes, except for "The Yaquis Revenge," in which the Native Americans exact revenge on a cruel mine operator, and the fact that Leidesdorff Street was named after a pioneer African American entrepreneur.

His wife was quite active as well, and was also involved in literature and cultural presentations. She kept a record of the meetings of the local Book Lovers' Club in the 1930s. When they met in early October 1935 at the Ricks's home, Mrs. Ricks discussed the etymology of the word "Africa," referring to Roman sources. At subsequent meetings, a discussion leader presented information on the flora and fauna of Africa, arguing that both cotton and coffee were indigenous to the continent; on African proverbs; on Ancient Egypt and the Egyptian constitution of 1923.

They also discussed contemporary politics. Late in winter 1935, Mrs. Ricks gave a presentation on "China," and the following winter—1936—she discussed "Mussolini and the League of Nations" shortly after Italy invaded Ethiopia to recapture the past glories of the Roman Empire.

The club's motto was "To study much, To play enough, To keep abreast of the times, To not be lost in the common herd." The weekly topics suggested the club members were quite sophisticated, familiar with the intellectual trends underlying the Harlem Renaissance. This included a familiarity with classical sources as well as with the latest historical findings from U.S. and African American authors and with the *Crisis*, the NAACP periodical. The origins of cotton and coffee have been noted, but even more surprisingly, club members were also familiar with and critical of the racist views in Thomas Jefferson's *Notes on the State of Virginia*.

They also suggested, moreover, "vastly more than has been supposed, . . . [that] African culture had to do with early exploration and colonization in America." Sudanic culture, they concluded, influenced Europe. Indeed, Black influence on Native Americans was so considerable that "perhaps" Africans came to the Americas before Columbus. As they were probably familiar with the work of the Harvard linguist Leo Weiner, they pointed out that many Indian words appeared to be related to words used by Africans.[50]

Sargent Johnson

In various ways these writers, club members, musicians and entertainers participated in the social, cultural, and intellectual currents that have received such attention under the rubric of the Harlem Renaissance. They responded creatively to the trends and circumstances of the times—war, migration, urbanization, and a fascination with folk culture and the exotic. Sculptor Sargent Johnson exemplified the spirit of this cultural movement in his various works, especially those patterned after West African masks, as well as in the heads he sculpted, and in his other artistic presentations. Johnson was influenced by other nationalities and ethnicities besides the African American, insofar as he studied Mexican and Native American art, and he spent considerable time south of the border after World War II.

Johnson was born in Massachusetts and grew up in New England and Virginia. For a time he lived with an aunt, May Howard Jackson, in Washington, DC. She was a sculptress who maintained a studio in her home and probably influenced her nephew artistically. He arrived in San Francisco for the Panama–Pacific Exposition in 1915, worked as a fitter, and enrolled in the A. W. Best School of Art.

As LeFall Collins argued, "Johnson was a product of two 'Negro' movements of self-redefinition, one less formal movement taking place in the late nineteenth century and the other—called the New Negro movement—taking place in the early twentieth century." Yet his artwork also reflected a complex multi-racial vision. His work, "Elizabeth Gee," (1927) represented the face of an Asian American girl, a neighbor, while "Mask Of A Girl," (1926), "Negro Woman" (1933), "Mask" (1930–1935), "Mask" (1933), "Mask" (1934), and "Female Egyptian Head," (1940) were clearly African influenced, and at least one, "Mask" (1934) was very abstract. "Primitive Head" (1945), "Mother and Child" (1947), and "Untitled," an abstract squarish sculpture suggesting two lovers, mirror other national and ethnic influences.[51]

In the autumn of 1935, Sargent Johnson stated his ideas in a *San Francisco Chronicle* article:

> I aim at producing a strictly Negro Art, . . . studying not the culturally mixed Negro of the cities, but the more primitive slave type as it existed in this country during the period of slave importation. Very few artists have gone into the history of the Negro in America, cutting back to the sources and origins of the life of the race in this country. It is the pure American Negro I am concerned with, aiming to show the natural beauty and dignity in that characteristic lip, that characteristic hair, bearing and manner.[52]

He also clarified that he aimed at pleasing the African American audience. "I wish to show that beauty not so much to the white man as to the Negro himself. Unless I can interest my race, I am sunk. And this is not so easily accomplished." He advised artists to "go South" instead of East or to Europe, from which they returned "imitators of Cezanne, Matisse, or Picasso." He concluded, "this attitude is not only a weakness of the artists, but of their racial public."

Johnson also criticized the fact that many artists indulged in "too much theorizing." He had only "one technical hobby to ride," as he:

> was interested in applying color to sculpture as the Egyptians, Greeks, and other ancient peoples did. I try to apply color without destroying the natural expression of sculpture, putting it on pure, in large masses, without breaking up the surfaces of the form, respecting the planes and contours of sculpturesque expression.

For Johnson, color was "a means of heightening the racial character of my work." He concluded, "The Negros [sic] are a colorful race. They call for an art as colorful as it can be made."

Johnson was one of the rare artists from the Bay Area who achieved an international reputation, but the careers of Ivie Anderson and Henry Starr suggested he was not alone in this respect. By themselves, their accomplishments are remarkable, and when you add those of lesser-known individuals, such as Ricks and Midge Williams, the true complexity and richness of this cultural milieu, though perhaps not as great as the Harlem Renaissance, becomes apparent.

Ricks, though he wrote about lynchings and such injustices, was influenced more by classical writers than by the culture of the Afro-Americans who inspired Claude McKay and Zora Neale Hurston. However, he could not have been unaware of the African topics presented by Mrs. Ricks and discussed by the Book Lovers' Club. The musicians and singers, on the other hand, were steeped in black cultural traditions, largely due to the influence of recordings, traveling shows, and artists who visited the West Coast.

Social forces that created the Harlem Renaissance shaped the cultural life in other cities, as well, and, remarkably in the distant Bay Area, in spite of its population of a few thousand African Americans until World War II. The fact that this region supported Morton and Oliver indicates it was familiar with and ready for the blues/jazz from the World War era—the same time as Chicago, which in itself is quite noteworthy given the southern, mid-western, and East Coast biases in the history of the music.

While scholars have noted the effects of the World War on black social and cultural life, the influences of the Spanish American war have been neglected. W. C. Handy, however, mentioned how his sojourn in Cuba gave him the habanera rhythm for the B section of his famous St. Louis Blues, and very likely, this war helped introduced African Americans to the guitar as well as Spanish and Afro-Cuban music and rhythms. We noted the number of West Indians who became musicians or, in the case of Lester Mapp, nightclub men in the Bay Area.

Afro-Americans in this metropolitan area experienced the vicissitudes of migration and, in some instances, immigration, just like the participants in the Harlem Renaissance—none of whom came from New York City, the sole exception being Countee Cullen. LeProtti and Anderson were native-born, but so many others came from the South in the early twentieth century, and they ranged up and down the coast, as noted, from Los Angeles to the Northwest. Urbanization, residencies in different cities, and formal education were at the core of their experiences. Rare individuals such as Ricks, and some younger high school graduates, enrolled at the University of California.

The NAACP and the *Crisis*, emerging before the war, influenced intellectual life and culture in the Bay Area as it did in other metropolises. It is noteworthy that this and other civil rights organizations and the *Crisis* possessed such meaning for black residents of the Bay Area, given the fact that while they suffered from racial discrimination in housing and employment, it was not as ubiquitous or as vicious and deadly in California as it was in the South—not for blacks, at least. The experiences of the Chinese, Japanese, and Mexicans were qualitatively different from those of blacks in the Far West.

Notes

1 William Nauns Ricks Papers, Bancroft Library; Herbert Bashford, KLX Reviewer, *Oakland Tribune* June 6, 1928, p. 6; "Exits and Entrances," *Oakland Tribune* September 11, 1925, p. 34; *Oakland Tribune* April 13, 1927, p. 25; see Anthony D. Hill with Douglas Q. Barnett, *The A to Z of African American Theater*, (Lanham, MD: The Scarecrow Press, 2009), pp. 19–20; James V. Hatch and Ted Shine (eds.), *Black Theatre USA: Plays by African Americans* (rev. and expanded ed.) (New York: The Free Press), pp. 95–132.

2 "Langston Hughes to Be Presented by Acorn Club," *Spokesman* April 30, 1932, p. 3; "Lecture Here to Be Hughes Social and Literary Fete," *Spokesman* May 7, 1932, p. 3; and "Carmel Residents to Hear Hughes," *Spokesman* May 28, 1932, pp. 1, 7.

3 "Neighbors Will Honor Artist Sargent Johnson," *San Francisco Spokesman* March 8, 1935, p. 1; see also "Noted Berk. Artist Gets NAACP Medal," *Spokesman* March 22, 1935, p. 1; Gordon Sproul, President of the University of California, bought one of his pieces; the German Ministry in Italy purchased a copy of "Sammy."

4 Byron "Speed" O'Reilly, "Star Stuff," *Spokesman* November 23, 1933, p. 2. On Turner, see Tom Stoddard, *Jazz on the Barbary Coast*, (Berkeley, CA: Heyday Books, 1998), pp. 137–148.

5 Byron "Speed" O'Reilly, "Star Stuff," *Spokesman* July 12, 1935, p. 2.

6 "Oakland, As Is!" *Defender* February 22, 1925, p. 8.

7 Stoddard, *Jazz*, pp. 21–27, 54–68. See also Herbert Asbury, *The Barbary Coast: An Informal History of the San Francisco Underworld* (Garden City, NY: Garden City Pub. Co., 1933).

8 Stoddard, *Jazz*, p. 26.

9 Stoddard, *Jazz*, p. 12; "Sam King of Pacific Street Is Dead," *San Francisco Chronicle* January 12, 1910, p. 10.

10 Stoddard, *Jazz*, p. 42.

11 Ibid., pp. 43–44. Reb Spikes Jazz Oral History Project Interview, Institute of Jazz Studies, Rutgers University, Newark, NJ, should also be consulted.

12 "Musician, World War Veteran Dies in S.F.," *Spokesman* March 26, 1932, p. 2.

13 Stoddard, *Jazz*, pp. 38–39.

14 "Stage and Screen," *Spokesman* February 13, 1932, p. 2.

15 "Duke Ellington Is Given Farewell Night at Apex," *San Francisco Spokesman* March 12, 1932, p. 3.

16 "Star Stuff," *Spokesman* March 29, 1934, p. 3.

17 "Henry Starr, Coast Radio Ace, to City," *Defender* August 4, 1934, p. 8.

18 Rob Roy, "Race's First Radio Ace Here," *Defender* September 1, 1934, p. 8.

19 "Browning, Stars [sic] Return to London," *Defender* February 19, 1938, p. 6.

20 "Star Stuff," *Spokesman* April 19, 1935, p. 2.

21 I wish to thank Tom Howard of the Gilroy Historical Museum, Fred Glueckstein of Sykesville, Maryland, and Phill Laursen for biographical details on Ivie Anderson.

22 "'Ragtime' Billy Tucker, 'Coast Dope,'" *Defender* June 20, 1925, p. 8.

23 *California Eagle* December 21, 1928, p. 24.

24 "S.R.O. Signs When Duke Plays in Loop," *Defender* February 21, 1931, p. 1; "Going Backstage with the Scribe," *Defender* April 25, 1931, p. 5.

25 Tippy Dyer, "Tipping You Off to the Doings in Columbus (Ohio)," *Defender* August 7, 1937, p. 21.

26 Almena Lomax, "The Duke and the Lady," clipping in Ivie Anderson file, San Francisco Public Library, San Francisco Room Collection (stamped May 24, 1970), San Francisco Public Library.

27 "Ivy Anderson Climbs Fame's Ladder," Oklahoma City *Black Dispatch* June 21, 1934, p. 8.

28 "Irene Belle Ruggles Junior Club," *Spokesman*, December 1, 1932.

29 "Mid-Nite Show Draws Numbers in Big Benefit," *Spokesman* June 7, 1934, p. 2.

30 "Star Stuff," *Spokesman* May 4, 1933, p. 2.

31 "Star Stuff," *Spokesman* December 21, 1933, p. 2.

32 "Star Stuff," *Spokesman* April 5, 1934.

33 Byron O'Reilly, "Star Stuff," *Spokesman* April 19, 1934, p. 2.

34 Byron O'Reilly, "Star Stuff," *Spokesman*, June 26, 1934, p. 2.

35 "Star Staff," *Spokesman.* September 13, 1934, p. 2; "Boy Slayer Faces Gun Law Charge," *San Francisco Chronicle* August 30, 1934, p. 1; "Star Stuff," *Spokesman* August 30, 1934, p. 2.
36 "Behind the Scenes with Harry," *California Eagle* September 28, 1934, p. 7.
37 Byron O'Reilly, "Star Stuff," *Spokesman* October 12, 1934, p. 2.
38 Folder 1, Letter of Langston Hughes to Roy Blackburn, August 26, 1936; Roy Blackburn Papers, Bancroft Library, UCB.
39 "Chicagoans Like Louis Armstrong," *Defender* June 22, 1940, p. 20; "Louis Armstrong To Quit the Cotton Club," *Defender* March 30, 1940, p. 21.
40 "Maxine Sullivan Quits," *Defender* March 23, 1940, p. 21.
41 "Armstrong Hits," *Defender* November 9, 1940, p. 21; see her photo in a San Francisco nightspot, "Drink, Midge?" *Defender* December 7, 1940, p. 20.
42 "Midge Williams Reported Much Improved Now," *Defender* May 24, 1941, p. 21.
43 Dan Burley, "Back Door Stuff," *Amsterdam News* July 4, 1942, p. 16.
44 "Radio Signs Singing Star," *Amsterdam News* December 26, 1941, p. 17.
45 Letter to Edith Wilson, September 17, 1919, Box 13 (or 20), Folder 6, William Nauns Ricks Papers, Bancroft Library.
46 Box 18 Folder 1; handwritten letter of Ricks to the Veterans Administration (n.d.), William Nauns Ricks Papers, Bancroft Library.
47 "Oakland Lair of Serpents Elects," *Oakland Tribune* December 23, 1925, p. 1; see also where he was commander of the Alexander camp. "Spanish War Veterans to Bow in Memory of Maine," *Tribune* February 17, 1930, p. 14.
48 "Memorial Day," dated April 30, 1914, *Oakland Tribune* May 31, 1914, p. 19.
49 Mrs. Eloise Bibb Thompson letter to Mr. W. N. Ricks, October 29, 1927, William N. Ricks Papers, Bancroft Library.
50 Ivan VanSertima, *They Came Before Columbus* (New York: Random House, 1976); *African Presence in Early America* (New Brunswick, NJ: Rutgers University, 1987).
51 Lizetta LeFall-Collins and Judith Wilson, *Sargent Johnson: African American Modernist* (San Francisco, CA: San Francisco Museum of Art, 1998), pp. 10–11.
52 Quoted in ibid., p. 15.

Further reading

Beasley, Delilah L. *The Negro Trail Blazers of California.* New York: Negro Universities Press, 1969.
Bryant, Clora, Buddy Collette, William Green, and Steve Isoardi, eds. *Central Avenue Sounds: Jazz in Los Angeles.* Berkeley, CA: University of California Press, 1998.
Chicago Defender, 1925–1940.
Daniels, Douglas Henry. *Pioneer Urbanites: A Social and Cultural History of Black San Francisco.* Philadelphia, PA: Temple University Press, 1980.
Forbes, Camille. *Introducing Bert Williams: America's First Black Star.* New York: Basic Civitas, 2000.
Hobbs, Richard S. *The Cayton Legacy: An African American Family.* Pullman, WA: Washington State University Press, 2002.
Hughes, Langston. *I Wonder As I Wander.* New York: Hill and Wang, 1956.
LeFall-Collins, Lizetta, and Judith Wilson. *Sargent Johnson: African American Modernist.* San Francisco, CA: San Francisco Museum of Art, 1998.
Oakland Tribune, 1912–1940.
Pastras, Phil. *Dead Man Blues Jelly Roll Morton Way Out West.* Berkeley, CA: University of California, 1949.

Pepin, Elizabeth, and Lewis Watts. *Harlem of the West: The San Francisco Fillmore Jazz Era.* San Francisco, CA: Chronicle Books, 2006.
Ricks Papers, Bancroft Library.
San Francisco Chronicle, 1910–1938.
San Francisco Spokesman, 1932–1935.
Stoddard, Tom. *Jazz on the Barbary Coast.* Berkeley, CA: Heyday Books, 1998.

6

HARLEM RENAISSANCE IN OKLAHOMA

Jean Van Delinder

The Harlem Renaissance in Oklahoma was influenced by its geographical location as a state bound in the combination of the Indian Territory and Oklahoma Territory. Oklahoma's mixture of peoples and cultures influenced a distinct black consciousness and artistic expression. The African Americans who settled in Oklahoma were descendants of the involuntary migration of Native Americans in the early nineteenth century and the voluntary migration of freedmen after the Civil War. This mixture of ethnic groups influenced a uniquely Oklahoma contribution to black arts and culture: a musical blend of country music, carried by the descendents of rural southerners, and jazz (swing). Though far removed from Harlem, "the Capital of the Black World," Oklahomans managed to create a unique Oklahoma sound that would influence larger metropolitan areas including Kansas City, Chicago, and New York. The most significant contribution of the Harlem Renaissance in Oklahoma is that it brought forth and nourished some of the best jazz musicians in the world.

As a national cultural experience, the Harlem Renaissance illustrates the flourishing of innovative, complex, and distinctively African American social structures and cultural traditions shaped by the African Diaspora. The diffusion of the Harlem Renaissance was tempered by local customs and ideas about race. Even though Oklahoma's African Americans had a very different topographical experience than that of Harlem's northern and urban experience, they developed a strong sense of community in opposition to racial prejudice. They also nurtured the development of a distinct African American cultural consciousness that found expression in numerous artistic forms, particularly in music.

Studying places such as Oklahoma, far removed from the geographical center of this African American literary, artistic and intellectual movement, brings into focus the importance of how locality and place shape creative expression.

Racial segregation in Oklahoma strongly influenced the creation of close-knit black communities in the state's largest cities, Oklahoma City, Tulsa and Muskogee. Black businesses along Second Street in Oklahoma City and the Greenwood District in Tulsa would bring together aspiring musicians, poets and writers. Writer Ralph Ellison's interest in jazz and other modern art forms was nurtured in his home town of Oklahoma City while playing in a jazz band and attending Frederick Douglass School. Forty miles northwest of Oklahoma City, Langston University was the only institution of higher learning for blacks in Oklahoma. Langston was home to the noted Harlem Renaissance poet Melvin Tolson, whose poem "Dark Symphony" not only won the National Poetry Prize in 1940 but would also become a focal point for a rising black consciousness on the cusp of the civil rights movement.

The chronology of the Harlem Renaissance in Oklahoma is circumscribed by the largely forgotten 1921 Tulsa Race Riot and that cultural icon of the Great Depression, the Dust Bowl Exodus in the 1930s. Though much has been written about the African American experience in terms of physical bondage (slavery) and racial segregation, little attention has been paid to the resulting racial discrimination in creating local communities that nurtured new beginnings. This chapter attempts to do that.

Early Beginnings

In order to understand the Harlem Renaissance in Oklahoma, it is important to first consider where Oklahoma fits in the broader context of American cultural values and racial attitudes. Though not a state until 1907, segregation and racial discrimination have long histories in Oklahoma, and blacks were subject to the racism of the times: a system of separation between blacks and whites. Geographically, the state is bisected roughly into east and west halves by the 98th meridian. The eastern half of the state, commonly referred to as "Indian Territory," was where blacks first arrived during the period of the forced migration of numerous southeastern tribes in the early nineteenth century.

During this period of forced migration or Indian Removal to the west, the status of African Americans was complicated; some African Americans were chattel slaves while others lived freely as citizens of the Five Civilized Tribes: Cherokee, Chickasaw, Choctaw, Creek and Seminole. Conflicts quickly arose when the slaveholding Cherokee and Creek tribes blamed a series of slave insurrections on the free black Seminoles, who had intermarried with tribal leaders. Of the Five Civilized Tribes, the Cherokees were the largest slave holders and had the most to lose as their economic structure was built on chattel slavery. By the time of the Civil War, Cherokee slaves numbered 4,600.

The Civil War brought havoc to the Five Tribes and created an excuse for the federal government to take away much of their lands through treaties for the purpose of moving other Indian peoples in neighboring states to the emerging "Indian Territory." The aftermath of the war also created conditions in which non-Indians would begin their systematic settlement of Oklahoma and the concurrent destruction of the reservations through the privatization of tribal lands.

In the aftermath of the Civil War and Reconstruction, land ownership among the tribes dwindled, while at the same time numerous all-black towns were founded, prompting black promoters to advertise for settlers throughout the South. After the Civil War, the towns of Boley, Red Bird, Rentiesville, Taft, and Langston were founded as a testament to black self determination. The freedmen of the southeastern Indian nations and the more recent arrivals from Tennessee and lower Appalachia came in search of economic opportunities and respite from racial prejudice.

An important oasis against racism in Oklahoma was Langston University, an institution of higher learning founded for African Americans. Langston's campus hosted prominent black intellectuals, orators, artists and musicians providing black Oklahomans with an opportunity to see and hear the important people and issues related to the Harlem Renaissance. Located ten miles east of Guthrie in Langston, Langston University was established in 1897 as the Colored Agricultural and Normal University (CANU). As the only higher learning institution in the state for African Americans, its curriculum provided training in industrial and agricultural arts, a normal or teachers' college, and a liberal arts course. By 1915 the student population had grown from 41 to 639.

As both black and white immigrants hungry for land poured into Oklahoma Territory they brought their most important possessions, which often included musical instruments. Scottish-Irish immigrants from the Southern Appalachian Mountains commonly brought fiddles, the basis of the Appalachian string band, an early form of country music. This more primitive form of country music, largely influenced by British and Irish folk music, is often referred to as "old-time music." This musical style was the result of interactions among musicians from different European and African ethnic groups over hundreds of years. Unsurprisingly, blacks and whites in rural communities in the South and later in Oklahoma not only worked together but also played music together. The cohabitation and extended contact continued between these different immigrant groups, nurturing unique cultural traits that would find an outlet for expression during the Harlem Renaissance.

By the early twentieth century, many of the all-black towns and settlements in larger communities in Oklahoma developed marching and concert bands. Oklahoma's major cities, such as Oklahoma City, Tulsa, and Muskogee, all had thriving black business districts and were important centers of culture for future Oklahoma jazz artists. Each of these cities will be considered in the follow-ing pages, beginning with Oklahoma City and the heart of its segregated business district, known as "Deep Deuce" or Northeast Second Street in Oklahoma City.

"Deep Deuce" Oklahoma City

Established after the Land Run of April 22, 1889, Oklahoma City became the state capital in 1910, when blacks comprised 10 percent of the city's population (6,546 out of 64,205). Because racial segregation had been established before statehood, excluding African Americans from schools, churches, and social groups, black Oklahomans created their own social world. Black businesses, clubs, fraternities, sororities, and social groups thrived, attracting an educated professional class who opened businesses.

Since racial segregation physically prevented African Americans from living in many parts of the city, by the 1920s the black community had clustered around the three hundred block of Northeast Second Street, which become known as "Deep Deuce," "Deep Two," or "Deep Second." During the day its businesses welcomed African Americans with safe and welcoming places to shop. At night, Deep Deuce was an important cultural center with a movie theater, nightclubs, supper clubs, and dance halls that catered to African American jazz musicians and enthusiasts. Deep Deuce also featured outstanding local talent, many of whom gained national acclaim—for example, Jimmy Rushing, Charlie Christian, and the famous traveling territorial band, the Oklahoma City Blue Devils. In addition, in the 1920s and 1930s numerous bands, including the Jolly Harmony Boys, Pails of Rhythm, and Ideal Jazz Orchestra, worked out of the city. Deep Deuce was the center of the African American community. It was where they held parades, New Orleans-style funerals, a Thursday night tradition called "maids night out," and a grand "street" fashion show involving the whole community as either spectators or participants.

An important political and intellectual feature of Deep Deuce was the office of the influential black newspaper *Black Dispatch*, located at 324 Northeast Second Street. Its editor, Roscoe Dunjee, the son of a professional black business-man who migrated to Oklahoma in 1892, championed the struggle for civil rights in Oklahoma on the pages of his newspaper for almost fifty years. Though Dunjee's formal education ended after attending Langston University for only one year, his keen intellect served to galvanize the black community toward challenging segregation. Dunjee served on the national board of directors for the NAACP, and for sixteen years he served as president of the Oklahoma State Conference of Branches of the NAACP, which included Guthrie, Tulsa, Chickasha, Muskogee and Oklahoma City. This pooling of resources resulted in several court cases challenging Oklahoma's segregation laws including *Sipuel vs. Board of Regents of the University of Oklahoma* (1948) and *McLaurin vs. Oklahoma State Regents* (1950), which challenged higher education, and *Hollins vs. State of Oklahoma* (1935), which focused on segregated juries.

Dunjee also sought to challenge segregation by developing black businesses and fraternal societies. He served as president of the local chapter of the National Negro Business League, an organization founded by Booker T. Washington in 1900. Dunjee understood that the path to black self-sufficiency was an economic one as well as a legal and political struggle. Dunjee also worked closely with his fraternal society, the Knights of Pythias, to develop future black leaders for business and industry.

The musical training of Oklahoma jazz musicians was due in part to the musical opportunities for studying music, singing and playing instruments. In the black Oklahoma City schools Douglass High School was particularly renowned for its music ensembles and marching band. This was largely due to the efforts of black music educators such as Zelia N. Page Breaux, Evelyn Sheffield, and Cornelius Pittman. Breaux, who at one time headed the music department at Langston University and later was Supervisor of Music for the Oklahoma Public Schools. Through her efforts she inspired the musical talents of Buddy Anderson, Jimmy Rushing, and Lemuel Johnson. Breaux and her colleagues also influenced local bandleaders Ernie Fields, Eddie Christian, Clarence Love and Al Dennie. Writer Ralph Ellison played in the Douglass High School Band, which was recognized as one of the best high school bands in the Southwest prior to 1954.

As the deepening of the Depression and Prohibition forced night clubs to close and jobs became scarce, Second Street in Oklahoma City became an important stopping place on the traveling jazz junket for musicians travelling to or from Kansas City or Chicago. Famous bands and musicians such as the Oklahoma City Blue Devils, Charlie Christian and Jimmy Rushing all came from the Oklahoma City area.

Oklahoma City Blue Devils

Founded in Oklahoma City in 1923, the Oklahoma City Blue Devils thrived until disbanded in 1933. The Blue Devils at various times included native Oklahomans Jimmy Rushing, Abe Bolar, Don Byas, and Lemuel C. Johnson. When bandleader Count Basie first heard them in Tulsa, Oklahoma in 1927, he later recalled that "Hearing them . . . was probably the most important turning point in my musical career so far as my notions about what kind of music I really wanted to try to play" (Daniels, 2006, 13). In the 1930s personnel from the Oklahoma City Blue Devils became the core of the Benny Moten band, which later formed the basis of Count Basie's swing combo, featured at the Reno Club in Kansas City by 1935.

Part of the reason the Blue Devils became legendary among the territorial bands was the new energy that they brought to jazz. Their brand of jazz was a blend of Oklahoma sounds combining ragtime, old time country and folk songs carried along with the various ethnic and racial groups that settled in the state. The Blue Devils are credited with beginning the "riff" structure that has become a characteristic feature of jazz. With the innovations and the abundance of soloist talent, such as Walter Page's string bass and Jimmy Rushing's charged big band vocal style, the Blue Devils were a prominent influence on jazz musicians for generations to come.

Charlie Christian

Charlie Christian was raised in Oklahoma City, where he studied with his father. He later played bass in Alphonso Trent's band, guitar in combos around Oklahoma and the Jeter Pillars orchestra in St. Louis. Christian is known for introducing single-string playing on the amplified guitar. He was not the first to use the electric guitar, but he was the first to put it in the front line in the solo spotlight. He played mostly single lines, like horn players. He had a warm, full sound that set a standard for the guitar. Christian joined the Benny Goodman band in September 1939.

Jimmy Rushing

Born in Oklahoma City, Jimmy Rushing's wide ranging vocal ability in jazz and blues brought him national notice while a member of the Oklahoma City Blue Devils. He is commonly acknowledged as one of the greatest of all big band singers. Rushing's singing style combines the brash energy of itinerant street singers and the more expressive blues-based swing, influencing big band singers for the next several decades. During the 1940s, Rushing became known as "Mr. Five-By-Five" for inventing the "blues shouter" style. Rushing's career included stints with Bennie Moten, Count Basie and Bennie Goodman's band.

Writer Ralph Waldo Ellison, who studied music alongside Jimmy Rushing, pursued a different artistic career. Though his jazz playing earned him a musical scholarship to Tuskegee Institute in Alabama, Ellison would make his mark as a writer. His father, Lewis Ellison, named him for the famous writer and philosopher, Ralph Waldo Emerson, because he wanted to inspire his son to be a poet. Though Ellison's father might have inspired his writing talents, it was his mother, Ida Ellison, who stirred his racial consciousness. After his father died when Ellison was three, Ida went to work as a domestic. In spite of the drudgery of long working hours and the financial hardships of having to support her family, Ida was active in the Oklahoma Socialist Party, which ranked as one of the top three state socialist organizations in America. Though the Socialist Party is largely known for its agrarian focus, in Oklahoma it organized anti-segregation demonstrations, and Ida was arrested numerous times for participating.

Though Ellison's seminal novel *Invisible Man* was published two decades after the Harlem Renaissance ended, his insightful articulation of the countless humiliations blacks suffered under racial segregation continues to haunt us today. His writings gave white Americans a glimpse of the complexity of the black experience that America's racial issues could no longer be completely ignored by national leaders.

Goin' to T-Town

Tulsa, also known as "T-Town," is Oklahoma's second-largest populated city and the most important city after Oklahoma City. Tulsa's origins lie in the late 1820s with the removal of the Creek from their ancestral homes in Georgia and Alabama. After arriving here in 1833 the Lower Creek Indian Tribe settled in present Tulsa, negotiating a treaty with the Cherokee positioning the boundaries between the two nations. After the St. Louis and San Francisco Railroad arrived in 1882, the city began to grow rapidly and while in 1890 Tulsa's population was approximately 1,000, by the 1910 federal census its population was 18,182.

The discovery of oil at Red Fork in 1901 and the discovery of another major oil field at Glenpool in 1905 quickly established Tulsa's boom town reputation, and it proclaimed itself the "Oil Capital of the World." The oil boom also drew African Americans from around the state and elsewhere. By 1910 African Americans comprised 10 percent of the population, creating a demand for black businesses, which quickly sprung up along Greenwood Avenue.

The delineation between black and white Tulsa was marked by the intersection of two streets, Greenwood and Archer. The first two blocks of Greenwood Avenue north of Archer was where the heart of the black business community was located. Its concentration of wealth quickly earned it the reputation as the "Black Wall Street." Like Deep Deuce in Oklahoma City, this area was a favorite place for black domestics to parade on Thursday nights and Sunday evenings, traditional "days off" for black workers living in white neighborhoods.

The rapid growth in Tulsa's black population and the limited choices in black residential areas due to racial segregation meant that most African Americans concentrated along or near Greenwood Avenue. By 1921, the black population had increased so much that it spread to surrounding streets, resulting in this segregated area of town being called the "Greenwood District." Black Tulsa also boasted two black schools—Dunbar and Booker T. Washington—one black hospital, and two black newspapers—the Tulsa *Star* and the Oklahoma *Sun*. The Greenwood District was also home to thirteen churches, several fraternal organizations, two black theaters and a black public library.

Tulsa's Greenwood District offered a number of jazz outlets, such as The Rhythm Club, Casa Dell, Rialto Theater, and The Hole. Ernie Fields, Al Dennie, and Clarence Love played in bands. Tulsa also produced numerous jazz luminaries, including Howard McGhee, Earl Bostic, and Cecil McBee.

Tulsa Race Riot

Tulsa's oil boom drew all types of speculators and during the first two decades of the twentieth century had a skyrocketing crime rate. Tulsa's reputation as a lawless town had people on both sides of the color line on edge. Though common prior to statehood, vigilantism started to increase once again as citizens lost faith in the police's ability to enforce the law. In the white community, this facilitated a rise in Ku Klux Klan membership. Many of Tulsa's government leaders, including the mayor, openly admitted to being Klan members. As Klan activity increased, so did the determination of African Americans to arm themselves in order to resist any attacks. On the pages of the black newspaper, Tulsa *Star*, influential editor A. J. Smitherman urged African Americans to use armed resistance against mobs. His message particularly resonated with returning World War I veterans.

In August 1920 a white mob lynched a white teenager accused of murder. Tulsa newspapers reported that the police stood by and watched as the lynching victim was taken from his jail cell at the county courthouse. Eight months later, on May 30, 1921, Dick Rowland, an African American shoe shiner, reportedly accosted Sarah Page, a white elevator operator in the Drexel Building. Page screamed when Rowland allegedly stepped on her toe as he entered the elevator.

On May 31, the afternoon paper, the *Tulsa Tribune*, reported that Rowland had been arrested for the attempted rape of Page, and by early evening a crowd had quickly gathered. At approximately 9:00 p.m., a group of twenty-five armed African American men, many of them World War I veterans, arrived at the courthouse offering to help the police protect Rowland. The sheriff sent them home, but about an hour later they returned in increased numbers after a rumor that whites were storming the courthouse. As they were leaving, there was an altercation with a white man and a riot started.

During the course of eighteen terrible hours on May 31 and June 1, 1921, Greenwood District was burned to the ground. Whites vented their rage, destroying more than one thousand homes and businesses. Due to the secrecy and cover-up after the riot, estimates of the number of riot deaths are difficult, but they range from fifty to three hundred. The violence only ended when National Guard troops were called in.

Even though the majority of Tulsa's African American population had been burned out of their homes by the riot, many remained to rebuild Greenwood. Among them was the family of the noted historian John Hope Franklin, who moved to Tulsa in 1925 so his father could set up his law practice. Franklin was born in the all-black town of Rentiesville, Oklahoma in 1915 and later graduated from segregated Booker T. Washington High School before going on to study at Fisk University and Harvard.

Muskogee

Located fifty miles southeast of Tulsa was another oil boom town, Muskogee, an important stop for territorial bands traveling from Tulsa and Oklahoma City. It was also the third largest center of black culture and arts. The cultural and business center of the black community was Second Street. Though smaller than its namesake in Oklahoma City, Second Street in Muskogee nurtured such jazz legends as Jay McShann, Claude "Fiddler" Williams, Barney Kessel, Don Byas, and Aaron Bell.

Jay "Hottie" McShann

Born in Muskogee in 1916, James Columbus McShann began work as a professional musician in 1931, playing blues and swing piano in Tulsa and the surrounding areas. Five years later, he moved to Kansas City and formed his own big band, including a young Charlie Parker on saxophone.

Conclusion

The Harlem Renaissance in Oklahoma flourished partly due to technological innovations in mass media (radio and movies) and improvements in mass transportation (railroads) that tied Oklahoma to the national intellectual and cultural life. Radio and movies facilitated exposure to creative arts and new musical sounds while the expansion of railroads made it much easier for musicians and other entertainers to travel around.

Oklahoma City, Tulsa, and Muskogee were part of the "jazz triangle," stopping off places for performers and musicians traveling to and from Chicago, Kansas City, and New Orleans. Langston University, the only college blacks could attend in the state, attracted scholars and creative artists.

Oklahoma's boom economy and resulting establishment of all-black towns in the late nineteenth century coincided with the rising consumerism of a strong black middle class, particularly in Tulsa. Racial segregation physically constrained African Americans in Oklahoma towns and cities, forcing them to live within specific residential areas and frequent black businesses. These commercial enterprises advertised in the numerous black newspapers that were founded, though only the larger metropolitan areas could attract enough circulation to stay solvent. The *Black Dispatch* in Oklahoma City had a circulation of 23,500 readers followed by the *Tulsa Eagle* with 4,200, while *Muskogee Independent* could raise only 200 subscribers. These black newspapers were important since they covered news and activities about their communities that white newspapers usually ignored.

By the 1920s, though the Harlem Renaissance was flourishing, racism in Oklahoma was deepening, with the rise of the Ku Klux Klan. Oklahoma's boom economy created a sense of lawlessness. This dissatisfaction with the rule of law came to the fore when 1921 Tulsa Race Riot destroyed the all-black Greenwood District. Caught in the middle between rising racism and vigilantism, black Oklahomans turned to their communities to strengthen their will and determination to be in control of their lives. They nurtured their sense of self-worth by creating their own economic, cultural and social institutions. The Harlem

Renaissance in Oklahoma was just one manifestation of the significant contributions of black arts and culture to American society.

Further Reading

Daniels, D. H. (2006) *One O'Clock Jump: The Unforgettable History of the Oklahoma City Blue Devils*. Boston, MA: Beacon Press.

Ellsworth, S. (1982) *Death in a Promised Land*. Baton Rouge, LA: Louisiana State University Press.

Franklin, J. L. (1982). *Journey Toward Hope: A History of Blacks in Oklahoma*. Norman, OK: University of Oklahoma Press.

Hirsch, J. S. (2002) *Riot and Remembrance: The Tulsa Race War and Its Legacy*. Boston, MA: Houghton Mifflin.

Johnson, H. B. (1998) *Black Wall Street: Roots, Riot, Regeneration and Renaissance of Tulsa's Historic Greenwood District*. New York: Eakin Press.

Wintz, Cary D. (1988) *Black Culture and the Harlem Renaissance*. Houston, TX: Rice University Press.

7

THE NEW NEGRO RENAISSANCE IN OMAHA AND LINCOLN, 1910–1940

Richard M. Breaux

In 1915, the all-African American Dan Desdunes Band cracked the color wall when upper middle class whites affiliated with the Union Pacific Railroad and other industries in Omaha, Nebraska, permitted the group to march in the annual Ak-Sar-Ben Parade. The Ak-Sar-Ben Parade was an annual fundraising event established by the all-white Knights of Ak-Sar-Ben, a disgruntled group of elite whites in Omaha that failed to secure the "Gateway City" as one of two cities that hosted the annual Nebraska State Fair. From 1872 to 1901, state officials alternated the Fair's host city between Omaha and Lincoln, but in 1901 Lincoln became the permanent home for the Nebraska State Fair and would serve as such until 2010. The Dan Desdunes Band had the city of Omaha, its near North Side, and the Midwest 'stompin' and dancing from 1915 until Desdunes died in 1929. The band played black formal events, black parades and pageants, and black athletic competitions through the 1920s. After Desdunes's death, members continued to perform individually and as the Dan Desdunes Band through the 1940s (Calloway and Smith, 64).

Dan Desdunes had migrated to Omaha from New Orleans in 1904 and was a part of the trickle of black migrants from the South to Omaha and Lincoln that turn into a flood and ushered in the Great Migration to the Cornhusker state between 1910 and 1940. Described as an Afro-Creole who attended grade school and later Straight University, Desdunes played violin, cornet, trombone, and the trap drums. He had organized a band in New Orleans, before taking on a number of odd jobs in Omaha. A gig as the director of the Colored Knights of Pythias eventually led Desdunes to form his own band. His story of relocation from the urban south to the urban north became one of the reasons that the Great Migration fed the birth of the New Negro arts and letters movement, Harlem Renaissance, or New Negro Renaissance, in Nebraska and the West.

This essay explores the New Negro arts and letters movement or the New Negro Renaissance in Omaha and Lincoln, Nebraska from 1910 to 1940. It uses a generous periodization for the New Negro Renaissance borrowed from the work of Ernest Allen, which extends the New Negro Renaissance from about 1919, and Cheryl Wall's *Women of the Harlem Renaissance*, which argues for a broader periodization to 1940 if we are to include black women as a part of this cultural movement (Allen, 48–50; Wall, 2). It draws upon my previous work on the New Negro arts and letters movement among African American collegians at white universities in the Midwest which included black expressive culture at the University of Nebraska at Lincoln (Breaux, 149). The scope of this chapter extends to blacks in Omaha and Lincoln, Nebraska, within universities such as the University of Nebraska, Omaha University, Creighton University, and the larger population of blacks in these cities. Over the years, blacks in Omaha and Lincoln refused to let whites, friend or foe, or blacks outside Nebraska define them or their social, cultural, and political experiences. To be truly self-determining, blacks in Lincoln and Omaha defined themselves, by themselves and for themselves. This means that blacks' struggle for racial equality in eastern Nebraska was culturally self-determining and therefore extremely similar to and uniquely different to black struggles in other states. As David Krasner argues, Black modern culture in Omaha and Lincoln was "a complex mixture of ideas and movements—migratory, urbanized, intellectualized, fragmentary, literary, oral, folk, jazz, blues, rhythmic, Western, and Afrocentric—that created a complex, hybrid form" (Krasner, 10). The dual purpose of modern black expressive culture was to challenge white's racist presumptions while drawing on blacks' "African roots and southern traditions."

The New Negro Renaissance in Omaha and Lincoln demands that we focus on aspects of black expressive culture such as journalism, music, theater, and photography that are underexplored in Harlem Renaissance literature compared to poetry, fictional novels, and the visual arts (especially painting and sculpture); yet a growing body of literature has begun to explore how black monthly magazines such as *The Crisis*, *Opportunity*, and the *Messenger* affirmed blacks' sense of the cultural equality to whites.

In his opening essay to *The New Negro* anthology, the black Howard University professor and godfather of the Harlem Renaissance, Alain Locke, directly related the explosion in African American expressive culture to this migration:

> The migrant masses, shifting from countryside to city, hurdle several generations of experience at a leap, but more important, the same thing happens spiritually in the life-attitudes and self-expression of the Young Negro, in his poetry, his art, his education and his new outlook, with additional advantage, of course of the poise and greater certainty of knowing what it is all about.
>
> (Locke, 4)

The Great Migration and New Negro arts and letters movement had a greater influence on Omaha and Lincoln in eastern Nebraska than any other cities in the state. In Omaha, the black population leaped from 4,426 to 10,315 from 1910 to 1920 and jumped to 11,123 by 1930. Ten years later, Omaha's black residents numbered 12,015. Lincoln's black population only increased from 733 to 896 from 1910 to 1920. Lincoln's black population peaked at 997 in 1930 and in 1940 dropped to 794.

The majority of blacks in Omaha came to live in the city's "Near North Side" and in South Omaha (which had been a separate city until it was annexed by Omaha in 1915). Before 1910, blacks in Omaha tended to reside in the city's Third Ward—a developing urban mix of a working-class residential area and a vice district. A combination of increased employment and business opportunities, middle-class flight among European immigrants, and attempts by blacks to move into more middle-class surroundings sparked the move to northeast Omaha or the Near North Side beginning in 1910. Black residents in the Near North Side and blacks and Latinos in South Omaha found themselves increasingly segregated by whites of all classes. The Near North Side is bordered by 16th Street on the east, 35th Street on the west, Cuming Street on the south, and Ames Street on the north. Twenty-Fourth Street, which stretches from north to south, emerged as a multi-racial business district and primary artery for black cultural life in Omaha. The center of black life was 24th and Lake streets where in 1913 young men such as Otto Hall were attracted to the pool halls and sporting houses and were seen "flaunting his new clothes, a 'box-backed' suit— 'fitting nowhere but the shoulders,' high-heeled Stacy Adams button shoes, and Stetson hat" (Haywood, 28). By 1923, 24th and Grant was home to Cecilia and Jimmy Jewel's Dreamland Ballroom where countless musicians played over the years. Similar establishments —such as Jim Bell's Club Harlem, Murphy's Egyptian Room, and the Grotto— also became favorites for local jazz, blues, swing, and ragtime lovers. South Omaha, whose black population never reached more than 717, was its own city before 1915 and its primary north-south artery was Twenty-Fourth Street also. It was bound by A Street in the north, Harrison Street in the south, by the Missouri River in the east, and by 36th Street in the west. Lincoln's relatively smaller black population was dispersed throughout eleven of its twelve wards; yet 60 percent of blacks resided in ward three. Blacks, like Mexicans, Jews, and Italians, crowded into the third ward, with working-class blacks heavily concentrated east of the University of Nebraska at Lincoln's main campus and north of "O" Street. More middle-class blacks lived to the south of campus. One scholar referred to this area north of O Street, squeezed between several railroad lines, as "a Black Heaven," but neither Lincoln nor Omaha were heaven for black folks (Mihelich, 65).

Neither Omaha nor Lincoln developed a significant population of African American professionals. Most blacks in these cities were working class, and the popularity of jazz, particularly in Omaha, reflected the working-class sensibilities of black migrants. Hayward Hall, also known as Harry Haywood, remembered, "Opportunities for educated Blacks were few, even in North Omaha's Black Community there were only a few professionals. In that community there were a few preachers, one doctor, one dentist and two teachers" (Haywood, 27–28). With meat packing and Union Pacific Railroad as the largest employers in Omaha, most blacks worked for Swift-Armour, Cudahy, Omaha, Hammonds, Union Pacific or in service industry jobs in local hotels, restaurants, or domestic service. In 1910, 1,590 out of 2,729 blacks, or 58 percent blacks employed in Omaha worked in domestic or personal service jobs; only 17, or 0.006 percent of blacks worked in professional jobs (which included teachers, doctors, and lawyers). Twenty years later the number of blacks in Omaha almost tripled, but 0.033 percent worked as professionals. Lincoln too, had very few professional African Americans in its community; blacks in Lincoln were crowded into the service work, and a few were fortunate enough to find civil service jobs. From the time Hayward Hall left South Omaha in 1913 until 1940, times had changed very little for blacks in Omaha and Lincoln. The author of the WPA study *The Negroes of Nebraska* summarized it best with the opening statement of the section, "The Negro Finds a Job," when he wrote, "In the industrial life of Nebraska Negroes are faced, as in their entire economic life, with the problem of an inferior status" (WPA, 21).

"They Can't Help Play Good Music:" Jazz and the Music of New Negroes in Nebraska

Jazz came to Omaha from New Orleans, up the Mississippi River and detoured at St. Louis, west and north up the Missouri River tributary. Scholar George Lipsitz argues that despite jazz historians' tendency to focus on New Orleans, Kansas City, Chicago, and New York, "Omaha was a rich source of inspiration and education about jazz all on its own" (Love, xx–xxi). In 1902, two years before Dan Desdunes came to Omaha from New Orleans, Springfield, Missouri-born barber and musician Josiah Waddle formed one of the first all-black bands in the Gateway City. Waddle was born in 1849, had moved around the Midwest and first arrived in Omaha in 1880. He was working class, and with little formal education he entered one of the most respectable professions open to black men —barbering. He made his living as a barber and continued to bounce around from Missouri, Kansas, Nebraska, and Minnesota, and established an all-white band in Winnipeg, Canada. In 1902, he returned to Omaha, opened another barber shop and organized a fifteen-piece band. Waddle's all-black band played county fairs, carnivals, and chautauquas throughout the region for the next twelve years and the Dan Desdunes Band soon rivaled it in the city and region. Josiah Waddle was not only interested in developing his own band, he began to mentor a host of young black musicians, including one of the first women-only black bands.

Many of Omaha's jazz bands never attained the notoriety of Kansas City's Bennie Moten Orchestra, but in the early 1920s younger people in Omaha began to prefer the more lively jazz style of bands such as Red Perkins and his Original Dixie Ramblers and Josiah Waddle's protégé, jazz trumpeter and big band leader, Lloyd Hunter. Born in the now defunct coalmining town of Muchakinock, Iowa in 1890, Frank Shelton "Red" Perkins moved his wife and child from Fort Dodge, Iowa where he worked as a porter in a barbershop to Omaha between 1917 and 1925. In 1925, with Omaha's jazz scene heating up and expanding, Perkins established the six-piece Original Dixie Ramblers from members of the Night Owls. Perkins was an astounding trumpeter and his band included trombonist Charlie "Big" Green. By 1931, Red Perkins and the Dixie Ramblers recorded *Old Man Blues* and *Hard Times Stomp* with Gennett (Russell, 68). In the same year, Omaha band Lloyd Hunter and the Serenaders recorded *Sensational Mood* on the Columbia-Vocalion label. Lloyd Hunter was born in May 1908 in South Omaha and was the second of seven children born to Inez and Stephen Hunter. By the time he turned twenty-one Hunter had established his own band and toured around the Midwest. Vocalist Victoria Spivey fronted the Serenaders and later took control of the band. Hunter had to put together another group with Tennessee-born Anna Mae Winburn, future director and vocalist for the International Sweethearts of Rhythm, on lead vocals (Russell, 68). Another well-known Omaha dancer and vocalist who regularly danced at the Ritz Theater and sang at Jim Bell's Club Harlem was Wynonie "Mr. Blues" Harris.

The 1920s and 1930s were the Golden Age of Jazz across the United States, especially in Omaha, and national and territorial bands played and packed Omaha's clubs. Talented vocalists and musicians were wooed away from their gigs with one band to play, sing, or occasionally front another band. In addition to Red Perkins and Lloyd Hunter's orchestras, Ted Adams and Sam Turner also formed jazz bands. According to Jazz historian Digby Fairweather, the rough living, hard drinking, funny man and trombonist Charlie "Big" Green started out playing carnival and tent shows in Omaha's Near North Side. In Omaha, he played with Red Perkins, but in 1924, he joined Fletcher Henderson's band. Green backed several blues women, soloed on Bessie Smith's "Trombone Cholly," and played with Ma Rainey's Georgia Minstrels (Fairweather *et al.*, 310–311; Russell, 68). The thirty-five year old Oklahoma-born Simon Harrold, who was once a drummer in Dan Desdunes's band, formed Simon Harrold and the Melody Boys after Desdunes's death in 1929. His notoriety carried over to his new band and he became so popular that students at Omaha University invited him to play at the freshmen homecoming dance in 1929 (Love, 12). Other local favorites were Warren Webb and the Spiders, which included Tommy "Dude" Love on the alto saxophone. Preston Love played one of his first gigs with the Spiders, not as a saxophonist but as a drummer when the band's drummer fell ill (Love, 12). When Anna Mae Winburn came to Omaha from Indiana, where she performed under the name Anita Door, she fronted Red Perkins and Lloyd Hunter's bands and Omaha's Cotton Club Boys. Initially, Winburn's place in jazz orchestras was stereotypical and bound by the limitations of being a woman in a so-called man's profession, but beginning with the International Sweethearts of Rhythm in 1941 she assumed the baton and proved that "girl-bands" as they were called could complete with the most accomplished all-male bands (Tucker, 170–172).

Omaha's most popular jazz band was the Nat Towles Dance Orchestra. Like Dan Desdunes, Nat Towles was born in New Orleans where he developed from a guitarist and violinist to a bass player. Towles was a member of the Original Tuxedo Jazz Orchestra, but in 1923 established the Nat Towles Creole Harmony Kings. As one of the most talented territorial bands, the Creole Harmony Kings famously battled a number of jazz and swing groups in Texas, Oklahoma, Kansas, and Nebraska. Towles decided to call Omaha home from 1936 to 1943, during which time his groups became the resident band at Omaha's Krug Park. A number of Towles's contemporaries consider his band on par with, if not "superior to the Count Basie Orchestra" (Russell, 69–70).

James Jewell's Dreamland Ballroom and Jim Bell's Club Harlem sustained white and black jazz fans and aficionados in Omaha, and the likes of Count Basie, Earl Hines, Duke Ellington, Jean Calloway, Fletcher Henderson, and a host of local bands kept the places jumping. The Dreamland Ballroom was a multi-purpose hall upstairs in the building purchased by James and Jewell at 2221–2225 North 24th Street. It served as a meeting hall for a number of African American civic and social organizations; tables and chairs were pushed off to the side when the hall was transformed into the ballroom. When Earl Hines and his Orchestra played the Dreamland in October in 1932, one reporter to the *Omaha Guide* recalled, "How beautiful the Sepias were under the colored lights. The people were incomparable in the art of dressing. Greens, Tans, Blues, Reds and all rushing to and fro laughing, talking and poking fun." Both C. Homer Burdette and Preston Love recalled that jazz fans and younger children who could not go to perform-ances stood on the fire escape of the north end of the building trying to catch a glance at the dancers and bands inside, and crowds of young people often stood outside the front door listening to music as patrons ascended the stairs to the Dreamland. By the time Hines and his band began to play:

> Several girls [were] surrounding a young lady clapping [their] hands while she did the snake hips . . . Then I looked around in time to see Earl Hines, Charles Allen at his left and William Franklin at his right. These gentlemen swayed the crowd singing "Sweet Sue." Mr. Hines band then strutted their stuff; 650 hearts were synchronized with joy by this incomparable orchestra.

Today, those familiar with North Omaha will know the Dreamland and the Jewel building as Love Jazz and Arts Center. The Dreamland, while possibly the most often remembered, was not the sole jazz club in town. Omaha native and saxophonist Preston Love remembered Jim Bell's Club Harlem complete with "a full line of chorus girls, a twelve-piece orchestra, and imported top-grade comedians, singers, emcees, and other acts for the floor show" (Love, 15). Like whites who travelled uptown to go the Cotton Club and Small's Paradise in Harlem, the popularity of Dreamland and Club Harlem drew more wealthy white crowds from Omaha's palatial Dundee neighborhood, who mingled with more working-class and middle-class blacks on 24th Street, especially when nationally known acts played the black clubs or the Omaha Civic Center.

Jazz was certainly the most popular form of music among younger blacks in Omaha and Lincoln, but older parents and middle-class families were as likely to listen to former Boston conservatory of Music student, George F. McPherson, blind pianist F. C. Curtis, or voice and piano teacher Mrs. Florence Pinkston-Mitchell, who all formally and classically trained massive groups of young black aspiring musicians and gave them the opportunity to perform on a number of special occasions and holidays over the years. Most of these musicians were not well known outside of Omaha, but musician and composer Maceo Pinkard arrived in Omaha and stayed just long enough to establish a theatrical company before he packed his bags and went to New York in 1919. Pinkard became as well known for his ballads and writing and producing the Broadway musical "Liza" in 1922 as for the increasing number of jazz and ragtime tunes he composed including his most famous composition "Sweet Georgia Brown." This classic, which was recorded by Louis Armstrong, Count Basie, Cab Calloway, and Ethel Waters, has since become synonymous with the Harlem Globetrotters (WPA, 42–43). While some historians refuse to acknowledge the importance of classical music to the New Negro Renaissance or dismiss it as a simple imitation of white expressive culture, both jazz and classical music complicated some blacks' and many more whites' ideals and blacks' cultural and intellectual abilities (Spencer, xxii; Anderson, 9–10).

The Black Press, Black Photographers and the New Negro

Historian D. G. Paz writes, "One reflection of the 'New Negro' was the growth of journalism." Few African Americans living during the New Negro Renaissance would disagree. As literary scholar Henry Louis Gates and historian David Levering Lewis point out, a New Negro consciousness, determined to challenge whites' myths about black cultural, social, and intellectual inferiority, existed long before the Harlem Renaissance. The black press, which flourished during the New Negro era and played an essential role in throwing down the gauntlet in this challenge, is a part of this long history. Nationally, the NAACP's *The Crisis*, the UNIA's *Negro World*, Chandler Owen and A. Philip Randolph's *The Messenger*, Cyril Briggs's *Crusader*, and the Urban League's *Opportunity* magazine presented a united front against white supremacy, yet represented a myriad of philosophical traditions that ranged from integrationist, nationalist, socialist and capitalist. On occasion, these publications included stories on Lincoln, Omaha, or its black residents. For example, Malcolm X's parents, Earl and Louise Little, regularly reported on UNIA activities in Omaha to the *Negro World*. Although blacks in Omaha had published three newspapers, the *Afro American Sentinel*, the *Omaha Enterprise*, and the *Progress*, as early as the 1890s, it was John Albert Williams's *Monitor* (1915–1929) and George Wells Parker's *New Era* (1920–1926) that led the fight against racism and racial segregation in Omaha and Lincoln and black communities in Nebraska during the first fourteen years of the New Negro Renaissance, and the *Omaha Guide* (1927–1958) and *Omaha Star* (1938–present) that ushered black Nebraskans from the 1930s into the Civil Rights era.

The only aspect of these newspapers that was the same was that all four papers were black weeklies, and often the editorial viewpoints and coverage reflected the racial and political views of their editors. The Reverend John Albert Williams, a bi-racial Episcopal priest born in London, Ontario in 1866, came to Omaha in 1891 and began publishing sermons in the *Omaha Enterprise* in 1895. First G. F. Franklin and later Thomas P. Mohammitt published the *Enterprise* from 1893 to 1914. The editors of the pro-Republican *Enterprise* constantly debated and competed with the more conservative pro-Democrat *Sentinel* for much of the 1890s, but their disappearance left a void in black Omaha, and for five years just after the blacks started migrating to Omaha in increasing numbers, only one newspaper, the *Monitor*, catered to blacks in Omaha.

Drawing on his experience as an occasional writer for the *Enterprise*, John Albert Williams founded the Omaha *Monitor* in 1915 and remained its editor until November 1928. The *Monitor* was the voice of black Omaha and despite the presence of smaller competitors, managed to have a longer tenure than all but two of the thirteen black newspapers published in the history of blacks in Lincoln and Omaha before 1940. New Negroism, racial uplift, and challenging whites' ideas about their own intellectual and cultural superiority to blacks became hallmarks of the *Monitor*. Through the *Monitor* Williams advocated the hiring of black teachers and regularly included coverage of middle-class black fraternal organizations and black church activities in Omaha. While the *Monitor* supported Republican candidates, neither it nor Williams shied away from shouldering up to socialist and socialism, particularly as the political left sought to draw class alliances across the color line. George Wells Parker founded the *New Era* in September 1920— after working several years as a reporter and business manager at the *Monitor*—to challenge what he considered the more racially moderate views of John Albert Williams at the *Monitor*. Parker, who attended Creighton University, first emerged as a journalist and advocated Pan-African ideals that were in their infancy in Omaha. Chapters of his well-known book, *The Children of the Sun*, first appeared in the *Monitor*; later these were published in their entirety with advertisements to purchase copies printed in the *Monitor* regularly. In 1917, Parker published, "The African Origins of Grecian Civilization," in the

Association for the Study of Negro Life and History's *Journal of Negro History*, reinvigorating a field of study pioneered by David Walker, Alexander Crummell, and Martin Delany, and later popularized by Afro-centric scholars such as Ivan Van Sertima, George James, Cheikh Anta Diop and others. As an early supporter of Marcus Garvey's Universal Negro Improvement Association, Parker had little trouble in finding validation for his idea of an organization that promoted a 1910s form of cultural nationalism and black economic self-determination. By 1923, Parker was no longer editor of the *New Era*, and he joined the chorus of black intellectuals who became mistrustful and critical of Marcus Garvey and the UNIA. The *New Era* ceased publication under the editorship of Count Wilkinson in 1926.

Just as the *New Era* and the *Monitor* shut down, Herman J. Ford, C. C. Galloway and B. V. Galloway's *Omaha Guide* stepped in to assume of mantle of leadership in the black press. The *Omaha Guide* was massive in size compared to *New Era* and the *Monitor*, and in addition to local and state politics it offered more coverage of Omaha's cultural life in the late 1920s and 1930s. Its most unique feature was its "Illustrated Feature Section," which included a number of fictional series such as Edward Lawson's "Marty Bell aka The Harlem Hurricane," an illustrated series about a boxer who was a Jack Johnson look-alike, "Roadhouse Racket" by William M. Johnson, short stories by Edward Worthy, and a serial by Nick Lewis, "The Clean Up," about a young black evangelist who fights crime in Harlem. As the sand began to shift under the nation's political tide Galloway endorsed no candidate for the 1936 presidential election, and some of his staff began to sympathize with the Communist Party as the various trials related to the Scottsboro incident unfolded. In 1938, the circulation manager and advertising manager at the *Omaha Guide*, S. Edward Gilbert and Mildred Gilbert-Brown left and established the *Omaha Star*. Eventually the *Omaha Guide* remained a supporter of Republican politicians, while the *Omaha Star* followed a number of blacks toward Franklin D. Roosevelt and the Democratic Party. After recovery from a fire in the 1940s, the *Omaha Guide* eventually shut its doors; the *Omaha Star* continues to serve Omaha's Near North Side.

Photographs by black photographers continue to be an often used, but under analyzed part of the Harlem Renaissance. John Johnson and Earl McWilliams were to black Lincoln what James Van Der Zee was to blacks in Harlem. John Johnson (1879–1953) was the son of a Civil War veteran Harrison Johnson (1849–1900) and his wife Margaret. The elder Johnson had escaped slavery and served in the First Nebraska Regiment as a private; he supported his family by working as a cook in a number of Lincoln hotels and as a turnkey at the Lancaster County Jail. John Johnson was born and raised in Lincoln, graduated from Lincoln High School in 1899 and attended the University of Nebraska at Lincoln for a short time before a varied career as a cart or wagon driver, a post office janitor, and a photographer. He was possibly assisted by another long-time black Lincoln resident, Earl I. McWilliams. Earl McWilliams (1892–1960) worked part-time as a photographer's assistant and finisher in the Elite photography studio's darkroom, which was owned by a white photographer named Alva Townsend (Zimmer and Davis, 62–63; Keister and Zimmer, 125–126). Photographer and photo historian Deborah Willis reminds us that the increasingly accessible and decreasingly expensive medium of photography meant that African American photographers could serve as "ambassadors" of an African American community's poor, working and middle classes and contrast their subjects and themselves with stereotypical images of blacks that appeared in print and film.

The photographs by John Johnson offer us insight into the lives of black Lincoln's middle class and those who had middle-class aspirations; they also capture the tension between middle-class blacks and a generation of young people determined to confront and expand black Lincolnites' and Omahans' ideals about acceptable dress and behavior among young people.

Few people outside of Lincoln and Omaha were familiar with Johnson's work, but his photographs were rediscovered in 1994 and have since received significant attention, first in 1999, then from 2003 to 2006 as a part of an Exhibits USA traveling exhibition, which included the following cities: Lincoln, Norfolk, Kearney, and Hastings, Nebraska; Oakland, California; Flint, Michigan; Hot Springs, Arkansas; Santa Clara, California; Alexandra, Virginia; Henderson, Nevada; Tulsa, Oklahoma; and Belton, Texas. An entire issue of the Nebraska State Historical Society's *Nebraska History* in 2003 and a collection of photographs published as *Images of America: Lincoln in Black and White, 1910–1925* by Douglas Keister and Edward F. Zimmer in 2008 brought John Johnson's work to an even larger audience.

The Birth of a Nation, the Lincoln Motion Picture Company, and the Silver Screen as Contested Space

In addition to the rise of the Invisible Empire of the Ku Klux Klan in Nebraska, showings of *The Birth of a Nation* became Lincoln's and the Omaha's other public nuisance. Some of the NAACP's most heated campaigns were its local branches' attempts to ban showings of the southern redemption classic. The NAACP branch in Omaha, chartered in Omaha and Lincoln in 1918, failed to get court injunctions to stop the showing of the film. The ban of the second half of *The Birth of a Nation* at the Rialto Theatre in 1918 became one of the Lincoln branches' major victories. In a public letter printed in the Omaha *Monitor*, local NAACP members thanked both Mayor J. E. Miller and Attorney General Willis E. Reed for "putting *The Birth of a Nation* out of commission." Attorney General Reed had taken up the expenses of getting an injunction through his office, thereby saving the Lincoln chapter the court costs. Although the Omaha branch of the NAACP failed to ban the film in 1915, the Omaha *Monitor* documented black communities' fight against the film as the battle unfolded in cities across the United States.

In response to the popularity of *The Birth of a Nation* and the dominance of white and black companies that cast blacks in negative racially stereotypical roles, brothers Noble and George P. Johnson founded the Lincoln Motion Picture Company in 1915. While some sources claim the Johnsons were from Omaha, Noble and George were born in Colorado Springs, Colorado in 1881 and 1885 (Stewart, 300). George moved to Omaha, Nebraska in 1913 after graduating from Hampton Institute and a brief stint as a real estate agent and newspaper publisher in Tulsa, Oklahoma. In Omaha, Johnson worked in the Post Office, and in 1915 he and his brother founded the Lincoln Motion Picture Company. Noble Johnson left school to travel with his father, worked at a number of ranching and mining companies until he found work as an actor and stunt man and moved to Hollywood. He gained roles as a character actor for Universal and Lubin Studios. In 1916, Noble and George Johnson, a group of African American businessmen, and one white cameraman incorporated the Company in Los Angeles with $75,000 in capital "for the purpose of producing Negro moving pictures that will reflect merit and credit upon the Race, as well as opening of the field of employment to Negroes and an opportunity to make profitable financial investments" (Stewart, 203). While Noble acted, produced, wrote and handled financial matters for Lincoln, George worked as a writer, producer, and distributor for Lincoln from Omaha. He used his knowledge about the US Postal Services to maximize the company's ability to distribute film. The Lincoln Motion Picture Company produced and distributed two films in 1916, *Realization of the Negroes Ambition* and *The Trooper of Troop K*, both of which challenged the Klansman, *The Birth of a Nation* school of thought that became increasingly popular in the early twentieth century.

All-black-cast films that presented African Americans in a complex but non-racially stereotypical light were the Lincoln Motion Picture Company's forte and a symbol of black cultural self-determination. *Realization of the Negroes Ambition* told the story of a Tuskegee Institute graduate whose experiences with racism in the oil industry leads him to return home, only to find his family's land is worth a fortune because of its oil deposits. *The Trooper of Troop K* similarly explores the life of a character named "Shiftless Joe," played by Noble Johnson, who enlists in the army, becomes a combat hero, and returns home to a hero's welcome. *The Law of Nature* (1917) contained a pro-western migration and settlement theme and reflected the notion that rural life in the West and in black towns held more promise and opportunity than the elusive urban North and Midwest (Stewart, 202–205; Cripps, 75–89; Bogle, 18–23). It also mirrored the spirit of self-determination in those black migrants who continued to establish black towns in Kansas, Colorado, Texas, Oklahoma and other states from 1877 to 1915. *American Colored Troops at the Front* (1918), *Our Colored Fighters* (1919) and *Our Colored Boys in Action Over There* (1921) all attempted to cast black soldiers in a different light than popular Hollywood and government films that featured blacks as lazy cooks, military drudges, and carefree members of military brass bands.

The Lincoln Motion Picture Company released at least two other films during its time in operation, *A Man's Duty* (1919) and *By Right of Birth* (1921).

Most of the time, money, and work that went into making the films were expended in Los Angeles, while in Omaha, George Johnson distributed Lincoln's films throughout the country and especially in the Midwest. Johnson listed his home and business address as 2816 Pratt Street. According to Jacqueline N. Stewart, George Johnson developed elaborate market surveys to gauge exhibitors' venue size, audience preferences, and formulas to divide box office receipts. He also developed much of the advertising and marketing material for the Lincoln Motion Picture Company and distribution, publicity, and booking networks that included Washington, DC, Atlanta, Chicago, New Orleans, New York, and Philadelphia (Stewart, 208–209; Bogle, 8–23). In Omaha, Boyd's Theater on 17th and Harney, the Auditorium on 15th and Howard, the Diamond Theater on 24th and Lake, and the Loyal Theater at 24th and Caldwell all played Lincoln and rival Oscar Micheaux's movies. George constantly worked to generate revenue and opportunities for Lincoln to cash in on the federal government's use of film as propaganda during World War I, although George was mostly interested in producing films that honored and celebrated rather than dishonored or disregarded African Americans' military efforts (Stewart, 210–218).

The Lincoln Motion Picture Company continued to make films until 1921 and operated until 1923, but with Noble Johnson's resignation in 1917, competition from other white and black film companies, and mounting production and distribution costs, George Johnson relocated to Los Angeles where the remaining Lincoln business partners lived and worked. In Los Angeles, George again found employment as a postal clerk, all the time continuing to write, produce and distribute the Company's films. As the financial burden became too much to bear, George established the Pacific Coast News Bureau, a company that distributed African American news of national importance, but it too had faded by 1927. Nonetheless, the idea of economic and cultural self-determination demonstrated by the Johnsons and the Lincoln Motion Picture Company laid the foundation upon which Oscar Micheaux and Ralph Cooper's Million Dollar Productions was built and was a symbol of black cultural and economic self-determination (Bogle, 165).

Little Theater, Black Theater and Drama in Lincoln and Omaha

The rapid and dominant emergence of film as a form of mass entertainment sparked a grassroots renaissance in the dramatic arts and play writing, returning theater to its more working-class roots; yet historians disagree on the exact place and time of the Little Theatre Movement's birth. Some suggest the Little Theatres sprang up in Chicago in 1912, while others note that "between 1912 and 1916, sixty-three organizations calling themselves Little Theatres sprang up in the

United States (Chansky, 5) All sources agree that the Little Theatre Movement and those involved in it did at least three things: 1) sought to reform and challenge the overly commercial growth of theater and film as reflected in populous political changes in the early 1900s; 2) created a space that activists "founded journals; renovated buildings; wrote plays and manifestos; taught playwriting; and produced, publicized, and acted in plays;" and 3) "generated the college theater major, the inclusion of theater in secondary school curriculums, and prototypes for non-profit producing (Chansky, 3–4).

In addition to those involved in the Little Theatre Movement, black high school and college students in Omaha and Lincoln established their own dramatic groups and occasionally appeared in roles with predominantly white theater groups. Two of the earliest groups among blacks in Lincoln or Omaha before 1920 were the Toussaint Dramatic Club in South Omaha and Du Bois Dramatic Club in North Omaha. Both met regularly, usually every week or every two weeks, and both rented out local theaters to host their annual productions. For example, the Toussaint Dramatic Club performed *The Way of the World* and the Du Bois Dramatic Club presented *The Starry Flag* at Omaha's Orpheum Theater in October 1916. Black characters and roles were often played by whites, sometime in blackface, other times not, in mainstream plays in Omaha and Lincoln. By 1936 a black Nebraska University student, J. R. Lillard, became the first black student to earn a place in the University Players drama club. In the university production of *Petrified Forest*, the *Lincoln Journal Star* reported that "J. R. Lillard, playing the part of Pyles, as usual turned in a brilliant performance. He is one of the few and far between members of the Players who can be relied upon at all times, regardless of the prominence of the part played." Two years later, students at Omaha University created the "Negro Dramatics Club" and performed Henrik Ibsen's *Ghost*, under the direction of the white mother and daughter team of Jean and Delores Jarmmin, of the Omaha University and University of Iowa drama departments.

Most plays that black students performed were those written by white Negrotarians whose names became attached with Harlem or the New Negro arts and letters movement; however, a few black students wrote and directed small productions of their own. Eugene O' Neil's *The Emperor Jones*, Marc Connelly's *Green Pastures* and DuBose and Dorothy Heyward's *Porgy* became debatable favorites among black students on white campuses. In 1929, a member of Alpha Kappa Alpha's Ivy Leaf Club at the University of Nebraska at Lincoln appeared with other black members of the University Players in a staged production of *The Emperor Jones*.

Local blacks and black and white students at the University of Nebraska applauded the student production of *The Emperor Jones*; local blacks in Lincoln openly criticized the proposed productions of *Porgy* at the university. First published as a novel in 1925, and later developed as a play and musical that attracted scores of whites and some blacks to the theater, *Porgy* is the story of crippled black beggar who witnesses a murder during a dice game and becomes enamored with the murderer's woman friend. When Crown, the murderer, returns to claim Bess, Porgy kills Bess's ex-lover, and escapes conviction because no one can believe a man in Porgy's condition could kill the brutish Crown. Porgy returns to Catfish Row only to discover that Bess becomes strung-out on "happy dust" and gets "turned-out" into a life as a New York City prostitute (Breaux, 155–156).

For some blacks, particularly those outside the arts, and among the black middle class, *Porgy* glorified the worst in black folk and urban street culture. Langston Hughes, a champion of creative license and artistic freedom, praised the theater adaptation of *Porgy*, but others, such as black actors and celebrities, later lambasted the play. In Lincoln, local black ministers organized against the production sponsored by the University Dramatic Club. Ministers claimed, "The play was a deliberate attempt to feature the race at its worst" (Kerns, 28). If the play continued on as scheduled, they charged, it would intimidate blacks in Lincoln and at the University of Nebraska, and it would damage the growing spirit of interracial cooperation in the city. Representatives of the Drama Department refuted the ministers' claims. They maintained that the play was "art with no thought of reflecting on the group," the cast was almost entirely made up of black students, and the suppression of the play would represent an attempt to squash students' artist expression (Kerns, 28).

A few blacks outside of the university in Omaha involved themselves in theater, although few if any were known outside eastern Nebraska. Former Omaha University drama department assistant Andrew Reed directed the Little Theatre at Omaha's National Urban League building and appeared in several productions at the Boyd Theater. Similarly, Cecelia Jewel, wife of Dreamland Ballroom owner James Jewel, acted and sang in performances at the Boyd Theater as well. Other blacks in Omaha joined the Y Players at the North Side YMCA, but by 1933 only the local branch of the Urban League and the Quack Club for girls continued to present annual plays (WPA, 42).

The debate about whether African Americans could create art for the sake of creating art or if art had to positively represent African Americans at their best, given the prevalence of racism, remains an issue rooted in intersections of race and class. Ultimately, this is a debate about cultural self-determination—a struggle over who gets to represent black folks: middle-class African Americans, working-class African Americans or both. Socioeconomic class remains the fault line that ran just beneath the surface of the New Negro Renaissance.

Black Poets, Authors, and Short Story Writers in Lincoln and Omaha

The poetry and short stories of Harlem's literati became a point of pride among blacks in Omaha and Lincoln, yet these black Nebraskans made their own contributions to the New Negro Renaissance. Those who had the time to write or paint tended to be more middle-class and/or have completed advanced formal schooling, and the plethora of poems published by black university students, especially at the University of Nebraska at Lincoln, reflects this class privilege. Some black students and alumni of Omaha University and the University of Nebraska at Lincoln began to plant the seeds of the New Negro Renaissance as early as 1911. William N. Johnson, a former student and football player at the University of Nebraska, wrote several poems and short stories for *The Crisis* including a story titled "The Coward," which told the story of Horton, a black plowman who reflects on his family's history as slaves and tenant farmers, and yet refuses to strike back at an abusive landlord (Breaux, 153).

Black men often dominate discussions and examinations of a New Negro Renaissance expressed through the arts, but black women students, particularly at the University of Nebraska turned out a number of poems and short stories. Zanzye H. Hill received her bachelor's degree from the University of Nebraska at Lincoln and became the school's first black women law school graduate in 1929. One year before she earned her law degree, Hill wrote a coming of age poem in AKA's *Ivy Leaf* titled "My Nantie." Zanzye Hill also published another poem in the same *Ivy Leaf* titled "At Dawning." Ruth Shores Hill, also a student at the University of Nebraska at Lincoln, wrote a poem that blended her creative spirit with a solicitation to get more literary contributions to AKA's *Ivy Leaf* (Breaux, 154).

These students' poems may not have reflected the more sophisticated style of those poets historians typically associate with the New Negro Renaissance, yet the poems by black women students share some of the themes and styles adopted by New Negro arts and letters movement women writers. Historian Cheryl Wall argues that the cultural milieu of the time forced black women to suppress their gender and privilege their race; nevertheless, black women poets were not only less race conscious but also less innovative in form when compared to black male writers of the time. This meant the black women poets rarely experimented with black vernacular, or cultural expressions such as jazz, blues, or spirituals (Wall, 12–13). This was certainly almost always the case with black women student poets at the University of Nebraska at Lincoln.

The poetry written and composed by black male college students showed much less sophistication than that produced by black women students. Men tended to write poems about romantic relationships such as "My AKA Sweetheart," "I'm Married Now," and "Kappa Alpha Psi Sweetheart," or rally songs about a particular fraternity or chapter of a fraternity. Most notably, Aaron Douglas, known more for his painting and visual art than his verse, penned "Pepper" "Eta Will Shine Tonight," and "A Tribute to Eta." The poems by Douglas and others demonstrate that among black students at white universities in Nebraska, black women rather than black men experimented with a variety of styles, forms, and black cultural expressions.

Omaha's greatest contributor to the New Negro Renaissance, like Omaha's most notable son, Malcolm X, spent only a year or two as a resident of the city, yet by the end of the New Negro Renaissance, Wallace Thurman had written for *The Messenger*, had conceived and printed *FIRE!! Devoted to the Younger Negro Artists* (1926), had authored *The Blacker the Berry: A Novel of Negro Life* (1929), had written the play *Harlem: a Forum of Negro Life* (1929), and had written and published the satirical *The Infants of Spring* (1934). Undoubtedly, Thurman was the most well-known Harlem Renaissance writer with a connection to Omaha or Lincoln. According to Thurman's own account, "Omaha, Nebraska was my next stopping off place. It was there that I finished grammar school and was a high school freshman" (Singh and Scott, 91–92). In relaying his story to fellow Harlem Renaissance writer Claude McKay he recalled that he:

> lived in Chicago, and Omaha, attended the University of Utah and the University of Southern California, edited and published a magazine in Los Angeles, known as *The Outlet*, which I used up all the money I had saved and could save for several years and convinced me that I must make a hasty hegira to Harlem which at the time was coming of age.
>
> (Singh and Scott, 163–164)

Much less well known were those literature scholars Marlon Ross refers to as the New Negro social science writers. These were the men and women in Lincoln and Omaha who, in the course of completing a master's thesis or a report for the Urban League or Workers Progress Administration, "hoped to situate the future of the race at the heart of modernity—making the race modern by granting it the status of the most systematically studied group in the country according to the most up-to-date social scientific methods" (Ross, 147). Community studies such as *The Negro in Omaha*, by Harrison J. Pinkett and the WPA's *The Negroes of Nebraska*, conducted with the assistance of John Johnson, Clyde Malone, Harrison Pinkett and others for the Omaha Urban League, "literally mapped the social and physical boundaries of black masses in northern cities," in an effort to challenge whites' ideals about whether blacks could be managed and could be productive citizens and producers of culture (Ross, 147).

New Negro Painters in Lincoln and Omaha

Aaron Douglas, like his friend and fellow *FIRE!!* collaborator Wallace Thurman, spent only a brief time in Nebraska. Douglas, also like Thurman, enjoyed the privileges of higher education and a middle-class existence. Born in Topeka, Kansas in 1899, after high school Douglas enrolled at the University of Nebraska at Lincoln where he became the golden-child of the art department and the lone black member of the department's art club (Kirschke, 2–8). Black intellectual traditions and news as presented in issues of *The Crisis* magazine provided Douglas with inspiration for his artistic subjects, and after graduating with his Bachelor of Fine Arts degree in 1922, German-American artist Reinhold Weiss would further influence Douglas's art deco-like style of painting and illustration. Douglas went on to become the New Negro Renaissance's signature painter and visual artist. His work graced several covers of the two most circulated monthly magazines in black America—*The Crisis* and *Opportunity* magazine. Douglas, along with Richard Bruce Nugent, provided the artwork and illustrations for *FIRE!!* magazine, a journal that explored black folk and urban street culture, black queer romances, and black sexuality. Douglas joined Nugent, Wallace Thurman, Langston Hughes, and Zora Neale Hurston in this project. In 1936, fourteen years after Aaron Douglas graduated from NU with a degree in fine art, the Nebraska Fine Arts Council honored the artist through the acquisition of his painting "Window Cleaning," which remains a part of University of Nebraska's permanent art collection. His murals remain the center piece of the 135th Street branch of the New York City Public Library's Schomburg Center for Research in Black Culture and as a professor of art at Fisk University Douglas trained and influenced the next two generations of black visual artists.

Lesser known painters gained regional recognition among African American Nebraskans. As early as 1907, Anna Jones-Burckhardt (1868–1945) won a bronze medal certificate for her hand-painted china at the Jamestown, Virginia, Tercentennial Exposition. This award and the china were loaned again to the Jamestown Settlement Museum for inclusion in the Celebrating Jamestown exhibit in 1998. Jones-Burckhardt was married to the Rev. Oliver J. Burckhardt, a one-time Pullman porter, waiter, Nebraska State Penitentiary Chaplain, and founding member of Lincoln's Chapter of the NAACP. She became celebrated artist in Lincoln, and taught art classes in her private studio to white and black children. In 1932, she was commissioned by the governor of Nebraska to retouch the painting of General Gillespie that hangs on the eighth floor of the state capitol building (WPA, 42). At least one of her water colors is still owned by the Nebraska State Historical Museum. By the late 1930s, only one other landscape and portrait painter, John Smith, had managed to make a name for himself in Nebraska. Smith also worked in the performing arts, but as a costume designer.

Conclusion

Whether one judges the New Negro Renaissance to be a failure or a success, the far-reaching influence of the Harlem Renaissance is undeniable. The New Negro Renaissance in Omaha and Lincoln, Nebraska demonstrate that historians' continued focus on black expressive culture in New York, Washington, DC, or Chicago only distorts and limits our understanding of the New Negro Renaissance as a mass movement for cultural self-definition, self-determination, and a challenge to white cultural supremacy in the first decades of the twentieth century in the United States.

Further Reading

Allen, Ernest. "The New Negro: Explorations in Identity and Social Consciousness, 1910–1922," in *1915: Cultural Moment*, ed. Adele Heller and Lois Rudnick (New Brunswick, NJ: Rutgers University Press, 1991).

Anderson, Paul Allen. *Deep River: Music and Memory in Harlem Renaissance Thought* (Durham, NC: Duke University Press, 2001).

Bogle, Donald. *Bright Boulevards, Bold Dreams: The Story of Blacks in Hollywood* (New York: Ballantine Books, 2005).

Breaux, Richard. "The New Negro Arts and Letters Movement Among Black University Students in the Midwest, 1914–1940," *Great Plains Quarterly* 24, 3 (Summer 2004): 147–162.

Calloway, Bertha and Alonzo N. Smith. *Visions of Freedom on the Great Plains: An Illustrated History of African Americans in Nebraska* (Virginia Beach, VA: Donning Company Publishers, 1998).

Chansky, Dorothy. *Composing Ourselves: The Little Theater Movement and the American Audience* (Carbondale, IL: Southern Illinois Press, 2004).

Cripps, Thomas. *Slow Fade to Black.* New York: Oxford University Press, 1977.

Fairweather, Digby, Ian Carr and Brian Priestly, ed. *A Rough Guide to Jazz* (New York: Penguin-Rough Guides, 2004).

Haywood, Harry. *Black Bolshevik: Autobiography of an Afro-American Communist* (Chicago, IL: Liberator Press, 1978).

Keister, Douglas and Edward Zimmer. *Images of America: Lincoln in Black and White, 1910–1925* (Charleston, SC: Acadia Publishing, 2008).

Kerns, J. Harvey. "Social and Economic Status of the Negro in Lincoln, Nebraska," (Lincoln, NE: The Race Relations Committee, 1933).

Kirschke, Amy Helene. *Aaron Douglas: Art, Race, and the Harlem Renaissance* (Jackson, MI: University Press of Mississippi, 1995).

Krasner, David. *A Beautiful Pageant African American Theater, Drama, and Performance in the Harlem Renaissance, 1910–1927* (New York: Palgrave, 2002).

Locke, Alain. *The New Negro: The Negro Voices of the Harlem Renaissance* (1925, New York: Atheneum, 1992).

Love, Preston. *A Thousand Honey Creeks Later: My Life in Music from Basie to Motown and Beyond* (Hanover, NH: University Press of New England, 1997).

Mihelich, Dennis N. "The Formation of the Lincoln Urban League," *Nebraska History* 68, 2 (Summer 1987): 63–73.

Paz, D. G. "The Black Press and the Issues of Race, Politics, and Culture on the Great Plains of Nebraska, 1865–1985," in Henry Lewis Scruggs, ed. *The Black Press in the Middle West, 1865–1985* (Westport, CT: Greenwood Press, 1996), 215–233.

Ross, Marlon. *Manning the Race: Reforming Black Men in the Jim Crow Era* (New York: New York University Press, 2004).

Russell, Ross. *Jazz Style in Kansas City and the Southwest* (Berkeley, CA: University of California Press, 1971).

Singh, Amritjit and Daniel M. Scott, eds. *The Collected Writings of Wallace Thurman* (New Brunswick, NJ: Rutgers University Press, 2003).

Spencer, Jon Michael. *The New Negroes and their Music: The Success of the Harlem Renaissance* (Knoxville, TN: University of Tennessee Press, 1997).

Stewart, Jacqueline Najuma. *Migrating to the Movies: Cinema and Black Urban Modernity* (Berkeley, CA: University of California Press, 2005).

Tucker, Sherrie. *Swing Shift: "All-Girl Bands" of the 1940s* (Durham, NC: Duke University Press, 2000).

Von Noteen, Eleanore. *Wallace Thurman's Harlem Renaissance* (Amsterdam: Rodovi, 1994).

Wall, Cheryl. *Women of the Harlem Renaissance* (Bloomington, IN: University of Indiana Press, 1995).

WPA (Worker Progress Administration) Nebraska Writer's Project. *The Negroes of Nebraska* (Omaha, NE: Urban League Community Center, 1940).

Zimmer, Edward and Abigail B. Davis. "Recovered Views: African American Portraits, 1912–1925," *Nebraska History* 84, 2 (Summer 2003): 62–63.

8

HARLEM RENAISSANCE WEST

Minneapolis and St. Paul, the "Twin Cities" of Minnesota

Carolyn Wedin

During the "Harlem Renaissance" period—roughly 1920–1940—while African Americans in Minneapolis and St. Paul and elsewhere in the Mississippi River-bordering state of Minnesota took courage and cheer and inspiration from the artistic and literary activities centered in Harlem, they also increasingly found their colleagues from the East Coast too parochial, too unconcerned with the impact of art on society, too urban-centered, and too pessimistic for Upper Midwest taste. If Alain Locke, "Mr. New Negro" himself after his editing of the ground-breaking anthology of that name, could by the end of the 1930s decry the tendencies of the Harlem-centered 1920s, how much more would that be the case for artists and art-devourers even further from New York City than Locke's Howard University in Washington, DC, and by then even deeper into the Depression than the city-folk out east. Thus when we speak of the "Harlem Renaissance" just a few miles west of the Mississippi, we find a surge of activity and consciousness occurring especially in the 1930s, coincident with the WPA programs of the New Deal.

Stacy I. Morgan, in his insightful and informative *Rethinking Social Realism: African American Art and Literature, 1930–1953*, points out the importance of support of the New Deal in the 1930s particularly in areas beyond New York City. African American visual and literary artists "began to place heightened emphasis on the role of the creative artist as an agent of democratic consciousness raising and social change," he says, suggesting that the creative movement labeled "Harlem Renaissance" or "New Negro" went from being centered around the eastern seaboard to covering the whole country, like seeds growing into plants and spreading even further into blooms. "Many African American artists, writers, and cultural critics adopted an antagonistic tone toward the Harlem Renaissance during the 1930s and 1940s," says Morgan, "for what they retrospectively perceived as its modernist 'decadence.'" Illustrative of this critical attitude are Wallace Thurman's satirical novel *Infants of the Spring*, 1932, passages in Langston Hughes's *The Big Sea* of 1940, and, though Morgan does not mention it, George Schuyler and his *Black No More* of 1931—interesting especially here because Schuyler was a speaker brought to the Twin Cities and the Phyllis Wheatley Settlement House in 1938 by an interracial group of individuals and civic organizations. Alain Locke, too, became critical in this way by World War II, for example when addressing the "labor-oriented" National Negro Congress (NNC) in 1937, when he criticized "aesthetic individualism and art for art's sake." The next year Locke accused Harlem Renaissance artists of going "exhibitionist instead of going documentarian" and getting "jazz-mad and cabaret-crazy instead of getting folk-wise and sociologically sober." Thus we expect to find foundation-building in the 1920s and more innovative creative activity in the 1930s, so let us look at what was happening from 1920 to 1940 in Minneapolis and St. Paul, Minnesota.

First, it is clear that creativity in the black community was considerably stronger than the low population of blacks in this time and place would lead one to expect. The population was small in comparison to urban centers to the east, particularly after the period of the "Great Migration" of the teens, during which people gravitated to cities east of the Mississippi. In 1930, the census reported 9,445 people in the State of Minnesota classified as Negroes, or four one-hundredths of a percent. Minneapolis housed 4,176 of that group in its total population of 464,356, or nine one-hundredths of the population in that city, and St. Paul included 4,001, or one and five-hundredths percent in its total population of 271,606. By way of contrast, in Chicago, the nearest urban center east of the Mississippi, and the place where artists from the Twin Cities tended to go first when leaving Minnesota, the black population went from about 44,000 in 1910 to more than 109,000 in 1920 and over 234,000 in 1930. (The migration of African Americans to the Twin Cities from Chicago did not occur until the early 1940s, with the development of the meat-packing industry in South St. Paul.) It can be hypothesized that the lower number and percentage of blacks in the Twin Cities as contrasted to a place such as Chicago or Detroit also meant, as Calvin Schmid says in his 1937 study of the *Social Saga of the Twin Cities* (Minneapolis, MN: Minneapolis Council of Social Agencies), that "the Twin Cities have thus far avoided many serious problems of racial adjustment with which so many northern cities have had to contend" and, we might add, made it possible for creativity in the arts and literature to take precedence over ongoing struggles against discrimination and racism. Over and over again in the papers of Roy Wilkins and others who moved from Minneapolis or St. Paul to other cities, such as Kansas City, comment is made about the lesser vehemence of discrimination in the former, though, of course, it was by no means absent. Derek Reveron, a black reporter, did a piece in 1980 called "City's aged blacks link today to past" based on interviews of by then old people who had grown up in the Twin Cities, and they, too, related instances of discrimination, but concluded that it was not nearly as bad as elsewhere.

Schmid points out some other statistical characteristics of the Twin Cities that could give rise to artistic and literary consumption and achievement. The black population over ten years of age in these cities had a comparatively much lower percentage of illiteracy—for example, 1.7 percent in Minneapolis, 1.2 percent in St. Paul, versus 16.3 percent for the rest of the country. Clustering of African Americans into specific areas also played a role, almost in the way the Harlem Renaissance grew out of Harlem, becoming a "Black Metropolis" and magnet in the 1920s. Among the elderly people Reveron interviewed in 1980 was one woman from Minneapolis who reported, "I was timid until other blacks moved into the area," and a man also from that city recalled that in the 1920s "all of your sporting life lived on the north side. That's where there were black cafes, cabarets, pool halls and those sorts of things." Indeed, in Minneapolis, the "Seven Corner" district and the Near North Side became black districts.

In St. Paul, that happened with the "Rondo" district, along the Rondo Avenue and adjacent avenues between Rice and Dale Streets. This section of the capital city—which was later in the 1960s bisected and dismantled by Interstate Highway 94—housed over half of the St. Paul black population in the period of which we are speaking. The Rondo district was unique in being very much lower middle class rather than lower class and with residential, mostly one-family homes with a low population density. Roy Wilkins, who grew up there, described it in 1927 as having tree-lined streets, good transportation, and a "riot of warm colors, feelings and sounds. . . . Music is in abundance from victrolas, saxophones, player pianos and hurry-up orchestras." It is not surprising that even the huge interstate highway system could not destroy it fully, since it retains an important community center that now houses an African American theater, and one can still sit at the corner window table (in what is now called Fabulous Fern's restaurant) where playwright August Wilson, of *Fences* fame, would later compose many of his plays. Growing up in Rondo forms the basis for more than one memoir—an example is Evelyn Fairbanks' *Days of Rondo*, with its descriptions of rent parties, story-telling, music (both church and "worldly") and "good-time houses," or "tippling houses," such as Good Daddy's. David Vassar Taylor points out a newspaper of 1926 that claimed Rondo Avenue was to St. Paul what State Street was to Chicago and Lenox Avenue to Harlem "because of the variety of cultural expression it exhibited."

The importance of the Rondo neighborhood in the history of the Twin Cities has not been allowed to disappear from current resident consciousness. In 1982, Marvin "Roger" Anderson and Floyd Smaller formed a group to "bring back a sense of community, stability, and neighborhood values of the old Rondo community," and to share "the contributions of African Americans and the rich cultural history of the Rondo community to the City of Saint Paul, and the great State of Minnesota; and to bring people together to celebrate the positive growth and diversity of our beloved Rondo community" (from Rondo Days website at www.rondodays.com). The group, which would become a community-based non-profit, has since the early 1980s sponsored a range of community events, including most notably the "Rondo Days Festival" in July each year, which in 2010 included a Drill, Step and Dance Competition, Senior Recognition Dinner, and Grande Parade. As the group's website says, "it doesn't matter if you grew up here or somewhere else, we were all affected by the loss of our beloved community," but the annual celebratory event "somehow lets the music in our hearts sing and live on, again."

Most of the literature in print out of Harlem in the 1920s reached Minnesotans through the two influential magazines of the period—the NAACP's *The Crisis*, where the novelist Jessie Fauset was the highly competent literary editor and became what Langston Hughes called a "midwife" to the Harlem Renaissance, and the Urban League's *Opportunity*, launched into literary and artistic competition with *The Crisis* by its editor, Charles S. Johnson, at a Civic Club dinner in March 1924, which was held to honor Fauset and her "first novel of the Renaissance," *There is Confusion*. In *The Crisis*, sections called "The Horizon," and "Music and Art" also reported on literary and artistic things occurring throughout the country, such as the April, 1922 mention of the activities of the IXL Dramatic Club in Minneapolis and the September, 1918 election of Roy Wilkins as president of Mechanic Arts High School literary society. Who knew that he would one day become editor of *The Crisis* and executive director of the NAACP? The St. Paul branch of the NAACP, the fifth in the country, was established in 1914, and an early activity was its attempt to close the showing in St. Paul of D. W. Griffith's 1915 film, *Birth of a Nation*. The Minneapolis branch, eleventh in the country, was formed in 1921. The Twin Cities Urban League was organized in 1923, and separated into separate units for the two cities in 1938. *The Crisis* and *Opportunity* were among the benefits of membership in these organizations.

These two magazines, together with books by African Americans, were also prominent features in the library of the Phyllis Wheatley Settlement in Minneapolis, with University of Minnesota graduate Rachel James as librarian. James also served as instructor of "Negro literature." The community centers played crucial roles in the 1920s and 1930s in helping the black population with economic and social questions, but also in providing space and expertise for discussions, training, and performances. The Phillis Wheatley House opened in Minneapolis in 1924 in a building at 808 Bassett Place North, which had been the site of a frame manufacturer and the Talmud Torah School. The first director was a Scotia Women's College graduate, W. Gertrude Brown, and the settlement sponsored classes in black history and culture as well as more practical and recreational things. St. Paul had several centers: Neighborhood House, dating from 1903 and nonsectarian from 1903 onward, at Indiana and Robertson Streets; Welcome Hall Community Center, next to its church sponsor, Zion Presbyterian, at St. Anthony and Farrington Avenues; The Christian Center, begun in 1926 and housed in a $40,000 building with classrooms, music rooms, library, and reading rooms at 603 West Central Avenue from 1927 until it burned down ten years later. As David Vassar Taylor writes, this impressive venture "sponsored many social, intellectual, cultural, and religious programs for its patrons." Finally, also in St. Paul, the Urban League, Community Chest, and YWCA organized successive centers, with the still-existing Hallie Q. Brown Community Center opening just before the stock market crash of 1929. That center is now at 270 N. Kent Street, and serves as the administrative body of the Martin Luther King Center, which also houses Penumbra Theater. In the statements of the Hallie Q. Brown Center's mission and core values, is the following:

> We believe an ideal community center is one where community members of all ages, abilities, races, cultures, and economic levels . . . are linked to the community's heritage and history [and] are involved in intergenerational and cross-cultural experiences that enrich and strengthen the community as well as benefit individuals and families.

From the 1930s on, this center was home to singers of both religious and popular music, with John M. Whitaker directing. It must also be pointed out that the community centers provided an outlet for African American women's work and performances of all kinds—something that tended not to be true in the social and service clubs or even in the churches.

The settlement houses, particularly the Phillis Wheatley house in Minneapolis, also housed a regular stream of visitors from Harlem and New York City and the East, at a time when Minneapolis hotels refused to take black guests. In 1926, Head Resident W. Gertrude Brown at the Phillis Wheatley House hired Ethel Ray as Associate Head Resident, convincing Ray to return to her native Minnesota from two years in New York City. Michiko Hase says Ray "brought the intellectual and artistic ferment of the Harlem Renaissance in which she had been intimately involved"—she had in fact been secretary to Johnson, the editor of *Opportunity*, and had worked with Langston Hughes, Arna Bontemps, Countee Cullen, James Weldon Johnson and others. Ray described some of the activities she led at the Phyllis Wheatley house—reading poetry, discussing books, "trying to keep up with things that were going on [in Harlem]" (Hase quoting from David V. Taylor's 25 May 1974 interview with Ethel Ray Nance, Minnesota Historical Society). And Ray recalled Cullen, Hughes, W. E. B. Du Bois, Zora Neale Hurston, and Marian Anderson visiting the Twin Cities. (In fact, as the newspaper *Twin Cities Herald* documents, Anderson came back over and over and over again, sometimes performing with musical groups from the settlements. Visitors to the Twin Cities who also stayed at Phyllis Wheatley include Roland Hayes, Mary McLeod Bethune, and Ethel Waters.) In 1928 Ray became the first African American policewoman in Minneapolis.

FIGURE 8.1 The organization of the Federation of Negro Women in the Twin Cities was fundamental in the development of the political and social milieu that nurtured the Harlem Renaissance and reflected the increasing determination of the New Negro to address social issues

Newspapers were also important disseminators of information and literature in the 1920s and 1930s. Many subscribed to the *Chicago Defender*, but local black newspapers and magazines played important roles as well. Cecil E. Newman, long-term editor of the *Twin Cities Herald*, tried in 1932 to establish a literary magazine that he called the *Timely Digest*. When it did not "take," he began in 1934 his own newspaper called the *Minneapolis Spokesman*, which came to be the longest-lived black newspaper in Minnesota, with the *Appeal*, from the nineteenth century, next in longevity. The *Appeal*, in fact, outlasted thirteen other newspapers between 1888 and 1919. The *Northwest Monitor*, an example from the 1930s and edited by William Helm, lasted only one year. As examples of literary material, Claude McKay's poem, "America" and the NAACP Chairman Mary White Ovington's syndicated "Book Chat" were published in the *Twin Cities Herald* in 1927.

Another set of framing institutions were the black churches of the Twin Cities, which "have always sponsored a wealth of soloists, quartets, and choirs," according to Judy M. Henderson, including at "religious revivals, public gatherings with music and preaching held at places such as Minneapolis's Nicollet Island." Among Baptist churches Minneapolis had Bethesda and Zion, St. Paul Mount Olivet and

Pilgrim, the latter dating from 1863. Methodist and other protestant churches included Border AME, St. Peter's AME, St. Thomas Episcopal, and Church of God in Christ in Minneapolis; Camphor Memorial United Methodist, St. James AME and St. Philips Episcopal in St. Paul.

Finally, the annual Festival of Nations provided considerable help and encouragement to African American artists, particularly in giving them an outlet for their works and performances. This event, begun in 1932 and sponsored by the International Institute of Minnesota, celebrates "cultural diversity with food, music, demonstrations, exhibits and dance" (http://festivalofnations.com). In one of its early years "a large mixed chorus of Negro voices, completed the American episodes"; "an exhibit of Negro art with a talented young sculptor from the Negro community working in the booth was interesting to many visitors to whom Negro art was entirely unknown"; and "a large group of young Negro tap dancers in rainbow hues" spread cheer at the Festival as in American life. Finally, in what is undoubtedly a reference to the ultimately very successful photographer for *Life* magazine, filmmaker and author, Gordon Parks, Alice Sickels in her 1945 *Around the World in St. Paul*, tells us that:

> [the] Negro exhibit chairman told the committee about one very practical result of their Festival contacts. One of their young men took some pictures of the school festivals, the Institute supplying the materials and paying him for his time. These were exhibited and a local businessman saw them and hired the young man to do some photography for him. Other stores called for his services, and soon he was able to give up his job as a railroad porter and open a photographic studio in Chicago, where he has been successful.

Sickels concludes this brief narration with the comment: "young people in the minority groups against whom there is stereotyped prejudice urgently need opportunities to be known as individuals."

As the 1930s advanced and the Great Depression deepened, the river of social programs pouring out of the Franklin Roosevelt administration of necessity increased. Disadvantage in the black community was there from the beginning. As David Taylor says:

> black people of Minneapolis and St. Paul had never fully participated in the prosperity of the 1920s. (As early as 1919, it was estimated that the median wage of a black male head of household in the Twin Cities was only $22.55 per week at a time when the United States Bureau of Labor Statistics regarded $43.51 per week as the amount necessary for a family of five.)

Then, as the Depression continued, the eleven railroad lines that served the Twin Cities began laying off the porters and redcaps who had depended on this employment for sustenance, and small black businesses were forced to close their doors. By 1938, the Urban League estimated that 69 percent of Twin City blacks were on some kind of federal assistance, either direct relief or assistance programs such as the Civilian Conservation Corps (CCC), or the many programs that came under the umbrella of the Works Projects Administration, including the Federal Writers' Project (FWP), the Public Works of Art Project, the Treasury Department's Section of Painting and Sculpture, the FAP, or Federal Arts Project in the Visual Arts, and the Federal Music Project. Though the percentage of African Americans employed in any of these programs was small, yet their activities in the community and state had a positive spillover effect on other artists. "Black cultural activity" funded by these programs included the group called the Twin Cities Jubilee Singers, which brought African American music, especially spirituals and popular and patriotic songs, to community churches and schools. The two dozen people in the group were paid semi-skilled laborers' wages of ninety-three dollars a month for their many hours per day of practice and their performances, under the direction of Samuel Herrod—not a lot, but better than nothing. Sculptor Robert Crump, from St. Paul and employed in the Federal Arts Project, created a statue of Leonidas Merritt that was erected in 1940 at Mountain Iron, Minnesota, and other works in the State. And Estyr Bradley Anderson was employed by the Federal Writers' Project to serve as social correspondent for the *St. Paul Recorder* and the *Minneapolis Spokesman.*

With these various frames in mind, let us turn now to some more specific examples of artistic creativity among African Americans in the Twin Cities between 1920 and 1940. Since music, as one of the few means of expression left for slaves brought from Africa, became such an important part of daily as well as cultural life, and is, in many ways, more accessible than other forms of art, we will begin there, with a surprising and somewhat humorous story. Beginning in 1914, the white women leaders of Minneapolis, particularly those who belonged to the Daughters of the American Revolution, or DAR, concluded that the Minneapolis City Hall should have chimes that could play patriotic music, particularly "The Star-Spangled Banner." They raised money from their own group, from other groups and individuals, from school children and churches, and at last in 1923, the chimes were installed and ready to ring out. And what was one of the first concerts on the chimes? On June 6 of the following year, as part of a Symphony Drive, Isham Jones, leader of a vaudeville orchestra, gave a concert of—"jazz music." Not very old at the time, with the first use of the words "jazz" or "jass" from Chicago in 1915, this kind of musical amalgam from Africa, from the American South, from popular song and from European concert music was not seen as particularly circumspect and stately when it rang out from Minneapolis City Hall. But what it definitely was was "Negro Music," and thus an interesting choice for a very public concert. Incidentally, by 1928 the Minneapolis chimes were heard throughout the United States on radio, and in 1933 the chimes fell silent due to budget cuts, leading to much lamenting in local articles and editorials.

We should probably keep in mind in the following that most music and musicians came in these years not from primary employment, but from informal activity, or moonlighting or volunteering. In 1926, Abram L. Harris, who would later get his doctorate at Columbia University and hold distinguished professorial appointments at Howard University in Washington, DC and the University of Chicago, came to Minneapolis for a year, as executive secretary of the Urban League. While there, he created mostly on his own a report on "The Negro Population in Minneapolis," the most important study on the city up to that time. Using people from the local Urban League chapter, he did interviews throughout the city with blacks, and with white employers and trade union leaders. Among the 275 "Men with Families" interviewed about their employment, there were a total of only four musicians. But music is likely longer-standing as an encouragement to black culture and identity than just the Harlem Renaissance period, and is more important to that period, too, than is usually hypothesized. As Samuel A. Floyd, Jr. writes in the introduction to his collection of essays:

> The Harlem Renaissance has been treated primarily as a literary movement, with occasional asides . . . about the jazz age and the performances of concert artists. But music's role was much more basic and important to the movement. In fact, the stance of the black leadership and scattered brief comments about music during the period suggest the primacy of music to the Renaissance philosophy and practice.

For a cohesive discussion of African American music in Minnesota, an excellent small booklet by Judy M. Henderson accompanies her CD of *African-American Music in Minnesota: From Spirituals to Rap*. We will begin with gospel, which early in the twentieth century absorbed secular music such as "the syncopated bass line of ragtime music" and, in the 1930s, with pianist Thomas A. Dorsey, the "father of modern gospel music," the blues. Gospel songs such as "Precious Lord, Take My Hand" became part of religious services elsewhere before they did in basically conservative Minnesota, where, as Henderson says, the African American community first thought of it as "music of the street" and less than dignified. But touring groups from Chicago and other urban northern cities introduced the music at revival meetings, and Minnesota musicians wrote them down as they heard them, rearranged them, memorized them, and eventually were able to include them in Sunday services. Henderson also describes what the church organist or pianist had to be able to do, usually unpaid—play hymns, spirituals, and gospel music, and often "improvise quietly in the background while a minister delivers a lengthy talk or prayer."

Turning to the secular, particularly jazz, Henderson notes that:

> much of Minnesota's early jazz was played by white musicians imitating the sounds of famous artists who toured the state, such as Count Basie,

Duke Ellington, and Lionel Hampton. [We could add Fletcher Henderson, "king of swing"; Cab Calloway and the Cotton Club Review; Earl Hines and his orchestra; and Louis "Satchmo" Armstrong]. Black players seldom played for white audiences, but white players joined their black counterparts at some clubs, including Minneapolis's Clef Club, for late-night jam sessions.

By the 1930s in Minneapolis people streamed to locations such as the Nest Club with El Herbert's Dixieland band; and the South Side Club, with Lester "Prez" Young on tenor saxophone. In the suburb of Wayzata, the Cotton Club opened in the late 1930s. In St. Paul, El Herbert, with Harry Pettiford, Hillard "Rook" Ganz, and others played at the Swing City nightclub, pianist Paul Cephus and the "Sepia Serenaders" at Allen's Tavern. Many clubs hosted black musicians, and the settlement houses and community centers sponsored groups—St. Paul's Hallie Q. Brown House had its "Merry Men of Rhythm" and the Minneapolis' Phyllis Wheatley Settlement had the "Downbeats." These groups began a regular "battle of the bands" fundraising contest, in highly decorated gymnasiums transformed into night clubs. From these contests came many subsequently successful performers, such as trumpeter Mel Carter, Sr. and saxophonist Percy Hughes, Jr. Henderson continues:

> Another talented family, the Pettifords, began playing in Minneapolis and small towns in the mid-1920s. Later, siblings Oscar, Marjorie, Harry, Ira, and others performed on their own throughout the area. Oscar Pettiford started a string trio that played Twin Cities nightclubs, including Swing City in the early 1940s. He later became a nationally famous jazz bassist, playing with the bands of Charlie Barnet, Dizzy Gillespie, Woody Herman, and Duke Ellington. An outstanding cellist as well, he also had his own jazz group in New York City. Marjorie Pettiford played with a popular black women's band, the International Sweethearts of Rhythm. . . . Harry Pettiford's energetic 1941 tenor-saxophone composition "Harry's Idea" [on CD] reflects the effortlessly improvisational nature of jazz, especially as performed by a member of this gifted family.

Another piece of jazz on Henderson's CD is by pianist Rufus Webster, who played in and arranged pieces for a group called the Four Jesters of Rhythm. The piece, as Henderson says, "shows off the magnitude of technique required of jazz musicians who played in bands of the 1940s."

"Concert music" was by no means absent. As mentioned earlier, Marian Anderson made many trips to the Twin Cities, always to anticipatory headlines, very large crowds and rave reviews from both black and white papers. When the DAR refused to allow Anderson to sing in their Constitution Hall in Washington, DC in 1939 and Eleanor Roosevelt resigned from the organization and arranged for Anderson to sing at the Lincoln Memorial instead, Cecil E. Newman, editor of the *Minneapolis Spokesman*, wrote his lead editorial on "Courageous Mrs. Roosevelt." And Roland Hayes was praised by the music editor of the *Minneapolis Tribune*, a white paper, as providing one of the very best concerts in the city ever.

Musical theater, drama, and dance, like other forms of art, combined visiting groups and productions with home-grown products. *Green Pastures*, by Marc Connelly, which had won the Pulitzer Prize and broken all Broadway records, brought its cast of a hundred to the Twin Cities in 1932 and performed for a week at the Metropolitan Theater. As Josephine Baker gained in fame in Paris, the *Twin Cities Herald* in 1927 wrote "remember when she was a chorus girl here in *Shuffle Along?*" Tap dancer Bill Robinson, "the Dark Cloud of Joy" or "the Man with the Laughing Feet" was joined by Ada Brown, "The Chocolate Kate Smith" and his fifty "Goin' to Town" beauties for a week at the Orpheum in 1933. And next door to Minnesotans, at 816 E. 36th Street, Minneapolis, resided the dancing team of Johnson and Dean (Mr. and Mrs. Charles Johnson), who introduced the city to the cake walk at the Lake Harriet pavilion in 1893, who had "played every civilized country on the globe" in "the world's greatest theatres," and who were performing at the Minnesota theater in the fall of 1939, over fifty years after originating their act. Phyllis Wheatley Settlement included Drama as one of its four departments, and produced an impressive list of plays, some original, some not.

African American visual artists during our time period included sculptor Robert Crump, already mentioned, and Henry (Mike) Bannarn, sculptor and painter. Grandson of a couple who came to Minnesota directly following the Civil War, Bannarn was academically trained at the Minneapolis School of Fine Arts and the Beaux Arts Institute of Design in New York City. He in turn trained others, teaching drawing at the Phyllis Wheatley House and sculpture at the Harlem Community Art Center. His work adorned the walls of the Wheatley House and the cover of its newsletter, "Meow"; he won first prize at the Minnesota State Fair for his sculptures; and his paintings were included in the New York and touring exhibits of the Harmon Foundation. We have also previously mentioned Gordon Parks, who spent his formative years with a sister and brother-in-law in St. Paul, and, as Maren Stange describes, dropped out of high school to work a series of Depression jobs—bartender, piano player, CCC lumberjack, basketball player, ranch hand, and bandleader, before he chanced upon a magazine of documentary photos from the Farm Security Administration photography project, left by a passenger on the train where he worked as a dining car waiter. He had found his calling—something that did not require college and allowed him to express his creativity, as he said. He viewed more photos at the Art Institute in Chicago when the train was in that city, took his own first published images in Seattle, and was hired to do fashion photography back in St. Paul. Finally, architect Cap Wigington was made municipal architect of the city of St. Paul in

1915, and left his mark on many a stone in that city. As David Taylor points out, he also did some fantastic ephemeral work, in the form of highly creative ice sculptures for the St. Paul Winter Carnival.

Local white reaction to the African American community became more visible and positive during the years we are looking at. Michiko Hase points out that more attention began to be paid in white newspapers during and just after World War I, indicated by the index of the Minneapolis *Journal*, which added the category "Negroes" at this time. The number of pages of entries in that division increased from one in 1918 to two in 1919 and more than two in 1920, and then dropped back to a half page for the rest of the decade. And while events such as the lynchings in Duluth, Minnesota, in 1920, called attention to extreme discrimination and danger for the African American, the Twin Cities retained a somewhat integrated stance, at least in the settlement houses, where, as Head Resident W. Gertrude Brown said, "It is a real pleasure to see all races use the House in harmony, and see the joy they get from working together" (Her Annual Report of 1929, quoted by Hase). Integrated organizations such as the Interracial Committee of Women's International League for Peace and Freedom and the Council of Churches of America also met there. In 1935 the NAACP's *The Crisis* included an article called "An Interracial Settlement House" about the Minneapolis Phyllis Wheatley. Mixed company was also part of what were called "black and tan" places—dance halls and cafes patronized by both races, though the latter were considered disreputable by many, and were "visited" by police more than once, for example, in April, 1931.

What is the legacy of the Harlem Renaissance period, 1920–1940, in the Twin Cities of Minneapolis and St. Paul? First, it must be said that here, as elsewhere during this time, artistic expression of all kinds increased both in volume and in prominence in the black community, and in that community's relation to the larger white population. But it must be added that in part because the percentage of black population here has remained small as contrasted with other cities, the "New Negro" spirit of cohesiveness and identity spreading its wings over the country from its nest in Harlem was less intense in these cities just west of the Mississippi than it was likely to be in cities with a higher black population. This comes out early and late. An early assessment is found in a short piece by Roy Wilkins written when he was twenty-two years old, called "Minnesota: Seat of Satisfaction." The article was originally published in *The Messenger*, the radical newspaper of labor activist A. Philip Randolph and economist Chandler Owen coming out of New York City, and controversial throughout its period of publication, from 1917 to 1928. Toward the end of this publishing period, *The Messenger* ran a series somewhat imitative of one that had appeared in *The Nation*, wherein each state of the union was described by an author or prominent person from that state. (Sinclair Lewis wrote about Minnesota in *The Nation*'s series.) *The Nation* said its purpose was "to counteract the excessively cosmo- politan, urban, and largely pessimistic view of America that was the seeming consensus of New York's young intellectuals." Wilkins, in his *Messenger* piece, begins with the usual praise for his home state, and then attacks the apathy of Minnesota African Americans. They do not take advantage of the educational opportunities in the state, he says; churches do not do anything, and there is no protest against increasing restrictions. "Satisfaction," as it turns out, is a two-edged sword.

An example of a later assessment is the article published in 1975 by Mary Jane Saunders in the St. Paul *Pioneer Press* entitled "Blacks Express Divided Opinion on Local Area." First she points out that the "total black population has remained comparatively small." Then she quotes various people from within and outside the state, including a young university student from out state, who describes "Minnesota niggers" who "act white, think white, date white, and lack a cohesive black community spirit." Five years later, Saunders published a piece on Twin City blacks in the corporate world, and one young interviewee described older blacks as more willing to play what he called the "schizoid personality," using one type of speech and language around whites, a different one to blacks. Lacking the numbers to form full, self-sufficient black communities, businessmen and others instead built support systems of social and religious and civic organizations.

But overall, this history does not lead us to such a negative conclusion. Perhaps the integration and mutual respect accorded blacks and whites in some of our story does not fit with some more militant time periods. Integration is not assimilation. Integration requires equally valued entities. It is clear to this writer, at least, that the 1920–1940 period greatly enhanced the regard among whites for black literature and art, and that integration as an ideal goal is still to be valued.

Further Reading

Carett, Kate. *Voices of Rondo: Oral Histories of Saint Paul, Historic Black Community.* Minneapolis, MN: Syren Book Company, 2005.

Carter, Ennis and Christopher DeNoon. *Posters for the People: The Art of the WPA.* Philadelphia, PA: Quirk Books, 2008.

Fairbanks, Evelyn. *Days of Rondo.* St. Paul, MN: Minnesota Historical Society Press, 1990.

Floyd, Samuel A., Jr., ed. *Black Music in the Harlem Renaissance.* Knoxville, TN: University of Tennessee Press, 1990, 1993.

Harris, Abram L., Jr. "The Negro Population in Minneapolis." In *Race, Radicalism, and Reform: Selected Papers Abram L. Harris,* ed. William Darity, Jr. New Brunswick, Oxford: Transaction Publishers, 1989. 64–99. First published Minneapolis, MN: The National Urban League Papers, 1926.

Hase, Michiko. "W. Gertrude Brown's Struggle for Racial Justice: Female Leadership and Community in Black Minneapolis, 1920–1940." Dissertation, University of Minnesota, 1994.

"The Heart of Bassett Place: W. Gertrude Brown and The Wheatley House." Minneapolis, MN: South Hill Films, 2006. DVD.

Henderson, Judy M. *African-American Music in Minnesota: From Spirituals to Rap.* St. Paul, MN: Minnesota Historical Society Press, 1994. (Booklet with CD.)

Morgan, Stacy I. *Rethinking Social Realism: African American Art and Literature, 1930–1953.* Athens and London: The University of Georgia Press, 2004.

North Star: Minnesota's Black Pioneers. Minneapolis, MN: Twin City Public Television, 2005. 90 Minutes. DVD.

O'Connor, Francis V., ed. *Art for the Millions: Essays from the 1930s by Artists and Administrators of the Works Progress Administration Federal Art Project.* Greenwich, CT: New York Graphic Society, 1977.

Sickels, Alice L. *Around the World in St. Paul.* Minneapolis, MN: University of Minnesota Press, 1945.

Spencer, Jon Michael. *The New Negroes and Their Music: the Success of the Harlem Renaissance.* Knoxville, TN: University of Tennessee Press, 1997.

Stange, Maren. "Gordon Parks: A World of Possibility." In *Bare Witness: Photographs by Gordon Parks.* Stanford, CA: Skira in Association with Iris & B. Gerald Cantor Center for Visual Arts at Stanford University. 2006. 9–27.

Taylor, David Vassar. *African Americans in Minnesota.* St. Paul, MN: Minnesota Historical Society Press, 2002.

——. *Cap Wigington: An Architectural Legacy in Ice and Stone.* St. Paul, MN: Minnesota Historical Society Press, 2002.

Wilkins, Roy (with Tom Matthews). *Standing Fast: The Autobiography of Roy Wilkins.* New York: Viking Press, 1982.

9

THE SAN ANTONIO/AUSTIN RENAISSANCE

Where "the Daddies of Jazz" Remembered the Alamo

Jeanette N. Passty

Decades of scholarly research and debate have brought us a wide range of perspectives regarding what Hubert Harrison's newspaper, *The Voice*, recognized in 1917 as the "New Negro Movement." Explorers of diversity and restorers of lost history have demonstrated that blacks, even while slaves, were intellectually astute and aesthetically proficient; that "from Emancipation" on, Washington, DC was the locus of "a proto-Harlem Renaissance" culture (Pierpont, 99); that the so-called "Renaissance" concept "overlooked," as Harrison himself argued in 1927 in the *Pittsburgh Courier*, "the stream of literary and artistic products that had flowed uninterruptedly from Negro writers from 1850 to the present" ("Harlem Renaissance").

While efforts continue to rediscover and redefine for future generations new milestones in the African American experience, in one area there is certainty: With slavery abolished, "education became the cherished goal of the Negro race" (Brawner, 2). Meanwhile, people of color in America were precluded by segregation from attaining that goal. As Episcopal Bishop James Steptoe Johnston, founder of St. Philip's Industrial School in downtown San Antonio in 1896, lamented, "It is the most difficult race problem a free people ever faced" (Norris, 43). To counteract their exclusion from the prevailing culture, blacks throughout the US—aided and abetted as they have been since Colonial times by people of faith and of conscience—invented a "parallel universe" for themselves. This was certainly true in South Texas, where colleges and universities, libraries, schools, churches, fraternities, sororities, businesses, and individuals created a cascading Renaissance in African American letters, arts, science and technology. Thus began a historic time when, as a prominent Prairie Lea educator has remarked, "Everyone had a Harlem" (Brown and Brown).

South Texas cities and towns benefited during this exemplary, post-Emancipation effort: In Austin the Congregational Church founded Tillotson Collegiate and Normal Institute (1881), a progenitor of Huston-Tillotson University; in Houston Pastor Jack Yates established a Baptist Academy (1885), which provided an alternative to the Colored High School of the public school system and became an antecedent of Texas State University for Negroes (later Texas Southern University) where muralist John Thomas Biggers came to prominence during the Harlem Renaissance and founded the art department. In Seguin the Black Baptist Church established Guadalupe College, destined in its all-too-brief lifespan (1884–1936) to become a junior college and then a fully accredited four-year institution until a corporate land grab, a devastating fire, religious discord, and the Great Depression reduced it to ruined buildings and a deserted campus. In San Marcos the Durham family—parents, children, and cousins—became a musical dynasty with an influence that extended beyond New York to Europe.

Rural areas were subject to the same cultural ferment. In the Gulf Coast Region of Texas, idealists and entrepreneurs made several attempts to found all black townships and farming communities. While these assumed prominence in Kansas, and remain popular tourist destinations in Oklahoma, such utopian efforts in Texas proved ephemeral. Many attempts at education and advancement in "the Lone Star State" were inhibited by the pervasive racism of the time. In Bastrop, as Captain C. L. Leonard, U.S. Air Force Ret. recalls, this would ultimately lead to:

> not one, not two, but three separate high schools. The white high school would receive new textbooks and send their used books to the Hispanic high school. The same practice was followed with basketball, football, and band uniforms, with athletic equipment, musical instruments. Then the Hispanic high school would send what they had used to us, at the black high school. And we were a *small* town . . .
>
> (Leonard)

As Bastrop went, so went the state capital: In 1933 to make way for the construction of a larger central library facility its diminutive predecessor was lifted from its foundation and moved to East Austin after the American Association of University Women (AAUW) helped residents successfully petition the city for a public library. This second-hand "Colored Branch" on Angelina Street, renamed the "Carver Branch" in 1947, a "1,896 square-foot" "wood-framed structure" with "brick veneer," was the only public library facility in Central-East Austin.

Anne Brawner's history of Guadalupe College in Seguin, which begins with "the background of Black education in Texas" explains how "harsh laws forbidding the instruction of slaves in the basic learning skills" were succeeded in the post-Emancipation era by an effort to levy on Negroes a special state tax for the establishment and maintenance of their children's schools, an endeavor regarded by whites first with hostility and then with indifference (Brawner, 2). Ernestine Ketchum Tanner, born in Slayden, Texas on the east bank of the San Marcos River in the early 1920s, explains in her memoir *Sharecropper's Daughter* (1998) how the primary and secondary schools she attended in Luling and Seguin counteracted scarcity with ingenuity: Children were involved in "drama and acting," with a "school closing play," using elaborately contrived crepe paper costumes, at the end of each academic year, as well as annual "scholastic league" competitions in spelling and public speaking, "every year at the county seat" (Tanner, 86–88, 98–99).

Tanner details how she and her classmates washed, dried, and dyed Bull Durham tobacco sacks, in colors created with "bluing" "boiled leaves, flowers, berries, or coffee," sometimes imprinting designs on them by using pressed leaves or flowers. "Some expressed unusual talent" in the creation of these small works of art, which, when dry, were stuffed with cotton, stitched together into ornamental pillows, and sold, with the proceeds used "to buy some equipment for the classroom for all to use and enjoy" (59–60). The children made vases from discarded jars and bottles, baskets and decorative doorstops from soda pop caps, ornamental pincushions from "bits of cloth" and "empty wasp or yellow jacket nests." They dug up and sculpted "clay," which when dried became:

> bowls and plates, as well as glasses, tables, and houses. . . . soldiers with guns and Indians with bows and arrows . . .. clay wells with buckets . . . the sides decorated by making the appearance of blocks. [We formed] mud animals . . . [such as] . . . Horses, pigs, and chickens. . . . Mud was rolled to make fences, pig pens, barns, [wood] piles or corded wood, and a farm. The farm could be built and fenced in with logs, there were cabins and barns stocked with cattle, horses and all.
>
> (Tanner, 60)

The same order of ingenuity was exercised to create in the Ketchum family's succession of seven homes a "place for family teaching," i.e. the front or back porch where the Bible was taught and the children were obliged to memorize and recite individual verses, and where Bessie and Tyler Ketchum improvised "a stage" for their eleven children: "[C]hairs would be placed in the yard, and each child was called on to [ascend the steps and] perform. He or she could sing a song or say a speech while others looked on from the yard below" (Tanner, 41).

The family frequently visited musical friends: a grandmother, her widowed son, and his children. Situated "just outside the school yard" in Luling, their home had a piano:

> Pianos were pretty rare in homes in those days. The oldest girl would play the piano, and we would gather around and sing. . . .

> The five children were extraordinary. The oldest boy became a famous gospel singer, and he carried the gospel songs to other areas. . . . [T]he oldest [sister] married a preacher, which created an opportunity for her to continue her singing. The third child, a girl, had one of the most beautiful voices one could hope to hear. She became a leader of choirs and contributed her voice and singing all over San Antonio.
>
> (Tanner, 103)

The fourth child, a boy, became a preacher; the fifth, a girl, remained as the guardian of the family homestead.

Opportunities to make and enjoy music were also available at "a clubhouse . . . that had been donated to the blacks for various celebrations in the town of Luling and its surrounding areas. . . . The main area is a large room. Dancing used to be done there during the nineteenth of June celebration." Outdoors at the same facility was "a little platform" and a place where "chairs . . . [could] be put . . . for programs in the open air" (Tanner, 102). It is tempting to speculate that during the Roosevelt Era this became the venue for the "widow with five children" from "a nearby town" who taught in an adult education program funded by the Works Progress Administration. She arrived early to call on prospective students and their families in their homes. She recruited many students by hosting Chautauqua-style public debates, after which "many stayed over" to attend her evening school classes (94). Ernestine took part in one such "heated debate":

> to determine who was the wisest, the one who invented the phonograph record or the one who invented the radio . . . I chose the man who invented the phonograph record because to me it was a mystery how the voice could be on a record. The speaker did not have to be present; the record could lay around, and one could always go back and hear something again.
>
> (Tanner, 94)

Ernestine Tanner's depiction of rural Texas in the Harlem Renaissance era also paints a lively picture of the Seguin "juke joints" (from Gullah "juke," i.e. "bad, wicked, disorderly," *American Heritage Dictionary*) where, stylish in the new "lay-away" clothes for which she had paid "twenty-five cents a week" with money earned as a washerwoman, she took part in the vibrant local night life:

> The blacks had their own places of recreation and entertainment. There was a long street with a line of cafes for this. . . . There was food and dancing. We usually went from one café to another, meeting others while talking and walking. All of the places had . . . fish, chicken, hamburgers, chili, hot dogs, soft drinks, and beer, . . . colorful tablecloths, . . . [and] juke boxes. Seguin, being near San Antonio and Randolph field, was near all the bases

in the area. Some of the partygoers who did not go to San Antonio went to Seguin.

(Tanner, 104–105)

"On Saturday nights, there was lots of action in Seguin," as Tanner recalls. "The food was good" (105), but the music was usually from recordings on 78 RPM discs, which could hold about three to three-and-a half minutes of continuous sound ("Gramophone record"). By contrast, in San Marcos, twenty-nine miles from Austin and twenty-one miles from Seguin, the music was live.

"Throughout the history of jazz," Dave Oliphant explains in his brilliant online survey of that quintessential Harlem Renaissance genre:

> Texans have contributed to the important movements in this native American music, beginning with blues, ragtime, and boogie-woogie in the early years of the twentieth century and continuing with hot jazz in the 1920s, swing in the '30s, bebop in the '40s. . . . [Whether] as composers, arrangers, or sidemen . . . a number of Texas musicians have figured as outstanding soloists and as leaders of vital, innovative groups of their own. Although Texas was the home to a large number of territory bands, most of the significant performances by Texans were recorded outside the state, principally in Chicago, New York, Kansas City, and Los Angeles. Yet wherever Texans have traveled, they have always taken with them something of their own musical heritage.
>
> (Oliphant, "Jazz")

The Durham extended family, a musical dynasty with roots in South Central Texas, was destined to become a major musical influence throughout the US and around the world. San Marcos, where future US President Lyndon Baines Johnson attended Southwest Texas State Teachers' College (1926–1927, 1928–1930), was the birthplace of virtuoso Eddie Durham (1906–1987), jazz guitarist, trombonist, composer, arranger, innovator of the "riff" (Club Kaycee, "Durham"), and pioneer of the "amplified guitar" (Oliphant, "Durham"). Eddie's father, Joseph Durham Sr., "played the fiddle at square dances." His oldest brother, Joe Jr., who had "served as musical director for Teddy Roosevelt's Rough Riders Cavalry Band during World War I," having first learned through correspondence lessons to read and notate music, taught these skills to his brothers, Eddie, Earl, and Roosevelt, and then organized them, his sister Myrtle who played piano, and later his cousins Allen Durham, Clyde Durham, and Herschel "Tex" Evans into the Durham Brothers Orchestra (Oliphant, "Durham").

Born in Denton, Texas in 1909, Evans, a composer and tenor saxophonist who had performed with Lionel Hampton and Buck Clayton, left a lasting musical legacy before he succumbed to heart disease in New York City at the age of thirty. From 1929 to 1932 he played with the Troy Floyd orchestra in San Antonio. Later he became "a featured soloist in Count Basie's Big Band" where he made definitive recordings of the "popular 'One O'Clock Jump'" as well as the hit "Blue and Sentimental." Composer of "Texas Shuffle" and "Doggin' Around," both popular "hits," Evans also should be credited with "starting his cousin, Joe McQueen's, interest in saxophone" ("Herschel Evans"), hailed by musicologist Brian Priestley as "the instrument which had come to the forefront in popular music and jazz" (5). McQueen, born in Dallas, Texas in 1919, had moved with his family to Oklahoma and was a tuba player in the Ardmore High School band. "Introduced to the [jazz] saxophone by his cousin, Herschel Evans, who played in Count Basie's band in the mid 1930s," McQueen quickly matured as a musician ("Joe McQueen"). At sixteen, he "began playing professional jazz"; at twenty-six, he became a band leader, helping to maintain the reputation of Ogden, Utah as a "hot spot for jazz music":

> In 1945, McQueen and his wife, Thelma, traveled to Ogden, Utah. He was at the time in a jazz band that dissolved when its leader gambled away the troupe's earnings *en route* from Las Vegas. McQueen reformed the band and stayed in Ogden. Ogden, Utah, in the near post-WWII era was a major stop on the railroad route west to San Francisco, California from Kansas City and beyond.
>
> ("Joe McQueen")

"In his early years" Joe McQueen "worked and played at the Porters and Waiters Club" and ultimately became a "truck mechanic and automotive technology instructor at Weber State University." However that—and other paid and volunteer jobs he has held—did not prevent him from becoming "the first African-American in Utah to play at previously white-only establishments and to have a mixed-race band" ("Joe McQueen"). Featured with that band in Ogden have been "jazz luminaries such as Charlie Parker, Chet Baker . . . Paul Gonsalves, Lester Young, Count Basie, Duke Ellington, Dizzy Gillespie, and others" ("Joe McQueen").

As of 2010, Joe McQueen, in recent years celebrated in a "documentary film," an Associated Press feature article, and a proclamation by the Governor of Utah, is continuing his work "as a full-time volunteer elder care worker; in this capacity he assists infirm senior citizens" ("Joe McQueen"). This extraordinary exponent of the Harlem Renaissance and the Durham jazz dynasty "continues to perform live in clubs in Ogden and record at the age of 90" ("Joe McQueen"), empowering the present generation as Brian Priestley (19) writes of Duke Ellington "listen to the details, and savor the craft and the soul that went into this music."

In 2002, April 18th was proclaimed "Joe McQueen Day" by the Governor of Utah. In 2003 in the South Texas "Corridor" between Austin and San Antonio, San Marcos designated August 19th as "Eddie Durham Day" and declared the neighborhood where he was raised to be a "Historical District." Rescued by community activists, one "modest building" there is now "a history museum detailing African American heritage in San Marcos" ("Calaboose"). But preservationists have been unable to prevent the demolition of many "homes dating back almost a century," including "what was believed to be the Durham family home" by developers who attempted to profit from the Dunbar neighborhood's "prime location near downtown" (Schwartz). Efforts by local blacks in the years since to create a Durham Family Archival Museum (Oliphant, "Durham"), pitted the minuscule Calaboose African American History Museum on MLK Drive—from 1885 until the 1940s a jail exclusively for "black and mentally challenged prisoners" and in World War II "a USO Center for black servicemen" —against the mighty Smithsonian Institution in Washington, DC. Both requested Eddie Durham's memorabilia from his daughter Marsha (Schwartz).

In a letter to the San Marcos City Council in support of Dunbar, "Phil Schaap, jazz director of the Lincoln Center in New York, wrote . . . 'This native of your city is a titan—perhaps *the* titan—of 20th century music'" (quoted in Schwartz; emphasis added). Speaking at nearby Texas State University, Dan Morgenstern, the Director of the Institute of Jazz Studies at Rutgers University who had interviewed Durham extensively "over a ten-year period in the 70s," hailed him as "a major player in the history of jazz." Morgenstern especially appreciates Eddie Durham's versatility. Durham . . . helped develop what we now know as Swing music, was a master trombonist, helped electrify the guitar and is perhaps best known for his musical arrangements. Even those who know little about jazz could identify one of Durham's most popular songs: Glenn Miller's "In the Mood" (Walker).

Durham began his itinerant professional career on guitar and trombone at ten and was touring the US and playing for circuses with the 101 Ranch Band by the time he was eighteen. By the time he was twenty, he had performed in Yankee Stadium and was touring the Southwest with a jazz group "before joining the Blue Devils . . . in 1928" Durham spoke "Spanish primarily until he was 12, and his early recordings with the Oklahoma City Blue Devils were in Spanish subtitles" (Walker). From 1929 to 1933 he "played with Bennie Moten out of Kansas City. . . [then] moved to New York in 1934" (Oliphant, "Durham") During the 1930s and 1940s "his early training in music theory" led to his composing and/or arranging music for "four important bands from Oklahoma, Missouri, and Tennessee: the Blue Devils, Bennie Moten, Count Basie, and Jimmie Lunceford" (Oliphant, "Durham"):

> The tunes Durham composed or arranged for these bands include such classics as "Moten Swing," "Swinging the Blues," "Topsy," "John's Idea," "Time Out," "Out the Window," "Every Tub," "Sent for You Yesterday," "One O'Clock Jump," "Jumpin' at the Woodside," "Lunceford Special," "Harlem Shout," and "Pigeon Walk."
>
> (Oliphant, "Durham")

During a prolific and distinguished musical "career [that] spread out over more than 60 years" (Walker), Durham also arranged music for Artie Shaw and Glenn Miller, among other white big bands of the Swing Era; Durham contributed to one of Miller's greatest hits, "In the Mood." He is primarily considered a key figure in working out arrangements in the famous Kansas City riff style (Oliphant, "Durham").

Significantly, aficionados who view the riff as "the foundation of the Kansas City sound" (Club Kaycee, "Durham"), also cite this definition from J. Bradford Robinson in *The New Grove Dictionary of Jazz* (1988):

> [a] short melodic ostinato, usually two or four bars long, which may either be repeated intact (strict riff) or varied to accommodate an underlying harmonic pattern. The *riff* is thought to derive from the repetitive call-and-response patterns of West African music, and appeared prominently in black-American music from the earliest times.
>
> (Club Kaycee, "Glossary")

By 1929, in an attempt to enhance the projection of his six-string guitar, Eddie Durham "began experimenting with homemade resonators and megaphones" (Oliphant, "Durham"). In one such endeavor, Eddie is said to have improvised a resonator that greatly increased the sound by cutting a segment out of a tin pan and positioning it inside the carved-out body of an acoustic guitar. He "made music history in 1935 when he recorded" his arrangement of "Hittin' the Bottle" with the Jimmie Lunsford Band using his "amplified guitar" (Walker), and he influenced "fellow Texan Charlie Christian, probably the most important guitarist in jazz history, who recorded electric guitar the following year" (Oliphant, "Durham"). For that reason, Siegel and Obrecht have hailed Eddie Durham as a "Pioneer of the Amplified Guitar."

San Antonio, forty-seven miles southwest of Eddie Durham's hometown, was destined to become a hub of the Harlem Renaissance in South Texas. There, in 1905, an effort led by black officers from Fort Sam Houston transformed the "Colored Community House" into a post-World War I library and assembly building financed by the War Services Board. In 1929, funded by $75,000 in bonds sold by the City of San Antonio, it became "the Colored Branch of the San Antonio Library and Auditorium." Listed in the National Register of Historical Places by the United States Department of the Interior and situated on the corner of Hackberry and Center Streets:

> The center was a focal point for educational, cultural, political, and social activities for San Antonio's African-American community. Nationally acclaimed artists such as Ella Fitzgerald, Lionel Hampton, Paul Robeson, Louis Armstrong, Charlie "Bird" Parker, Dizzy Gillespie, Benny Carter, Cab Calloway, and Billy Eckstein performed at the Center.
>
> ("Carver Community Cultural Center," Official website)

Long since renamed "The Carver Community Cultural Center," and governed by a 501 (c) (3) organization, the facility remains a venue for national talent, includes a School for Visual and Performing Arts, continues its long tradition of community outreach, and now describes itself as:

> an historical center of the community's African-American culture. Named in honor of internationally esteemed agricultural chemist George Washington Carver, the Carver embodies this great man's philosophy and spirit:
> "Start where you are, with what you have.
> Make something of it. Never be satisfied."
> ("Carver Community Cultural Center—About")

As the Alamo City Renaissance shifted into high gear, local talent as well as performers who traveled what whites called "the minstrel circuit" and blacks called "the chitlin' circuit" enlivened clubs and churches with instrumental and vocal music both secular and sacred, with British and American poetry, oratory, and drama, and with dance. According to local legend, even the staid Second Baptist Church, then on Center and Chestnut Streets, became the birthplace of black cinema in Texas when Spencer Williams, a young would-be producer, director, screen writer with a hand-cranked camera, used it as a setting for his Bible-based silent film, *Go Down Death*, starring ingénue Geraldine Stain (Hinton).

San Antonio demographics made it possible for jazz and swing to flourish in the Alamo City. As cornet player and jazz band leader Jim Cullum Jr. explained prior to a February 2007 concert at the Carver, "San Antonio might seem like a jazz backwater, but, when Jack Teagarden was playing here [in 1921] it was very, very, very early in the development of jazz." Retired newsman and jazz aficionado Sterlin Holmesly has recorded how "Millard McNeal had the first black jazz band in San Antonio in 1923. He played for Gov. Ma Ferguson at the Governor's Mansion" (quoted in Beal). Jim Cullum agrees, "It all started with Millard McNeal," whose music The Jim Cullum Jazz Band has transcribed and performed. The Alamo City's "large Hispanic population and not so much of the Baptist influence as other towns in Texas" explains why "There's always been something happening here." Jim Cullum commends Don Albert, who "had the first band to call themselves a swing orchestra," and Boots Douglas for the "amazing recordings" they made with their bands (quoted in Beal).

Had "Professor" Cullum extended his commentary to include "the Texas blues tradition" viewed by historian Gunther Schuller as "probably much older than the New Orleans idiom that is generally thought to be the primary fountainhead of jazz" (quoted in Oliphant, "Jazz"), he could also have mentioned:

> three women singers from [nearby] Houston—Beulah T. (Sippie) Wallace, Victoria R. Spivey, . . . and Maggie Jones of Hillsboro. . . . All four of these figures, "in using some of the finest jazz musicians of the day as their

accompanists, . . . made possible some of the earliest recorded jazz breaks by [such] great artists" [in the 1920s] as Armstrong, Oliver, Fletcher Henderson, Sidney Bechet, Johnny Dodds, Henry "Red" Allen and J. C. Higginbotham.

(Oliphant, "Jazz")

The Landing on the *Paseo del Rio* in San Antonio, where Jim Cullum has spent more than half a century "researching, performing, and presenting" jazz "repertoire" of the 1920s and 30s" ("Riverwalk Jazz") is near a historic venue for controversial blues singer/guitarist Robert Johnson, who became the subject of "a myth that, like Faustus, he had sold his soul in order to acquire his musical genius." In a single three-day session, at the Gunter Hotel on East Houston Street just off the Riverwalk near the Alamo, Johnson made "his only album ever recorded in San Antonio" (Gray). The technical and societal hardships endured by black musicians of Johnson's day were formidable, as Jim Cullum reminds us; nevertheless, artistry prevailed:

[A]nd you have to remember these were one-take tracks probably recorded in a hotel. There was a high level of creativity and interesting original tunes. . . . There are great solos, good rhythm. . . . And think about the problems these guys faced. It was the Depression. Everybody was broke. And then you had the segregation these guys had to deal with.

(Beal)

With a reminder that "in the 1920s and 1930s when stereotypes would likely suggest San Antonio was still part of the Wild West, it was, instead, the home of sophisticated jazz and swing," columnist Jim Beal's "S.A.'s Jazz Age," references Sterlin Holmsley's "extensive collection of jazz oral histories" preserved at UT San Antonio's Institute of Texan Cultures. Beal also catalogs the clubs that are commemorated in that archive: "Shadowland, The Horn Palace, The Keyhole, the New Keyhole, the Avalon Grill, the Chicken Plantation." Some of these clubs became "nationally known," and also "the nice cats," "the daddies of jazz," such as trombonist Jack Teagarden, along with "Don Albert Dominique, Troy Floyd, Boots Douglas, Alvin Acorn, Herb Hall, Louis Cottrell, L. D. Harris," who played in them.

Not included in Beal's richly retrospective and valuable survey of "the daddies of jazz" is Big Band-Era pianist James Garnet Hopkins who "outlived them all." Hopkins, who died in a San Antonio nursing home on March 16, 2010, at 101 years of age:

played with a lot of famous musicians of the 1930s and '40s, among them bandleader Tommy Dorsey, trumpeter and vocalist Louis Armstrong, pianist Earl Hines, trombonist Jack Teagarden, and guitarist T–Bone Walker. . . . By the 1930s, he was playing with several jazz and dance bands.

(Ayala)

As Ayala notes, worn down by the rigors of cross-country travel and travail, Hopkins:

came back to the Alamo City and established the James Hopkins Orchestra, playing Texas and Mexican border cities. . . . [He also] performed at the legendary Eastwood Country Club, which booked the most famous performers in the "Chitlin Circuit" and encouraged integration in a city still intensely segregated.

Implicit in Elaine Ayala's beautifully written *San Antonio Express-News* tribute to Hopkins is the fact that his life and career benefited significantly from three San Antonio religious institutions that enriched and empowered African Americans and Hispanics before, during, and after the Harlem Renaissance Era: St. Peter Claver Catholic School, St. Philip's Episcopal Church, and St. Philip's College.

St. Peter Claver Church and School, "named for the . . . Jesuit saint who devoted his life to helping slaves" ("Healy-Murphy"), and the Sisters of the Holy Spirit and Mary Immaculate who served there and later in Oaxaca, Mexico and Laredo, Texas, were founded by Mother Margaret Mary Healy-Murphy, widow of businessman and Corpus Christi Mayor John Murphy when:

On Pentecost Sunday, May 29, 1887, Mrs. Murphy attended Mass at St. Mary's Church in downtown San Antonio. Father John Maloney, OMI read a letter from the Bishops of the United States, asking the Church to reach out to African Americans, for whom little education was available. Mrs. Murphy took this message to heart. . . . She sold some property . . . and with the proceeds purchased property on the corner of Live Oak and Nolan Street in downtown San Antonio.

("Healy-Murphy")

Despite "great hardships in the early operation of the school," there were "sixty children . . . enrolled" by January 1989. Within three years, "two hundred students were enrolled. The school had grown into an academy with both day and boarding students" ("Healy-Murphy"). A few years later James Hopkins was sent there from his home, sixty miles away:

Born in Seguin in 1908, the musically gifted Hopkins went to St. Peter Claver Catholic School as a boarder. Established by Margaret Mary Healy-Murphy, it served black children.

(Ayala)

James Hopkins's exact course of study is unknown, but the corporate tradition of the first school he attended is obvious from the account of another of the school's alumni, Nettie P. Hinton, who, among her other posts served as US Customs Service Desk Officer for Asia, Africa, and the Pacific Basin:

> From pre-primer through the twelfth grade, I attended St. Peter Claver Catholic School. . . . [I]t was small, historically Black, and nurturing. . . . [T]here were no hard sciences, but we received an absolutely marvelous grounding in the liberal arts. We all played instruments and sang; we all learned European and Mexican folkloric dance. We all performed Shakespearian plays and Gilbert and Sullivan operettas; we all had numerous opportunities to recite or to speak in public. The sisters intended to make every St. Peter Claver graduate marvelously articulate.
>
> That was the school's crowning achievement. I came away from there with the love of the written word: of literature, of history, of the social sciences.
>
> Thanks to those nuns, I went out into the world with a love of what is right,
>
> With a love of—Yes!—democracy.
>
> (Nettie Patricia Brooks Hinton, quoted in Passty, "Lion")

Like many St. Peter Claver graduates before and after her, Nettie Hinton then went on to study at nearby historically black-Hispanic serving St. Philip's College. She was not from the Harlem Renaissance Era. However, the following transcription is from an August 1995 interview of Woodrow F. Wilson an alumnus who did live through that historic time:

> I was a student here [in Medical Records Technology] from 1936 to 1937. Every week, my mother, who worked in Luling, Texas, would mail me a letter with a dime taped to its corner. I would take the dime and go to that [Mrs. Baird's] bakery down the street. With four cents I would buy myself a loaf of bread, and then go somewhere where no one could see me eat it. Then, with the other six cents, I would buy my pencils and my papers for school. . . . You know what Miss Bowden gave us for supper every night? Peanut butter and [maple] syrup. . . . Miss Bowden didn't have any bread. . . . But every Sunday—how she managed it in those hard times I don't know—she had an apple and an orange for each one of us. . . . That was our Sunday dinner, an apple and an orange. And then Miss Bowden would lock us out of the cafeteria, and she wouldn't unlock the door again until Monday morning. . . .
>
> [Nevertheless,] we had a lot of fun. Miss Bowden gave a mandatory dance every night. And she had a Victrola. And everybody from the College came, but they would mostly sit in corners because a lot of them didn't

know how to dance. But then Miss Bowden would come up to them and take them by the hand. She knew *all* those dances—waltzes and fox trots and rumbas and such. And she would teach us and dance with us, and then we would dance with each other.

(Woodrow F. Wilson, quoted in Passty, "Bishop")

It is noteworthy that, when St. Philip's College Co-Founder Artemisia Bowden, the daughter of former slaves and the longtime friend and correspondent of Mary McLeod Bethune, taught Harlem Era music and dance to Woodrow and his classmates at St. Philip's College, she was fifty-eight. Those who saw her dance could appreciate the way in which "Tango is learned from the feet up, but danced from the heart down" (Cusumano, 31).

Elaine Ayala's obituary of James Garnet Hopkins, mentioned above, notes that he had "a magnificent bass voice," that he served as "a longtime organist and singer at St. Philip's Episcopal Church" and that he "also sang with the . . . St. Philip's College Community Choir." At the time of its founding in 1895 by Episcopal Bishop James Steptoe Johnston as the "First Episcopal Church for Black People . . . in the Diocese of West Texas" the church was situated in La Villita on what became the San Antonio Riverwalk. A former second lieutenant in the Confederate Army, James Johnston had fought under John Bell Hood and Jeb Stuart, spent a year as a Union Army prisoner of war, owned a plantation, lost his cotton crop to a leaf disease, studied law, been ordained, and founded Douglas MacArthur's alma mater, the Texas Military Institute. Expelled in his youth from one college, a wartime dropout from another (Temple), Johnston nevertheless had a passion for religion and for education.

After its founding, St. Philip's Church endured seven decades of struggle to survive, before, during, and after the Harlem Renaissance Era:

> St. Philip's had as its first place of worship, the historic Little Church of La Villita in downtown San Antonio. At that site a Parochial Day School for Girls, later to become co-educational, was begun. This school was the beginning of what is now St. Philip's College.
>
> Subsequent to its beginning at La Villita, St. Philip's Church was relocated several times—to facilities on Dakota Street in 1917, to temporary use of upstairs rooms in a hardware store on West Commerce Street at Grimes, to its present location on Pecan Valley Drive in 1963.
>
> ("History of St. Philip's Church")

In all of these locations, St. Philip's Church has continued its century-long practice of "worship . . . in the great Anglican tradition." It takes its liturgy from the *Book of Common Prayer*, its "congregational hymns and choral anthems" from the *Anglican Hymnal*, and its "spiritual songs" from generations of African

American musical tradition which have recently been collected into *Lift Every Voice and Sing: An African-American Hymnal*, "under the supervision of the Office of Black Ministries of the Episcopal Church," by the late Dr. Horace Clarence Boyer.

Thus, in 2002, when James Garnet Hopkins, the last surviving Alamo City "daddy of jazz," sat down at the console of the organ brought to St. Philip's Church by his predecessor, Kathryn Walker Morgan, founder of the Theater and Fine Arts Program at St. Philip's College and godmother of the author of this chapter, he was more than happy to play James Weldon Johnson's words and John Rosamond Johnson's music for the "Negro National Anthem," so that they might echo in our hearts forever.

Further Reading

Ayala, Elaine, "Hopkins played piano with big band-era musicians." *My SA*, March 20, 2010.

Beal Jr., Jim. "Feature, S.A. Life: S.A.'s Jazz Age." State & Metro Edition, *San Antonio Express-News*, February 18, 2007, p. 01j.

Biemiller, Lawrence. "A Post-and-Beam Mystery at William and Mary." *The Chronicle of Higher Education*, June 4, 2010. Volume LVI, Number 37, A8–A9.

Brawner, Anne. "Guadalupe College: A Case History in Negro Higher Education 1884–1936," Master's Thesis, Southwest Texas State University, Department of History, 1980.

Brown, Judy, and Dr. Ronald Brown. Interview. April 18, 2010.

"Calaboose African American History Museum" (Museum-issued leaflet). 2009.

"Carver Community Cultural Center." Official website of the City of San Antonio Community Initiatives. www.thecarver.org/.

"Carver Community Cultural Center—About." www.thecarver.org/about.html.

"Carver Museum and Cultural Center." Austin City Connection: Parks and Recreation Department. www.ci.austin.tx.us/carver/history.htm.

Club Kaycee. "Durham, Eddie." *Kansas City Jazz History*. University of Missouri-Kansas City, 1996.

Club Kaycee. "Glossary." *Kansas City Jazz History*. University of Missouri-Kansas City, 1996.

Cohen, Harvey G. *Duke Ellington's America*. Chicago, IL: University of Chicago Press, 2010.

Cusumano, Camille. "For the Love of Tango: Why I packed up my dancing shoes and headed to Buenos Aires." [With] Photographs by Patrick Bennett. *Texas Journey: The Magazine for AAA Members*. July/August 2010, pp. 29–31.

"Eddie Durham." *Oxford African American Studies Center*. www.oxfordaasc.com/.

"Gramophone Record." *Wikipedia*. http://en.wikipedia.org/wiki/Gramophone_record #78_rpm_recording_time.

Gray, Jennifer. Personal Conversation, June 3, 2010. See also Peter Guralnick, "Robert Johnson: King of the Delta Blues Singers," CD album liner notes, Sony Music Entertainment/Columbia Records, 1937, 1961, 1998; www.deltahaze.com/Robert%20 Johnson.html.

"Harlem Renaissance." *Wikipedia*. http://en.wikipedia.org/wiki/Harlem_Renaissance.

"Healy-Murphy Center Home Page: About Us." www.healymurphy.org/index.cfm?
   fuseaction=about_History.

"Herschel Evans." *Wikipedia.* http://en.wikipedia.org/wiki/Herschel_Evans.

Hinton, Nettie Patricia. Telephone Conversation of October 12, 2009.

"History of St. Philip's Episcopal Church: 1895-Present." www.stphilips-sat.org/about.
   html.

"Joe McQueen." *Wikipedia.* http://en.wikipedia.org/wiki/Joe_McQueen.

"John T. Biggers." *Wikipedia.* http://en.wikipedia.org/wiki/John_T._Biggers.

Keller, Irene. "Humorous Satirical Dialogue Created by American Women Writers in the
   Second Half of the Nineteenth Century and in the Second Half of the Twentieth
   Century" (Chapters on Harriet Jacobs and Sojourner Truth). Electronic Dissertation,
   Indiana University of Pennsylvania, 2009. http://hdl.handle.net/2069/217.

Leonard, Captain C. L., U. S. Air Force, Ret. "Veterans' Day Speech at St. Philip's College."
   Sponsored by Drs. Deborah Byrd and Jeanette Passty, November 11, 2004.

Messer, Kate X. "The Calaboose African-American History Museum & San Marcos MLK
   Historic District." *The Austin Chronicle.* Arts: June 20, 2003. www.austinchronicle.com/
   gyrobase/Issue/print.html?oid=oid:164554.

Norris, Clarence Windzell, "St. Philip's College: A Case Study of a Historically Black Two-
   Year College," Dissertation, University of Southern California School of Education,
   January 1975.

Oliphant, Dave. "Durham, Eddie (1906–1987)" *The Handbook of Texas Online.* (n.d.)
   www.tshaonline.org/handbook/online/articles/DD/fduqk.html.

Oliphant, Dave. "Jazz." *The Handbook of Texas Online.* www.tshaonline.org/handbook/
   online/articles/JJ/xbjyb.html.

Osofsky, Gilbert. *Puttin' on Ole Massa: the slave narratives of Henry Bibb, William Wells Brown
   and Solomon Northup.* New York: Harper & Row, 1969.

Passty, Jeanette N. "'Bishop, I Am Wedded to My College!' The Life and Work of
   Dr. Artemisia Bowden," paper presented at the Fifth Annual "American Women Writers
   of Color Conference," Salisbury State University, October 6, 1995 (Video broadcast
   Channel 12; excerpt on CNN).

Passty, Jeanette N. "The Lion Writes Her Story: Nettie Patricia Brooks Hinton takes
   Washington and then the World." *Palo Alto Review*, Fall 1998, pp. 3–11.

Passty, Jeanette N., "'A Pearl of Great Price': Socio-Literary Activism in the Life and
   Writings of Olga Samples Davis," *South Texas Studies.* Victoria, Texas: Victoria College
   Press, 2000, pp. 65–82. Rev. and rpt. College Station: Texas A&M University Press
   (to appear) 2011.

Pierpont, Claudia Roth. "Black, Brown, and Beige: Duke Ellington's Music and Race in
   America." *The New Yorker*, May 17, 2010, pp. 96–103.

Priestley, Brian, "DUKE ELLINGTON: Never No Lament . . . The Blanton-Webster
   Band, 1940–1942," CD album liner notes, Bluebird/RCA Victor/BMG, 2003.
   (Adapted from Brian Priestley's essay, *The Early Forties Recordings* from *The Duke Ellington
   Centennial Edition: The Complete RCA Victor Recordings, 1927–1973*).

"Riverwalk Jazz: About Jim Cullum." Texas Public Radio Station KSTX. www.tpr.org/
   programs/riverwalkjazz.html.

Schwartz, Jeremy. "San Marcos to honor jazz legend, native son Durham." *EJAZZNEWS.*
   Posted by Editor on Monday, June 02, 2003—06:07 AM. www.ejazznews.com/
   modules.php?op=modload&name=News&file=article&sid=1372.

Siegel, Joel A. and Jas Obrecht. "Eddie Durham: Charlie Christian's Mentor, Pioneer of the Amplified Guitar." *Guitar Player* (August 1979).

Tanner, Ernestine Ketchum. *The Plight through Seven Houses: A Sharecropper's Daughter.* Pittsburgh, PA: Dorrance Publishing Co., Inc., 1998.

Temple, Louann Atkins. "Johnston, James Steptoe." *Handbook of Texas Online.* http://tshaonline.org/handbook/online/articles/JJ/fjo35.html.

Theisen, Olive Jensen. *Walls That Speak: The Murals of John Thomas Biggers.* Denton: University of North Texas Press, to appear November 2010. http://web3.unt.edu/untpress/catalog/detail.cfm?ID=342.

Walker, Jeff. "The Jazz Master: Eddie Durham to be honored at Feb. 6 tribute." *San Marcos Daily Record.* January 30, 2009. www.sanmarcosrecord.com/features/x1169230280/The-Jazz-Master?keyword=topstory.

Yardley, Jonathan. "Harvey G. Cohen's 'Duke Ellington's America.'" Review. *The Washington Post*, May 30, 2010.

10

THE BLACK RENAISSANCE IN THE DESERT SOUTHWEST

Bruce A. Glasrud and Cary D. Wintz

The African American cultural and political reawakening of the 1920s and 1930s, frequently referred to as the Harlem Renaissance but also as the New Negro movement, played out in other parts of the nation including the desert Southwest particularly in the states of Arizona, Nevada, New Mexico, Utah, and the far western portion of Texas. This section of the nation included the cities of Albuquerque, El Paso, Las Vegas, Phoenix, Salt Lake City, and Tucson. Remote and isolated from major centers of population such as Kansas City, Chicago, New York, and Boston, to some extent the cultural renaissance in the Southwest took its own shape, but it was patterned after that of the nation's larger cities. In form and substance it was, not surprisingly, more like the renaissance in other western cities than that of the East Coast.

Harlem, a vibrant, intoxicating enclave in the nation's largest city was, by the 1920s, filled with new migrants from the south as well as sophisticated, energetic middle class black residents. Despite the terminology, however, the Harlem Renaissance was not so much a creation by native Harlemites as it was a movement fueled by transplants from the west and south seeking new experiences in the Mecca city. Many of the prominent participants in the Harlem Renaissance grew up in the West, later moving to Harlem to participate in that exhilarating urban and cultural experience; they included Langston Hughes, Wallace Thurman, Aaron Douglas, and Arna Bontemps.

However, the long distances, the expense, and the breaking of family ties (especially for black women) prevented many black westerners from relocating to New York. Instead, despite innumerable obstacles, they created and participated in regional and local renewals in their own home communities. Although the art and literary efforts of the period often take center stage, the music of the era was a vital output and could be viewed at the Cotton Club in Harlem or at smaller replicas across the nation such as in Las Vegas. In the desert Southwest, though, the music and entertainment continued to derive from private fraternal groups and from the churches.

The background of the southwestern community of African Americans is essential to our understanding of the southwestern renaissance experience. Blacks initially arrived in the Southwest with Spanish explorers, then as traders and trappers—for example, Edward Rose and James Beckwourth. During the latter nineteenth century black soldiers, often called the Buffalo Soldiers, served in the Southwest and were stationed at places such as Fort Bliss, Fort Huachuca, Fort Douglas, and Fort Duncan. Upon completing their service, a few black soldiers remained in the Southwest, including the well-known black graduate of West Point, Henry O. Flipper. Other African Americans arrived in the Southwest as cowboys, riding with Texas or eastern New Mexico herds as they ranged northward. They too remained in New Mexico and Arizona or moved westward to Nevada and Utah and helped establish black communities. John Swain, an honored black cowboy from Tombstone, rose up the ladder as a black cowboy; he became a foreman and ultimately owned land and cattle of his own. Other African Americans in the Southwest came to the region as miners, prospectors, lumbermen or as small farmers and businessmen.

As in the West, blacks in the Southwest also developed self-contained all-black communities. Many left the South to escape violence and discrimination; they sought freedom and an opportunity to live with dignity and pride while maintaining a self-sufficient life for themselves and their families. In New Mexico black communities emerged in Blackdom, in Vado, and likely in Dora. Arizona black communities arose in Mobile, McNary, and Randolph. In Las Vegas, Nevada, the Westside essentially became an all-black community. The separation and self-sufficiency sought in the all-black communities was seldom accomplished. Land that was available for blacks was not always suited for agricultural endeavors. Water rights changed or were never clear. Water was farther underground than blacks were told. The wind always blew, or seemed to anyway. And nature was a constant threat, with blizzards and droughts that ruined even well-established families.

The black percentage of the population in these territories and states remained small and continued so into the 1920s even as the cultural rebirth began. Even by 1940, the end of the New Negro movement, the African American population of these four southwestern states totaled only 21,564. Of the four, Arizona's black population was the largest, at 14,993, and Nevada's the smallest, at 664—perhaps a consequence of Nevada's stature by the end of the nineteenth century as the "Mississippi of the West." The population of Las Vegas was only 64 as late as 1940, although 218 blacks did reside in Reno. On the other hand, only the black population of New Mexico and Utah declined during the years of the New Negro Movement—New Mexico from 5,733 in 1920 to 4,672 in 1940, and Utah from 1,446 to 1,235. The city in the Southwest with the largest black population,

Phoenix, had a population of over four thousand African Americans in 1940. The next largest city was El Paso with 2,188 black residents.

Part of the lure of the desert Southwest, however, derived from that feature. There were few black friends, but community support and self-help were constants for black residents. Openness and space suggested freedom and merged in creating an enjoyable, sustainable life. Even though segregation eventually emerged in some instances, it was not rooted in the society in the way that Jim Crow and its laws and traditions ruled the black community of the Deep South. Anti-black violence existed, but in a more benign and less threatening atmosphere.

In spite of the small population, during the 1920s and 1930s a few African American southwesterners successfully pursued careers in writing that corresponded to the emerging renaissance in Harlem and the remainder of the nation. The African American literary renaissance in the Southwest was epitomized by four authors/writers—three African American women, one from El Paso, one from Silver City, New Mexico, and one from Fort Worth—Bernice Love Wiggins, Anita Scott Coleman, and Lillian B. Horace. The fourth author was a black male, Wallace Thurman, from Salt Lake City.

The period produced a few articulate poets who came from middle-class, college-educated backgrounds. The poetry ranged widely in topics, philosophy, and approach. The most successful of the southwestern black women poets undoubtedly was Bernice Love Wiggins, whose father J. Austin Love was also a well-known poet. Born in Austin, Texas in 1897, Wiggins was reared in El Paso. As early as 1925 Bernice Love Wiggins published a volume of poetry entitled *Tuneful Tales*. She dedicated a poem to Paul Laurence Dunbar, was referred to as Texas's Dunbar, and in her poetry emphasized the ordinary black community. Wiggins's delightfully sarcastic poem "Church Folks" was included in J. Mason Brewer's collection, *Heralding Dawn* and originally was published in *Tuneful Tales*. Her poetry appeared in a number of publications, including the *El Paso Herald*, the *Chicago Defender*, and the *Houston Informer*. But her marvelous poetry stopped; in 1936 she moved to California and after her departure was not heard from again.

The violence directed toward African Americans in the 1920s led El Paso poet Wiggins to ask whether black women mistakenly sent their sons to war; in her poem "Ethiopia Speaks" she asked:

> Why not take it back?
> Until in the South, the "Land of the Free,"
> They stop hanging my sons to the branch of a tree,
> Take it back till they cease to burn them alive,
> Take it back till the white man shall cease to deprive
> My sons, yea, my black sons, of rights justly won,
> 'Til tortures are done?

(Wiggins, 38–39)

Wiggins's poetry almost vanished also; finally in 2000 her volume of poetry, *Tuneful Tales*, was reprinted in a book edited by Maceo Dailey Jr. and Ruthe Winegarten.

The only published black southwestern novelist during the early years of the twentieth century was Lillian B. Horace (for more on Horace see Chapter Two). Born Lillian B. Amstead in 1886, Horace spent her formative years and much of her adult life in Fort Worth, "where the West began." In 1916 (one year after Marcus Garvey arrived in New York) Horace self-published her novel *Five Generations Hence*, a fitting precursor to the emerging Harlem Renaissance movement in the Southwest. Horace also worked for the Texas Commission on Inter-racial Cooperation, maintained a diary, wrote and published a biography, completed but was not successful in publishing another novel (*Annie Brown*), and published articles for the *Eastern Star*. Espousing education and independence for African American women and concerned with the lack of freedom for blacks in the United States, Horace's protagonist in *Five Generations Hence* was an Afro-Texas school teacher whose vision called for blacks to go back to Africa "five generations hence."

New Mexico resident Anita Scott Coleman—one of the most prolific black women short story writers of the first half of the twentieth century—had a varied and unique heritage. Her life began in Mexico; she was born in Guaymas, Sonora in 1890. Anita Scott Coleman grew up in New Mexico, matriculated at New Mexico Teachers College in Silver City, taught school, married, and in 1926 moved to Los Angeles. In New Mexico she lived on a ranch; her father had been a black soldier in the late nineteenth century. Coleman published award-winning short stories, essays, and poems in national magazines such as *Half-Century Magazine*, *The Crisis*, *The Messenger*, *The Competitor*, and *Opportunity* during the 1920s and 1930s. She published her first stories in 1919 and 1920, and before her career closed she published thirty known short stories; at least two others received awards but were not published. She later issued a volume of poetry, *Reason for Singing* (1948) and, posthumously, a children's book, *Singing Bells*.

While Coleman's strength as a writer is in the short story genre, her poetry is effective and powerful. In "Idle Wonder," for example, the speaker muses about white views of their black maid. In "Portraiture" she states that:

> Black men are the tall trees that remain
> Standing in a forest after a fire.
>
> (*The Crisis*, June 1931, 199)

Many of her other poems reflect her desire to speak well of the black race, including "The Shining Parlor," "Black Faces," and "America Negra." Her poem "Baptism" won first place in the 1940 Robert Browning Poetry Contest at the University of Redlands.

Coleman's short stories and her poetry reflect concerns of women and African Americans during the early twentieth century. She wrote about passing, lynching, racism, sexism, and family. She emphasized the struggle of black women. Even though Anita Scott Coleman remained in New Mexico and California, she participated in the Harlem Renaissance through her writings and her acquaintances such as Wallace Thurman. As happened with too many women writers of these years, she died ignored in 1960 (the same year as Zora Neale Hurston) and, until recently, was frequently excluded from discussions of the writers of the Harlem Renaissance.

The fourth southwestern desert author differed from the three already mentioned. Wallace Thurman was male, did not like the West, became well known during the Renaissance period, and participated in the Renaissance at its base —Harlem. Born in Utah (in 1902), Thurman spent his early years in Salt Lake City (and Boise and Omaha) before moving to Los Angeles to attend college (University of Southern California). In Los Angeles he met Arna Bontemps, and in 1925 he relocated to Harlem. Thurman worked with and edited journals, including the magnificent *FIRE!!*, and published three novels, notably *The Blacker the Berry*, set partially in Boise, Idaho. Thurman became known as one of the leading writers of the Harlem Renaissance but tragically died in 1934 at the age of thirty-two.

Thurman provides us with considerable insight into his abilities, his prescience, and his view of African Americans in the West in an article on Utah, "Quoth Brigham Young: This Is the Place," for the collection of articles entitled *These "Colored" United States*. He argues that blacks have not been influential enough anywhere to refer to a black state but contends that there are black cities:

> When it comes to such localities as Harlem, the south side black belt of Chicago, the Central Avenue district of Los Angeles, the Seventh Street district in Oakland, the North 24th Street district in Omaha, the Vine Street district in Kansas City . . . and similar districts in Houston, El Paso, . . . et cetera one might write of these as colored cities, for it is there that the Aframerican spirit manifests itself, achieving a certain individuality that is distinguishable from that achieved in similar white districts . . .
>
> (Lutz and Ashton, 1996, 264–265)

Thurman is quite critical of Utah and of African Americans residing in Utah (as well as white Utahans). Segregation prevailed in Utah and he noted that the only thing separating Utah from Georgia was that Utah did not have Jim Crow railroad cars as did Georgia. Nonetheless Thurman decided that Utah was not any worse than neighboring states, and that probably he was lucky; he might, he averred, have been born in Texas, or Georgia, or Tennessee, or Nevada, or Idaho.

One of the aspects of black life that Thurman noted in Salt Lake City was the lack of African American publications—as he asserted, not even a church bulletin. Likely, since he noted that publications such as *The New Republic* and *The Nation* could not be purchased in Salt Lake City, prominent national African American publications *The Crisis*, *The Messenger*, or *Opportunity* could not be located in that city as well. Those black periodicals—the heart of the black renaissance—could be found in Phoenix, in El Paso, in Albuquerque, and in Silver City, New Mexico, at least until Anita Scott Coleman moved from Silver City to Los Angeles. Such magazines and outlets gave residents of those cities information and knowledge of events and peoples connected with the Harlem Renaissance and the literary and artistic output of the movement.

Although no black publications derived from Salt Lake City or Las Vegas, black owned and edited publications were published in other cities of the Southwest. National magazines such as *The Crisis* and *The Messenger* existed for political purposes as well as cultural and social issues. Local publications sometimes followed that broad path. In Albuquerque *The Southwestern Plaindealer*, started in 1924 by owner/editor S. T. Richards, emphasized that blacks in New Mexico ought to support the Democratic Party. Richards, a school teacher from Arkansas who arrived in New Mexico in 1912, became a successful entrepreneur and builder. One property—the Ideal Hotel—was the first place of public accommodation for blacks in Albuquerque. Anita Scott Coleman published an excerpt from her essay, "Arizona and New Mexico," in the *Southwest Review*, an African American publication from Albuquerque edited by S. W. Henry. Also published in Albuquerque late in the 1930s was the black-owned *Western Voice*.

None of the southwestern African American newspapers were of long duration but they were significant nevertheless. They sometimes published stories or poems from local residents and referenced visits to the community of nationally and regionally prominent individuals, including those connected to the Harlem Renaissance. At least three black-owned papers emerged in Arizona during the years between World War I and World War II. *The Arizona Gleam*, founded and edited in 1931 by Mrs. Winston Hackett, soon was purchased by George Rodgers, a businessman who operated an insurance company, the Western Mutual Benefit Association. One issue of the *Gleam* featured a story about Kansas-reared, Harlem Renaissance standout Langston Hughes. Black-owned and operated, the *Phoenix Tribune* spoke out against the bombastic Ku Klux Klan and its actions in Phoenix during the years 1918 to 1925. Edited by a Texas born teacher, Arthur R. Smith, by 1933 the *Phoenix Tribune* apparently revived. Three years later the *Phoenix Index* arrived. Its slogan was "Don't Spend Your Money Where Colored People Are Not Welcome." As the story about Hughes indicated, these newspapers could be important sources of information informing the local black community of the Harlem Renaissance.

The black newspapers could not have been published without the support and patronage of a significant population. That, too, is why the southwestern (as well as other sections of the nation) renaissance of the 1920s and 1930s settled in the region's cities. In the far-West Texas town of El Paso conditions existed for a political, cultural, and social rebirth. As early as 1910 blacks in El Paso formed a chapter of the NAACP. It continued actively and in the 1920s stood behind

Dr. Lawrence A. Nixon as he fought the Texas Democratic white primary. Nixon won his two cases in the United States Supreme Court, *Nixon vs. Herndon* (1927) and *Nixon vs. Condon and Knolle* (1932). Ultimately the state of Texas won other cases that overturned the *Nixon* decisions. Not until 1944 was the white primary completely overturned.

African Americans in El Paso featured a many-sided experience; the African American community was progressive, talented, diverse, and enduring. In 1915 black women established the Phyllis Wheatley Club that provided community and civic service.

Many highly motivated black leaders emerged, including Henry O. Flipper, Lawrence A. Nixon, and Bernice Love Wiggins. Black churches, fraternal groups, and businesses enabled members of the black community to meet, entertain, and support one another. Black soldiers stationed at nearby Fort Bliss added to the mixture as well as providing social activities and support. Segregation meant a black school such as the Douglass High School could be a meeting place for political and cultural events, and in 1931 the school leaders sponsored a poetry reading given by prominent Harlem Renaissance writer Langston Hughes. Perhaps it was Hughes's trip to El Paso that encouraged him to write the poem, "West Texas," with its final stanza, West Texas "ain't no place for a colored man to stay!" (Rampersad and Roessel, 1994, 252). Music and dances provided entertainment; El Paso's Blues Syncopators performed locally and in other locations in West Texas. El Paso blacks eagerly listened to traveling jazz bands such as the Oklahoma City Blue Devils. El Paso did not have a black-owned newspaper for many years, though —until Marvin E. Williams founded *The Southwest Torch Newspaper* in 1937 (it later became *The Good Neighbor Interpreter* published by Leona Washington).

Good neighbors included the neighboring states of New Mexico and Arizona. Where Wallace Thurman indicated his displeasure with his home state of Utah, Anita Scott Coleman, who wrote the article on "Arizona and New Mexico —the Land of Esperanza" for *These "Colored" United States*, vigorously extolled the virtues of her part of the Southwest. Although at the age of thirty-six she left New Mexico for Los Angeles, it was to join her husband who had located a printer's job in that city. Coleman praised the climate, the geography, the vegetation, the animals, and the natural resources. She mentioned the black history of the region, beginning with Estevan's incursion in 1538. Coleman also included reference to the hunters, the soldiers, and the lesser known. Most blacks resided in the towns, she pointed out. African American homeseekers form "a small yet valiant army in the land of esperanza." "And over it all," she notes, "the joyous freedom of the West" (Lutz and Ashton, 1996, 30). And Coleman had reason to be pleased; from her home in Silver City she was able to contact and convince national publishers to accept her stories and her poetry.

The largest city in New Mexico was Albuquerque, and with its two northern neighbors—Santa Fe and Taos—it became a center in the desert Southwest for

FIGURE 10.1 Jean Toomer first visited Taos in 1925 at the invitation of Mable
Dodge Luhan. He returned in the mid-1930s, marrying his second
wife, Marjorie Content, there in 1934. This photo depicts Toomer at
his writing desk in his rented house in Taos, in the summer of 1935.
Photograph by Marjorie Content, Courtesy Jill Quasha, New York.
Copyright Estate of Marjorie Content

activities related to the Harlem Renaissance. As Coleman phrased it, "one is almost
persuaded to say, that the brains and the brawn of the Negro population is gathered
in Albuquerque" (Lutz and Ashton, 1996, 29). Blacks in the city early organized
a chapter of the NAACP when in 1914 five men and one woman established
the critical civil rights organization. They followed with other support groups
including clubs for African American youths, women, and men. In Albuquerque

the renaissance touched frequently and eventfully. Anita Scott Coleman's own writings brought attention to New Mexico. Black businesses sold and featured national periodicals of the Renaissance while at least three black-owned newspapers/ magazines were published from Albuquerque during these years. Nightclubs provided entertainment. Musicians lived and performed in the city. Others traveled to the city from outside; Denver's George Morrison Jazz Orchestra visited Albuquerque and influenced a budding local musician, John Lewis. From the 1920s to World War II the black businesses thrived despite discrimination, and perhaps partially because of segregation. Establishments such as the legendary swing club, Chet and Pert's, catered to the small but growing black community.

A portion of the New Mexico relationship to the Harlem Renaissance centered upon New York City expatriate and Taos salon staple, Mabel Dodge Luhan. Carl Van Vechten, a white New York City supporter of the Harlem Renaissance and some of its renowned authors visited Luhan in New Mexico. Van Vechten took photographs of Harlem Renaissance personnel during the later stages of the Renaissance. Due to the influence of Edward Leuder, who authored Van Vechten's University of New Mexico Press biography, many photos are located at the University of New Mexico. Luhan had a striking physical interest in Jean Toomer, an outstanding black writer of the early renaissance whose work *Cane* (1923) was well received. Toomer visited with and stayed at Luhan's house. This dalliance led Langston Hughes to write a poem, "A House in Taos," that was critical of the trio involved—Dodge Luhan, her husband, and Toomer. "A House in Taos" also was a critique of white patrons and their relationships with black authors. Toomer would return to Taos in the mid-1930s. He married his second wife, Marjorie Content, in Taos, and the couple spent several summers there.

With the largest black population (2,366 in 1930 and 4,263 in 1940) in the desert Southwest, Phoenix's African American community was also an active community. Black members opposed the KKK, they fought a losing battle against segregated schools, and they also opposed racist movies or films. A movie, *The Nigger*, scheduled to be shown in Phoenix in 1915, raised the ire of the black community, and the city commission passed an ordinance censoring such movies. It was not shown. The same thing happened with *The Birth of a Nation* a year later. However, Hollywood promoters brought a band and showed the film for a twenty-week period. The theater manager was fined fifty dollars.

Black Phoenicians kept abreast of national developments; they could purchase copies of the *Chicago Defender*, *Dallas Express*, *New York Age*, *The Crisis*, and other African American newspapers and journals at J. W. Snell's restaurant. They joined national organizations such as the NAACP, the National Urban League, and the National Negro Business League. A division of Marcus Garvey's UNIA began in Phoenix and one formed in the neighboring community of Mesa as well. The Elks and the Masons provided fraternity as well as meeting places for the black community. Race-owned night clubs enabled entertainment and knowledge of the music and writings from other black communities of the Renaissance era. Band concerts, carnivals, and holidays such as Juneteenth were attended and celebrated at Eastlake Park, a segregated park for blacks in Phoenix. Music was a big part of these get-togethers.

Racial conditions in Tucson were similar to those in Phoenix, except on a somewhat smaller scale. However, by 1940 Tucson counted nearly 1,700 African American residents, larger than most other cities of the desert Southwest. Black Tucsonians early organized to enhance and protect their rights; in 1918, nine years after the NAACP organized nationally, according to Harry Lawson, Tucson blacks led by Creed Taylor established a local of the NAACP. Black women joined forces, in 1932 establishing the Eureka Club. Night life was available, including attendance at the Beau Brummel, which began in 1936. Fraternal Clubs also sponsored evening events and dances. Luther King, a black classical soloist performed at the Temple of Music and Arts. Later to be a prominent African American classical composer, Tucson-born Ulysses Kay performed two classical concerts during the 1930s. In Tucson, as in most of the remainder of the desert Southwest, blacks were not allowed in white-owned clubs. Segregation in Tucson, as in other cities, meant that blacks needed to support each other and to establish their own businesses. In Tucson restaurants, night spots, barber shops, and beauty parlors operated by and for blacks promoted conversation, relaxation, and the exchange of ideas. Tucson's Renaissance experience was slightly different from other southwestern cities; although active, involved, and interested, the black residents were less involved in literary and artistic activities than in Phoenix.

The Las Vegas of the 1920s and 1930s was not the lively hot spot that it is today, nor did it offer the fruits of national renaissance efforts. Yet, the small black community energized itself. By 1920 approximately fifty African Americans, principally railroad workers, called the Westside section of Las Vegas home. Card games were run out of a black barbershop in the 1920s. By the 1930s at least two cafes existed. Fresno-born Clarence Ray arrived in 1922 to work on the railroad, but stayed only a short time; he returned in 1925 to his first job of running poker games at the Miner's Club. Later, three men—Ray, Bill Jones, and Clarence Reed—started a black gambling house, the "Navasota;" it was the first club to hang a gaming license issued to blacks. The Navasota also became a temporary place to stay for black workers at Hoover Dam. A local chapter of the NAACP started in 1927 with a majority of Las Vegas blacks as members. Prominent national black leader, orator, writer, and educator William Pickens helped the local NAACP blacks achieve positions as construction workers on the Hoover Dam. Eventually forty-four African Americans (out of some five thousand) worked on the dam. Their presence in Westside, the black section of Las Vegas, fueled excitement and entertainment and nightlife activities in Westside.

Prior to gambling's legalization, legal divorces, and the end of prohibition in the early 1930s, a dozen or so blacks owned property in what became downtown

Las Vegas. However, soon after, they sold or lost their holdings, and Westside became the place in which blacks could purchase property. Las Vegas movie theaters were segregated. Blacks stopped at clubs for social interaction and liba-tion. The most popular meeting place in Westside was the Mitchell Ranch; it became the hub of social, political, and religious activity. Las Vegas's version of the Cotton Club arrived in the late 1930s, but it was not similarly elaborate. By then a few black entertainers traveled to town. If they performed at a Las Vegas hotel or club, they could not stay there; they were likely to be found in the late evening at a club in Westside. As she reported in *The Raw Pearl*, Pearl Bailey first performed in Las Vegas in 1941, the end of what was the Harlem Renaissance period.

Even though Nevada's entire population during the 1920s and 1930s was quite small, in 1940 Reno's black population reached 218, considerably more than that of Las Vegas. African Americans in Reno also learned about and paid attention to the renaissance and "New Negro" spirit alive in the West. In 1935, for example, the AME Church of Reno presented the enlightening play, *Ethiopia at the Bar of Justice*, with a cast of about twenty. The play was performed at the Civic Auditorium in that city.

Westward-bound African Americans also visited in the Salt Lake City region even before the Mormons settled in Utah. By the twentieth century blacks found work with the railroads, in coal mining, and in domestic and personal services. Segregation set the bounds of their activities, their livelihoods, but created an opportunity for black-owned businesses such as hotels, rooming houses, and cafes or restaurants. They organized and joined national associations. Blacks in Salt Lake City established a chapter of the NAACP in 1919; in Ogden, Utah, a division of the UNIA, Marcus Garvey's well-known organization, was created by blacks in that Utah community. Fraternal groups existed—two prominent ones in Salt Lake City were the Masons and the Elks. On the other hand, the Utah Ku Klux Klan spread racism and hatred, sometimes endangering or threatening the lives of black citizens of Utah. In 1925 a black man was brutally lynched in a small community beyond Salt Lake City.

Blacks persevered despite the discrimination, and participated in a renaissance spirit in the Utah city. A Porters and Waiters Club existed for railroad workers. Salt Lake City residents established a literary club. Black musicians performed, and whites flocked to hear the black performers, but the artists could not enjoy the food or beds at the clubs. Los Angeles jazz men performed, bringing their own particular version of western jazz. In 1929, after publication of *The Blacker the Berry*, Wallace Thurman returned to reside in the city for a time. Black visitors to the city included traveler and Harlem Renaissance leader Langston Hughes; Hughes referred to Salt Lake City in his poem "One Way Ticket," as he noted that "he's picked up his life and heading on a one way ticket" to get to the West and out of the South with its segregation and lynching. Thurman's potential destinations included Bakersfield, Los Angeles, Oakland, Salt Lake City, and Seattle. Hughes also visited El Paso and Albuquerque and ventured through other parts of the desert Southwest.

If the Harlem Renaissance movement did not flourish during the 1920s and 1930s in the desert Southwest of New Mexico, Arizona, Nevada, and Utah, it nevertheless played a vital role in the lives of urban residents in those states. A few black authors/writers—including Bernice Love Wiggins, Lillian B Horace, Anita Scott Coleman, and Wallace Thurman—enthralled their readers. Musicians, primarily playing blues and jazz, displayed their talents and provided a vivid form of entertainment and listening enjoyment. Although discrimination and segregation existed in this desert locale, it was neither as dangerous nor as omnipresent as that of their former southern locales. Black residents organized to resist the discrimination, occasionally in divisions of Marcus Garvey's UNIA, but more often with the NAACP. Perhaps the chief limitation to black life in the desert Southwest was the small black population. On the other hand, blacks came to the Southwest for the openness, the feeling of freedom, and the vast spaces. Although more limited than the Renaissance in Harlem, or even in Los Angeles, the New Negro movement captured the souls of blacks (and many whites) in the desert Southwest as it did in such major cities as Chicago and New York.

Further Reading

Bailey, Pearl. *The Raw Pearl*. New York: Pocket Books, 1973.

Bracey, Earnest N. "The African Americans." In *The Peoples of Las Vegas: One City, Many Faces*. Edited by Jerry L. Simich and Thomas C. Wright, 78–97. Reno, NV: University of Nevada Press, 2005.

Burke, Flannery. *From Greenwich Village to Taos: Primitivism and Place at Mabel Dodge Luhan's*. Lawrence, KS: University Press of Kansas, 2008.

Coleman, Anita Scott. "Idle Wonder." *Opportunity* (May 1938): 150.

Coleman, Ronald G. "Blacks in Utah History: An Unknown Legacy." http://historytogo. utah.gov/people/ethnic_cultures/the_peoples_of_utah/blacksinutahhistory.html.

Coray, Michael S. "African-Americans in Nevada." *Nevada Historical Society Quarterly* 35 (Winter 1992): 239–257.

Dailey, Jr., Maceo C., and Kristine Navarro, eds. *Wheresoever My People Chance to Dwell: Oral Interviews with African American Women of El Paso*. Baltimore, MD: Black Classic Press, 2000.

Geran, Trish. *Beyond the Glimmering Lights: The Pride and Perseverance of African Americans in Las Vegas*. Las Vegas, NV: Stephens Press, 2006.

Glasrud, Bruce A., and Laurie Champion, eds. *Unfinished Masterpiece: The Harlem Renaissance Fiction of Anita Scott Coleman*. Lubbock, TX: Texas Tech University Press, 2008.

Harris, Richard E. *The First 100 Years: A History of Arizona Blacks*. Apache Junction, AZ: Relmo Publishers, 1983.

Kossie-Chernyshev, Karen. "What Is Africa To Me? Visions of Africa in Lillian Jone's *Five Generations Hence* (1916): A Gendered Means to a Political End." *East Texas Historical Journal* 49.1 (Spring 2011): 135–146.

Lawson, Harry. *The History of African Americans in Tucson: An Afrocentric Perspective*. 2 volumes. Tucson, AZ: Lawson's Psychological Services, 1996, 2000.

Luckingham, Bradford. *Minorities in Phoenix: A Profile of Mexican American, Chinese American, and African American Communities, 1860–1992*. Tucson, AZ: University of Arizona Press, 1994.

Lutz, Tom, and Susanna Ashton, eds. *These "Colored" United States: African American Essays from the 1920s*. New Brunswick, NJ: Rutgers University Press, 1996.

Overstreet, Everett Louis. *Black Steps in the Desert Sands: "A Chronicle of African Americans' Involvement in the Growth of Las Vegas, Nevada"*. Las Vegas, NV: privately printed, 1999.

Rampersad, Arnold, and David Roessel, eds. *The Collected Poems of Langston Hughes*. New York: Random House, 1994.

Richardson, Barbara J., comp. *Black Directory of New Mexico—Black Pioneers of New Mexico: A Documentary and Pictorial History*. Rio Rancho, NM: Panorama Press, 1976.

Wiggins, Bernice Love. *Tuneful Tales*. Edited by Maceo C. Dailey and Ruthe Winegarten. 1925. Lubbock, TX: Texas Tech University Press, 2002.

11

HARLEM RENAISSANCE IN DENVER

George H. Junne, Jr.

What is the Harlem Renaissance and when did this explosion of African American social, political, literary and artistic creativity occur? Known as the "New Negro Movement, the New Negro Renaissance, and the Negro Renaissance," the Harlem Renaissance flourished during the 1920s and 1930s, but "had no clearly defined beginning or end."[1] As some have asserted, the term "New Negro Renaissance" more aptly described the "literary and artistic activity in African American communities throughout the United States" because many of its contributors lived and worked outside of Harlem.[2] For instance, writer Anita Scott Coleman, born in Mexico and raised in New Mexico, was a major contributor to black publications but is little known today. Black writers, artists and activists in Los Angeles, Dallas, Seattle, Helena, Phoenix, Denver, and many other communities sometimes still receive little recognition. By default, Harlem has become the symbolic location for the period.

According to award-winning academic David Levering Lewis and others, the Harlem Renaissance was more than a movement that involved culture, as it also incorporated politics and economics. Lewis places the date of the Harlem Renaissance between the years 1917 and March 19, 1935, the date of the Harlem riot. He also posits that the NAACP and the National Urban League were responsible for jump-starting the "New Negro Arts Movement" with their associated publications, *The Crisis* and *Opportunity* magazine.[3]

It was in Harlem—"the undeclared capital of Black intellectual life—[that] black artists began to rally their forces" as artists, musicians, painters, poets and writers organized to protest the quality of life for African Americans.[4] Furthermore, Denver had its intellectual and cultural triumphs that garnered both local and national attention. What is usually missing in Harlem Renaissance history is the fact that African Americans in Denver (originally Denver City) and other communities in the West were involved in social, artistic, philosophical and political activities that affected those in the East. At the same time, activities of the Harlem Renaissance were affecting black westerners.

January 9, 1867, proved to be a landmark date for African Americans in Colorado. According to *Harper's Weekly*, the bills to admit Nebraska and Colorado as states both contained amendments to "impose Negro suffrage as a condition." The next day the US Senate passed the Territorial Suffrage Act "prohibiting the denial of civil or political rights in the Territories on account of color." The House concurred and forwarded the bill to the President to approve.[5] Those actions did not end discussions and arguments surrounding black male suffrage in Colorado, but did precipitate events that could not be turned around. Black men voted for the first time in the territory on April 1,1867, in the Denver election, the same day the Ku Klux Klan held its first national convention and the same year Congress granted African Americans in DC the right to vote.

By the 1890s, Denver's small middle class black population began to move in the Five Points Neighborhood area and thrived. As the original white community of Germans, Irish and Jewish residents moved on to the Capitol Hill and Curtis Park areas, African Americans began to migrate to the neighborhood, which was near the jobs they held near the industrial and rail yards by the Platte River. By the end of the nineteenth century, three black newspapers served those residents. Sarah Breedlove married newspaper reporter Charles J. Walker and became known as Madame C. J. Walker, opening her hair care products marketing and manufacturing business in 1907 before moving east and becoming the first black woman millionaire.

Noted African American poet and novelist Paul Laurence Dunbar relocated temporarily to Harman, Colorado in 1899 with his wife and mother on the advice of his physician, who believed Colorado's climate would help the poet battle pneumonia. Harman is now contained within Denver's Cherry Creek Neighborhood but during Dunbar's stay, its residents would ride horses across the fields to Denver proper. While there, Dunbar wrote his second novel, *The Love of Landry*, about a woman recovering from tuberculosis in Colorado. Meanwhile, he continued to correspond with his friend, Edward Arnold. Because Dunbar gave Arnold one of the first copies of the work, the latter treasured it. Dunbar also described Denver to his friend:

> This wonderful country, as he described it, "with great rolling illimitable plains, and bleak mountains standing up like hoary sentinels guarding the land" was beautiful beyond description. Speaking of Denver, he wrote: "The city where so many hopes are blighted, where so many dreams come true, where so many fortunes go up and so many lives go down. Denver, over which nature broods with mystic calm, and through which humanity struggles with hot strenuous life."[6]

While in Denver, Dunbar wrote articles for the *Denver Post*, and he incorporated some of his experiences in *The Love of Landry*. Although some critics feel that *Landry* is Dunbar's poorest novel, one finds that at least he attempted "to introduce the topic of the second-class status of Negroes." At the same time, Dunbar "was becoming more and more concerned with racial issues during the course of his brief, five-year career."[7]

The *Denver Sunday Post* published a Dunbar article titled "The Hapless Southern Negro" on September 17, 1899. While on a tour in the South to look into "the condition of the people themselves," he noted the deplorable condition of blacks, their mortgaged homes and other economic problems they were facing. He also noted "they have industry" and will work and they are industrious. Dunbar predicted that if black people moved west they would make the area wealthy. Further, "He [black people] will go on your farms and ranches and into your mines . . . and the mountains at night shall hear his Southern song transferred to the West."[8]

On September 13, 1899, *The Denver Daily News* published an article in which Dunbar pondered on how he could best serve black people at the time. It appears while he was in Denver, he was solidifying some principles that would influence black consciousness in his later works such as "Douglass" and "The Fourth of July and Race Outrages."

One of the major figures of the Harlem Renaissance was Dr. W. E. B. Du Bois, a founder of the NAACP in 1909. Two years later, on Monday, May 22, *The Denver Independent*, a black newspaper, sponsored him to present an address at Denver's Peoples' Tabernacle. The talk's title was "The History of the Negro Race."

The year 1915 would be a significant one for activism. In May of that year, black citizens formed The Colored Protective League of Colorado, organized to fight, according to its Constitution and By-Laws, the false impression "that the Negro race is a child-race, not capable of self-leadership, and therefore not to be dealt with as other races. . . ." Among other goals were materially advancing African Americans to "secure full civil and political rights" and providing legal redress for "Colored persons who are persecuted."

It appears that the racist silent film, *The Birth of a Nation*, galvanized Denver's black population and led to protests beginning in 1915. Following the national lead of the NAACP, the *Denver Star* printed a front-page editorial titled "What the People are Saying," attacking the film. Copied from the NAACP's monthly publication *The Crisis: A Record of the Darker Race*, this was the beginning of a series of articles to rally the black community. Supported by President Wilson and screened for the Supreme Court, *Birth* contained most of the racist stereotypes of African Americans still evident today. Denver's City Council often banned racially inflammatory films and plays, but *Birth* continued to play almost uninterrupted. Even so, Black Denver was not acquiescing to racism. In 1915, four years after Du Bois's 1911 visit to the city they organized a Denver chapter of the NAACP.

The early twentieth century brought a period of profound social, political, cultural, religious, and economic changes and challenges for African Americans, particularly in the East. Among those who responded to these challenges was Marcus Garvey and his UNIA. The UNIA established branches in both cities and rural communities that "inspired Garvey to motivate a significant number of African American citizens migrating from the South" to other areas of the United States, included Colorado.[9] He therefore decided to tour the West to promote his ventures because of the rising black population in some cities. The *Salt Lake Telegram*, January 29, 1921, noted an increase of Denver's black population to 6,085 or 12.1 percent. The white population, according to the Census Bureau, reached 249,652, up 20.6 percent.

The year before Marcus Garvey traveled to Colorado, the East Denver branch of the UNIA initiated a fundraising drive. United under the slogan "the world cannot be made safe for democracy until Africa has been made safe for negroes," the UNIA announced its goal was to raise $50,000 within thirty days, beginning September 2, 1921. The group explained that the funds would be used "to further a movement to return Negroes of Colorado and other states to Liberia and to Christianize the African continent."[10]

In May 1922, Marcus Garvey and then secretary Amy Jacques were in Colorado Springs. They married a few months later and Garvey visited Denver, along with his new wife, Amy Jacques Garvey. Beginning in September 1924, Garvey began a cross-country tour to promote the sale of stock in the Black Cross Navigation and Trading Company and "to unify UNIA membership."[11] While in Denver, he delivered two addresses at Fern Hall on October 5. *The Colorado Statesman*, in an ad captioned "Look Who is Coming," answered: "Hon. Marcus Garvey, Provisional President of Africa, and President General of the Universal Negro Improvement Association."

The two African American weekly newspapers, *The Colorado Statesman* and the *Denver Star*, were the primary news sources for Denver's black community. D. D. Rivers, the *Statesman*'s publisher, "was committed to including as many names as possible in his newspaper because he knew that this might be the only time a Black citizen ever saw his or her name in print." The *Star*'s editor, George Ross, was both an attorney and an "ardent champion of civil rights." On both of their watches, they covered news such as visits from Garvey and others in depth.[12]

Between Garvey's visits to Denver, one of the preeminent writers of the Harlem Renaissance wrote a flowery article about Denver and its African American population for the November 1923 issue of *The Crisis*. Jessie Redmon Fauset did her undergraduate work at Cornell University where she earned election to Phi Beta Kappa. After she received her MA degree in French at the University of Pennsylvania, W. E. B. Du Bois offered her a position as literary editor on

FIGURE 11.1 The NAACP meeting in the Five Points office of Dr. Clarence Holme's in 1920. The NAACP was instrumental in bringing Harlem Renaissance figures such as W. E. B. Du Bois and Jessie Fauset to Denver

The Crisis in 1919. In 1924, she published *There is Confusion*, the first of her four Harlem Renaissance novels.

Fauset's article "Out of the West" contains headshots of important members of Denver's black community; other photograph titles include "White Friends of Black Denver" and "Some Colored Homes." She noted the Shorter AME Church with its membership of 1,000, the 450 pupils in Sunday School "and a choir which is nationally known." She also mentioned the Zion Baptist Church plus other organizations such as the YMCA (colored branch), the Phyllis Wheatley Center of the YWCA with its 309 members and the five troops of 125 Boy Scouts. Another paragraph described Engine Company Number 8, Denver Fire Department, and another "colored institution." She also described the schools and business enterprises in some detail. By focusing on the commonalities between blacks and whites, Fauset was subverting the prevailing stereotype that one group was culturally and intellectually superior to the other and one could observe that phenomenon in Denver.

During the 1920s Denver experienced its share of racial strife, some of which was connected to activities of the Ku Klux Klan. Klan activities were not unusual in Colorado, particularly Denver. The revitalized Invisible Empire of the Ku Klux Klan "was in numbers and political influence the most powerful social movement of the 1920s and probably the most significant crusade of the American right-wing." The most powerful klonkaves in the West were in Colorado, Texas, California and Oregon, and they used politics as a means of controlling their targets —Blacks, Jews, Catholics, immigrants and lawbreakers. Klan members elected those to office who could control certain elements. When needed, they also resorted to "(B)oycotts, cross burnings, and night riding."[13]

In June 1925, the NAACP met in Denver to "beard the Colorado Klan in its den." Conference attendees included the famous Charles Edward Russell, Oswald Garrison Villard, W. E. B. Du Bois, James Weldon Johnson, and Walter White, who planned to fight "the local brand of 100 percent Americanism through exposing ignorance, prejudice, and bigotry on the national front." One outcome of Klan activity was that it led to the development of the Denver Council of Churches plus interracial and interfaith activities, including Brotherhood Week in which ministers exchanged pulpits.[14]

The most prominent manifestation of the arts among African Americans in Denver during the 1920s and 1930s involved in music. This began even before the emergence of the Harlem Renaissance. Opera composer Harry Lawrence Freeman produced his first opera, *The Martyr*, while living in Denver in 1893. He moved there while in his early twenties. He formed the Freeman Grand Opera Company to stage his productions and presented *The Martyr* at Denver's Deutsches Theater and other cities around the country. Freeman moved to New York during the second decade of the twentieth century and worked with Bob Cole, J. Rosamond Johnson and James Weldon Johnson; he also established his Freeman School of Music and the Freeman School of Grand Opera.

One reason for the expansion of music in Colorado and in particular, Denver, was that the western states of California, Colorado, Oregon, and Washington had a high proportion of their population engaged in the music profession as teachers and musicians. In 1900, Colorado vied with California, Massachusetts, and New York for the number of musicians and teachers of music as a percentage of population. The year 1910 saw Colorado successfully vying not only with these states but also with Illinois, Utah, Oregon, and Washington. In 1910, Denver was included in the list of the ten most musical of US cities having a population of over 100,000 persons.[15]

An important contributor to classical music in Denver was soprano Emma Azalia Hackley, singer, musician, and music educator. Raised in Detroit, Hackley eloped to Denver with husband Edwin Henry Hackley, a journalist and attorney, in 1894. They had met at a Sissieretta Jones concert, and Edwin became editor of *The Colorado Statesman*. Hackley studied music at the University of Denver and at the same time became involved in issues of civil rights. She wrote columns for the women's section of the *Statesman* and founded the Denver branch of the Colored Women's League. She and her husband also organized the Imperial Order of Libyans, a fraternal organization for combating racial prejudice. In 1900, Mrs. Hackley was the first African American to graduate from the University of Denver's School of Music. She taught in that school's extension program and performed with the Denver Choral Society while directing local choral groups. Also skilled in the piano and violin, Hackley began a cross-country tour in 1901 and then settled in Philadelphia. While there she founded the 100-voice People's Chorus, later renamed the Hackley Choral Society. Using money from her concerts, she studied in Paris and established a scholarship fund so that African Americans could study abroad. She and her husband separated in 1909 but she continued to sing duets with black musicians and composers and feature works of black composers. Hackley traveled the country into the 1920s, even appearing again in Denver.

The January 2, 1915 issue of the *Denver Star* announced the following appearance: "Mme E Azalia Hackley, the Nation's Charming Singer and Musical Educator." It stated that she was visiting friends in Denver and would be staying for ten days before leaving for the west coast. The paper also proclaimed, "Welcome to our city, Madame we read of you in Boston."

The Hackleys were a prime example of an upper-crust African American family in the West, not only of Denver. Both came from elite families—"Old Detroiters"—who were also politically active. Edwin Hackley had attended the University of Michigan, was admitted to the bar, and was a clerk in the county recorder's court in Detroit. His wife grew up in an all-white neighborhood where her family was the only exception. While in Denver the couple formed a Whist Club and entertained their set. Like many other upper-class black families, the Hackleys attended the Church of the Redeemer, an Episcopal church. Unlike in the East, however, high status in the West was more related to wealth than to family background and education. Culture and refinement still meant a lot to aristocratic Denver blacks, but to the public, initiative and individual effort counted far more. As residents of Denver, the Hackleys "demonstrated the extent to which members of the black upper class who moved west took with them the style, values, and views of social life drawn from older societies in the East."[16]

During the 1920s in Harlem, jazz was a music that drew whites to the neighborhood. For many, it was the rare opportunity for blacks and whites to interact, even on a segregated basis. For instance, the famous Cotton Club, "The Aristocrat of Harlem," was segregated while it featured black entertainers such as Duke Ellington, Cab Calloway, the Nicholas Brothers, and other famous celebrities. However, African Americans were not allowed inside unless they were featured in the reviews or were waiters, dishwashers, janitors or those who performed drudgework. The owner who opened the establishment, Owney "Ollie" Madden, did so from his cell in Sing Sing Prison.

Other Harlem clubs featuring black entertainers but catering for white audiences also existed. In other less prestigious establishments, blacks and whites met on more of an equal basis, not only to listen to the music but also to create both formal and informal relationships. One could note similar observations in the Five Points area of Denver:

> As they crossed the boundaries of Five Points to listen to jazz music, whites in Denver not only entered Denver's black community, but also participated in a national urban phenomenon. As one Denver journalist commented, "Fashionable whites went clubbing in Five Points, just as New Yorkers traveled uptown to Harlem to dance." For many, whites crossing into a "black" space seemed at once dangerous and exhilarating. Black entertainment districts often became liminal spaces, places where visitors were encouraged—and even expected—to disregard some of the social expectations that usually constrained their behavior. When whites entered spaces they had coded "black," they operated under a different set of cultural expectations.[17]

Famous clubs in Five Points included the Casino, Benny Hooper's Ex-Serviceman's Clubs, the Rossonian and Lil's After-Hours. Many considered the Rossonian to be the best jazz club between St. Louis and San Francisco. Over the years Louis Armstrong, Ella Fitzgerald, Billie Holiday, Duke Ellington, Count Basie and Denver's own George Morrison held court. George Morrison's orchestra, variously called "The Greatest Orchestra in the World" and "The Colored Paul Whiteman and His Twelve Rigadooners," would, over the years, include future bandleaders Jimmy Lunceford on flute, Andy Kirk, plus vocalist and drummer Hattie (High-Hat) McDaniel, an East High graduate who went on to win the 1939 Academy Award for Best Supporting Actress in *Gone with the Wind*. Morrison also helped to start the career of the famous White Denver orchestra leader, Paul Whiteman, whom he recommended to Victor Phonograph Company. In a column titled "In the Footlights Glow" from a Denver newspaper circa 1925, the reporter noted Hattie McDaniel appearing "in a series of syncopated comedy songs."[18] The "favorable" article went on to report the following:

> George Morrison's jazz band, occupying headline position on the bill, comprises an aggregation of negro syncopators with all the qualifications and characteristics of the darky jazz artist.

Jazz violinist and orchestra leader Morrison gave his first recital in November 1914, receiving "strong applause." According to a report in the November 21 *The Denver Star*, "Prof. Geo. Morrison, a thorough Western violinist who has struggled and fought his way to recognition, gave one of the most inspiring musical recitals by his pupils at [People's] Presbyterian church last Thursday night, than that church has ever witnessed before." Many of the works were classical in nature, reflecting the depth of Morrison's training.

In 1920, Morrison traveled to New York to play at the Carleton Terrace Supper Club where he played classical violin solos, recording for Columbia Records under the name Morrison's Singing Jazz Orchestra. While at the Club one evening after playing a composition of famous Austrian-born violinist Fritz Kreisler, "a tall distinguished man walked up to him and handed him his card. It was Fritz Kreisler." Kreisler asked Morrison if he had any difficulties with any of the passages and Morrison said he did "with the flying staccato in the Mendelssohn Concerto." Kreisler then invited Morrison to his home and gave him six free lessons.[19]

Hattie McDaniel attended school in Denver, one of two black children in her elementary school. Encouraged by one of her white teachers, Louise Poirson, to recite poetry and sing in class, she joined J. M. Johnson's Mighty Modern Minstrels in 1910 at age thirteen, plus the Spikes Brothers Comedy Stars. In April 1916, she and sister Etta McDaniel, featured as "The McDaniel Sisters & Co.," starred in the two-act musical farce "Goin' Back to Memphis" with George Morrison's full orchestra providing the music. She toured with her father's minstrel show and in 1920, joined George Morrison and the Melody Hounds, billed as the female Bert Williams. She also toured with Morrison when he worked with the Shrine and Elks Indoor Circuses in Denver, Salt Lake City and Texas, plus on the Pantages vaudeville circuit throughout the western states and Canada. Morrison changed the name of his orchestra to "George Morrison and His Twelve Rigadooners" with McDaniel still the lead singer. One newspaper advertised for an upcoming concert:

> "You'll Wanta' Hear Hattie M'Daniels Sing 'Crazy Blues'"
> "Sweet Daddy!"
> S-o-m-e music——[20]

Radio broadcasting was just beginning. Later in her life, she would be one of the litigants in a housing case that would set a precedent for the 1948 Supreme Court case of *Shelly vs. Kraemer*, ending restrictive covenants in housing.

On December 15, 1924, the radio station KOA in Denver aired its first broadcast, marking the beginning of McDaniel's extended radio career. McDaniel was the first black person to sing at the station, making her one of the first, if not the first, black person to sing on radio in the nation.[21]

Morrison and his orchestra played live concerts on the radio for KLZ in Denver. His group also played engagements at the Lakeside Amusement Park, nicknamed "The Playland of Denver." *The Boulder News-Herald*, dated April 15, 1930, ran an article on Morrison titled, "Ex-Local Negro Jazz Band Leader Making a Success of Work." It revealed Morrison and his musicians and singers were chosen from a field of 157 applicants to play the Lakeside venue, and WMAQ of Chicago planned to establish a national link for live broadcasts on Sundays between 1:00 and 3:00 p.m.[22] Morrison and his orchestra are prime examples of Denver's major contribution to the Harlem Renaissance.

The Rossonian began as the Baxter Hotel and catered almost exclusively to Whites until real estate agent A. H. W. Ross purchased it in 1928 and changed the name. Its clientele became both black and white under the new black ownership. During the 1920s and 1930s, Denver had a flourishing jazz scene. Located across from Benny Hooper's, The Rossonian claimed to be a "sophisticated jazz club":[23]

> The Points was the bee's knees and the cat's meow, a place to settle in and sip some (at times) legal hooch and listen as a canary on stage sang to the hypnotic beat of a skin tickler. The musical mash, "the sweet brutality of hopes and dreams, both achieved and dashed, and the freedom to let loose with heart and soul," everything got played in the Points.[24]

African Americans around the country, including Denver, valued play and recreation. A major problem was funding, so they turned to community members and churches for support. Because many were poor, fundraising efforts sometimes did not produce the desired revenue. The black communities also had a handful of entrepreneurs who opened pool halls and organized plays, musical productions, and other social gatherings, many times drawing on local black talent.

Benny Hooper served in World War I and saved his paychecks. Upon his return to Denver, his hometown, he decided to open the Ex-Serviceman's Club downtown because there was no hotel in which blacks, particularly servicemen, could stay. Mayor Stapleton went to Hooper one day, put his arm around him and said he should find a new location. Hooper therefore opened his new business in Five Points as the Deluxe Recreation Parlor and Ex-Serviceman's Club. During the 1930s, Hooper opened a dancehall next door so that people could dance to popular jazz music. There was balcony seating for 1,000 patrons:

> Hooper donated the use of the dance hall and many of its proceeds to the various churches, charities, and civic groups of which he was a member: the YMCA, the NAACP, and the Zion Baptist Church all held functions there.. . .A beloved member of the black community, Hooper was the proud recipient of several plaques honoring him as the Unofficial Mayor of Five Points.[25]

Hooper was also able help feed those in need in a unique manner. During the Depression years, there were many jackrabbits around the city limits of Denver. Hooper organized some of the World War I veterans and had them hunt the animals and bring them to his billiard parlor. Any hungry person who wanted them could just go there and pick them up from the sidewalk in front of the business. One resident remembered that it did not matter what color the person was and people came from all over the city. At the end of the 1930s, Hooper founded the Wallace Simpson Flying School where black men could receive flight instruction, and a few became Tuskegee Airmen in World War II.[26]

Besides his black clientele, whites also went to Hooper's club to enjoy jazz and the atmosphere. Musicians who played in the basement, nicknamed "The Hole," included drummers Kenny "Stix" McVey and Willie Hunter, trumpeter Leonard Chadwick who also played with King Oliver, Jimmy Lunceford and the Blue Devils, and sax player Paul Quinchette, who later played with Count Basie.[27] Lunceford, whose family moved to Denver before he entered high school, would move to New York in the 1930s, and the groups he led would play regularly at the Lafayette and Apollo theaters plus the Cotton Club. Again, some from the Denver area were influencing the Harlem Renaissance in the East.

During George Morrison's youth in Boulder, Colorado, he organized a boys' string band that played dances in mountain towns and mining camps. It was the only music group available in many of those areas. He moved to Denver on the eve of the twentieth century and left to obtain a music degree from Chicago's Columbia Conservatory of Music, learning the violin. He was barred from the position of concertmaster for the Denver Symphony because he was African American. As a violinist and arranger, he worked with small bands and was finally able to organize the George Morrison Orchestra in Denver, "which dominated the dance band business there for many years."[28]

Besides Lunceford, Kirk, McDaniel, and pianist Alphonso Trent, Ferdinand "Jelly Roll" Morton, famed pianist, composer-arranger and bandleader, played with Morrison's Orchestra for a short period from early 1921 until that summer, following his engagement in Casper, Wyoming. After Denver, he played through Colorado Springs and Pueblo on his way to Los Angeles. For eleven years, Morrison's group was the house band in Denver's Albany Hotel, also playing the Cathedral Ballroom. The group traveled around Colorado as well as to New Mexico and Wyoming. They also toured the West and East on the Pantages circuit. Venues included high school proms, and the group was the official band for Cheyenne Frontier Days. According to jazz historian Ross Russell, the longevity of the George Morrison Orchestra "was the longest of any band in the Southwest, apart from the Moten-Basie tradition, overlapping the two wars and spanning the interval between them."

By the mid-1920s, Morrison had given up much of his touring and had opened the Casino, a jazz club, and was the bandleader. He also taught music at Whittier Elementary School, Cole Junior High School and Manual High School. Newspaper articles from Kansas City, Kansas, show Morrison did travel to that area to perform in 1934. In the late summer, Morrison, his son George Morrison, Jr., and his daughter Marian May Morrison would be performing in Topeka.

Over a year later the same Kansas City newspaper announced that Morrison would be assisting in Denver's Glenarm YMCA membership campaign and provided a very positive short biography.[29]

Where did African American visitors, including musicians, stay when they traveled to Denver? This was during the time when they were not allowed to stay in Denver hotels, so local African Americans, including the Morrisons, would find room for them at their houses, or they could stay at the Rossonian or the jazz club. Quentin Harrison, owner of the Rossonian Hotel, said that black performers and entertainers were not allowed to stay in other Denver hotels. Paul Robeson, Duke Ellington, the Harlem Globetrotters, Count Basie, Sarah Vaughan, and countless others stayed at the Rossonian. At the same time, white people would line up to get in to hear the black performers, clearly demonstrating the absurdity of segregation. Harrison said that on some evenings he "couldn't see a Black face in there."[30] Denver's black population battled for human rights for years before it became a fact of life.

Bandleader and bassist Andy Kirk, who would gain fame as Andy Kirk and the Clouds of Joy, was raised in Denver from age six and studied with Wilberforce Whiteman, the father of the famous orchestra leader Paul Whiteman. At age twenty, Kirk became a tuba player for the George Morrison Orchestra, his first professional job according to *The Cleveland Call-Post*, May 8, 1943. Kirk became enamored with jazz after hearing Jelly Roll Morton in Denver during the early 1920s, leaving the George Morrison Orchestra to pursue his jazz interests in 1925. The Clouds of Joy included the famed Mary Lou Williams and played for the dance audience. Kirk's success was based on his combining "the jazz ideas of the southwestern bands with the easy beat of the George Morrison Orchestra."[31]

By 1929, Denver's black population had grown to an estimated 7,000, increasing from 3,923 in 1900. Purported to be "the largest manufacturing city between the Missouri River and the Pacific Coast," Denver had seven railroad systems that serviced the meat slaughter and packing industries, the largest sheep market in the world, and the attendant stockyards. Ford also built an assembly plant. Still, there was discrimination against hiring African American employees. The 1929 Denver survey showed that of the 214 industries surveyed with their 23,062 employees, only thirty-one had black workers, totaling 314. Only eight plants had more than ten.

As the African American population of Denver increased, job discrimination prevailed. Excuses ranged from "It is not the policy of this company to employ Negro labor," to "the highly technical nature of the work," to "The Negroes are employed as janitors." For the 2,371 men employed in 1920, the largest number (278) worked as janitors and sextons. For the 1,200 women, the largest group (629) worked as servants. By 1929, the City and County of Denver employed sixty African Americans and the State of Colorado offices employed thirty-five. It was in the federal offices that they saw more of an opportunity, with eighty African Americans working there, sixty-six working for the Post Office and one employed as a Deputy US Marshal for the Denver district.[32] Although Denver might not have had the severe racism found in other areas of the country, there were still major problems that needed addressing during the rise of the Harlem Renaissance.

At first, the YWCA attempted to find employment for the black community. To further assist, the Denver Colored Civic Association, established in 1925, worked with the Department of Labor. Even into the late 1920s, most of the jobs for African Americans were in the service area and included cooks, chauffeurs, janitors, elevator operators, porters and kitchen helpers in tearooms, clubs, and hotels. Most jobs open to black women were for domestic assistants in homes and maids in hotels and stores. Every so often, there would be a call for skilled laborers.[33]

Denver African Americans had difficulty in many public spaces, but according to the laws of the time, there was supposed to be equality. If someone discriminated, the person could be taken to court, but that did not occur very often. If it did, the violator was fined the minimum amount. In April 1929, for instance, an African American was not allowed to ride in the elevator in Denver's Brown Palace, although he was the governor's messenger and the governor was residing there. The situation received a lot of publicity and *The Denver Star* urged the black community not to take such insults but to fight back:

> What happened to Jackson can, and will, happen to our men and women at any time a servant desires to insult. Act! Act!!! This happens in Denver, Colorado, where our statutes on civil rights in public places point out in no uncertain language the duties and responsibilities of hotel owners and managers, etc.; where violation of this statute carries with it a criminal penalty or a civil responsibility.[34]

Denver's African American community would continue to protest discrimination and segregation into the 1930s through direct action, as their children did in August 1932 when they attempted to integrate the beach at Washington Park. The manager of Denver's parks warned them to leave. The Safety Manager first acknowledged their right to be there but then warned them, "If you go into the lake you will be acting at your own peril." The blacks responded that they were citizens, so the Safety Manager should have the police protect them:

> They then went swimming. Whites quickly left the water, armed themselves with sticks and stones, and advanced on the newcomers who fled toward the trucks which [they] had brought with them. Two of the trucks would not start. Unable to make a quick exit, the African-Americans were pursued and beaten as nearly a thousand onlookers watched. The police arrested seventeen people, ten blacks and seven whites who had encouraged the blacks to assert their rights.

The Denver Post placed the blame of the so-called riot on a convenient outside agitator, Communists. As the Harlem Renaissance was waning in the mid-1930s, "Denver in 1932, still in the shadow of its Klan days of the 1920s, was not ready to provide equal protection of the law to all."[35] However, the reason why blacks were not allowed in swimming areas was steeped in a deep fear.

Many whites, because of prejudice and ignorance, did not want to swim with blacks or have their children swim with them. Playgrounds and parks might be desegregated, but desegregating pools and sometimes bathing beaches were "a line in the sand" for some whites.

Denver African Americans received a civil rights victory, as announced in the October 1, 1932 issue of *The Colorado Statesman*. In a case brought against the city of Denver by the NAACP and attorney George Ross, District Court Judge Charles C. Sackman struck a blow against discrimination stemming from one swimming pool case. The city had to remove signs at the 20th and Curtis Streets bathhouse and pool "telling when colored bathers might use the pool."

Famous entertainers playing to Denver audiences during the early 1930s included basso-baritone Paul Robeson and tenor Roland Hayes, singers with international reputations. Robeson's baritone was heard three years earlier, according to a story in the March 14, 1931 edition of *The Colorado Statesman*, reprinted from the *Rocky Mountain News*. The *News*'s music critic reported specifically that his rendition of folk songs were "more moving than the musical expressions of any other race of people. And Robeson is able to give them as no other singer of this generation."

Later that year "Denver fell under the magic spell of the artistry of Roland Hayes" at City Auditorium, during which the audience sat spellbound. The critic proclaimed, "Hayes is a master artist. His diction in German, Italian, French or English is clear and distinct, while his pianissimo work is exquisite." Special room was made for those in wheelchairs, on stretchers and on crutches and the audience gave him several ovations.[36]

Visual art was also important to Denver's African American community, which had its share of talented people. There was also an interest in national art figures, demonstrated by the show at Denver's Chappell House February 4–10, 1935. Formed in 1919, the Denver Interracial Commission, as part of Interracial Week, brought the Harmon Foundation's "Art of the Negro" collection to Mile High City. Watson Bidwell, Denver Art Museum Docent, wrote an article for the February 9 edition of the *Colorado Statesman* that praised the talented group. In part, he wrote that the show "was a very good representative demonstration of contemporary art, which is made the more significant because of its racial background."

There were a number of noted persons who presented lectures in Denver, ensuring that Denver's black community continued to stay informed on a variety of topics. Famous scientist Dr. George Washington Carver, head of Tuskegee Institute's agricultural research department and a 1923 recipient of the NAACP's

Spingarn Medal, spoke at Shorter AME. The title of Carver's address was "Great Creator, What Is a Peanut? Why Did You Make It?" Attendees from Denver and around the state, including high school and university students, were enthralled, according to *The Colorado Statesman*, February 20, 1932. The reporter saw Carver's presentation not only as intellectually informative but also as helping "to make clear the way for successful adjustment of certain conditions in our civil, domestic and intellectual life." The mind of the "wizard of chemistry" and others like him ought to help to develop mutual respect among people.

In the area of recreation, African Americans living in the Denver area were more privileged than many in other areas of the country, but it could still be difficult. In 1920, Denver's blacks were allowed to use only two of the city's playgrounds. But beginning in 1922, they could travel to the mountain resort community of Lincoln Hills, Gilpin County. By 1926, they could travel to Wink's Lodge and stay in the fifteen cabins or the three-story inn. Lincoln Hills was one of the few African American resort communities in the United States, a welcoming oasis away from segregation and prejudice. African Americans could buy land plots for $5 down and $5 a month for a grand total of $50:

> If visitors were lucky, they'd bump elbows with Zora Neale Hurston, Lena Horne, Count Basie, Duke Ellington, Ella Fitzgerald, Langston Hughes and other luminaries visiting Winks Lodge or Winks Tavern, both built by O. W. "Wink" Hamlet, the African American entrepreneur who galvanized the Lincoln community . . .[37]

Denverites could travel to Lincoln Hills by car or take the hour-long train ride. Some built their own cabins in the area rather than renting from Obrey Wendell "Wink" Hamlet. Vacationers also included women and girls who were members of the Phyllis Wheatley YWCA attending its summer camp—Camp Nizhoni. Programs for the visitors, many who lived in Five Points, gave them "a chance to enjoy the mountains and featured events such as swimming in the river, sunbathing and hiking and camping in the fresh mountain air."[38]

Unlike other areas of the country, overt violence against them was minimal, yet Denver's black newspapers covered those events and the drive to enact federal anti-lynching laws. Numbers of reported lynchings in various states between the 1880s and the 1960s were: Colorado 2; Pennsylvania 6; Maryland 27; Texas 352; Georgia 492; and Mississippi 538. Black newspapers also began to cover the rise of Nazi Germany and the precarious position of blacks there. For example, a front-page story in the Colorado *Statesman* dated February 24, 1934, was titled "Sterilization of Negroid Children Urged in Germany." In addition, front-page articles included those on the Scottsboro Boys, the political activities of US representative Oscar De Priest and snippets on African Americans who were making entrees into management and educational positions nationwide.

The Harlem Renaissance, according to some, ended in 1935. Not only was it the year of the Harlem Race Riot (dubbed the first modern race riot by some) but there were also other significant events that ensured the position of African American writers and artists.

While New York City's Mayor LaGuardia's report on the riot laid its cause on poverty and discrimination, it still concluded that "ignorant and unsophisticated peasant people without experience with urban life" were at least partially responsible. However, neither the *Denver Post* nor the *Colorado Statesman* published a story on that incident, raising the question of how significant it was to Coloradoans. What might have been more significant to Black Denverites was a photograph and short biography of United States Senator Edward P. Costigan of Colorado in the June 1935 issue of *The Crisis*. Along with New York Senator Robert F. Wagner, Costigan, a Harvard graduate and Denver attorney, supported an unsuccessful anti-lynching bill in Congress, gaining nationwide support of black communities.

At the same time, the Works Progress Administration (WPA) announced its support of black artists and writers. According to David Levering Lewis, "Writers William Attaway, Ralph Ellison, Margaret Walker, Richard Wright, and Frank Yerby would emerge under its aegis, as would painters Romare Bearden, Jacob Lawrence, Charles Sebree, Lois Maillou Jones, and Charles White." Arna Bontemps would head the writers' unit for which many of them worked. The WPA's Federal Theater Project's Negro Unit supported black drama, and black plays began to open on Broadway, including Langston Hughes's successful theatrical production, *The Mulatto*. Around the country all-black theater companies were being formed and were producing their own shows. African Americans were also achieving on political, economic and educational fronts.

As the Harlem Renaissance ended, The "Swing Era" began—Ella Fitzgerald's star was rising and Count Basie formed his own band. George Gershwin's American folk opera *Porgy and Bess* received its first performance, and Marian Anderson debuted at New York Town Hall. The Museum of Modern Art opened its exhibition *African Negro Art* and Mary McLeod founded the National Council of Negro Women (NCNW) and the center of the Renaissance began to move west to Chicago. In the upcoming years, the role of Denver in the Harlem Renaissance would be almost forgotten and World War II would take center stage for all Americans.

Notes

1 Cary D. Wintz, "The Harlem Renaissance," in *Harlem Speaks: A Living History of the Harlem Renaissance*, ed. Cary D. Wintz (Naperville, IL: Sourcebooks, 2007), 8.

2 Cary D. Wintz and Paul Finkleman, eds., *"Encyclopedia of the Harlem Renaissance*, (New York: Routledge, 2004), s.v. "New Negro Movement."

3 David Levering Lewis, "The Harlem Renaissance," in *Cornerstones: An Anthology of African American Literature*, ed. Melvin Donalson (New York: Saint Martin's Press, 1996), 763.

4 Eileen Southern, *The Music of Black Americans*, 3rd ed. (New York: W. W. Norton, 1997), 340.

5 "Domestic Intelligence," *Harper's Weekly*, January 26, 1867.

6 Edward F. Arnold, "Some Personal Reminiscences of Paul Laurence Dunbar," *The Journal of Negro History* 17, no. 4 (October 1932): 405, www.jstor.org/stable/2714556 (accessed January 2, 2010).; and Lynda Faye Dickson, "The Early Club Movement among Women in Denver: 1890–1925," (Ph.D. diss., University of Colorado at Boulder, 1982), 73.

7 Charles R. Larson, "The Novels of Paul Laurence Dunbar," *Phylon* 29, no. 3 (3rd. Quarter, 1968): 257–260, www.jstor.org/stable/273490 (accessed January 2, 2010).

8 Gossie Harold Hudson, "Paul Laurence Dunbar: Dialect Et La Negritude," *Phylon* 34, no, 3 (3rd Quarter, 1973): 242–243, www.jstor.org/stable/274182 (accessed January 4, 2010).

9 Ronald J. Stephens, "Methodological Considerations for Micro Studies of UNIA Divisions: Some Notes Calling on an Ethno-Historical Analysis," *Journal of Black Studies*: 284, http://jbs.sagepub.com/cgi/content/abstract/39/2/281 (accessed January 4, 2010).

10 "Making Africa Safe for Negroes," *Aspen Democrat-Times*, August 23, 1921, www.coloradohistoricnewspapers.org/.

11 Robert A. Hill, ed., *The Marcus Garvey and Universal Negro Improvement Association Papers*, (Berkeley, CA: University of California Press, 1989), 6: lvii.

12 Joan Reese, "Two Enemies to Fight," *Colorado Heritage* 1 (1990), 3–4.

13 Robert A. Goldberg, "Beneath the Hood and Robe: A Socioeconomic Analysis of the Ku Klux Klan Membership in Denver, Colorado, 1921–1925," *Western Historical Quarterly* 11, no. 2 (April 1980: 181).

14 James A. Atkins, *Human Relations in Colorado, 1858–1959* (Denver, CO: Offices of Instructional Services, 1961), 88–89.

15 Henry J. Harris, "The Occupation of Musician in the United States," *The Musical Quarterly* 1, no. 2 (April 1915): 308–311, www.jstor.org/stable/737852. The other cities in the "top ten" were Boston, Kansas City (MO), Los Angeles, Minneapolis, Oakland, Portland (OR), San Francisco, Seattle and Spokane.

16 Willard B. Gatewood, *Aristocrats of Color: The Black Elite, 1880–1920* (Bloomington, IN: Indiana University Press, 1990), 137–138.

17 Tracy Elizabeth Ainsworth, "Strange Brew: Women and Blacks in Denver During Prohibition" (Master's thesis, University of Colorado, 1998), 95.

18 "In the Footlights Glow," c. 1925, George Morrison Collection, MSS ARL55 Rg8B, Blair-Caldwell African American Research Library, Denver Public Library.

19 "George Morrison Biography," George Morrison Collection, MSS ARL55 Rg8B, Blair-Caldwell African American Research Library, Denver Public Library.

20 "You'll Wanta' Hear Hattie M'Daniels Sing 'Crazy Blues,'" George Morrison Collection, MSS ARL55 Rg8B, Blair-Caldwell African American Research Library, Denver Public Library and Sheldon Harris, *Blues Who's Who: A Biographical Dictionary of Blues Singers* (New York: De Capo Press, 1979), 360.

21 Darlene Clark Hine, ed., *Black Women in America*, 2nd ed. (New York: Oxford University Press, 2005), s.v. "McDaniel, Hattie."

22 "Ex-Local Negro Jazz Band Leader Making Success of Work," George Morrison Collection, MSS ARL55 Rg8B, Blair-Caldwell African American Research Library, Denver Public Library.

23 Ainsworth, "Strange Brew," 95–94.

24 Elena Brown, "All That Jazz," *Denver Magazine*, February 2, 2009.

25 Ainsworth, "Strange Brew," 79–80.

26 Moya Hansen, "Pebbles on the Shore: Economic Opportunity in Denver's Five Points Neighborhood, 1920–1950," *Colorado History* 5 (2001): 113.

27 Ainsworth, "Strange Brew," 93.

28 Ross Russell, *Jazz Style in Kansas City and the Southwest* (New York: Da Capo Press, 1997), 66–67.

29 "George Morrison in Recital," *Plaindealer* (Kansas City, Kansas), August 3, 1934; and "Denver Music Leader to Assist Y.M.C.A. Campaign," *Plaindealer*, September 27, 1935.

30 Billie Arlene Grant, Ernestine Smith, and Gladys Smith, *Growing Up Black in Denver*, 3rd printing (Denver, CO: B. A. Grant, 1988), 46–47.

31 Russell, *Jazz Style in Kansas City and the Southwest*, 163.

32 Ira De A. Reid, *The Negro Population of Denver, Colorado: A Survey of Its Economic and Social Status* (New York, The Denver Interracial Committee, 1929), 1. Reid was an African American sociologist who also wrote articles for *Opportunity*.

33 Dickson, "The Early Club Movement," 118.

34 James Rose Harvey, "Negroes in Colorado" (Master's thesis, University of Denver, 1941), 67–68.

35 Stephen J. Leonard, "Black-White Relations in Denver, 1930s-1970s," *The Midwest Review* 12 (1990): 56.

36 "Magic Artistry of Roland Hayes Grips Listeners," *The Colorado Statesman*, November 14, 1931.

37 Claire Martin, "A Resort to Remember," *Denver Post*, February 15, 2009.

38 Laura M. Mauck, *Five Points Neighborhood of Denver* (Charleston, NC: Arcadia Publishing, 2001), 61.

12

BLACK RENAISSANCE IN HELENA AND LARAMIE

Hatched on Top of the Rocky Mountains

Charlotte Hinger

Taylor Gordon, Montana's best known African American participant in the Harlem Renaissance, wrote in his autobiography, *Born to Be*, that race had never been the big "ghost" in his life because he had been "laid on top of the Rocky Mountains, hatched out by the Broiling Sun, a suckling of Honey Bluebacks and educated by the Grizzly Bear, with all the beauty and fresh air Nature can provide for her children."

Gordon's belief that his Western heritage made all the difference in his attitude toward racial issues was shared by other African Americans who grew up in sparsely populated mountain and plains regions. Although African American children who grew up in Montana and Wyoming experienced less prejudice than blacks clustered in cities, this same expectation of acceptance on their individual merits caused problems if they moved east of the Mississippi. Not only were many unaware of the intensity and scope of collective white prejudice toward their race, they were unprepared to handle the complexity of intra-racial negotiations.

For instance, Era Bell Thompson, in her autobiography, *American Daughter*, wrote about her isolated North Dakota childhood. When she moved east as an adult she felt profoundly alienated from both whites and blacks in more populous communities. Thompson was saddened by a black landlord's hostility toward her visiting white friends, and bewildered by the resentment of other African Americans when she obtained a teaching job. Both Gordon's and Thompson's childhood experiences were intensified because they were born into the only black families in very small communities.

Gordon was born in White Sulphur Springs, Montana in 1893. His account of early years in this small community is peculiarly lacking in racial awareness or the experience that writer and educator W. E. B. Du Bois referred to as "double consciousness, this sense of always looking at one's self through the eyes of others." Gordon's recollections of pranks and friendship when he was growing up contain few references to being black. On the other hand, he was very proud of his western identity. When he reached adolescence and wanted to be looked upon as a man, he went to a dance in cowboy boots, leather cuffs, a Stetson hat, and a bag of Bull Durham tobacco in his breast pocket.

Gordon was a tenor and at the height of his career sang at Carnegie Hall. He also pursued acting and appeared in the plays *Shoot the Works, The Gay Divorcee*, and *The Emperor Jones*. He was introduced to music through his family. His brother Bob collected musical instruments and played the violin, banjo, and off-beat instruments, such as the Duolyne harp that Gordon described as "freakish." His mother had a spectacular singing voice. Blues was coming into its own during his childhood. Some critics asserted that blues was the "profane twin" of the Baptist Church's pattern of call and response. His description of his mother's voice rhythmically rising and falling in time to her movements over a wash tub suggests she shared the country's fascination with these repetitive twelve-bar three-chord blues compositions.

Conservatives protested the "Africanizing" of American culture through the distinctly African American contribution of jazz, ragtime, and blues. For a time when jazz became a national craze, it looked as though the music would bring the races closer together. Jazzmania increased through admiration for James Reese Europe, a black band leader whose music became the rage in France during World War I. Europe started a worldwide demand for jazz. New York gave his regiment, the Hellfighters, a victory parade in New York upon its return from World War I. Some scholars pinpoint the beginning of the Harlem Renaissance with this exuberant recognition.

In the beginning, jazz was exclusively associated with African Americans. The incursion of whites into this musical genre came later. The proliferation of jazz was reinforced by prohibition. Speakeasies were everywhere and white and black communities intermingled to a degree unthinkable before passage of the Eighteen Amendment.

Even before the Volker Amendment, Gordon exploited opportunities offered by the underbelly of Montana society. During his childhood, he became a "page and cash" boy for Big Maude when she started a new house, Palace of Joy, in a district known as "sporting line." Gordon acquired customers from all walks of life who needed a go-between to obtain booze. He later claimed he fitted "right into the network perfectly on account of the pigment of my skin." His cloak of invisibility bestowed by race indicated the extent of even western society's depersonalization of blacks.

In his early teens, Gordon made money driving passengers between White Sulphur Springs and Dorsey. However, one night his employer burned out the crankshaft bearing in the old "Maytag two-seated bus," so he was unemployed.

FIGURE 12.1 This caricature depicts Taylor Gordon along with Carl Van Vechten and his actress wife Fania Marinoff. Taylor Gordon was the Montana native who achieved the greatest fame in Harlem during the late 1920s. This image was likely made during one of the many Harlem Renaissance gatherings that Van Vechten hosted in the late 1920s to introduce black writers and artists to the New York City arts world. It also represents the party scene that characterized the Harlem Renaissance during its heyday

By that time, he had decided that White Sulphur Springs had "lost its thrill." He wrote that he knew "everybody by their whole names, nicknames and businesses, as well as their habits. I knew all the ranches, mountain trails, hunting grounds, fishing holes, vacant mines and beautiful caves." So he went to the state capital of Montana—Helena—in search of more excitement. Montana's total population was 12,000, with approximately 1,800 African Africans in the entire state. Helena's black population was around 400. While there, Gordon claimed to have visited "all of the buildings in the city, the Capitol, Assay Office and Library." He took in the fair, then afterwards decided the town had lost all its "speed and pep" and that Helena was not as a big city should be, so he went back to White Sulphur Springs.

Despite Gordon's dismissal of Helena's lack of vitality, the town had emerged from a gold-mining camp in 1864 to become an established black community that encouraged racial uplift and supported artistic endeavors. An outstanding African American photographer, James P. Ball, who moved from Helena to Seattle before Gordon was born, made a substantial contribution to the visual arts. There are eighty of Ball's photos at the Montana Historical Society museum. He often photographed minorities and documented historical events. Among his portraits are three of William Biggerstaff, who was hanged for killing another African American man. The first is an elegant pose with Biggerstaff dressed in a suit. The second shot is of the hanging itself, followed by a view of the man in the coffin. For three months, his son, James Presley Ball, Jr., published a newspaper, *The Colored Citizen.*

Gordon arrived in Helena during the reign of Joseph B. Bass, the vigorous thirty-eight year old editor and publisher of the *Montana Plaindealer.* Bass, who launched the paper in 1906, was an enthusiastic advocate for the arts. He came to Helena from Kansas where he had worked for the *Topeka Plaindealer.* From the first issue, March 16, 1906, Bass gave significant coverage to cultural events and laid a foundation for the subsequent New Negro movement. This edition began with a lengthy reprint from the *Denver Post* commenting on the life and recent death of the renowned poet, Paul Laurence Dunbar. Dunbar was hailed as "the first poet to arise out of the African race in America."

The writer argued that Dunbar's books and poetry provided an answer to "ignorant bigots" dithering over the future of blacks, and insisted that the fate of the race would be settled by simply allowing Negros to enjoy the opportunities opened up by the abolition of slavery. Dunbar displayed a rare ability to implement a number of voices. Although a number of his poems were in dialect and delved into homey details of life in black households, an equal number of poems were quite formal. He explored racial themes and was held in high esteem by many of the country's black leaders.

In a subsequent issue, Bass wrote in the *Plaindealer* that Dunbar was the world's greatest Negro poet and his achievements in the literary world were all the more gratifying because he had no "white blood in his veins." He then suggested that James Ephraim McGirt of North Carolina was a likely successor to Dunbar. Both poets' work ranged from dialectical presentations to formal compositions. Although "local items" were a standard addition to all newspapers, these columns in the *Plaindealer* were often headed by poetry—composed either by Bass or others whose work appealed to the editor.

Bass's mission was to advocate "the principles of Peace, Prosperity and Union." Although he was quick to speak out on issues affecting African Americans, in the beginning his tone was far less strident than a number of black editors, and certainly that of his more militant Kansas counterparts. True to his commitment to racial uplift, he continued to give extensive coverage to cultural events. However, Bass could not keep politics and the arts in separate spheres. When these two entities intersected on either a national or state level, Bass responded immediately and unleashed his ability to compose scathing rhetoric. He was well-schooled in this technique as it was often employed by the infamous Kansas editors who had acquired a national reputation for vindictiveness through their caustic prose.

In this first issue, Bass urged readers to ignore a new play, *The Clansman*, and its "unprincipled author," Thomas Dixon. The play portrayed black males as brutes and rapists. However, in a subsequent issue he abandoned his belief that the impact of the play could be minimized by giving it little publicity. He denounced the blatantly racist author in a bitter editorial. He predicted that the "infamous and hell-inspiring play," would stir up "strife, prejudice and race hatred." He was right. D. W. Griffith's ground-breaking movie, *The Birth of a Nation*, based on *The Clansman*, was one of the most controversial films in this nation's history.

When *The Birth of a Nation* was released in 1915, Bass was living in California and the editor of his wife's paper, the *California Eagle*, which was the state's oldest black newspaper. Bass participated in a legal campaign to stop production of the film. Although he was unsuccessful, he and his wife, Charlotta Amanda Spears Bass, joined forces in a number of anti-discrimination causes. Over the years, Bass became increasingly militant and incurred the wrath of California's Ku Klux Klan. When *The Birth of a Nation* was shown in Montana, blacks in both Butte and Helena protested against its inflammatory theme.

As was the case with most black communities across the nation, crusades against racism originated in the church. In Helena, the St. James African Methodist Episcopal Church played a central role, and Bass was a member. St. James organized a literary society in November 1906. The lively debates included current topics, such as President Theodore Roosevelt's action in discharging the 26th infantry battalion. Their programs included recitations, musical solos, and the presentation of formal papers.

Bass came from the vibrant black community of Topeka, Kansas, where the long-established church of St. John had affected Kansas politics for decades. Bass was a staunch member. St. John's literary society, which provided a lively forum for the accomplishments of the black community throughout the state and supported many cultural events. Perhaps it is no accident that Helena's St. James literary society was organized shortly after Bass's arrival. No doubt he was influenced by the extraordinary speakers and politicians who presented papers at Topeka.

In 1908, despite African Americans' perception of racial tolerance in the West, the *Plaindealer* reported a Jim Crow incident involving a black musician that went all the way to the state supreme court. According to Bass, William J. Holland, a vocalist and pianist who came to Helena to give a concert, was arrested for wearing the insignia of the Benevolent Protective Order of the Elks. The colored Elks was a new organization with around 100,000 members nationwide. Bass argued that "If Elkdom is a good thing for the white man it is perhaps likewise a good thing for the black man . . ." He and others certainly objected to Holland's arrest simply for wearing a pin. However, wearing the pin was in defiance of a recent law forbidding non-Elks from claiming membership in the organization.

In fact, Holland was a member of the new rapidly growing colored Elks organization. Holland was prosecuted and convicted in the lower courts, but pursued the verdict to the state supreme court and won. Bass presented Holland as an elegant gentleman who innocently wore the Elk insignia.

However, William Lang, who wrote about Helena's African American community in "The Nearly Forgotten Blacks on Last Chance Gulch, 1900–1912," gave a considerably more lively account of the Holland incident. Lang wrote that Holland "played ragtime piano in a Clore Street brothel," and "wore large and flashy diamonds, with clothes to correspond." Although the photo of Holland published in the *Plaindealer* a year later was that of a neat conservative black man in a well-tailored suit, Bass also wrote that Holland was known as "King Do-Do," the "king of spenders," and was often seen in the company of Joe Gans, an African American boxer who was the lightweight champion of the world from 1902 to 1908. In a span of three months, Bass reported, Holland spent $16,000 gambling.

Holland's ability as a ragtime pianist reflected a movement that originated in New Orleans and was spreading across the country. Americans were acquiring radios, and ragtime, which some regarded as the "soul of the Negro," was one of the first popular offerings. Few black households in Helena could afford a radio. In fact, as late as 1930, only four black families had acquired sets: Joseph Wheeler, a porter in a hotel; Aaron Stitt, a janitor in a bank; Arthur Palmer, a porter in a hotel; and Julian Anderson, retired, who lived with his wife, Mattie, in the house of another black couple.

Helena African Americans had a band that made its first appearance at a parade in July 1908. D. H. Harris was the director, J. H. Taylor assistant director, Eugene Clark secretary, H. Salsbury Treasurer, and J. B. Bass was the business manager. Participants were W. Cole, a waiter, 1st trombone, Gus Mason tenor saxophone, Charles Johnson piccolo, E. Johnson alto saxophone, and Joseph Brown drums. The following men were not listed on the 1910 census: Joseph Lewis tuba, H. Price drums, J. W. Day clarinet, Joseph Smite alto saxophone, and H. Dillard piccolo. By the 1930 census only the following men still lived in Helena: Taylor, an express man who later became a porter at a hotel, Salsbury, a dry cleaner, Charles Johnson, an engineer, and E. Johnson, a janitor.

Other musical groups were the Silver-Toned quartette usually consisting of W. D. Cole, H. C. Simmons, William Knott, and Gus Mason. However, the members changed from time to time. There was also a small orchestra led by Miss Alma Bass as 1st mandolin, William Mason 2nd mandolin, H. Salsburg guitar, and D. Harris cornet. Both groups, in addition to the band, played frequently for the St. James Literary Society.

In addition to publicizing musical events on a local level Bass was quick to write about national issues that involved music. He gave a great deal of space to a controversial appeal from Emmett J. Scott, of the famed Tuskegee Institute in Alabama, to President Roosevelt to replace the white bandmasters in the "four Negro regiments in the United States Army." Scott had originally written to William Howard Taft, Roosevelt's secretary of War. However, after eighteen months he appealed directly to the president, who issued a directive stating "whenever there is a vacancy for bandmaster in a white regiment, transfer a white bandmaster from a colored regiment to it; and fill the place by the assignment of a colored man." He continued, "as soon as it can be done without injustice, I wish all the colored regiments supplied with colored bandmasters."

Helena's African Americans organized a baseball team, the Helena Giants in April 1906. Bass was elected business manager, Ward Cole captain, J. C. Brown was secretary, and Gus Mason served as treasurer. Team members included Joseph Marshall, Willie Wooley, Ward Cole, Joseph Brown, Clover Smith, Joseph Smith, James Howard, Gus Mason, Charles Graves, and Joseph Lewis. Three of its members—Marshall, Brown, and Cole—occasionally went to Missoula and played with that town's team.

In addition to supporting cultural activities and blacks' contributions to the arts, Bass published social commentary. Originally he was an ardent supporter of Booker T. Washington, the "Wizard of Tuskegee," who advocated a policy of cooperation and accommodation. Later he embraced the more militant ideas of W. E. B. Du Bois, who launched the NAACP and advocated a more aggressive approach to gaining civil rights for blacks. In keeping with his admiration for poets, Bass regarded Du Bois's *The Souls of Black Folk* as among some of the finest literature of his race. He promoted Du Bois's lists of the five rights both white and black men should consider basic: the right to individuality, the right to public courtesy, the right to opportunity, the right to peace, and the right to the truth.

As was the case with many black newspapers, the Montana *Plaindealer* was short-lived. Economics forced the paper to cease publication in the later part of 1911. Some scholars have speculated that Bass's inherent activism may have been the reason subscriptions declined to the Montana *Plaindealer*. However, to Bass, the central issue was that the "Negro people have had to fight for every recognition which has come to them during all the forty years since the Civil War."

Gordon left for the East one year before the *Plaindealer* ceased publication. He soon learned that the sense of place offered by regional identity would never trump the reality of racial discrimination in the long run. One of Gordon's most poignant chapters in *Born to Be* tells of leaving Montana when he was seventeen and being exposed to segregation for the first time. While working as a chauffeur, he went into a cafe and was told "we don't serve colored people in here." He had never heard the phrase before—honestly did not understand—and proceeded to order pie and milk. The irate waiter finally made it plain that black persons could not eat in the same establishments as white. Gordon was shocked to discover that in other regions of the country evaluation of his worth as a human being was based on the color of his skin.

Through his early years in Montana, Gordon became an astute observer of human nature. His humorous accounts of incidents during his childhood demonstrated a well-honed ability to strike the most intelligent stance with various community figures. This trait stood him well when he struggled to adjust to the range of attitudes toward blacks he encountered in the north. There are a number of passages in his autobiography that deal with the difficulty of a Montana boy forced to cope with the unwritten rules of racial interaction, which most African Americans learned in childhood. He left Montana for the East during one of the most exciting times in history for African Americans. Black power would not unite again in such an effective manner until the 1960s when this energy took a more militant political form.

African American women in Wyoming began fighting for civil rights before the Renaissance. However, political activity increased during this period of racial awareness. Although Wyoming was famous for being the first in the nation to institute suffrage for women on a state level, the movement did not include blacks. Throughout the nation, black women's struggle for voting rights faced discrimination on all fronts: race, class and gender. Black women were devastated when their contributions were rejected by white women who feared inclusion of African Americans in the suffrage movement would result in rebellion against their cause. This lack of acceptance prompted the formation of a vibrant network of African American women's clubs in Wyoming at a local and state level.

The black federated women's clubs concentrated on goals concerning quality of life for black women. Suffrage was but one of the rights sought. Many of these women had honed their organizational skills through previous involvement in the criteria pursued by white women's clubs. Wyoming blacks were more focused on education and cultural uplift than on collective efforts to gain recognition through the arts.

During the time when the Harlem Renaissance was at its height, a much darker movement was taking place. The Ku Klux Klan was making inroads in nearly every state in the union. Wyoming was one of the few states that resisted the Klan. In fact, when the Imperial Wizard, Hiram Evans, was scheduled to speak in Casper, local members were unable to find a meeting hall and enough community participation to warrant his stopping. Evans cancelled his speech.

Cheyenne blacks incorporated the Afro-American Club in 1905. The purpose of the club was to provide reading rooms, billiard rooms, restaurants, and other rooms as became necessary to provide recreation, diversion, and amusements for its members. The articles to incorporate were approved, but the corporation was dissolved July 18, 1927. Another popular Cheyenne gathering place was the Black and Tan Club owned by Lola West. African Americans could go there to drink, eat dinner, and socialize with their friends. The Cheyenne community was often entertained by the 9th Cavalry Band, which was attached to Fort Francis E. Warren.

Laramie was on the route traveled by a number of bands when the Great Depression seized the country. These bands entertained both blacks and whites and went from state to state hoping for bookings. The East could no longer support the black bands that inundated more populous areas. Not all performers appreciated this change in venue from the East to the West. Benny Goodman objected that the West had the reputation for being boring.

Bands passing through Laramie included those of Alphonse Trent and George Morrison. Trent's band had a number of exceptionally talented innovative musicians. Many famous musicians, white and black, played at the Elk Mountain Hotel. Even the great Louis Armstrong played there. The Elk Mountain Hotel had a famous "springy floor," constructed of oak flooring layered over widely spaced pine log moorings.

Harriet Elizabeth Byrd, Wyoming's first African American state legislator, recalls the wonderful musicians who provided entertainment for black servicemen stationed at Fort Warren who came to the USO. At this time the USO clubs were segregated. Sammy Davis, Jr., a well-known singer and entertainer, was based at the fort. He was upset over the lack of attention the "colored" USO club received compared to the one frequented by whites. He was instrumental in persuading musicians and artists to come to the club. The prestigious black entertainer even persuaded the famous actress Bette Davis to visit the base.

Sammy Davis, Jr.'s autobiography is riddled with accounts of prejudice he encountered at Fort Warren, despite his credentials as an entertainer. Although most of his ill-treatment came at the hands of white southern soldiers, no doubt his impression of Wyoming was colored by this experience. He had been raised by his father and uncle in the relatively color-blind venue of show business. Davis endured daily taunts with racial slurs. His initial response to these attacks was "immense anger growing within me until my legs were shaking and it was impossible to keep them still."

He was subjected to relentless physical attacks and destruction of property. A small group of men who delighted in tormenting him crushed a beloved, prized watch that his father and uncle had sacrificed to buy him when he was drafted. Even within this hostile environment he discovered "My talent was the weapon, the power, the way for me to fight. It was the one way I might hope to affect a man's thinking."

Despite Elizabeth Byrd's pleasant recollections of Sammy Davis, Jr.'s contributions to the black USO when he was stationed at Fort Warren, she, too, endured her share of discrimination in Wyoming. She attended an integrated high school because there were few black families in the community and the city certainly could not afford to maintain a separate institution. Her father was chief of police in Cheyenne under five different mayors. However, when it was time for his daughter to attend college, he learned the University of Wyoming had established segregated dormitories. She attended West Virginia State College instead. Byrd was further dogged by segregation when she was denied a teaching position in Wyoming because of her race.

Taylor Gordon had a spectacular career until his slow decline into mental illness. He entertained kings and queens in Europe and performed in America's most prestigious concert halls. His fascinating autobiography has passages that show his progression into confusion and deterioration. Ironically, this slide into despair and helplessness coincided with the end of the Harlem Renaissance. The entire music industry came close to collapsing during the nation's economic decline in the Great Depression. Even phonograph records were burned to provide warmth. After a series of stays in institutions, Gordon eventually returned to Montana to live out his days.

In 1934, a brilliant black statistician, Charles E. Hall, brother of Abram T. Hall, Jr., the African American politician who organized Graham County, Kansas, published an 850-page book of tables reporting every imaginable detail about African Americans. *The American Negro: His History and Literature* was set in approximately five point type, and Hall presented this work to the Department of Commerce. In his table "Negro Population of Cities and Other Urban Places 1920 and 1930," he lists Helena as having 220 blacks in 1920 and a mere 131 in 1930. Laramie, Wyoming had only 46 in 1920 and 109 in 1930. Clearly, both towns lacked the population for an effective group response to the infusion of new energy that characterized the Harlem Renaissance. Nevertheless the spirit of the New Negro movement spurred western blacks to emulate their eastern counterparts and develop individual talents.

In 1930, there were only 528 men and 127 gainfully employed African American men and women over ten years old in the entire state of Montana. Of these, only six black men and one black woman reported their occupations as musicians or teachers of music. Wyoming reported four black male musicians and four women out of a population of 536 men and 160 women.

The Harlem Renaissance was a time of intense creativity for African Americans. They mitigated the crippling implementation of segregation resulting from the 1896 *Plessy vs. Ferguson* decision by establishing their own institutions. They built banks, formed baseball teams, and developed a vibrant culture of black writers, artists, and musicians. The spirit of the New Negro infused visual arts, literature, the performing arts, and politics. Through this transformation blacks began appreciating their own potential and rich traditions. Blacks developed an extraordinary culture separate and independent from the surrounding white community. Ironically, through this explosion of talent and inspiration, whites began to upgrade their perception of the ability of African Americans to affect the arts.

The West lacked the population to support a collective movement. Nevertheless, through their isolation from blatant racial discrimination, western African Americans were free of the "double consciousness" that hampered those raised in the South and East. Gordon's assertion that being "laid on top of the Rocky Mountains" was a great blessing was borne out by the westerner's fearless approach to racial matters. Talented blacks fortunate enough to be "educated by Grizzly bears" and "hatched by the broiling sun," fused the energy of the New Negro with the spirit of the West.

Further Reading

Anoke, Akua Duku and Jacqueline Brice-Finch. *Get It Together: Readings About African American Life*. New York: Longman, 2003.

Chalmers, David M. *Hooded Americanism: The History of the Ku Klux Klan*. Durham, NC: Duke University Press, 1987.

Cohen, William. *At Freedom's Edge: Black Mobility and the Southern White Quest for Racial Control*. Baton Rouge, LA: Louisiana State University Press, 1991.

Craig, Lulu Sadler. *Craig Manuscript Collection*. Hill City, KA: Graham County Historical Society Archives.

Davis, Sammy Jr. and Jane and Burt Boyer. *Sammy, an Autobiography*. New York: Farrar, Straus and Giroux, 2000.

Frazier, Thomas R. *Readings in African-American History*. Belmont, CA: Wadsworth/ Thompson, 2001.

Gaspar, David Barry and Darlene Clark Hine, eds. *More Than Chattel: Black Women and Slavery in the Americas*. Bloomington, IN: Indiana University Press, 1996.

Glasrud, Bruce A. and Laurie Champion. *The African American West: A Century of Short Stories*. Boulder, CO: University of Colorado Press, 2000.

Gordon, Taylor. *Born to Be*. Lincoln, NE: University of Nebraska Press, 1995.

Hall, Charles E. *The American Negro, His History and Literature: Negroes in the United States, 1920–1932*. New York: Arno Press, 1969.

Hine, Darlene Clark, William C. Hine, and Stanley Harrold. *The African-American Odyssey*. Upper Saddle River, NJ: Prentice Hall, 2002.

Katz, William Loren. *Black West: A Documentary and Pictorial History of the African American Role in the Westward Expansion of the United States*. New York: Harlem Moon, 2005.

Lang, William L. "Helena, Montana's Black Community, 1900–1912." In *African Americans on the Western Frontier*, edited by Monroe Lee Billington, and Roger D. Hardaway, 198–215. Boulder, CO: University Press of Colorado, 1998.

Lemann, Nicholas. *The Promised Land: The Great Black Migration and How It Changed America*. New York: Alfred A. Knopf, 1991.

Lhamon, W. T., Jr. *Raising Cain: Blackface Performance from Jim Crow to Hip Hop*. Cambridge, MA: Harvard University Press, 1998.

Locke, Alain, ed. *The New Negro*. New York: Atheneum, 1968.

Logan, Onnie Lee. *Motherwit*. New York: Dutton, 1991.

Montana Plaindealer. (Helena, MT) March 16, 1906–September 1, 1911.

Porter, Kenneth W. *The Negro on the American Frontier*. New York: Arno Press, 1971.

Ravage, John. *Black Pioneers: Images of the Black Experience on the North American Frontier*. Salt Lake City, UT: University of Utah Press, 1997.

Rice, Marc. "Frompin' in the Great Plains: Listening and Dancing to the Jazz Orchestras of Alphonso Trent, 1925–1944." In *African Americans on the Great Plains*, edited by Bruce A. Glasrud and Charles A. Braithwaite, 256–272. Lincoln, NE: University of Nebraska Press, 2009.

Riley, Peggy. "Women of the Great Falls African Methodist Episcopal Church, 1870–1910." In *African American Women Confront the West, 1600–2000*, edited by Quintard Taylor and Shirley Ann Wilson Moore, 122–139. Norman, OK: University of Oklahoma Press, 2003.

Taylor, Alrutheus A. "Negro Congressmen a Generation After." *The Journal of Negro History* 7 (April 1922): 127–171.

Taylor, Quintard. "The Emergence of Black Communities in the Pacific Northwest: 1865–1910." *The Journal of American History* 64 (Autumn, 1979) 342–354.

Taylor, Quintard. *In Search of the Racial Frontier: African Americans in the American West*. New York: W. W. Norton & Company, 1998.

Taylor, Quintard and Shirley Ann Wilson Moore, eds. *African American Women Confront the West, 1600–2000*. Norman, OK: University of Oklahoma Press, 2003.

Terborg-Penn, Rosalyn. *African American Women in the Struggle for the Vote, 1850–1920*. Bloomington, IN: Indiana University Press, 1998.

Trotter, Joe William, Jr. *The African American Experience*. Boston, MA: Houghton Mifflin Company, 2001.

Winz, Cary D. and Paul Finkelman. *Encyclopedia of the Harlem Renaissance*. New York: Routledge, 2004.

Wood, Forrest G. "On Revising Reconstruction History: Negro Suffrage, White Disfranchisement, and Common Sense." *The Journal of Negro History* 51 (April 1966): 98–113.

13

A RENAISSANCE IN SEATTLE AND PORTLAND

Kimberley Mangun

Even as the Renaissance gained momentum in Harlem, a concurrent move-ment was taking shape some 2,400 miles to the west. Blacks living in Seattle and Portland welcomed William Pickens, Oscar De Priest, A. Philip Randolph, and other national leaders who toured the country. Citizens debated topical issues such as the Volstead Act and gave lectures and piano recitals. They participated in musical comedies, attended masquerade balls, and greeted the celebrated singers Roland Hayes and Marian Anderson. And they traveled between Seattle and Portland, less than 200 miles apart, to share culture, religion, and politics. While white leaders in those cities worked to dispel the frontier-town images that many easterners still had of Portland and Seattle, black citizens focused on circumventing Jim Crow restrictions and creating a strong community of their own in the Pacific Northwest. In this way, they were able to tap into the Renaissance and participate in a period that has been described as an "intellectual and artistic cross-fertilization."

This cross-fertilization was simultaneously embraced and fostered by the recording industry, radio, nightclubs, publishing houses, and black periodicals. For example, *The Crisis*, the monthly magazine of the National Association for the Advancement of Colored People, regularly featured the talents of black authors; "The Negro Speaks of Rivers," considered by many to be Langston Hughes's greatest work, was published in that journal in 1921. Hughes recited the poem during a program at Portland's Bethel African Methodist Episcopal (AME) Church in May 1932. Beatrice Morrow Cannady, publisher of *The Advocate*, was delighted to finally meet the poet, whom she described as young, good-looking, and vivacious. She had often read selections from *The Weary Blues*, his first collection of poetry, during radio broadcasts she gave in conjunction with Negro History Week. The broadcasts over KGW, KEX, KOIN, and other stations owned by Portland's white newspapers enabled Cannady to share the Renaissance with black and white listeners alike, and she wrote that she had received letters from people living along the Pacific Coast asking about the poems and their author.

Black newspapers such as *The Advocate*, published in Portland from 1903 until about 1936, and *The Northwest Enterprise* and *Cayton's Weekly*, both produced in Seattle, were important during the Renaissance. Not only did the periodicals keep local blacks—who numbered less than 5,000—informed about upcoming events and activities that were not covered by the white press but they also documented the rich intellectual and cultural history in Seattle and Portland during the early 1900s. This record demonstrates that the Renaissance soon reached the Pacific Northwest, and helps dispel the myth that black people in the Northwest contributed little to the region's history.

In fact, Seattle's rich musical history can be traced to June 10, 1918, when Miss Lillian Smith's Jazz Band played at a fundraiser for the local NAACP branch at Washington Hall. Many shows were subsequently held there, but the heart and soul of the city's thriving black jazz scene—which peaked between 1937 and 1951—was centered a few blocks away at Jackson Street and 12th Avenue. One musician who impacted Seattle's culture was pianist Evelyn Bundy, whose band has been called one of the earliest and most influential local jazz ensembles. She formed her group while still in high school; following her graduation in 1926, she changed the name from the Garfield Ramblers to the Evelyn Bundy Band. The group played at a variety of events in 1928 and 1929. For example, when the steamship *H. F. Alexander* arrived in Seattle to resume its seasonal service between that city and San Francisco, Bundy's band was hired to play at a dance to welcome the ship's one hundred black employees.

One article notes that dancing offered people "a reprieve from the harsh economic realities and the drudgery of earning a living doing monotonous tasks" in menial jobs. Although the article discusses this in terms of the famous Savoy Ballroom, the nightclub that filled an entire Harlem block, the importance of dance in Seattle is evident in the sheer number of events that were advertised in *The Northwest Enterprise*. "Social dance . . . was a way for people to celebrate, to escape, and to express their identity"; that was true of participants as well as influential musicians such as the clarinetist Oscar Holden.

Holden, often called the patriarch of Seattle jazz, arrived in the city with Jelly Roll Morton's band in 1919 and decided to remain. He soon formed his own group and played gigs after his day job as a pipe fitter at Todd Shipyards. One regular engagement was at Doc Hamilton's Barbecue Pit, which equaled Harlem's Cotton Club as a Prohibition-era hangout. People in Seattle also had opportunities to enjoy Holden's incomparable orchestra in 1929–1930 when the group played at a Thanksgiving dance, a Christmas frolic, and a masquerade dance on New Year's Day. Another frolic at Washington Hall—which was acquired by Historic Seattle in 2009 and saved from demolition—featured the Jimmy Adams Band.

FIGURE 13.1 Black-oriented popular entertainment was an integral feature of the Harlem Renaissance. In January 1928 African Americans in the Pacific Northwest attended shows like this musical revue, which depicted slave life and featured music and dancing. As an additional feature attendees had the opportunity to win a sporty new car. *Northwest Enterprise*, January 6, 1928

Adams had been a member of Evelyn Bundy's Band with brother Wayne, who later joined Earl Whaley's group.

Whaley was a bandleader from the San Francisco Bay Area who played alto saxophone. After settling in Seattle, he formed the Red Hot Syncopators, one of the first swing bands on the West Coast. *The Northwest Enterprise* promised pleasure lovers an unusually good time at the Alhambra Club, where a dance celebrating the election was planned for a Tuesday night in March 1930. Whaley and the Syncopators were furnishing the music; Sally Harper, a lyric tenor, and Eddie Rucker were scheduled to sing. Rucker was known as a jive artist, according to one writer, and one of the wildest entertainers performing in Los Angeles then.

Soprano Estelle Slater Jackson, whose brief career included performing in concerts around the country and doing chorus work for Hollywood films, also made Seattle her home for a time. She gave a farewell recital at Mt. Zion Baptist Church, whose choir she had directed, in March 1930. The *Enterprise*'s columnist reported that the church "was crowded . . . by an enthusiastic audience" who hoped to hear her perform once more before she left for Los Angeles. "Mrs. Jackson who has been acclaimed one of the leading sopranos of the race was in fine voice and presented a well balanced program of sacred and spiritual numbers," noted the columnist.

Large-scale events also were popular. Seattle's grandest musical production may have been *Ethiopia at the Bar of Justice*, a pageant that featured 130 of Seattle's leading black singers and actors. An article in the *Enterprise* noted that the production was "the biggest and most impressive musical and dramatic under-taking ever attempted by the colored people of the Pacific Northwest." Not only did it have the large cast but it also promised to "concentrate and glorify in one stage presentation the whole history of the American Negro." Following the two performances in May 1927, an *Enterprise* columnist observed that it was nearly impossible for her to find sufficient adjectives to "properly describe this beautiful pageant of Negro progress."

Other productions presented in Seattle between 1928 and 1930 included: *The Old Kentucky Home*; *The Awakening*, a springtime pageant that featured 110 young participants and special costumes and stage settings; *Gypsy Rover*, a musical comedy staged by the Mt. Zion Baptist Choir; *The Prodigal Son*; *The Transformation*, a two-act comedy; and *Simon Peter and His Wife's Mother*, a Biblical drama in three acts that was presented by the Dumas Dramatic Club.

In May 1929, Portlanders capitalized on an engagement of *Hearts in Dixie*, the motion picture that launched Stepin Fetchit's career, by preparing a seven-act stage show at the Rivoli Theatre. Local performers did "dialect readings," a group of children did a dance routine, and others sang before the midnight screening of the film.

Two years later, Stepin Fetchit became an *Advocate* subscriber when he stopped in Portland to perform at the Paramount Theatre. Then he made his first appearance in Seattle. The actor born Lincoln Theodore Perry had a long film career that was alternately celebrated—he was the first black performer to sign a deal with a major studio—and criticized—his career was built on playing stereotypical roles. Nevertheless, the *Enterprise* published a large sketch of the performer above an article that described him as the famous colored tap dancer and screen comedian. Fetchit was in town to headline a program at the Fox Paramount Theatre; one of his films, *The Prodigal*, was playing concurrently at the theater. His arrival also represented an opportunity to hold a dance. For fifty cents, people could meet Stepin Fetchit and dance to music by Cecil Finley's California Stompers, a local group that played at many clubs on Seattle's south side.

Events in Seattle and Portland also emphasized progress and achievements by blacks, a key theme of the Harlem Renaissance. In October 1926, for example, Seattle's Mt. Zion Baptist Church hosted a six-night Fair and Industrial Show. Highlights of the full program included music by Seattle's most talented individuals, a discussion of the historical progress of the race, and a Business and Professional Night. *Enterprise* editor William H. Wilson gave the main address and introduced representatives of every Negro-owned business in the city. The show's final night was marked by the selection of Seattle's "most useful Colored Citizen" and subsequent awarding of a gold medal, a joyful occasion similar to the NAACP's annual presentation of its highest honor, the Spingarn Medal for distinguished merit and achievement.

A similar event was held in Portland after *Advocate* editor Cannady returned from the Fourth Pan-African Congress, held in New York City in August 1927. Eager to make the most of her experience at the Congress, convened by W. E. B. Du Bois to address race relations in the United States and around the world, she decided to organize a unique educational meeting to discuss Negro progress. The free, two-day event at Portland's Central Library featured her report on the recent Congress; spirituals and other music by Negro composers; exhibits of books and magazines by and about black people; lectures by individuals such as Nettie Asberry, president of the Washington State Federation of Colored Women's Clubs; and recitations of work by Paul Laurence Dunbar and other Negro poets. The conference attracted national attention by publications including *Legislative Counsellor*, the organ of the Woman's Legislative Council of Washington, which noted that the program had emphasized the wonderful progress made by American Negroes since Emancipation.

Recitals were very popular in Seattle. Advertisements and articles for the various events and performers make clear that the city was an active participant in the artistic cross-fertilization that was occurring at the time; stories and ads also frequently read like a who's who of black entertainers. Contralto Belle Salter Tyler returned to Seattle in March 1927 to perform at Mt. Zion Baptist Church. An advance article in the *Enterprise* noted that her appearance would be one of the distinct musical events of the season. Tyler had lived in Seattle for some years before moving to St. Paul, Minnesota, to continue her vocal training with some of the East's leading teachers. One month later, Thornton Lewis Evans, described as the foremost colored baritone of the Pacific Northwest, sang at the Valhalla Temple. In June 1927, mezzo-soprano Lena Louise Johnson, who lived in nearby Tacoma and had starred in *Ethiopia at the Bar of Justice*, performed for an appreciative audience at the First AME Church. And Dock Snellings, the so-called Singing Postman whose songbook ranged from classical music to spirituals, appeared in Seattle in February 1928. The baritone was touring the Pacific Coast when he stopped to perform for a large audience at the First AME Church.

Carl Diton, who was completing a two-year term as president of the National Association of Negro Musicians in 1928, gave a recital at Bethel AME Church that May. An *Enterprise* article described him as the race's most versatile musician. Readers were encouraged to show their support for him by attending the free event, which was sure to eclipse any similar affair ever presented in Seattle. Six months later, Florence Cole-Talbert performed at the Olympic Theater. A review in the *Enterprise* noted that she upheld her reputation as one of America's foremost prima donnas; arias were interpreted with reverence, and her versions of *Big Lady Moon* and *Slumber Song* were superb.

A short article in the *Enterprise*'s "Seattle Notes and Gossip" column informed readers of an upcoming concert by Lorenza Jordan Cole. Advertisements and additional brief stories published in the weeks before the September 1928 concert promised a delightful program, and noted that the Woman's Century Theater would be a Mecca for music lovers. But there was more to the story. Mary White Ovington, a founder of the NAACP, was in Seattle then to talk about the organization. On the last day of her visit, the secretary of the local branch asked Ovington if she would listen to a young pianist play. Ovington initially declined because she was ill and was already scheduled to give four talks that day, among other activities. Fortunately, she later changed her mind. "Lying on a couch in [Cole's] pleasant room, I was prepared to hear an aspiring but mediocre player," Ovington recalled in her book, *Black and White Sat Down Together*. "But after a few minutes I sat up. Lorenza Jordan Cole was no ordinary pianist." This private concert prompted Ovington to help pay for Cole's education at the New York Institute of Musical Arts. Her assistance was important, as well as unusual: Recent reappraisals of the Harlem Renaissance have noted that men received most of the patronage then. The corresponding lack of financial and professional support for women made it more difficult for them to publish poetry or short stories, and fewer of their plays were produced.

Some individuals, such as ragtime pianist Eubie Blake, came to Seattle as part of the Orpheum Theater circuit. Blake, considered to be one of the most important figures in early twentieth-century black music, needed little introduction before arriving in the city in November 1928. The musical he collaborated on with Noble Sissle had been the sensation of 1921; pieces such as *I'm Just Wild About Harry* and *Love Will Find a Way* were instant hits and *Shuffle*

Along launched the careers of Josephine Baker and Paul Robeson. Blake performed in *Shuffle Along, Jr.* in Seattle. The *Enterprise* called the revue "a typical Eubie Blake offering, with Mr. Blake singing those songs for which he is so justly famous and providing his own accompaniment for them." Ada Brown also appeared at the Orpheum Theater in RKO's *Collegiate Revue*. Brown, described as "pear shaped and gregarious with a resounding contralto voice," had begun her career nearly two decades earlier in Chicago. By the time she visited Seattle, she had toured in Europe and recorded the popular song, *Evil Mama Blues*.

Forbes Randolph's Kentucky Jubilee Singers played at the Orpheum in May 1928. The chorus had been founded in the mid-1870s, a period when dozens of jubilee troupes toured the country on the heels of the wildly successful Fisk University Jubilee Singers. The original group performed for two decades before it apparently disbanded. Entrepreneur Forbes Randolph revived the name early in 1928 and selected an eight-member chorus from hundreds of applicants in Harlem. According to the *Enterprise*, all of the singers were college men with a musical background; three were described as former opera singers who had had European training.

Many individuals, such as Ada Brown and Eubie Blake, passed through Seattle and Portland once they had achieved some measure of success. Others, such as Howard Biggs, Shirley Graham McCanns, and William Duncan Allen, Jr., launched their careers in the Pacific Northwest. Biggs, called Seattle's phenomenal boy pianist, gave a concert at the First AME Church in that city at the end of April 1928. An *Enterprise* columnist predicted a bright future for the ten-year-old, provided he was given a chance to thrive. The concert aimed to help with that; funds were collected to pay for his continuing musical education. Biggs would go on to have a stellar career in jazz and rhythm and blues as a pianist, arranger, and composer for groups such as The Ravens; an advertisement in *The Billboard 1944 Music Year Book* called him "A Pianist That's Different." Biggs also worked for RCA Victor and Sunbeam Music and was musical director for Regal Records.

Shirley Graham McCanns, who would become W. E. B. Du Bois's second wife, established a reputation in Portland in 1926–1927 as a composer, singer, and conductor. For a time she directed the choir at Mount Olivet Baptist Church and a group called the Roland Hayes Quartette. She also did some speaking at area churches and the YWCA about topics including the role of Negro music in the development of mankind. She left Portland to travel in France, and later worked at Howard University as a music librarian and as a music teacher at Morgan State University in Baltimore. In July 1932, her opera *Tom-Tom* debuted in Cleveland. *TIME* reported that nearly 15,000 people attended the premiere of the first Negro opera to be staged and performed by an all-black cast; it also was the first opera by a black woman to be produced.

William Duncan Allen, Jr. was another local success story. One month after graduating from Portland's Jefferson High School, Allen left for Ohio to study piano at Oberlin College's Conservatory of Music. He graduated in June 1928, and then did some postgraduate work at the Juilliard School of Music. He returned to Portland for a visit during the summer of 1929. The *Enterprise*'s Portland correspondent reported that music lovers in her city were eagerly anticipating a recital at Bethel AME Church: "He is recognized as one of the most brilliant pianists of the race and next Friday night [he] will present a diversified program sure to meet the approval of his audience." People in Seattle also had the opportunity to hear Allen in concert when he visited Mt. Zion Baptist Church in September 1929. He gave another recital at a Seattle church two years later; his sister, Nellie Allen, a talented pianist in her own right, performed too.

Also noteworthy was Susie Revels Cayton, an activist, journalist, and writer whose father, Hiram Revels, was the first black man elected to the US Senate. Susie Revels began writing for *The Seattle Republican* in January 1896. Six months later, she relocated to Washington and married the newspaper's publisher, Horace Cayton, who later founded *Cayton's Weekly* and the short-lived *Cayton's Monthly*. She served as associate editor of the *Republican* and regularly contributed articles to the newspaper. Susie also enjoyed writing short stories and published many of them in the *Republican* and *Seattle Post-Intelligencer* during the early 1900s. Her husband proudly observed in 1917 that she was a "splendid short story writer" and could have ranked among the country's best authors if she had had more time to devote to her craft.

Black churches, intimate venues for recreation as well as religion, were invaluable to the growing Renaissance in the Pacific Northwest. Even though color lines in Portland and Seattle were not as rigidly enforced as they were in the South, de facto racism and segregation existed in both cities. Hotels owned by white proprietors refused black guests, restaurateurs could decline to serve patrons, and theater owners often required blacks to sit in balconies and refused to rent their facilities to event organizers. So, churches were a haven for many of the era's most popular performers and speakers. For example, the Williams Colored Singers, known for their harmonies and interpretation of spirituals, performed at Seattle churches several times during the Renaissance. In November 1927, the choir of four men and four women sang at Mt. Zion Baptist Church. The singers returned to that church in January 1929. According to the *Enterprise*, the group had "recently returned from a European trip where they won the plaudits of the continent."

The noted tenor Roland Hayes also earned accolades abroad before he gained the respect of Americans. To ensure a good turnout for a 1918 concert, Beatrice Cannady, editor of *The Advocate*, closed her office and went from person to person to tell them about the talented performer. About a thousand people, white and black, reportedly attended Hayes's performance at the Masonic Temple and Auditorium in downtown Portland. After all of the bills were paid, Cannady had $150 remaining, just enough to pay Hayes and his accompanist and cover their expenses. Thereafter, Hayes performed numerous times in the Pacific Northwest during the Renaissance. He was scheduled to return to Portland in March 1925 as part of the Elwyn Artist Series, which featured some of the most popular performers of the day. Cannady began advertising the concert months in advance; she assured people that ticket prices were reasonable and urged individuals not to delay their purchase because the event was sure to sell out. She promoted another concert in 1931, when he began his tour in the Northwest rather than in the East, as she had previously reported in *The Advocate*. Following his concert, she wrote that the audience remained for some time, hoping to induce Hayes to sing just one more number.

Hayes sang at Meany Hall for the Performing Arts on the University of Washington campus in March 1927. "Hayes is not only a great artist, he is an inspiration," reported the *Enterprise*. He returned two years later for a concert at the Metropolitan Theater. Again he enthralled his audience, who "relished with the artist the warmth and color of the group of Negro spirituals" he had selected for the program. The tenor also performed in Seattle in March 1930, his sixth concert in the city, according to the *Enterprise*. "The singer never was in better form," observed a columnist. Hayes returned to Meany Hall in October 1931. By then, the newspaper noted that little needed to be said about the famous tenor's skill or popularity.

Marian Anderson also performed many times in Seattle, and always to great acclaim. Her first trip to the Pacific Coast was in 1929. That June, she appeared twice with the American Philharmonic Orchestra at an outdoor summer-concert series at the University of Washington Stadium. "Not only does Miss Anderson possess a voice of unusual beauty and power, but she also has a personality that instantly wins her audience, making them her enthusiastic friends," noted the *Enterprise*. She was invited to give two more performances at the Stadium in August. The fact that she was the sole entertainer who had been asked to return was proof, according to the *Enterprise*, that the race was finally being acknowledged for its contributions to music and art. However, white-owned hotels in Seattle refused to accommodate her. Anderson returned to Seattle in January 1931 and again delighted her listeners. The newspaper's columnist felt "she should be awarded a place among the finest singers of all time. Her sincerity, her sense of musical values and her purity of diction make every given breath an artistic delight."

Seattle and Portland benefited greatly from this national artistic cross-fertilization. But the cities also gained from sharing a talented group of local individuals. One of those people was Jessie Coles Grayson, billed as Portland's Famous Contralto in an ad for a May 1929 concert at Mt. Zion. Following the recital, the *Enterprise*'s columnist wrote that Grayson had given one of the finest concerts ever presented in Seattle. "Mrs. Grayson proved herself an artist in every sense of the word. She is a master of contralto voice which she uses effectively and without exaggeration."

And in November 1929, Dr. Jonathan L. Caston, pastor of Portland's Mount Olivet Baptist Church, gave a free talk at Mt. Zion about "Facing the Color Bar From the Black Man's Side." According to the *Enterprise*, Caston had given this talk several times to groups including the Portland Chamber of Commerce, and each time it had "occasioned much comment, favorable and otherwise."

Portland and Seattle also shared the talented Elmer C. Bartlett, a former organist for the First AME Church in Los Angeles. In August 1929, the *Enterprise* reported that he was organizing a chorus of 200 to sing at a concert at Garfield High School Auditorium. Two years later, Bartlett organized a similar concert at Portland's Civic Auditorium, now known as Keller Auditorium. *The Morning Oregonian*'s music columnist wrote that an appreciative audience had asked for numerous encores. Bartlett apparently was so taken with Portland that he decided to remain. He began advertising instruction in piano, harmony, voice, and pipe organ for students of all levels. By July 1932, his students were ready to give a recital at Bethel AME Church; a front-page article in *The Advocate* noted that the program promised to be most interesting, in part because many original compositions by Negroes were going to be performed for the first time in Portland. Bartlett also directed the Bethel choir at a number of events, and the group performed Negro spirituals during KWJJ's Jubilee Hour one Sunday night in 1932. That summer he directed the Portland Negro Chorus, composed of the Bethel choir and other singers, in a series of concerts dubbed "Spirituals Under the Stars." Black as well as white people were observed in the large audience at Multnomah Civic Stadium, now called PGE Park.

But the Renaissance in the Northwest was not solely an artistic cross-fertilization; it also was a time for intellectual discussions with visitors and locals alike. In May 1921, for example, Bishop Robert E. Jones discussed "The Democracy of Love" at Seattle's Mt. Zion Baptist Church. Jones, a leader in New Orleans and editor of the *Southwestern Christian Advocate*, was the first Negro to be elected a bishop in the Methodist Episcopal Church. And Henry Allen Boyd was in the middle of an extensive speaking trip through the West when he gave a free lecture, titled "Think," at Mt. Zion in March 1927. Boyd, an ordained Baptist minister and editor of *The Globe* in Nashville, Tennessee, told the audience that Negroes "must address themselves to a big program of construction and must win for themselves credit for the achievements of the race." In a talk to Portlanders, Boyd advised "the race to take advantage of educational opportunities," to "use their brains to create businesses for themselves," and to "give literature to their children that will build the right character and inspire them to become great and glorious in the Master's Cause."

Politicians and activists also included the Pacific Northwest in their speaking tours. The *Enterprise* observed that Seattle was fortunate to have Kelly Miller, the writer, orator, race leader, and dean of Howard University, visit in June 1927. Miller discussed the "Inherent Manhood of the Negro" with a small audience at Renton Hill Hall. "The speech," noted the *Enterprise*, "was a masterpiece of eloquence, diction and logic."

Illinois Congressman Oscar De Priest visited Seattle in September 1929. *Enterprise* editor William Wilson wrote that his coming should be an inspiration to men and women of color, and he urged people to attend the event with their children. Following De Priest's visit, a front-page story announced that he had thrilled his audience at the Third Avenue Theater by delivering a rousing talk about citizenship and school segregation. He also paid "tribute to the hard working class of Negroes who made sacrifices and supported every endeavor for the advancement of their race." De Priest then went to Portland, where an estimated 800 blacks turned out to hear his ninety-minute discussion of "race prejudice, discriminatory measures adopted in some southern states against the negro . . . and failure of the country to enforce the 14th amendment." De Priest and his party returned the following day to Seattle, where they boarded the *H. F. Alexander* for California and other speaking engagements.

William Pickens, field secretary for the NAACP, and Mary White Ovington, chairman of the organization's board of directors, visited the West in 1928. Pickens gave a lecture in April at Seattle's Labor Temple, where a large crowd listened to his discussion of "American Race Prejudice." According to the *Enterprise*, Pickens "carefully explained the danger of segregation, in that it not only crushes the spirit of the Negro people, but it also keeps the white citizen down with the Negro." In Portland, Pickens had a very full schedule that included talks to the City Club, students at Lincoln High School, and the NAACP branch. He continued on to Los Angeles, where he and Cannady planned to attend and speak at the NAACP's 19th Annual Conference.

Ovington visited Portland after the conference ended in July. She gave numerous talks to the City Club and other white groups, met with ministers, and spoke to reporters with the local white newspapers. She stopped in Seattle, too. As noted earlier, she came down with a cold during her stay, but did not disappoint any of her audiences. Editor and Seattle NAACP Branch President Horace Roscoe Cayton introduced her to the audience at Mt. Zion Baptist Church. He reported that she "stressed the necessity of Negroes fighting through organization to gain full citizenship rights and privileges."

Pickens did another long speaking tour of the country in 1930. He started his three-month trip in St. Louis, and then traveled to Missouri, Nebraska, and Wyoming before dipping down into Colorado and the Southwest. Next, Pickens traveled the length of California—giving talks along the way in cities including San Diego, Oakland, and Sacramento—before making stops in the Pacific Northwest. He finally arrived in Portland in May. An *Advocate* headline proclaimed: "Pickens Triumphs! Crowds Pack Bethel to Hear Famous Orator." Cannady reported that more than 700 people squeezed into the AME church to hear Pickens talk about "Abraham Lincoln, Man and Statesman." He continued to Seattle, where more than 300 people heard him discuss the mission, goals, and accomplishments of the NAACP.

Editor and labor organizer A. Philip Randolph spoke to groups in Seattle on two consecutive nights in March 1929. "Unlike many orators Randolph does not resort to witticisms and anecdotes to interest an audience," observed the

Enterprise's columnist; instead, "he holds and thrills his hearers by power of his argument and eloquence." Randolph told the crowd at Mt. Zion Baptist Church about the Brotherhood of Sleeping Car Porters and the union's importance to Negro workers, and stressed the need for better wages and working conditions. Randolph visited Portland in July 1932 as part of a cross-country trip that included stops in Missouri, Colorado, Utah, Washington, and California. Beatrice Cannady was one of the individuals who welcomed him to Mount Olivet Baptist Church, where he delivered an address on "The Negro in the Economic Crisis." Randolph discussed the Depression and reiterated the need for black men to organize and pool their power. He was still fighting for federal recognition of the Brotherhood of Sleeping Car Porters, the labor union he created to help protect exploited employees of the Pullman Palace Car Company. Cannady wrote in *The Advocate*: "The race needs more men like Randolph with guts and back-bone to represent it before the eyes of the world."

Another individual with the courage to speak his mind was George S. Schuyler, described by the *Enterprise*'s Portland correspondent as the most promising of all the younger Negro writers and lecturers. "Those who have read Mr. Schuyler's 'Views and Reviews' in the *Pittsburgh Courier* know just what a treat is in store," she wrote. He made his first visit to the Pacific Coast in March 1928, two years after publishing his controversial article, "The Negro Art Hokum," in *The Nation*. In that piece he disputed the uniqueness of the Harlem Renaissance and argued that there was no distinct Negro art or literature because writers and artists were products of their environment: "The Aframerican is subject to the same economic and social forces that mold the actions and thoughts of the white Americans. He is not living in a different world as some whites and a few Negroes would have me believe," he wrote. His article raised fundamental questions about the construction of blackness, identity, culture, and community, topics that still resonate today.

Although Harlem became the Renaissance's "symbolic capital and its institutional center of gravity," this focus on place has obscured other, related renaissance movements—such as those in Seattle and Portland—and the creative work people were doing to build community, celebrate accomplishments, and affirm identity. By documenting this record in their respective newspapers, editors Beatrice Morrow Cannady, William H. Wilson, and Horace Roscoe Cayton helped readers take part in the cultural citizenship that the philosopher Alain Locke and other black intellectuals envisioned in the early 1900s. The editors also welcomed, and interacted with, many of the Renaissance's key participants, and believed their visits could have an impact on race relations locally.

In March 1920, editor Cayton reflected on recent talks by Mary Talbert, the clubwoman and civil-rights activist from Buffalo, New York: "The addresses . . . were, in a way, masterpieces and the overcrowded house enjoyed her every word," he wrote in *Cayton's Weekly*:

> I regret, however, that the white citizens of this community never seem to feel sufficiently interested in the noted colored speakers, who . . . visit this city on lecture tours, as they say things of as much, if not more so, interest to the white man as the black man.

Beatrice Cannady also contemplated the status of race relations in Portland. At one point she told a white reporter that it was critical to present gifted singers, poets, musicians, politicians, and speakers to Portlanders to counteract front-page stories of crimes allegedly committed by blacks and dispel the myth that black people had played no role in America's cultural heritage. One writer has noted that Seattle's musical legacy was obscured by race, class, and gender: White reporters and cultural observers failed to see the vibrant scene and the important contributions musicians were making to jazz history, and clubs were located in a black neighborhood where few white people traveled. Those who did go to a mixed-race club such as the Black and Tan at 12th and Jackson ("black and tan" was the general term for a club that allowed white and black patrons) often went to satiate their curiosity rather than partake in the "unfolding drama of an American music culture in the making." However, for the 5,000 blacks living in the Pacific Northwest in the early 1900s, the Renaissance was not only an opportunity to connect with a passionate movement taking place in Harlem but also a chance to start a cultural and civil-rights movement of their own that would hit its stride in the years after World War II.

Further Reading

The Advocate (Portland, OR). *The Northwest Enterprise, Cayton's Weekly, Cayton's Monthly* (Seattle, WA).

Barros, Paul de. *Jackson Street After Hours: The Roots of Jazz in Seattle* (Seattle, WA: Sasquatch Books, 1993).

Diaz, Ed, ed. *Horace Roscoe Cayton: Selected Writings* (Seattle, WA: Bridgewater-Collins, 2002).

Diaz, Ed, ed. *Stories by Cayton: Short Stories by Susie Revels Cayton, a Seattle Pioneer* (Seattle, WA: Bridgewater-Collins, 2002).

Hobbs, Richard S. *The Cayton Legacy: An African American Family* (Pullman, WA: Washington State University Press, 2002).

Mangun, Kimberley. *A Force for Change: Beatrice Morrow Cannady and the Struggle for Civil Rights in Oregon, 1912–1936* (Corvallis, OR: Oregon State University Press, 2010).

Taylor, Quintard. *The Forging of a Black Community: Seattle's Central District from 1870 Through the Civil Rights Era* (Seattle, WA: University of Washington Press, 1994).

14

HARLEM RENAISSANCE IN SAN DIEGO

New Negroes and Community

Charles P. Toombs

The manifestation of the spirit of the Harlem Renaissance in San Diego was prompted by similar motives and dreams as that of the Harlem Renaissance in East Coast and Midwest cities and yet it also had significant differences. African Americans in San Diego, like their counterparts nationally, seized the opportunity to define themselves (and in the process to debunk racial stereotypes of blacks), to establish organizations and businesses, and to actively respond to an environment of steadily increasing racism, discrimination, and segregation. In carrying out the above, black San Diegans relied much less on whites and white patronage and, instead, created a thriving and vibrant black community.

African Americans began moving to the Southwest as early as 1804. John Brown, a sailor, is the "first known black from the United States to set foot in San Diego," in 1804, and "When California entered the Union in 1850 only eight blacks in a total population of 798 resided in [San Diego] county. In 1870 there were only seventeen, but by 1880 there were fifty-five" (Madyun and Malone, 1). It is important to mention that even the above number may be misleading or under-reported since there was the "tendency of African-Hispanics to be listed as white or as Mexican rather than Black" (*Centre City Development Corporation: Downtown San Diego African-American Heritage Study*, CCDC 2004, II-3). Major migration trends are noted following the end of the Civil War and Emancipation. For example, Clayborne Carson, Emma J. Lapsansky-Werner, and Gary B. Nash remark that:

> Between World War I and 1930, an estimated 2 million black people left the South. Some headed for border states such as Missouri and Illinois.
> . . . Still others formed separate black communities in far-flung sections of

the United States or even abroad. Large cities, such as Chicago, Detroit, New York, Washington, and Los Angeles, together absorbed more than 800,000 black newcomers in this period.

(346)

Reasons for African American migration to the Southwest, and Southern California in particular, are not unlike the reasons for black migration out of the South to other areas: southern terrorism and tyranny (especially the tremendous rise of the number of lynchings of black men, women, and even children), lack of economic opportunity and autonomy, Jim Crow-ism, neo-slavery (share-cropping system), black disfranchisement, and the desire to locate a "Promised Land," where political, economic, cultural, and racial freedom might be a possibility. In addition to the masses and the working class's desire to locate a context where a modicum of freedom might be found, the educated and professional classes were also seeking geographical and cultural spaces where its talents and ambitions might be realized. For either class, an escape from an entrenched racist environment was central to their motivation to leave the South (and Midwest too with the rise of the Ku Klux Klan there, beginning in the second decade of the twentieth century). Homer Hawkins, in his "Trends in Black Migration from 1863 to 1960," argues that black migration to the Southwest United States was also made in conjunction with the expansion of numerous railway systems" and these "systems gave rise to a large number of land speculators who made a concerted effort to induce individuals to go west and settle land. The appeals of the land speculators had an effect on the black population of the South" (140). Furthermore, black population growth (as well as the general population growth) was increased "in 1885 with the laying of lines for the California Southern Rail . . . in San Diego" (CCDC II-5). San Diego and Los Angeles were geographical and cultural sites that attracted the black migrating population. These cities were different from those of the East Coast and Midwest cities to which most southern blacks migrated. For one, in Southern California, African Americans discovered they were not the only marginalized people of color, for people of Mexican descent, Asian descent, and Native Americans were marginalized by color, caste, and class. Therefore, diverse people of color were targets of white racism and so no one group was singled out. That is, the racial playing field was not just black and white. Gail Madyun and Larry Malone suggest that for blacks migrating to San Diego they found most public venues were segregated and thus "their status in San Diego was no better or worse than that of other blacks living outside the South" (2). While this is largely true, white San Diegans had other people of color to racially target and thus racism against African Americans was somewhat diffused. Furthermore, San Diego had a small but significant black presence prior to the migration of blacks in the late 1800s and early 1900s. When blacks migrated to San Diego, other blacks, who were beginning to create a viable black community, were present to receive them.

How the New Negro creates community in San Diego and establishes its voice is related to its cousin in Harlem but is also distinctly different. For one, as Alain Locke proclaims in *The New Negro*, his groundbreaking essay that announces the call and the articulation of the issues and concerns African Americans must confront and deal with in the 1920s, "the New Negro will be a 'thinking' being and will be motivated by a 'group psychology'" (3, 10). In this sense, New Negroes in San Diego respond to the call and carry out the spirit and cultural direction or agenda as its East Coast brethrens. And because the numbers of blacks are so much smaller in San Diego than in East Coast and Midwest cities, blacks rely much more on each other in San Diego. In many ways, blacks in San Diego are far closer to the West African ethos of the communal self or kinship. John Mbiti, for example, writes that "The community must . . . make, create or produce the individual; for the individual depends on the corporate group. . . . The individual can only say: 'I am, because we are; and since we are, therefore I am'" (108–09). That is, Harlem or New Negro cultural expression in San Diego is "more black," and a significant black insular community is established. There is less reliance on white patrons or benefactors to launch and sustain this new Negro movement. Indeed, with the exception of whites attending dance and musical perform-ances at the Creole Club, buying black art, and seeking the black consumers' dollar (even the "Officials of the City of San Diego" and "San Diego County Officials," the mayor, city council, board of supervisors, etc. place ads in the *Colored Directory*), they have little to do with New Negro cultural production and political and social activity in San Diego.

Because African Americans migrated to San Diego for work and social opportunities, it is useful to examine the types, variety, and kinds of work, business, and social opportunities that were present in San Diego or that blacks created once in the city between World War I and World War II. This examination is important because the Harlem Renaissance, as generally conceived, is not only about Talented Tenth cultural expression and cultural production; it is also about opportunities and creation of culture and resistance to social and racial oppression that is generated by the black masses. Although the Talented Tenth and its involvement in the arts and politics generates much of the discussion of the New Negro Movement, what everyday black people were able to accomplish within the landscape of the "Promised Land," in Harlem and in other Eastern and Midwestern cities, is equally important, and, arguably, makes the larger movement possible, as Alain Locke so succinctly puts it when he writes, "In a real sense it is the rank and file who are leading, and the leaders who are following" (7). The same is true in San Diego.

In the 1920s, Black San Diegans are employed in a variety of occupations, and some are business owners. Although as might be expected in a segregated city, blacks are overwhelmingly employed in service and domestic positions (cooks, washer-women, maids, laborers, and shoeshine operators), they are, as mentioned in the 1925–1926 *Colored Directory*, "found in all walks of life. In business and professions, merchants, mechanics, and men of leisure [sic]" (54). Examples of the diversity of black employment and business can be gleaned from the numerous advertisements listed in the *Colored Directory*. The usual businesses that make up any black community in the 1920s are there, such as barber shops, beauty shops, small restaurants, ice cream parlors, candy shops, morticians and funeral homes, shoe repair shops, laundry and dry cleaners, but also listed are pharmacies, clothing stores, furniture stores, tailors, jewelry companies, music stores, pawn shops, loan companies, pool halls, music shops, photographers, flower shops, auto repair shops, car dealerships, and plumbers—and Robert North (with his picture) is listed as the owner and breeder of thoroughbred race horses. Dr. F. C. Calvert (MD from the University of Michigan) and Dr. F. T. Moore (MD from Meharry Medical College) are also listed, with their photos. Although not all of the businesses listed in the *Colored Directory* can absolutely be verified as being owned by blacks, clearly many of them were, and the others certainly catered to the black consumer. In a short essay in the 1925–1926 *Colored Directory*, the African American population (which lists its number as 4,000) is proud of its accomplishments and the Douglas Hotel is touted as an example of black progress:

> Built in November, 1924, by George A. Ramsey and the late Robert Rowe, representing an expenditure of $100,000 which stands as a monument to the enterprise of the colored people of the city [sic]. This hotel is owned and controlled by members of the race.
>
> (52)

In the 1931–1932 *Colored Directory*, in addition to the business advertisements, an essay is included that makes clear that some of the leading businesses are black owned. The essay states that E. W. Anderson has had several successful businesses and in 1932 he "has the contract for hauling rubbish for the city of Coronado" (76). William Dyson is mentioned as "one of the city's most successful real estate brokers" (76). Eva Jessie Smith is noted for being one of San Diego's finest artists and has her work exhibited in galleries and in some of the homes of San Diego's most elite citizens, black and white (78). Herman Herbert is owner of the Transfer and Express Line and is "a well known, respected business man of the city, having operated a first class hotel in San Diego before entering this business" (78). Catherine Campbell has a restaurant, specializing in southern cuisine, especially fried chicken, located in the Dew Drop Inn (78). H. E. Howell operates San Diego's only black loan office, and he "makes a specialty of paying the public's taxes, bonds, electric, gas, and telephone bills. This makes it convenient for those who are employed [sic]" (80). George Ramsey is "proprietor of California's most popular and widely advertised Douglas Hotel and Nite Club" (80). James Tate owns and operates Tate's Funeral Home, and C. C. Gadson, another prominent business owner, has the most extensive stock of hair care and personal hygiene products (82). In addition to the above sampling of businesses, four blacks are employed as fire fighters and one as a police officer (80). Dr. F. C. Calvert is mentioned as a physician and surgeon. In the 1935–1936 *Colored Directory*, a new resident, Dr. A. Antonio Da Costa, is noted as a "skilled surgeon" (73). By 1935, black women are making inroads into the health care profession. For example, twelve women graduated from Dr. Carmody's School of Practical Nursing and they established the County Association of Colored Nurses.

During the 1920s and 1930s African Americans in San Diego are represented in a variety of employment, business, and professional activities. Beyond these activities, blacks devote time and resources to participate in and advance social organizations such as lodges and clubs that provide opportunities not only for socializing but also for political and racial strategizing. Examples of these are Paul Laurence Dunbar Lodge, Mount Olive Lodge, Negro Women's Council, Sisters of the Helping Hand, Household of Ruth, San Diego Lodge, Balboa Lodge, The Ladies Book Club, the Booster Club, The City Colored Employees' Social Club, and the Colonel Duncan Post, among others. Black women are equally represented. Group solidarity and common interests are emphasized in these organizations, which, according to Alain Locke, W. E. B. Du Bois, Marcus Garvey, and others, is one hallmark of the New Negro. An attention to the group is also noted with black churches. Many scholars have noted that throughout black people's history in America, the black church is often the only institution black people control and often, perhaps beyond their homes, the only place where they can be truly authentic and free, free to express their language, values, hopes, and dreams without reacting to white authority and censure. As with the diversity of work and employment experiences of African Americans in San Diego, black churches represent several denominations, such as Bethel AME, First Street Baptist, Phillips Temple CME, Mount Zion Baptist, Seventh Day Adventist, and Church of the Living God, Calvary Baptist Church, Apostolic Faith Mission, Independent Church of God in Christ, to mention a few. Black churches are also known for their liberation theology. That is, within black churches its members blend religious teachings and beliefs to assist with their liberation from racial oppression in the secular world. In this sense, black churches and their group efforts to assist in combating racial oppression are also political institutions. Equally important is the fact that within black churches class differences become diffused, and thus tensions between "high" (Talented Tenth, educated, middle and upper classes) and "low" (uneducated, the masses) are lessened. Indeed, San Diego's New Negro Movement displays much less of these class tensions than in cities east of the Mississippi.

And San Diego, in spite of the reasons that attracted blacks to migrate there, was no different from Harlem or Eastern and Midwestern cities that also attracted a migrating black population. Although some expressions of overt racism, Jim Crow-ism, and terrorism might have been a bit less than in the South, nevertheless, it was present. For example the Ku Klux Klan had a major national resurgence in the 1920s and in San Diego County the KKK targeted Mexican immigrants and Jews, and the climate for all people of color changed for the worse. One of its targets was the significant presence of blacks in downtown San Diego, and, as a result, blacks began to slowly move to Southeast San Diego (Larralde and del Castillo in CCDC II-10).

It is during the late 1910s and the 1920s in San Diego that black political organizations begin to form and to create agendas to combat racism and discrimination. This is a time and an opportunity for African Americans to use all available resources and talents to define who they are, to articulate what they want, and to resist racial and social oppression. Just as the NAACP is central to the Harlem Renaissance's political and resistance efforts east of the Mississippi, it is important in San Diego too. In "Struggle for Equality in 'America's Finest City': A History of the San Diego NAACP," it states that W. E. B. Du Bois came to San Diego in 1913 and then again 1917 as a part of his tour of Western states to recruit members. Du Bois thought the black citizens of the city were "thoughtful," "kindly," and "thrifty" (1). The San Diego Branch of the NAACP was approved in 1919 with fifty-four founding members (1). That the NAACP became an effective organization against racial oppression is recorded in the following from "Struggle for Equality in 'America's Finest City': History of the San Diego NAACP" in which a member of the black masses, and not of the Talented Tenth, assumes race leadership:

In February 1924, then San Diego NAACP president Elijah J. Gentry, "a shoe shiner," forwarded a frank assessment of the racial climate in San Diego to NAACP field secretary James Weldon Johnson, the celebrated writer and poet. "Colored people [in San Diego] are not allowed in restaurants, nor to drink soda water in drugstores, nor can they rent bathing suits at any bathing house or beach in this city," Gentry revealed. He affirmed that despite the small number of blacks in the area and the perception of racial tolerance, this place was nonetheless "a very prejudice[d] city. Not only was there reason to complain about the situation within city limits but . . . when branch officials looked across the border they protested against signs in Tijuana shops warning "colored not wanted." . . . just three years after Gentry's grim communication to Johnson the branch scored its first major civil rights victory. On September 7, 1927 it gleefully fired off a telegram to officials in New York City that read: "The San Diego Branch of the National Association for the Advancement of Colored People was victorious in the fight for admittance of colored girls as nurses in the San Diego County Hospital."

(1)

Similar NAACP victories occurred throughout the 1920s and 1930s. In addition to black San Diegans' involvement in the NAACP, they also formed locally based organizations and political action groups to resist oppression and to advocate for civil rights. There was the Young Men's Republican Club, The San Diego Negro Men's Democratic Club, The San Diego Race Relations Society, among others. In 1926 a division of Marcus Garvey's UNIA was established. The UNIA, as a counter to the NAACP with its middle class preoccupations and assumptions, is more representative of the black masses, is nationalist in its agenda, and promotes race pride and race beauty.

While much of the above discussion attempts to contextualize New Negro history and expression in San Diego, the movement is, of course, a cultural and aesthetic one. In New York, for example, the six major leaders of the Harlem Renaissance (W. E. B. Du Bois, Alain Locke, Charles Johnson, Jessie Fauset, Walter White, Casper Holstein, and James Weldon Johnson) articulate a cultural mandate for the younger artists to carry out that, as David Levering Lewis argues, is elitist and focused on "a cultural nationalism of the parlor" and "civil rights by copyright" (*When Harlem Was in Vogue*, xvi). San Diego New Negro expression and cultural production might be argued as being more democratic, creating a balance between Talented Tenth, middle class cultural values and assumptions and those of the black masses. Indeed, the more significant cultural expression produced in San Diego is more closely tied to the black masses, and their participation in its venues is paramount. In this regard, black San Diegans seem less interested in reacting to or impressing white people or seeking their approval.

Music, dance, and places where these can occur are San Diego's most important aesthetic contribution to the Harlem Renaissance or New Negro Movement of the 1920s and 1930s. In addition to providing a space where African American talent can be displayed and expressed, these were sites where blacks could socialize and express who they were in relative safety from the larger racist city of San Diego. Although several hotels were either owned or leased by blacks or were places that welcomed them as guests (Ideal Hotel, Clermont Hotel, Anita Hotel, and the Simmons Hotel), the one that towers above the others is the Douglas Hotel, located at 206 Market Street in the heart of downtown. Leland T. Saito remarks that the Douglas Hotel's "existence was a stark reminder of racial exclusion and segregation" in San Diego (8). Moreover, this hotel embodies the spirit of the Harlem Renaissance both because of what happened in it and because of its owner, George A. Ramsey, who was the unofficial mayor of black San Diego. According to "Who's Who in San Diego" in the *1931–1932 Colored Directory*, Ramsey and the Douglas Hotel are described in this way:

> Mr. George Ramsey, proprietor of California's most popular and widely advertised Douglas Hotel and Nite Club, is one of California's best known business men. . . . He is an experienced horseman and formerly was a partner to the late Robert Rowe. Their famous stables were known throughout Southern California and race circles for their fast horses. The beautiful hotel located at Second and Market Streets, was built in 1924 and is the finest

hotel owned by colored people on the Pacific Coast. The Nite Club was opened to the public in March, 1930, and is San Diego's most popular amusement place. You can tune in any night from 11:00 p.m. to 12:00 p.m. and hear their peppy numbers over KFSD, San Diego [sic]. Mr. Ramsey has engaged the best orchestra and entertainers available . . .

(80)

The hotel became, according to Michael Austin, the "only place of quality lodging and entertainment for Black visitors to the city of San Diego during a period of intense segregation in the United States" (quoted in Saito, 5). Entertainment is not the Douglas Hotel's only contribution to African American life from its opening to its closing in the late 1950s (it was demolished in 1985). It provided employment for blacks in its restaurant, card room, billiard rooms, and dry cleaners, and employed barbers and bell boys, among others. Michael Austin emphasizes that:

There was a lot of tourism in San Diego during that period, and there were plenty of jobs, mostly service-oriented, for black people . . . but the most prized work was at the Douglas because it paid relatively high wages and its success ensured job security . . . People valued their jobs there

(quoted in Saito, 6)

Located within the Douglas Hotel was The Creole Palace with its Nightclub Revue, which became generally known as the" Cotton Club of the West" and as the "Harlem of the West." The Creole Palace was integrated, welcoming whites but not catering to them; it was primarily a place for blacks to be entertained and to entertain themselves. The Creole Palace attracted most of the major entertainers of the Jazz Age; many of these entertainers came to Los Angeles and then on to San Diego, and vice versa. Jazz musicians, singers, dancers, comedians, show girls in colorful and meticulously designed costumes (the "Creole Cuties"), and carefully produced burlesque and cabaret revues were mainstays at the Palace, which had "a seating capacity of several hundred" (DjeDje and Meadows, 250). The San Diego Historical Society, in its archives, has a photograph of the Palace's "Nightclub Revue 2" singers and dancers, and in the photograph, the title of the Revue 2's show is "Harlem after Dark." Musicians such as Bessie Smith, Count Basie, Duke Ellington, and jazz bands appeared at the Palace in both its jazz club and dance room, where in addition to jazz, blues, boogie-woogie and Charleston music was presented. Jacqueline Cogdell DjeDje and Eddie S. Meadows emphasize in *California Soul: Music of African Americans in the West* that although major jazz performers of the era came to the Creole Palace, San Diego did not produce "an indigenous jazz style" such as occurred in New York, Chicago, and New York (248). Nevertheless, the cultural production at the Creole Palace was on par with black musical and performing production nationally in the 1920s and 1930s.

African American aesthetic production in San Diego was not limited to performance. San Diegans made contributions to the visual arts and literature, but here their production is not on par with that produced in cities east of the Mississippi in terms of quantity and, perhaps, quality as well, at least as far as current research has been able to discern. In the visual arts, two artists are represented: Eva Jessie Smith and Sargent Johnson, who, while not a resident of San Diego, had a small connection to the city, at the tail end of the Harlem Renaissance. Smith, who is listed in both the 1931–1932 and 1935–1936 *Colored Directories*, is described as being "one of America's renowned Colored artists" and is known for her Ceramics. Her work "has been highly commended by art critics for its originality of design and harmony of color" (78, 74). Moreover her work was exhibited in the Little Art Gallery of San Diego, Fine Arts Gallery, and Athletic Club of San Diego. Some of her customers were Mrs. Reginald Poland, Director of the Fine Arts Gallery, and Mrs. Ridges of Point Loma, so clearly her work were received well by whites (78, 74). Archival research failed to uncover any photographic images of her work.

Sargent Johnson arrived in San Francisco in 1915 and lived most of his life in the Bay area until his death in 1957. His works reflected the life experiences of blacks that he knew or who were around him. Johnson was at his most original and highest level of production during the Harlem Renaissance and the themes of his sculpture, portraits, masks, and drawings focused on mother-child relationships and the everyday experiences of blacks. In 1939, the San Diego Fine Arts Gallery added his terracotta head "Ester" to its collection.

Two San Diego black woman writers, Ruby Berkley Goodwin and Bessie A. Cobb, make contributions to African American literature of the late Harlem Renaissance when their works appear in an anthology that includes several of the major poets of the period, *An Anthology of Contemporary Verse: Negro Voices*, 1938. Goodwin is listed in the 1929 "Who's Who in Colored America," and Robert Fikes calls her a "Renaissance Woman" in his *The Black in Crimson: A History and Profiles of African Americans at SDSU"* (San Diego State University). He notes that Goodwin graduated from what was then San Diego State Teachers College in 1922 and went on to a distinguished career in writing, poetry, non-fiction, and journalism, in addition to a career on stage and screen, and as personal secretary and publicist for actress Hattie McDaniel of *Gone with the Wind* fame and countless other movies.

Goodwin has five poems in the above-mentioned anthology. Her poems are noteworthy for their ability to evoke the persona's mediation of a barely disguised anger and frustration with apparently romantic and personal foes and with constraining social and racial borders and reality from which it must contend. In either case, whether the persona's conflict and tension is with the personal or social, the poems reveal and maintain elements of hope and optimism that are represented in song, dream, or an appeal to God. Although not particularly experimental or innovative, as might been observed in the poetry of Langston

Hughes, Countee Cullen, or Claude McKay, "I Sing" and "Race Prejudice" more than any of her other poems in the anthology capture a bit of the Harlem Renaissance agenda as articulated by its leaders, particularly Du Bois, as editor of *The Crisis*, to use literature to assist in the acquisition of civil rights, to combat discrimination and segregation, and to do so by creating literature that is on par with that produced by white writers. In "I Sing," the persona laments that "I Sing— / For far too many wrongs are left unrighted / As black folks bend before the scourge of hate" (62). Not only does the persona express the condition of blacks in the 1930s. The persona insists that if only one person hears the song and its "pleading cadence" then "Cheerfully I can look beyond the pain; / Knowing that my song was not breathed in vain" (62). In this sense the poem pays homage to the significance of cultural expression or venting in African American experience; that is, if one expresses the pain, whether the outside world really changes or not, the pain or suffering is lessened, if only temporarily. "I Sing," then, is a variation of the Blues. "Race Prejudice," beyond its evocative title, captures what the Great Migration and the New Negro has been able to accomplish:

> Time was, I was confined to one small spot, . . .
> But now I've scattered everywhere.
>
> (63)

And, Goodwin concludes that as he has scattered, he has shed his defenselessness and become powerful and dangerous.

Cobb's one poem in the anthology, "Change," while slight, is important in that it shows promise, as she was only twenty and a student at San Diego State College. After her graduation from San Diego State College she went on to receive a master's degree from Atlanta University and became a freelance writer.

The Harlem Renaissance or New Negro Movement in San Diego has its unique character that is punctuated with black people as the agents who create their own agencies to carry out a complicated agenda that responds to a site of racial discrimination and segregation in a time when real change is possible. The 1920s and 1930s represents a time in San Diego history and culture when African Americans seized the opportunity to define and advance themselves in an era when segregation, Jim Crow-ism, and other intolerance against black people was rampant. Within the geographical and cultural space of San Diego, African Americans were entrepreneurs, business owners, workers in skilled and unskilled positions, professionals, members of social, religious, and political organizations, musicians, dancers, actors, writers, and artists. African Americans established a firm cultural base that would allow for future development and progress. Tied to these accomplishments is an attention to the group and what the group needs to lead productive, diverse, and worthy lives. By paying more attention to collective goals, New Negro expression in San Diego is less dependent upon whites to advance and sustain its efforts. As a consequence of this independence, New Negroes in San Diego were less impacted by the Great Depression, when in Eastern and Midwestern cities, white patrons pulled their financial support from black artists and a big thrust of the Harlem Renaissance was over. New Negro actions in San Diego thrived well into the late 1950s.

Further Reading

Carrico, Richard L. and Stacey Jordan. *Centre City Development Corporation: Downtown San Diego African American Heritage Study*. San Diego, CA: Mooney and Associates, 2004.

Carson, Clayborne, Emma J. Lapsansky-Werner, and Gary B. Nash. *The Struggle for Freedom: A History of African Americans*. New York: Pearson, 2007.

Colored Directory. 1925–1926, 1931–1932, and 1935–1936. Archives. San Diego City Library. California Collection. Accessed 20 July 2010.

DjeDje, Jacqueline Cogdell, and Eddie S. Meadows, eds. *California Soul: Music of African Americans in the West*. Berkeley and Los Angeles, CA: University of California Press, 1998.

Fikes, Robert. *The Black in Crimson and Black: A History and Profiles of African Americans at SDSU*. San Diego, CA: San Diego State University Library and Information Access, 2010.

Hawkins, Homer C. "Trends in Black Migration from 1863 to 1960." *Phylon* 34.2 (1973): 140–152.

Lewis, David Levering. *When Harlem Was in Vogue*. New York: Oxford University Press, 1989.

Locke, Alain. *The New Negro: Voices of the Harlem Renaissance*. 1925. New York: Touchstone, 1997.

Madyun, Gail, and Larry Malone. "Black Pioneers in San Diego: 1880–1920." *The Journal of San Diego History* 27.2 (1981).

Mbiti, John. *African Religions and Philosophy*. New York: Praeger, 1969.

Murphy, Beatrice M., ed. *Negro Voices: An Anthology of Contemporary Verse*. New York: Henry Harrison Poetry Publishers, 1938.

Saito, Leland T. "African Americans and Historic Preservation in San Diego: The Douglas and the Clermont/Coast Hotels." *The Journal of San Diego History* 54.1 (2008): 1–15.

"Struggle for Equality in 'America's Finest City': A History of the San Diego NAACP." California State Conference: National Association for the Advancement of Colored People. August 10, 2010.

A SELECTED BIBLIOGRAPHY

Bruce A. Glasrud and Cary D. Wintz

Ainsworth, Tracy Elizabeth. "Strange Brew: Women and Blacks in Denver During Prohibition," Master's thesis, University of Colorado, 1998.

Allmendinger, Blake. *Imagining the African American West*. Lincoln, NE: University of Nebraska Press, 2005.

Barr, Alwyn. *Black Texans: A History of African Americans in Texas, 1528–1995*. Second edition. Norman, OK: University of Oklahoma Press, 1996.

—— and Robert A. Calvert, eds. *Black Leaders: Texans for Their Times*. Austin, TX: Texas State Historical Association, 1981.

Beeth, Howard and Cary D. Wintz, eds. *Black Dixie: Essays on Afro-Texan History and Culture in Houston*. College Station, TX: Texas A&M University Press, 1992.

Billington, Monroe Lee, and Roger D. Hardaway. *African Americans on the Western Frontier*. Boulder, CO: University Press of Colorado, 1998.

Bracey, Earnest N. "Anatomy of Second Baptist Church: The First Black Baptist Church in Las Vegas." *Nevada Historical Society Quarterly* 43 (Fall 2000): 201–213.

Brady, Marilyn Dell. "Kansas Federation of Colored Women's Clubs, 1900–1930." *Kansas History* 9 (1986): 19–30.

—— "Organizing Afro-American Girls Clubs in Kansas in the 1920s." *Frontiers* 9 (1987): 69–73.

Breaux, Richard M. "The New Negro Arts and Letters Movement Among Black University Students in the Midwest, 1914–1940." *Great Plains Quarterly* 24.3 (Summer 2004): 147–162.

Brewer, J. Mason, ed. *Heralding Dawn: An Anthology of Verse*. Dallas, TX: June Thomason, 1936.

Bringhurst, Newell G. *Saints, Slaves, and Blacks: The Changing Place of Black People Within Mormonism*. Westport, CT: Greenwood Press, 1981.

Broussard, Albert S. *Black San Francisco: The Struggle for Racial Equality in the West, 1900–1954*. Lawrence, KS: University Press of Kansas, 1993.

Bryant, Clora, Buddy Collette, William Green, and Steve Isoardi, eds. *Central Avenue Sounds: Jazz in Los Angeles*. Berkeley, CA: University of California Press, 1998.

Carroll, Anne Elizabeth. *Word, Image, and the New Negro.* Bloomington, IN: University of Indiana Press, 2005.

Chaudhuri, Nupur. "'We All Seem Like Brothers and Sisters': The African-American Community in Manhattan, Kansas, 1865–1940." *Kansas History* 14 (1991–1992): 270–288.

Clayton, Lawrence, and Joe Specht, eds. *The Roots of Texas Music.* College Station, TX: Texas A&M University Press, 2003.

Cox, Bette Yarbrough. *Central Avenue: Its Rise and Fall (1890-c. 1955), Including the Musical Renaissance of Black Los Angeles.* Los Angeles, CA: Beem, 1993.

Crudup, Keith Jerome. "African Americans in Arizona: A Twentieth Century History." Ph.D. dissertation, Arizona State University, 1998.

Daniels, Douglas Henry. *Pioneer Urbanites: A Social and Cultural History of Black San Francisco.* Berkeley, CA: University of California Press, 1990.

——. *Lester Leaps In: The Life and Times of Lester "Pres" Young.* Boston, MA: Beacon Press, 2002.

——. *One O'clock Jump: The Unforgettable History of the Oklahoma City Blue Devils.* Boston, MA: Beacon Press, 2006.

Davis, Cynthia, and Verner D. Mitchell, eds. *Western Echoes of the Harlem Renaissance: The Life and Writings of Anita Scott Coleman.* Norman, OK: University of Oklahoma Press, 2008.

Davis, Frank Marshall. *Livin' the Blues: Memoirs of a Black Journalist and a Poet.* Edited by John Edgar Tidwell. Madison, WI: University of Wisconsin Press, 1992.

De Barros, Paul. *Jackson Street After Hours: The Roots of Jazz in Seattle.* Seattle, WA: Sasquatch Books, 1993.

De Graaf, Lawrence B., Kevin Mulroy, and Quintard Taylor, eds. *Seeking El Dorado: African Americans in California.* Seattle, WA: University of Washington Press, 2001.

Dickson, Lynda Faye. "The Third Shift: Black Women's Club Activities in Denver, 1900–1925." *Women and Work* 6 (1997): 217.

Dinerstein, Joel. *Swinging the Machine: Modernity, Technology, and African American Culture between the World Wars.* Amherst, MA: University of Massachusetts Press, 2003.

DjeDje, Jacqueline Cogdell, and Eddie S. Meadows, eds. *California Soul: Music of African Americans in the West.* Berkeley, CA: University of California Press, 1998.

Driggs, Frank, and Chuck Haddix. *Kansas City Jazz: From Ragtime to Bebop—A History.* New York: Oxford University Press, 2005.

Durham, Philip, and Everett L. Jones. *The Negro Cowboys.* Lincoln, NE: University of Nebraska Press, 1965.

Early, Gerald. *Black Heartland: African American Life, the Middle West, and the Meaning of American Regionalism.* 2 volumes. St. Louis, MO: Washington University, 1996–97.

Fabre, Geneviève, and Michael Feith, eds. *Temples for Tomorrow: Looking Back at the Harlem Renaissance.* Bloomington, IN: University of Indiana Press, 2001.

Farnsworth, Robert M. *Melvin B. Tolson, 1898–1966: Plain Talk and Poetic Prophecy.* Columbia: University of Missouri Press, 1984.

Fauset, Jessie. "Out of the West." *The Crisis* 27 (November 1923): 11–18.

Fitzgerald, Roosevelt. "The Evolution of a Black Community in Las Vegas, 1905–1940." *Nevada Public Affairs Review* 2 (1987).

Flamming, Douglas. *Bound for Freedom: Black Los Angeles in Jim Crow America.* Berkeley, CA: University of California Press, 2005.

——. *African Americans in the West.* Santa Barbara, CA: ABC-CLIO, 2009.

Fontenot, Chester J., Jr. "Oscar Micheaux, Black Novelist and Film Maker." In *Vision and Refuge: Essays on the Literature of the Great Plains*. Edited by Virginia Faulkner and Frederick C. Luebke, 109–125. Lincoln, NE: University of Nebraska Press, 1982.

Gillette, Michael L. "The NAACP in Texas, 1937–1957." Ph.D. dissertation, University of Texas, 1984.

Gioia, Ted. *West Coast Jazz: Modern jazz in California, 1945–1960*. Berkeley, CA: University of California Press, 1992.

Glasrud, Bruce A., ed. *African Americans in the West: A Bibliography of Secondary Sources*. Alpine, TX: Sul Ross State University, Center for Big Bend Studies, 1998.

——. "From Griggs to Brewer: A Review of Black Texas Artists, 1899–1940." *Journal of Big Bend Studies* 15 (2003): 195–212.

——. "The Harlem Renaissance in Texas and the Southwest." In *Encyclopedia of the Harlem Renaissance*. Edited by Cary D. Wintz and Paul Finkelman, 2 volumes, 521–525. New York: Routledge, 2004.

—— and Laurie Champion, eds. *The African American West: A Century of Short Stories*. Boulder, CO: University Press of Colorado, 2000.

—— and Laurie Champion, eds. *Unfinished Masterpiece: The Harlem Renaissance Fiction of Anita Scott Coleman*. Lubbock, TX: Texas Tech University Press, 2008.

—— and Merline Pitre, eds. *Black Women in Texas History*. College Station, TX: Texas A&M University Press, 2008.

—— and Charles A. Braithwaite, eds. *African Americans on the Great Plains: An Anthology*. Lincoln, NE: University of Nebraska Press, 2009.

Gordon, Taylor. *Born to be Free*. 1929; Lincoln, NE: University of Nebraska Press, 1995.

Govenar, Alan B. and Jay E. Brakefield. *Deep Ellum and Central Track: Where the Black and White Worlds of Dallas Converged*. Denton, TX: University of North Texas Press, 1998.

Grant, Billie Arlene, Ernestine Smith and Gladys Smith. *Growing Up Black in Denver*, 3rd printing. Denver, CO: B. A. Grant, 1988.

Hansen, Moya. "Pebbles on the Shore: Economic Opportunity in Denver's Five Points Neighborhood, 1920–1950." *Colorado History* 5 (2001): 95–128.

Hebert, Janis. "Oscar Mischeaux: A Black Pioneer." *South Dakota Review* 11 (Winter 1973): 62–69.

Henderson, Judy M. *African-American Music in Minnesota: From Spirituals to Rap*. St. Paul, MN: Minnesota Historical Society Press, 1994.

Hobbs, Richard S. *The Cayton Legacy: The African American Family*. Pullman, WA: Washington State University Press, 2002.

Horace, Lillian B. *Five Generations Hence*. N.c.: privately printed, 1916.

Hughes, Langston. *Not Without Laughter*. New York: Alfred A. Knopf, 1930.

——. *The Big Sea: An Autobiography*. 1940. New York: Hill and Wang, 1993.

Hunt, Darnell, and Ana-Christina Ramon, eds. *Black Los Angeles: American Dreams and Racial Realities*. New York: New York University Press, 2010.

Isoardi, Steven L. *The Dark Tree: Jazz and the Community Arts in Los Angeles*. Berkeley, CA: University of California Press, 2006.

Jack, Tom. "The Omaha Gospel Complex in Historical Perspective." *Great Plains Quarterly* 20.3 (Summer 2000): 225–234.

Johnson, Michael K. "Migration, Masculinity, and Racial Identity in Taylor Gordon's Born To Be." In *Moving Stories: Migration and the American West, 1850–2000*. Edited by Scott E. Casper and Lucinda M. Long, 119–142. Reno, NV: Nevada Humanities Committee, 2001.

——. *Black Masculinity and the Frontier Myth in American Literature*. Norman, OK: University of Oklahoma Press, 2002.

——. "'This Strange White World': Race and Place in Era Bell Thompson's *American Daughter.*" *Great Plains Quarterly* 24.2 (Spring 2004): 101–112.

Katz, William Loren. *The Black West: A Documentary and Pictorial History of the African American Role in the Westward Expansion of the United States*. New York: Simon & Schuster, 1987.

Kirschke, Amy Helene. *Aaron Douglas: Art, Race, and the Harlem Renaissance*. Jackson, MI: University Press of Mississippi, 1995.

Laurie, Clayton D. "The U.S. Army and the Omaha Riot of 1919." *Nebraska History* 72.3 (1991): 135–143.

Lay, Shawn, ed. *The Invisible Empire in the West: Toward a New Historical Appraisal of the Ku Klux Klan of the 1920s*. Urbana, IL: University of Illinois Press, 1992.

Lewis, David Levering. *When Harlem Was in Vogue*. New York: Vintage Books, 1982.

MacMahon, David R. "The Origins of the NAACP in Omaha and Lincoln, Nebraska, 1913–1926." Master's thesis, Creighton University, 1993.

Marshall, Marguerite Mitchell. *An Account of Afro-Americans in Southeast Kansas, 1884–1984*. Manhattan, KA: Sunflower University Press, 1986.

Matsumoto, Valerie J., and Blake Allmendinger. *Over the Edge: Remapping the American West*. Berkeley, CA: University of California Press, 1999.

Menard, Orville D. "Tom Dennison, The Omaha Bee, and the 1919 Omaha Race Riot." *Nebraska History* 68 (Winter 1987): 152–165.

Mihelich, Dennis N. "The Formation of the Lincoln Urban League." *Nebraska History* 68 (Summer, 1987): 63–73.

——. "The Lincoln Urban League: The Travail of Depression and War.*" Nebraska History* 70 (Winter, 1989): 303–316.

——. "The Origins of the Prince Hall Mason Grand Lodge of Nebraska." *Nebraska History* 76.1 (Spring 1996): 10–21.

——. "A Socioeconomic Portrait of Prince Hall Masonry in Nebraska, 1900–1920." *Great Plains Quarterly* 17.1 (Winter 1997): 35–48.

Mock, Charlotte. *Bridges: New Mexican Black Women, 1900–1950*. Albuquerque, NM: New Mexico Commission on the Study of Women, 1985.

Moore, Deedee. "Is There Anything Gordon Parks Can't Do?" *Smithsonian* 20 (April 1989): 147–164.

Moore, Shirley Ann Wilson. *To Place Our Deeds: The African American Community in Richmond, California, 1910–1963*. Berkeley, CA: University of California Press, 2000.

Murphet, Julian. *Literature and Race in Los Angeles*. Cambridge, MA: Cambridge University Press, 2001.

Notten, Eleonore van. *Wallace Thurman's Harlem Renaissance*. Atlanta, GA: Rodopi, 1994.

Patrick, Elizabeth Nelson. "The Black Experience in Southern Nevada." *Nevada Historical Society Quarterly* 22 (Summer 1979): 128–140.

——. "The Black Experience in Southern Nevada, Part II." *Nevada Historical Society Quarterly* 22 (Fall 1979): 209–220.

Patterson, Cheryl R. "Aspects of Negro Life, from Topeka to Harlem, Forming Aaron Douglas." Master's thesis, University of Kansas, 1999.

Pepin, Elizabeth, and Lewis Watts. *Harlem of the West: The San Francisco Fillmore Jazz Era*. San Francisco, CA: Chronicle Books, 2006.

Porter, Kenneth Wiggins. "Micheaux, Oscar." In *Dictionary of American Negro Biography*. Edited by Rayford W. Logan and Michael R. Winston, 433–434. New York: W. W. Norton, 1982.

Quantic, Diane Dufva. "Black Authors in Kansas." *Kansas English* 55 (December 1969): 14–16.

Ragar, Cheryl R. "Harlem Renaissance in the United States—Kansas and the Plains States." In *Encyclopedia of the Harlem Renaissance*. Edited by Cary D. Wintz and Paul Finkelman, 512–514. New York: Routledge, 2004.

Ravage, John W. *Black Pioneers: Images of the Black Experience on the North American Frontier*. Salt Lake City, UT: University of Utah Press, 1997.

Reed, Tom. *The Black Music History of Los Angeles: Its Roots—A Classical Pictorial History of Black Music in Los Angeles from the 1920s to 1970*. Los Angeles, CA: Black Accent on L.A., 1992.

Rice, Marc. "Frompin' in the Great Plains: Listening and Dancing to the Jazz Orchestras of Alphonso Trent, 1925–44." *Great Plains Quarterly* 16.2 (Spring 1996): 107–115.

Riley, Glenda. "American Daughters: Black Women in the West." *Montana: The Magazine of Western History* 38 (Spring 1988): 14–27.

Russell, Ross. *Jazz Style in Kansas City and the Southwest*. Berkeley, CA: University of California Press, 1968.

Scott, Mark. "Langston Hughes of Kansas." *Kansas History* 3 (Spring 1980): 3–25.

Sharp, Wanda F. "*The Black Dispatch*: A Sociological Analysis." Master's thesis, University of Oklahoma, 1951.

Sides, Josh. *L.A. City Limits: African American Los Angeles from the Great Depression to the Present*. Berkeley, CA: University of California Press, 2003.

Smith, Catherine Parsons. "Harlem Renaissance in the United States: California and the West Coast." In *Encyclopedia of the Harlem Renaissance*, edited by Cary D. Wintz and Paul Finkelman, 2 volumes, 505–507. New York: Routledge, 2004.

Smith, Gloria L. *Black Americana in Arizona*. Tucson, AZ: Gloria L. Smith, 1977.

Stoddard, Tom. *Jazz on the Barbary Coast*. Chigwell: Storyville, 1982.

Taylor, David Vassar. "John Quincy Adams: St. Paul Editor and Black Leader." *Minnesota History* 43 (Winter 1973): 282–296.

——. "Pilgrim's Progress: Black St. Paul and the Making of an Urban Ghetto, 1870–1930." Ph.D. dissertation, University of Minnesota, 1977.

——. *African Americans in Minnesota*. St. Paul, MN: Minnesota Historical Society Press, 2002.

Taylor, Quintard. *The Forging of a Black Community: Seattle's Central District from 1870 through the Civil Rights Era*. Seattle, WA: University of Washington Press, 1994.

——. *In Search of the Racial Frontier: African Americans in the American West, 1528–1990*. New York: W. W. Norton, 1998.

—— and Shirley Ann Wilson Moore, eds. *African American Women Confront the West, 1600–2000*. Norman, OK: University of Oklahoma Press, 2003.

Thompson, Audrey. "Great Plains Pragmatist: Aaron Douglas and the Art of Social Protest." *Great Plains Quarterly* 20.4 (Fall 2000): 311–322.

Thompson, Era Bell. *American Daughter*. 1946; St. Paul, MN: Minnesota Historical Society, 1986.

Tidwell, John Edgar. "Frank Marshall Davis, Ad Astra, Per Aspera." *Kansas History* 18 (Winter 1995/1996): 270–283.

Tolbert, Emory J. *The UNIA and Black Los Angeles: Ideology and Community in the American Garvey Movement*. Los Angeles, CA: Center for Afro-American Studies, UCLA, 1980.

Tolson, Melvin B. *The Harlem Group of Negro Writers*. Edited by Edward J. Mullen. Westport, CT: Greenwood, 2001.

Tyler, Bruce M. *From Harlem to Hollywood: The Struggle for Racial and Cultural Democracy, 1920–1943*. New York: Garland Publishing, 1992.

Tyler, Deidre Ann, ed. *Our Corner of the World: African American Women in Utah Tell Their Stories, 1940–2002*. Lanham, MD: University Press of America, 2005.

Vanepps-Taylor, Betti Carol. *Forgotten Lives: African Americans in South Dakota*. Pierre, SD: South Dakota State Historical Society, 2008.

Whitaker, Matthew. "In Search of Black Phoenicians: African American Culture and Community in Phoenix, Arizona, 1868–1940." Master's thesis, Arizona State University, 1997.

Widener, Daniel. *Black Arts West: Culture and Struggle in Postwar Los Angeles*. Durham, NC: Duke University Press, 2010.

Wiggins, Bernice Love. *Tuneful Tales*. Edited by Maceo C. Dailey, Jr. and Ruthe Winegarten. 1925. Lubbock: Texas Tech University Press, 2002.

Wilson, Noel. "*The Kansas City Call*: An Inside View of the Negro Market." Ph.D. dissertation, University of Illinois, 1968.

Wintz, Cary D. "Langston Hughes: A Kansas Poet in the Harlem Renaissance." *Kansas Quarterly* 8 (Spring 1976): 58–71.

———. *Black Culture and the Harlem Renaissance*. College Station, TX: Texas A&M University Press, 1996.

———, ed. *The Harlem Renaissance, 1920–1940: Interpretation of an African American Literary Movement*. 7 Vols. New York: Garland Publishing, 1996.

———, ed. *The Harlem Renaissance: A History and an Anthology*. Malden, MA: Blackwell Publishing, 2003.

———. *Harlem Speaks*, Naperville, IL: Sourcebooks, Inc., 2007.

——— and Paul Finkelman, eds. *The Encyclopedia of the Harlem Renaissance*, 2 Vols. New York: Routledge, 2004.

Wood, Roger and James Fraher. *Down in Houston: Bayou City Blues*. Austin, TX: University of Texas Press, 2003.

Yancey, James C. "The Negro in Tucson—Past and Present." Master's thesis, University of Arizona, 1933.

Young, Joseph A. "Oscar Micheaux's Novels: Black Apologies for White Oppression." Ph.D. dissertation, University of Nebraska, 1984.

Young, Mary E. "Anita Scott Coleman: A Neglected Harlem Renaissance Writer." *CLA Journal* 40 (March 1997): 271–287.

CONTRIBUTORS

Richard M. Breaux is Assistant Professor of Ethnic Studies at Colorado State University. He is currently working on a book manuscript titled, 'These Institutions Belong to the People': New Negro College Students in America's Heartland, 1900–1940." His *Great Plains Quarterly* article, "The New Negro Arts and Letters Movement Among Black University Students in the Midwest, 1914–1940," was reprinted in *African Americans on the Great Plains* (Bruce A. Glasrud and Charles Braithwaite, editors).

Charles Orson Cook teaches American History in the Honors College at the University of Houston; he earned his Ph.D. in history at the University of Houston. Cook has special interests in nineteenth century popular culture and American race relations. Among his publications is *Horatio Alger: Gender and Success in the Gilded Age: Two Novels by Horatio Alger*. Cook is one of several collaborators on a new book, *African Americans and the Presidency: The Road to the White House*. In the summer of 2010, two of his essays—one on James Weldon Johnson and another on Colin Powell—were featured in an anthology entitled *Major Documents of African Americans*.

Douglas Henry Daniels is professor of black studies and history at the University of California at Santa Barbara. He is the author of *Lester Leaps In, Pioneer Urbanites: A Social and Cultural History of Black San Francisco*, and *One O'clock Jump: The Unforgettable History of the Oklahoma City Blue Devils*.

Douglas Flamming is professor of history at the Georgia Institute of Technology in Atlanta. His award-winning books include *Creating the Modern South: Millhands* *and Managers in Dalton, Georgia, 1884–1984, Bound for Freedom: Black Los Angeles in Jim Crow America,* and *African Americans in the West.*

Bruce A. Glasrud is Professor Emeritus of History, California State University, East Bay, retired Dean, School of Arts and Sciences, Sul Ross State University, and a Fellow of the Texas State Historical Association. A specialist in the history of blacks in the West, Glasrud has authored or co-authored eighteen books including *The African American West: A Century of Short Stories, Buffalo Soldiers in the West,* and with Cary D. Wintz, *African Americans and the Presidency: The Road to the White House* (Routledge).

Charlotte Hinger is a novelist and western Kansas Historian. She earned an MA in history at Fort Hays State University. Her historical novel, *Come Spring,* (Simon and Schuster) won the Western Writers of America Medicine Pipe Bearer's award. Her article, "'The Colored People Hold The Key': Abram Thompson Hall, Jr.'s Campaign to Organize Graham County," (*Kansas History,* Spring 2008) won the Westerners International 2009 Coke Wood Award. Hinger has published a number of mystery short stories, and historical articles focusing on the American West. *Deadly Descent,* the first book in a new mystery series published by Poisoned Pen Press in 2009, won the Arizona Book Award for Best Mystery/Suspense. She is working on her second mystery and an academic book about nineteenth-century African American politicians in Kansas and their impact on the settlement of the West.

George H. Junne, Jr. heads the Africana Studies Department at the University of Northern Colorado. His research emphases include African Americans in the US West and the history of the African American community of Dearfield, Colorado. He is also a summertime paleontologist with the University of Michigan. Among his publications are *Afro American History: A Chronicle of People of African Descent in the United States* (1996), and *Blacks in the American West and Beyond—America, Canada and Mexico: A Selectively Annotated Bibliography* (2000).

Kimberley Mangun is an Assistant Professor in Communication with a Ph.D. from the University of Oregon. Mangun's book, *A Force for Change: Beatrice Morrow Cannady and the Struggle for Civil Rights, 1912–1936,* was published by Oregon State University Press (2010). Her work has been published in *American Journalism, Oregon Historical Quarterly, Pacific Northwest Quarterly, African American National Biography, BlackPast.org,* and other print and online publications.

Jeanette N. Passty is Associate Professor of English at St. Philip's College in San Antonio, Texas and a recipient of that College's 2003–2004 Teaching Excellence Award, as well as the 2003 NISOD Medallion for Excellence in Teaching and Leadership from The University of Texas at Austin. She was a contributor to

American Women Writers: A Critical Reference Guide from Colonial Times to the Present, and author of an American Library Association "Outstanding Academic Book of 1988–89," *Eros and Androgyny: The Legacy of Rose Macaulay.* The most recent of her numerous creative works, scholarly papers, and published articles—co-authored with research chemist William C. Davis—is "Creating the Spark: A Journey with Henry Ford, George Washington Carver, Wernher von Braun, and Rosalyn Yalow" (Fall & Spring 2008–89, *Palo Alto Review*).

Michael Phillips received his doctorate in history from The University of Texas at Austin in 2003, and since 2007 has taught American history at Collin College in Plano. His first book, *White Metropolis: Race, Ethnicity and Religion in Dallas, 1841–2001* was published by the University of Texas Press and won the 2007 T. R. Fehrenbach Award for best work on Texas History. UT Press published his second book, *The House Will Come to Order: How the Texas Speaker Became a Power in State and National Politics* (co-written with Patrick Cox) in 2007.

Marc Rice is an Associate Professor of Musicology at Truman State University and is the area chair of the Perspectives of Music program. He has extensively published on gender and race issues concerning jazz in the Midwest. His work can be found in the journals *American Music, Musical Quarterly*, and the forthcoming *Encyclopedia of African American Music.* He has also conducted fieldwork in Louisiana, tracing the Cajun music revival, and is currently preparing a manuscript on the Nueva Cancion movement in Latin America.

Charles P. Toombs (Ph.D., Purdue University) is associate professor of Africana Studies, San Diego State University. His areas of specialization and research include Africana literature, American literature, and Black Queer Studies. He is President of the San Diego State University California Faculty Association (CFA). His works in progress include: *The Harlem Renaissance and American Modernism* (co-authored with Dr. Svitlana Pukhnata, Ukraine); *The Early Fiction of Alice Walker;* and *In Your Space and Staying: A Black Gay Man Aesthetic.*

Jean Van Delinder is associate professor of sociology, with affiliated appointments in American Studies, Africana-African American Studies, and Women's Studies at Oklahoma State University. She received her Ph.D. in sociology from the University of Kansas. Her book, *Struggles Before Brown: Early Civil Rights Protests and Their Significance Today* (2008) examines the early years of the civil rights movement in the Midwest. Van Delinder has also published several articles in leading journals.

Carolyn Wedin is professor emeritus of English at the University of Wisconsin, Whitewater. Wedin is a frequent lecturer and speaker, and her publications include *Inheritors of the Spirit: Mary White Ovington and the Founding of the NAACP* and *Jessie Redmon Fauset, Black American Writer.*

Cary D. Wintz is Distinguished Professor of History at Texas Southern University and is a specialist in black political history and the Harlem Renaissance. Wintz is the author of nearly twenty books, including *Harlem Speaks, Black Culture and the Harlem Renaissance, African American Political Thought, 1890–1930*, and with Bruce A. Glasrud, *African Americans and the Presidency: The Road to the White House* (Routledge). He also served as an editor of the Oxford University Press five-volume *Encyclopedia of African American History, 1896 to the Present*.

INDEX

African Americans and the Presidency

Edited By
Bruce A. Glasrud and Cary D. Wintz

"The election of Barack Obama to the presidency is a landmark moment in American history. But it's a moment that was made possible by the steady, determined work of so many individuals—some recognized, but the majority working quietly out of the spotlight to bring about change. From the 1954 Brown v. Board of Education decision to the 2008 election, it's been a long distance race and a team effort. This book illuminates the course of that race and documents the contributions of many who laid the groundwork for Obama's victory."

Rev. Jesse Jackson, Founder and President, RainbowPUSH Coalition

"This is a wonderfully surprising and important collection of essays that illuminates a quest that was once seen as a fool's errand, but became a reality with the election of Barack Obama. Glasrud and Wintz rediscover and re-interpret a little known history where African Americans demanded access to America's highest political offices. This collection brings to life the story of Frederick Douglass, Shirley Chisholm, Jesse Jackson and many other African Americans who attempted to use the political system to shame, prod, or force America to confront its tortured racial history."

Lonnie Bunch, Director, National Museum of African American
History and Culture, Smithsonian Institution

"This volume documents the mostly forgotten political campaigns of African Americans who have run for the nation's highest office. With fresh insights and historical discoveries of campaigns that have long been neglected in the nation's history, *African Americans and the Presidency* provides a lens to understand Barack Obama's successful path to the White House. No one interested in blacks' political struggle for dignity and recognition should neglect this book. It is simply a gem."

Frederick C. Harris, co-author of *Countervailing Forces in
African-American Civic Activism, 1973–1994*

African Americans and the Presidency tells the untold story of how "outsider" campaigns for the presidency have carved out new strategies for black empowerment. This worthy and provocative book gives all readers an inside look and gave me a new appreciation of the history in which I am proud to have played a part."

Dr. Lenora B. Fulani

African Americans and the Presidency explores the long history of African American candidates for President and Vice President, examining the impact of each candidate on the American public, as well as the contribution they all made toward advancing racial equality in America. Each chapter takes the story one step further in time, through original essays written by top experts, giving depth to these inspiring candidates, some of whom are familiar to everyone, and some whose stories may be new.

Presented with illustrations and a detailed timeline, *African Americans and the Presidency* provides anyone interested in African American history and politics with a unique perspective on the path carved by the predecessors of Barack Obama, and the meaning their efforts had for the United States.

ISBN 13: 978-0-415-80391-5 (hbk)
ISBN 13: 978-0-415-80392-2 (pbk)
ISBN 13: 978-0-203-86433-3 (ebk)

Available at all good bookshops
For ordering and further information please visit:
www.routledge.com

RELATED TITLES FROM ROUTLEDGE

Origins of the Black Atlantic

Edited By
Laurent Dubois and Julius S. Scott

"This excellent set of essays gathered and introduced by Laurent Dubois and Julius Scott will become a classic of its kind—useful to scholars, teachers, and readers of history as long as we want to understand the world of race and class we live in."

Marcus Rediker, author of *The Slave Ship: A Human History*

"Any course on Atlantic revolutions would benefit from this anthology. It provides an important counter-weight to more Euro-centric accounts of the Age of Revolution by showing how enslaved people understood and re-imagined their role within the societies that had enslaved them."

John D. Garrigus, author of *Before Haiti: Race and Citizenship in French Saint-Domingue*

"Laurent Dubois and Julius Scott have put together an up-to-date collection of the most interesting literature on the formation of the Black Atlantic, which could easily form the core of a course on the subject. They have been particularly careful to find literature that reveals the dynamic nature of Afro-Atlantic culture and its engagement with the political and cultural dimensions of the Americas."

John Thornton

"An extraordinarily rich and skilfully assembled collection, and well suited to classroom use, this represents a valuable contribution to an increasingly sophisticated field."

Journal of American Studies

Between 1492 and 1820, about two-thirds of the people who crossed the Atlantic to the Americas were Africans. With the exception of the Spanish, all the European empires settled more Africans in the New World than they did Europeans. The vast majority of these enslaved men and women worked on plantations, and their labor was the foundation for the expansion of the Atlantic economy during the seventeenth and eighteenth centuries.

Until relatively recently, comparatively little attention was paid to the perspectives, daily experiences, hopes, and especially the political ideas of the enslaved who played such a central role in the making of the Atlantic world. Over the past decades, however, huge strides have been made in the study of the history of slavery and emancipation in the Atlantic world. This collection brings together some of the key contributions to this growing body of scholarship, showing a range of methodological approaches, that can be used to understand and reconstruct the lives of these enslaved people.

ISBN 13: 978-0-415-99445-3 (hbk)
ISBN 13: 978-0-415-99446-0 (pbk)

Available at all good bookshops
For ordering and further information please visit:
www.routledge.com